بسم الله الرحمن الرحيم

IN THE NAME OF

ALLAH

THE ALL-COMPASSIONATE, ALL-MERCIFUL

THE DAY OF RESURRECTION

- Title: THE DAY OF RESURRECTION
- Author: Dr. 'Umar S. al-Ashqar
- Arabic Edition 1 (1990)
- Translated from Arabic Edition 6 (1995)
- English Edition 2 (2005)
- Translator: Nasiruddin al-Khattab
- Editor: Huda Khattab
- Layout: IIPH, Riyadh, Saudi Arabia
- Cover Designer: Haroon Vicente Pascual, Arlington, U.S.A.
- Filming: Samo Press Group

ISLAMIC CREED SERIES 6

The Final Day

THE DAY OF RESURRECTION

In the Light of the Qur'an and Sunnah

القيامة الكبرى

Dr. 'Umar S. al-Ashqar

Translated by:
Nasiruddin al-Khattab

الدار العالمية للكتاب الإسلامي

INTERNATIONAL ISLAMIC PUBLISHING HOUSE

King Fahd National Library Cataloging-in-Publication Data

Al-Ashqar, Umar S.

The Day of Resurrection in the light of the Qur'an and Sunnah. / Umar S. al-Ashqar; translated by Nasiruddin al-Khattab - 2nd ed., .- Riyadh, 2005

...p ; 22 cm **(Islamic creed series 6)**

1- Resurrection (Islamic creed) I- Nasiruddin al-Khattab (trans.) II- Title III- Series

243 dc 0082/23

Legal Deposit no. **0082/23**
ISBN Hard Cover: **9960-672-80-8**

International Islamic Publishing House (IIPH)
P.O.Box 55195 Riyadh 11534, Saudi Arabia
Tel: 966 1 4650818 – 4647213 – Fax: 4633489
E-Mail: iiph@iiph.com.sa – iiphsa@gmail.com
www.iiph.com.sa

CONTENTS

PUBLISHER'S NOTE

All thanks and praise are due to the All-Gracious and All-Merciful, Lord of the Universe. Allah's blessings and peace be upon the last of the prophets and messengers Muhammad, his family, his Companions and all those who follow in his footsteps.

Tawheed, *Risaalah* and *Aakhirah* are the bases of the teachings of Islam. The belief in the oneness of Allah, is the foundation. Allah sent His messengers for the guidance of mankind. It culminated with Muhammad son of 'Abdullah, the seal of all messengers and prophets. None can attain true salvation except those believing and following the teachings of the last Prophet. Life on earth is only a transitory period and not an end in itself. The world will cease to exist. Mankind and Jinn will thereafter be resurrected to account for their deeds in the world and will be rewarded or punished accordingly. The Hereafter will be devoid of death and will be permanent.

Professor 'Umar Sulayman al-Ashqar, has earned laurels for his benign efforts to make the fundamental dogmas of Islam understandable to all and sundry - scholars, researchers and laymen. This is the second part of *The Final Day* sub-series of his *'Aqeedah* (Islamic Creed) Series. He discusses the issue of resurrection in detail relying on the basic texts of the Qur'an and Sunnah, copiously quoting both. He has also examined the deviant opinions exhaustively and has summarized the views of *Ahl as-Sunnah wa'l Jama'ah* quoting only the most reliable and authentic sources on the subject. A number of editions of the Arabic original have been published and more are on the way. This speaks of the popularity of this noble work.

We are happy to publish it in a number of languages in order to acquaint our readers with the significance of this aspect of Islamic belief. This English version was rendered by brother Nasiruddin al-Khattab who translated his other works also.

May Allah bless with acceptance the efforts of the author, the translator and all those associated with its publication.

Muhammad ibn 'Abdul-Muḥsin Al-Tuwaijri

General Manager
International Islamic Publishing House, IIPH
Riyadh, Saudi Arabia

TRANSLATOR'S FOREWORD

Belief in the Day of Resurrection is one of the central tenets of Islamic faith. It is a belief that was preached by all the Prophets from Adam to Muhammad (may the blessings and peace of Allah be upon them all). This belief gives meaning to the life we are living, for it shows us that we are not created without purpose, simply to live and die, and with death ends the story.

The notion that our existence is without purpose is widespread among many different nations. This is the underlying belief that makes people pursue material gains and physical pleasures, regardless of ethical guidelines or morals. Their thoughts may be summed up in the phrase, "eat, drink and be merry, for tomorrow we die." They think that the end of this life is the absolute end and that they have only one opportunity to seize pleasure, so they strive to do so, no matter what the cost.

Not believing in the Hereafter renders any moral principle pointless. Why should a person sacrifice any pleasure he might achieve in this world, if there is no compensation in the Hereafter? This line of thought explains the chaos of worldly life, the abuse of nature, the greed and destructive behaviour of man against his own self, his fellow-man and the world around him.

Belief in the Day of Resurrection and the final Judgement is a belief that makes sense of a sometimes incomprehensible world. Almost on a daily basis, we see evil committed by people on every level from the individual to the global, and all too rarely do we see justice done in this world. But Islam tells us that on that Day, all scores will be settled with the utmost justice, and none shall be treated unfairly.

This belief also makes the individual focus on what is in his ultimate best interests, guiding his actions in ways that will benefit him and bring him happiness in this world and the next. On the broader social level, this belief imposes controls on human greed and restrains people from committing transgressions for which they would ultimately have to answer.

Islam tells us that this life is no more than a transitory phase, ending with our death. When we die, we enter the realm of the eternal, in which there will be no more death. But the quality of that eternal life depends on our belief and conduct in this short worldly life. Hence the person who believes in the Hereafter as described in the teachings of Islam will be very careful not to jeopardize his eternal future.

The Qur'an and Sunnah present a very vivid picture of the Hereafter, from the blowing of the Trumpet, the collision of the stars, the death of all living things except Allah, through the Reckoning and the weighing of man and his deeds, to the final gathering of creatures into the Fire of Hell or the Gardens of Paradise. These are all matters of the Unseen which are known only to Allah, matters of which we can have no knowledge except that which Allah, by His mercy, tells us in His Book or through the words of His Prophet (ﷺ) (Blessings and Peace be upon him).

Dr. 'Umar al-Ashqar takes us on a journey through the texts of the Qur'an and Sunnah, tracing the events of that Day in detail and acquainting us with classical Islamic scholarship on this central tenet of our faith. This is a book which deserves to be on Muslim bookshelves in homes, schools and Islamic centres, for it deals with a topic of vital importance to every believer.

May Allah, (سبحانه وتعالى) (the Exalted), reward the author for his efforts to educate the ummah on the basic principles of their faith. May He guide us all to the Straight Path and keep us safe from the terrors of that Day.

Naṣiruddin al-Khaṭṭab

AUTHOR'S FOREWORD

Praise be to Allah for Whom nothing is impossible, for He is Able to do all things. He encompasses all His creatures with His knowledge and subdues them by His might and wisdom. He created His slaves from nothing, and to nothing will they return, then He will bring them back to life again when He wills to resurrect them.

And I send blessings and peace upon His Chosen slave, His selected Messenger, the one who will be granted intercession and the station of praise and glory (*Al-Maqaam al-Mahmood*), and upon all his family and Companions and those who follow them in truth until the Day of Judgement.

This is the second book in which we speak of the Last Day. The topic here is the Resurrection. It consists of fourteen chapters, preceded by an Introduction. The Introduction offers a definition of *Al-Qiyaamah* (The Resurrection).

Chapter 1 mentions the names of the Day of Resurrection and lists the most well-known of these names. It also discusses the reason why there are so many names for this Day.

Chapter 2 discusses the destruction that will befall mankind when the Trumpet is blown and Allah (ﷻ) causes all living things to die. Here I quote the texts which describe the Trumpet, the angel who will blow on it, the Day on which the Trumpet will be blown, the number of times the Trumpet will be blown, and those who will not swoon when all living creatures swoon.

Chapter 3 discusses how the Resurrection will happen and the state of Allah's slaves at that time.

Chapter 4 deals with the description of the land in which mankind will be gathered (for the Judgement).

In Chapter 5, I discuss the evidence that points to the Resurrection, and refute those who disbelieve in it.

Chapter 6 is a discussion of how the Prophets spoke about the Resurrection, for they all mentioned it and spoke about it. In this chapter I also discuss how the People of the Book view the Day of Resurrection today.

Chapter 7 deals with the terrors of the Day of Resurrection. Here I quote the texts of the Qur'an which speak of the earth being ground to powder, the mountains being blown away, the seas bursting forth and overflowing, the heavens shaking and being cleft asunder, the sun being wound round and losing its light, the moon being eclipsed, and the stars falling.

Chapter 8 discusses the state of people on that Day, when they will be divided into three categories: the *mushrik kuffaar* (disbelievers and the polytheists), the disobedient sinners and the pious righteous ones. The humiliation of the *kuffaar* is described, and the fact that their deeds will be to no avail. I mention some of the sins for which the sinners will be punished on that great Day. I describe how the pious will be safe and secure on the Day of great terror, and list some of the deeds which will earn people safety and salvation.

Chapter 9 discusses the great intercession and the station of praise and glory (*Al-Maqaam al-Mahmood*) which will be granted only to the Messenger (ﷺ) out of all of mankind, when he will intercede with his Lord (*Rabb*) to save His slaves from the terrors of the gathering in which they find themselves. So Allah will judge among His slaves, then the people of Paradise will be taken to Paradise and the people of Hell will be taken to Hell.

Chapter 10 deals with the Reckoning and reward/punishment. This is a lengthy chapter which speaks about the meaning of *Al-Ḥisaab* (the reckoning), the scenes of Judgement, those who will be questioned on that Day, the principles according to which the reckoning will be carried out, the matters concerning which people will be questioned, and the first deeds concerning which people will be brought to account.

This chapter describes the three kinds of reckoning: discussion (of one's sins), pointing out (of sins), and rebuking.

Chapter 11 discusses how scores will be settled among people in cases of wrongdoing and injustice, and how this settling of scores will be achieved.

Chapter 12 deals with the Balance or Scale and what the belief (*'Aqeedah*) of *Ahl as-Sunnah* is concerning it. Here we look at what things will be weighed in it, and what actions weigh heavily in the Balance.

In Chapter 13, I quote the *aḥaadeeth* which speak of the Cistern of the Prophet (ﷺ), how big it is, how sweet its water is, and who will be allowed to drink from it and who will be turned away.

Chapter 14 deals with the scene of the gathering to Paradise and Hell. Here we discuss *Aṣ-Ṣiraat* (a bridge over Hell) and outline the belief of *Ahl as-Sunnah* concerning it.

I ask Allah to include us among those who are victorious and are saved on that Day, to overlook our mistakes and to forgive us our sins, and to elevate our status. May He shade us with His shade on the Day when there will be no shade except His, for He is the All-Hearing, Ever-Near, Always-Responsive. May Allah bless His slave and Messenger Muhammad and his family and Companions, and grant them peace.

Dr. 'Umar Sulaymaan al-Ashqar

INTRODUCTION

Definition of *Al-Qiyaamah al-Kubra* (The Greater Resurrection)

There will come a day when the Ever-Living, Self-Sustaining will cause all life and living beings to perish, in fulfilment of His words:

﴿كُلُّ مَنْ عَلَيْهَا فَانٍ ﴿٢٦﴾ وَيَبْقَىٰ وَجْهُ رَبِّكَ ذُو الْجَلَالِ وَالْإِكْرَامِ ﴿٢٧﴾﴾

﴾Whatsoever is on it [the earth] will perish. And the Face of your Lord full of Majesty and Honour will remain forever.﴿ *(Qur'an 55: 26-27)*

﴿... كُلُّ شَيْءٍ هَالِكٌ إِلَّا وَجْهَهُ ... ﴿٨٨﴾﴾

﴾...Everything will perish save His Face...﴿ *(Qur'an 28: 88)*

Then there will come a time when Allah will restore and resurrect His slaves. He will make them stand before Him and bring them to account for their previous actions. On that Day the people will be faced with immense terrors from which none will be able to escape except those who have prepared themselves for that Day with faith and righteous deeds. At the end of that Day, people will be driven to their ultimate destination, Paradise or Hell.

This Day is the Day of Resurrection.

CHAPTER ONE
THE NAMES OF THE DAY OF RESURRECTION

Allah (ﷻ) has called this Day - on which this universe will be destroyed and the Resurrection and Reckoning will take place - by many names. A number of scholars have endeavoured to list these names. Al-Ghazaali and Qurṭubi counted them and listed fifty names, as Ibn Ḥajar al-'Asqalaani mentioned.[1]

Qurṭubi listed these names and explained their meanings, but he took the interpretation of them from the book *"Siraaj al-Mureedeen"* by Ibn al-'Arabi, who may have added things by way of comments.[2]

Some scholars listed them without commenting on them, such as Ibn Najaaḥ in *"Subul al-Khayraat"*, Abu Ḥaamid al-Ghazaali in *"Al-Iḥyaa'"*, and Ibn Qutaybah in *"Uyoon al-Akhbaar"*.[3]

We will limit ourselves here to the most well known names, with a brief discussion of the meaning of each one.

THE MOST WELL KNOWN NAMES FOR THAT DAY

1 - *Yawm al-Qiyaamah* (The Day of Resurrection)

This name is mentioned in seventy *aayaat* (verses) of the Qur'an, such as:

﴿ ٱللَّهُ لَآ إِلَٰهَ إِلَّا هُوَ لَيَجْمَعَنَّكُمْ إِلَىٰ يَوْمِ ٱلْقِيَٰمَةِ لَا رَيْبَ فِيهِ... ﴿٨٧﴾ ﴾

﴿Allah! *Laa ilaaha illa Huwa* [none has the right to be

---

[1] *Fatḥ al-Baari*, 11/396.

[2] *At-Tadhkirah* by Qurṭubi, 233.

[3] Ibid, 232.

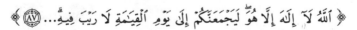

worshipped but He]. Surely, He will gather you together on the Day of Resurrection about which there is no doubt...﴾ *(Qur'an 4: 87)*

﴿ ... وَنَحۡشُرُهُمۡ يَوۡمَ ٱلۡقِيَٰمَةِ عَلَىٰ وُجُوهِهِمۡ عُمۡيٗا وَبُكۡمٗا وَصُمّٗاۖ ... ﴿٩٧﴾ ﴾

﴿...And We shall gather them together on the Day of Resurrection on their faces, blind, dumb and deaf...﴾ *(Qur'an 17: 97)*

﴿ ... إِنَّ ٱلۡخَٰسِرِينَ ٱلَّذِينَ خَسِرُوٓاْ أَنفُسَهُمۡ وَأَهۡلِيهِمۡ يَوۡمَ ٱلۡقِيَٰمَةِۗ ... ﴿٤٥﴾ ﴾

﴿...Verily, the losers are they who lose themselves and their families on the Day of Resurrection...﴾ *(Qur'an 42: 45)*

The root of the word *qiyaamah* in Arabic is *qaama / yaqoomu* (to stand, rise). It appears in the feminine form (with the ending *-ah*) to give more emphasis to its meaning, as is the custom of the Arabs in their speech. It is so called because of the great events which will happen (*yaqoomu fihaa*) on that Day, as described in the texts. One of these events is when the people will stand before the Lord of the Worlds.

2 - *Al-Yawm al-Aakhir* (The Last Day)

As in the *aayaat* (verses):

﴿ ... وَلَٰكِنَّ ٱلۡبِرَّ مَنۡ ءَامَنَ بِٱللَّهِ وَٱلۡيَوۡمِ ٱلۡأٓخِرِ وَٱلۡمَلَٰٓئِكَةِ وَٱلۡكِتَٰبِ وَٱلنَّبِيِّـۧنَ ... ﴿١٧٧﴾ ﴾

﴿...But *Al-Birr* is [the quality of] the one who believes in Allah, the Last Day, the Angels, the Book, the Prophets...﴾ *(Qur'an 2: 177)*

﴿ ... ذَٰلِكَ يُوعَظُ بِهِۦ مَن كَانَ مِنكُمۡ يُؤۡمِنُ بِٱللَّهِ وَٱلۡيَوۡمِ ٱلۡأٓخِرِۗ ... ﴿٢٣٢﴾ ﴾

﴾...This [instruction] is an admonition for him among you who believes in Allah and the Last Day...﴿
(Qur'an 2: 232)

﴿ إِنَّمَا يَعْمُرُ مَسَٰجِدَ ٱللَّهِ مَنْ ءَامَنَ بِٱللَّهِ وَٱلْيَوْمِ ٱلْءَاخِرِ ... ﴿١٨﴾ ﴾

﴾The mosques of Allah shall be maintained only by those who believe in Allah and the Last Day...﴿
(Qur'an 9:18)

Sometimes it is called *Al-Aakhirah* (the Hereafter) or *Ad-Daar al-Aakhirah* (the Home of the Hereafter), as in the *aayaat* (verses):

﴿ ... وَلَقَدِ ٱصْطَفَيْنَٰهُ فِى ٱلدُّنْيَا ۖ وَإِنَّهُۥ فِى ٱلْءَاخِرَةِ لَمِنَ ٱلصَّٰلِحِينَ ﴿١٣٠﴾ ﴾

﴾...Truly, We chose him in this world and verily, in the Hereafter he will be among the righteous.﴿
(Qur'an 2: 130)

﴿ ۞ فَلْيُقَٰتِلْ فِى سَبِيلِ ٱللَّهِ ٱلَّذِينَ يَشْرُونَ ٱلْحَيَوٰةَ ٱلدُّنْيَا بِٱلْءَاخِرَةِ ۚ ... ﴿٧٤﴾ ﴾

﴾Let those [believers] who sell the life of this world for the Hereafter fight in the Cause of Allah...﴿
(Qur'an 4: 74)

﴿ تِلْكَ ٱلدَّارُ ٱلْءَاخِرَةُ نَجْعَلُهَا لِلَّذِينَ لَا يُرِيدُونَ عُلُوًّا فِى ٱلْأَرْضِ وَلَا فَسَادًا ۚ ... ﴿٨٣﴾ ﴾

﴾That home of the Hereafter [i.e. Paradise], We shall assign to those who rebel not against the truth with pride and oppression in the land nor do mischief by committing crimes...﴿ *(Qur'an 28: 83)*

﴿ ... وَإِنَّ ٱلدَّارَ ٱلْءَاخِرَةَ لَهِىَ ٱلْحَيَوَانُ ۚ لَوْ كَانُوا۟ يَعْلَمُونَ ﴿٦٤﴾ ﴾

﴾...Verily, the home of the Hereafter - that is the life indeed [i.e. the eternal life that will never end], if they but knew.﴿ *(Qur'an 29: 64)*

This Day is called the Last Day, because it is the Day after which there will be no more days.

3 - *As-Saa'ah* (The Hour)

Allah (ﷻ) says:

﴿ ... وَإِنَّ ٱلسَّاعَةَ لَآتِيَةٌ فَٱصْفَحِ ٱلصَّفْحَ ٱلْجَمِيلَ ﴿٨٥﴾ ﴾

﴾...And the Hour is surely, coming, so overlook [O' Muhammad], their faults with gracious forgiveness.﴿ *(Qur'an 15: 85)*

﴿ إِنَّ ٱلسَّاعَةَ ءَاتِيَةٌ أَكَادُ أُخْفِيهَا ... ﴿١٥﴾ ﴾

﴾Verily, the Hour is coming - and I am almost hiding it...﴿ *(Qur'an 20: 15)*

﴿ يَٰٓأَيُّهَا ٱلنَّاسُ ٱتَّقُوا۟ رَبَّكُمْ ۚ إِنَّ زَلْزَلَةَ ٱلسَّاعَةِ شَىْءٌ عَظِيمٌ ﴿١﴾ ﴾

﴾O' mankind! Fear your Lord and be dutiful to Him! Verily, the earthquake of the Hour [of Judgement] is a terrible thing.﴿ *(Qur'an 22: 1)*

Qurṭubi said:

"*As-Saa'ah* in Arabic refers to an unspecified portion of time. Customarily it is used to refer to one of the twenty-four parts into which the night and day are divided, which are the basis of time. When it is mentioned in general terms, with the *alif* and *laam* (of the definite article *al-*, in this case the "generic *al-*"), it refers to the current time, i.e. now. The Resurrection is called *As-Saa'ah* either because it is close at hand, for everything that is coming is near, or as an indication of the tremendous, heart-stopping events that will happen on that Day. It was also said that it is called the Hour because it will come suddenly, in an instant..."[4]

4 - *Yawm al-Ba'th* (The Day of Resurrection)

Allah (ﷻ) says:

﴿ يَٰٓأَيُّهَا ٱلنَّاسُ إِن كُنتُمْ فِى رَيْبٍ مِّنَ ٱلْبَعْثِ فَإِنَّا خَلَقْنَٰكُم مِّن تُرَابٍ ... ﴿٥﴾ ﴾

﴾O' mankind! If you are in doubt about the Resurrection, then verily, We have created you [i.e. Adam] from dust...﴿ *(Qur'an 22: 5)*

﴿ وَقَالَ ٱلَّذِينَ أُوتُوا۟ ٱلْعِلْمَ وَٱلْإِيمَٰنَ لَقَدْ لَبِثْتُمْ فِى كِتَٰبِ ٱللَّهِ إِلَىٰ يَوْمِ ٱلْبَعْثِ ۖ فَهَٰذَا يَوْمُ ٱلْبَعْثِ ... ﴿٥٦﴾ ﴾

﴾And those who have been bestowed with knowledge and Faith will say: 'Indeed you have stayed according to the Decree of Allah, until the Day of Resurrection; so this is the Day of Resurrection...'﴿ *(Qur'an 30: 56)*

Ibn Manẓoor said: "*Al-Ba'th* refers to when Allah will revive the dead and bring them forth on the Day of Resurrection."[5]

5 - *Yawm al-Khurooj* (The Day of Coming Out)

Allah (ﷻ) says:

﴿ يَوْمَ يَسْمَعُونَ ٱلصَّيْحَةَ بِٱلْحَقِّ ۚ ذَٰلِكَ يَوْمُ ٱلْخُرُوجِ ﴿٤٢﴾ ﴾

﴾The Day when they will hear *Aṣ-Ṣayḥah* [shout] in

[4] *At-Tadhkirah*, 216.

[5] *Lisaan al-'Arab*, the root *ba -'ayn - tha* (1/230).

truth, that will be the Day of coming out [from the graves, i.e. the Day of Resurrection].› *(Qur'an 50: 42)*

﴿ يَوْمَ يَخْرُجُونَ مِنَ ٱلْأَجْدَاثِ سِرَاعًا كَأَنَّهُمْ إِلَىٰ نُصُبٍ يُوفِضُونَ ﴿٤٣﴾ ﴾

‹The Day when they will come out [*yakhrujoon*] of the graves quickly as racing to a goal.› *(Qur'an 70: 43)*

﴿ ...ثُمَّ إِذَا دَعَاكُمْ دَعْوَةً مِّنَ ٱلْأَرْضِ إِذَآ أَنتُمْ تَخْرُجُونَ ﴿٢٥﴾ ﴾

‹...Then afterwards when He will call you by a single call, behold, you will come out [*takhrajoon*] from the earth [i.e. from your graves for reckoning and recompense].› *(Qur'an 30: 25)*

It is so called because on that Day people will come out of their graves when the Trumpet is blown.

6 - *Al-Qaari'ah* (The Striking Hour)

Allah (ﷻ) says:

﴿ ٱلْقَارِعَةُ ﴿١﴾ مَا ٱلْقَارِعَةُ ﴿٢﴾ وَمَآ أَدْرَىٰكَ مَا ٱلْقَارِعَةُ ﴿٣﴾ ﴾

‹*Al-Qaari'ah* [the striking Hour, i.e. the Day of Resurrection]. What is the striking [Hour]? And what will make you know what the striking [Hour] is?›
(Qur'an 101: 1-3)

﴿ كَذَّبَتْ ثَمُودُ وَعَادٌۢ بِٱلْقَارِعَةِ ﴿٤﴾ ﴾

‹Thamood and 'Aad people denied the *Qaari'ah* [the striking Hour of Judgement]!› *(Qur'an 69: 4)*

Qurṭubi said: "It is so called because it strikes the heart with terror. Or it is said that they were stricken with the calamities of time, i.e. its terrors and distress."

7 - *Yawm al-Faṣl* (The Day of Judgement, Day of Decision)

Allah (ﷻ) says:

﴿ هَٰذَا يَوْمُ ٱلْفَصْلِ ٱلَّذِى كُنتُم بِهِۦ تُكَذِّبُونَ ﴿٢١﴾ ﴾

﴾[It will be said]: 'This is the Day of Judgement which you used to deny.'﴿ *(Qur'an 37: 21)*

﴿ هَٰذَا يَوْمُ ٱلْفَصْلِ جَمَعْنَٰكُمْ وَٱلْأَوَّلِينَ ﴿٣٨﴾ ﴾

﴾That will be a Day of Decision! We have brought you and the men of old together!﴿ *(Qur'an 77: 38)*

﴿ إِنَّ يَوْمَ ٱلْفَصْلِ كَانَ مِيقَٰتًا ﴿١٧﴾ ﴾

﴾Verily, the Day of Decision is a fixed time.﴿

(Qur'an 78: 17)

It is so called because on that Day Allah will judge or decide (*yafṣil*) between His slaves in that concerning which they differed and disputed. Allah (ﷻ) says:

﴿ إِنَّ رَبَّكَ هُوَ يَفْصِلُ بَيْنَهُمْ يَوْمَ ٱلْقِيَٰمَةِ فِيمَا كَانُوا۟ فِيهِ يَخْتَلِفُونَ ﴿٢٥﴾ ﴾

﴾Verily, your Lord will judge [*yafṣil*] between them, on the Day of Resurrection, concerning that wherein they used to differ.﴿ *(Qur'an 32: 25)*

8 - *Yawm ad-Deen* (The Day of Recompense)

Allah (ﷻ) says:

﴿ وَإِنَّ ٱلْفُجَّارَ لَفِى جَحِيمٍ ﴿١٤﴾ يَصْلَوْنَهَا يَوْمَ ٱلدِّينِ ﴿١٥﴾ وَمَا هُمْ عَنْهَا بِغَآئِبِينَ ﴿١٦﴾ وَمَآ أَدْرَىٰكَ مَا يَوْمُ ٱلدِّينِ ﴿١٧﴾ ثُمَّ مَآ أَدْرَىٰكَ مَا يَوْمُ ٱلدِّينِ ﴿١٨﴾ يَوْمَ لَا تَمْلِكُ نَفْسٌ لِّنَفْسٍ شَيْـًٔا ۖ وَٱلْأَمْرُ يَوْمَئِذٍ لِّلَّهِ ﴿١٩﴾ ﴾

﴾And verily, the *Fujjaar* [the wicked, disbelievers, polytheists, sinners and evildoers] will be in the blazing Fire [Hell], Therein they will enter, and taste its burning flame on the Day of Recompense, And they [*Al-Fujjaar*] will not be absent therefrom. And what will make you know what the Day of Recompense is? Again, what will make you know what the Day of Recompense is? [It will be] the Day when no person shall have power [to do anything] for another, and the Decision, that Day, will be [wholly] with Allah.﴿ *(Qur'an 82: 14-19)*

﴿ وَقَالُوا۟ يَٰوَيْلَنَا هَٰذَا يَوْمُ ٱلدِّينِ ﴿٢٠﴾ ﴾

﴾They will say: 'Woe to us! This is the Day of Recompense!'﴿ *(Qur'an 37: 20)*

In Arabic, the word *deen* means recompense and reckoning. (This Day) is so called because Allah will reward or punish His slaves and will bring them to account for their actions on that Day.

9 - *Aṣ-Ṣaakhkhah* (The Trumpet-Blast)

Allah (ﷻ) says:

﴿ فَإِذَا جَآءَتِ ٱلصَّآخَّةُ ﴿٣٣﴾ ﴾

﴾Then when there comes *Aṣ-Saakhkhah* [the (second) blowing of the Trumpet on the Day of Resurrection].﴿ *(Qur'an 80: 33)*

Qurṭubi said: "Ikrimah said: '*Aṣ-Ṣaakhkhah* is the first blast of the Trumpet, and *Aṭ-Ṭaammah* is the second blast. Aṭ-Ṭabari said: 'I think it is from (the phrase) *ṣakhkha fulaan fulaanan* (so-and-so made so-and-so deaf).' Ibn al-'Arabi said: '*Aṣ-Ṣaakhkhah* is that which causes deafness, and it is so loud as to be heard.' This is the utmost eloquence, as the young people say, "The caller makes you deaf even if you can hear him."

By Allah (ﷻ) the tumult of the Day of Resurrection will make people deaf to this world and will make them hear the matters of the Hereafter."[6]

Ibn Katheer said: "Al-Baghawi said: '*Aṣ-Ṣaakhkhah* means the tumult of the Day of Resurrection. It is so called because it will penetrate their ears to such an extent that it will nearly make them deaf.'"[7]

10 - *Aṭ-Ṭaammat al-Kubraa* (The Greatest Catastrophe)

Allah (ﷻ) says:

﴿ فَإِذَا جَآءَتِ ٱلطَّآمَّةُ ٱلْكُبْرَىٰ ﴿٣٤﴾ ﴾

﴾But when there comes the greatest catastrophe [i.e. the Day of Recompense].﴿ *(Qur'an 79: 34)*

It is so called because it is the most terrifying and alarming thing of all, as Allah (ﷻ) says:

﴿ ...وَٱلسَّاعَةُ أَدْهَىٰ وَأَمَرُّ ﴿٤٦﴾ ﴾

﴾...And the Hour will be more grievous and more bitter.﴿ *(Qur'an 54: 46)*

Qurṭubi said: "*Aṭ-Ṭaammah* means overwheleming - as you say *tamma ash-shay'u* if it overwhelms and takes over. Because it will overwhelm everything, this Day alone has this name which is true. Al-Ḥasan said: '*Aṭ-Ṭaammah* is the second blast of the Trumpet.' It is also said that this is when the people of Hell will be driven to Hell."[8]

---

[6] *Tadhkirat al-Qurṭubi*, 227.

[7] *Tafseer Ibn Katheer*, 7/217.

[8] *Tadhkirat al-Qurṭubi*, 227.

11 - *Yawm al-Ḥasrah* (The Day of Grief and Regrets)

Allah (ﷻ) says:

﴿ وَأَنذِرْهُمْ يَوْمَ الْحَسْرَةِ إِذْ قُضِيَ الْأَمْرُ وَهُمْ فِي غَفْلَةٍ وَهُمْ لَا يُؤْمِنُونَ ﴿٣٩﴾ ﴾

﴿And warn them [O' Muhammad] of the Day of grief and regrets, when the case has been decided, while [now] they are in a state of carelessness, and they believe not.﴾ *(Qur'an 19: 39)*

It is so called because of the intensity of the grief and regret that people will feel on that Day. The *kuffaar* - the disbelievers - will regret their lack of faith:

﴿ ... حَتَّىٰ إِذَا جَاءَتْهُمُ السَّاعَةُ بَغْتَةً قَالُوا يَا حَسْرَتَنَا عَلَىٰ مَا فَرَّطْنَا فِيهَا... ﴿٣١﴾ ﴾

﴿...Until all of a sudden, the Hour [signs of death] is on them, and they say: 'Alas for us that we gave no thought to it.'...﴾ *(Qur'an 6: 31)*

Listen to how the *kuffaar* will regret it when the punishment comes upon them:

﴿ أَن تَقُولَ نَفْسٌ يَا حَسْرَتَىٰ عَلَىٰ مَا فَرَّطتُ فِي جَنبِ اللَّهِ وَإِن كُنتُ لَمِنَ السَّاخِرِينَ ﴿٥٦﴾ أَوْ تَقُولَ لَوْ أَنَّ اللَّهَ هَدَانِي لَكُنتُ مِنَ الْمُتَّقِينَ ﴿٥٧﴾ أَوْ تَقُولَ حِينَ تَرَى الْعَذَابَ لَوْ أَنَّ لِي كَرَّةً فَأَكُونَ مِنَ الْمُحْسِنِينَ ﴿٥٨﴾ ﴾

﴿Lest a person should say: 'Alas, my grief that I was undutiful to Allah [i.e. I have not done what Allah has ordered me to do], and I was indeed among those who mocked [at the truth!]' Or [lest] he should say: 'If only Allah had guided me, I should indeed have been among the *Muttaqoon* [the pious].' Or [lest] he should say when he sees the torment: 'If only I had another chance [to return to the world], then I should indeed be among the *Muhsinoon* [good-doers].'》 *(Qur'an 39: 56-58)*

The sorrow and regret that the *kuffaar* - disbelievers - feel will reach their peak when the masters and followers disown one another:

﴿ وَقَالَ ٱلَّذِينَ ٱتَّبَعُوا۟ لَوْ أَنَّ لَنَا كَرَّةً فَنَتَبَرَّأَ مِنْهُمْ كَمَا تَبَرَّءُوا۟ مِنَّا ۗ كَذَٰلِكَ يُرِيهِمُ ٱللَّهُ أَعْمَٰلَهُمْ حَسَرَٰتٍ عَلَيْهِمْ ۖ وَمَا هُم بِخَٰرِجِينَ مِنَ ٱلنَّارِ ﴿١٦٧﴾ ﴾

《And those who followed will say: 'If only we had one more chance to return [to the worldly life], we would disown [declare ourselves as innocent from] them as they have disowned [declared themselves as innocent from] us.' Thus Allah will show them their deeds as regrets for them. And they will never get out of the Fire.》 *(Qur'an 2: 167)*

And the believers will feel regret on that Day because they did not do more deeds of righteousness and piety.

12 - *Al-Ghaashiyah* (The Overwhelming)

Allah (سبحانه وتعالى) says:

﴿ هَلْ أَتَىٰكَ حَدِيثُ ٱلْغَٰشِيَةِ ﴿١﴾ ﴾

《Has there come to you the narration of the overwhelming [i.e. the Day of Resurrection]?》 *(Qur'an 88: 1)*

It is so called because its terrifying events will overwhelm the people and cause them grief. One of the aspects of this meaning is that the Fire will overwhelm the *kuffaar* and encompass them from above and from beneath their feet, as Allah (ﷻ) says:

﴿ يَوْمَ يَغْشَىٰهُمُ ٱلْعَذَابُ مِن فَوْقِهِمْ وَمِن تَحْتِ أَرْجُلِهِمْ ... ﴿٥٥﴾ ﴾

﴾On the Day when the torment [Hell-fire] shall cover them from above them and from underneath their feet...﴿ *(Qur'an 29: 55)*

﴿ لَهُم مِّن جَهَنَّمَ مِهَادٌ وَمِن فَوْقِهِمْ غَوَاشٍ ... ﴿٤١﴾ ﴾

﴾Theirs will be a bed of Hell [Fire], and over them coverings [of Hell-fire]...﴿ *(Qur'an 7: 41)*

13 - *Yawm al-Khulood* (The Day of Eternal Life)

Allah (ﷻ) says:

﴿ ٱدْخُلُوهَا بِسَلَٰمٍ ذَٰلِكَ يَوْمُ ٱلْخُلُودِ ﴿٣٤﴾ ﴾

﴾Enter you therein in peace and security - this is a Day of eternal life!﴿ *(Qur'an 50: 34)*

That Day is called the Day of eternal life because the people will go to their place of eternal abode: the *kuffaar* will abide forever in Hell, and the believers will abide forever in Paradise. Allah (ﷻ) says:

﴿ وَٱلَّذِينَ كَفَرُوا۟ وَكَذَّبُوا۟ بِـَٔايَٰتِنَآ أُو۟لَٰٓئِكَ أَصْحَٰبُ ٱلنَّارِ ۖ هُمْ فِيهَا خَٰلِدُونَ ﴿٣٩﴾ ﴾

﴾But those who disbelieve and belie Our *Aayaat* [proofs, evidences, verses, lessons, signs, revelations, etc.] - such are the dwellers of the Fire. They shall abide therein forever.﴿ *(Qur'an 2: 39)*

﴿ وَأَمَّا ٱلَّذِينَ ٱبْيَضَّتْ وُجُوهُهُمْ فَفِى رَحْمَةِ ٱللَّهِ ۖ هُمْ فِيهَا خَٰلِدُونَ ﴿١٠٧﴾ ﴾

﴾And for those whose faces will become white, they will

be in Allah's Mercy [Paradise], therein they shall dwell forever.﴾ *(Qur'an 3: 107)*

14 - *Yawm al-Ḥisaab* (The Day of Reckoning)

Allah (ﷻ) says:

﴿ ... إِنَّ ٱلَّذِينَ يَضِلُّونَ عَن سَبِيلِ ٱللَّهِ لَهُمْ عَذَابٌ شَدِيدٌۢ بِمَا نَسُوا۟ يَوْمَ ٱلْحِسَابِ ﴿٢٦﴾ ﴾

﴾...Verily, those who wander astray from the path of Allah [shall] have a severe torment, because they forgot the Day of Reckoning.﴿ *(Qur'an 38: 26)*

﴿ وَقَالَ مُوسَىٰٓ إِنِّى عُذْتُ بِرَبِّى وَرَبِّكُم مِّن كُلِّ مُتَكَبِّرٍ لَّا يُؤْمِنُ بِيَوْمِ ٱلْحِسَابِ ﴿٢٧﴾ ﴾

﴾Moosa [Moses] said: 'Verily, I seek refuge in my Lord and your Lord from every arrogant who believes not in the Day of Reckoning!'﴿ *(Qur'an 40: 27)*

This Day is called the Day of Reckoning, because on this Day Allah will bring His slaves to account. Qurṭubi said:

"The meaning of *Al-Ḥisaab* (the Reckoning) is that Allah will count people's deeds, good and bad, and will count His blessings (that He bestowed). Then He will weigh the elements of good and evil (in each action), and whichever outweighs the other will determine whether that action is recorded as good or evil. It is narrated that the Prophet (ﷺ) said:

"There is not one among you but Allah will speak to him directly without any mediator."

15 - *Al-Waaqi'ah* (The Event)

Allah (ﷻ) says:

﴿ إِذَا وَقَعَتِ ٱلْوَاقِعَةُ ۝١ ﴾

﴿When the Event [i.e. the Day of Resurrection] befalls -﴾ *(Qur'an 56: 1)*

Ibn Katheer said: "It is so called because it will definitely come to pass."[9]

The root of *waqa'a* in Arabic means "took place" or "existed".

16 - *Yawm al-Wa'eed* [The Day Whereof Warning (had been given)]

Allah (ﷻ) says:

﴿ وَنُفِخَ فِى ٱلصُّورِ ۚ ذَٰلِكَ يَوْمُ ٱلْوَعِيدِ ۝٢٠ ﴾

﴿And the Trumpet will be blown - that will be the Day whereof warning [had been given] [i.e. the Day of Resurrection].﴾ *(Qur'an 50:20)*

- because it is the Day of which He had warned His slaves, and warning means telling of the punishment when an offence takes place.

17 - *Yawm al-Aazifah* (The Day that is Drawing Near)

Allah (ﷻ) says:

﴿ وَأَنذِرْهُمْ يَوْمَ ٱلْءَازِفَةِ إِذِ ٱلْقُلُوبُ لَدَى ٱلْحَنَاجِرِ كَـٰظِمِينَ ... ۝١٨ ﴾

﴿And warn them [O' Muhammad] of the Day that is drawing near [i.e. the Day of Resurrection], when the hearts will be choking the throats...﴾ *(Qur'an 40: 18)*

It is so called because it is close at hand, as Allah (ﷻ) says:

---

[9] *Tafseer Ibn Katheer*, 6/507.

﴿ أَزِفَتِ ٱلْـَٔازِفَةُ ۝٥٧ لَيْسَ لَهَا مِن دُونِ ٱللَّهِ كَاشِفَةٌ ۝٥٨ ﴾

﴿The Day of Resurrection draws near. None besides Allah can avert it [or advance it or delay it].﴾ *(Qur'an 53: 57-58)*

The Hour is very near, for everything that is coming is near, even if it is still far away. And after its signs appear, the Hour is even closer.

18 - *Yawm al-Jama'* (The Day of Assembling)

Allah (ﷻ) says:

﴿ وَكَذَٰلِكَ أَوْحَيْنَآ إِلَيْكَ قُرْءَانًا عَرَبِيًّا لِّتُنذِرَ أُمَّ ٱلْقُرَىٰ وَمَنْ حَوْلَهَا وَتُنذِرَ يَوْمَ ٱلْجَمْعِ لَا رَيْبَ فِيهِ ... ۝٧ ﴾

﴿And thus We have revealed to you [O' Muhammad] a Qur'an in Arabic that you may warn the Mother of the Towns [Makkah] and all around it, and warn [them] of the Day of Assembling of which there is no doubt...﴾ *(Qur'an 42: 7)*

It is so called because on this Day Allah will assemble all of mankind together, as He (ﷻ) says:

﴿ ...ذَٰلِكَ يَوْمٌ مَّجْمُوعٌ لَّهُ ٱلنَّاسُ ... ۝١٠٣ ﴾

﴿...That is a Day whereon mankind will be gathered together...﴾ *(Qur'an 11: 103)*

19 - *Al-Ḥaaqqah* (The Inevitable)

Allah (ﷻ) says:

﴿ ٱلْحَآقَّةُ ۝١ مَا ٱلْحَآقَّةُ ۝٢ ﴾

﴿The Inevitable [i.e. the Day of Resurrection]! What is the Inevitable?﴾ *(Qur'an 69: 1-2)*

It is so called - as Ibn Katheer says - because on this Day the promise and the warning will be fulfilled.[10]

Bukhari said in his *Ṣaheeḥ*: "It is the Inevitable because on that Day there will be reward and punishment and the reality of things will become apparent. And *Al-Ḥaqqah* and *Al-Ḥaaqqah* are the same thing." Ibn Ḥajar said in his comment on Bukhari's words: "He took this from the words of *Al-Farraa'*, who said in *Ma'aani al-Qur'an*: *Al-Ḥaaqqah* means the Resurrection. It is so called because on that Day there will be reward and punishment and the reality of things will become apparent. Then he said, *al-ḥaqqah* and *al-ḥaaqqah* both mean the same thing. Aṭ-Ṭabari said: it is called *al-ḥaaqqah* because it is certain. Others said: it is called *al-ḥaaqqah* because, then the reward and punishment will be given to the people of Paradise and the people of Hell, respectively. Again it is so called because then the *kuffaar* - disbelievers - will be defeated who went against the Prophets. And it is said (in Arabic) *ḥaaqaqtuhu fa ḥaqaqtuhu* (I debated with him and defeated him in argument). And it is also said that it is so called because it is *ḥaqq* (true) and there is no doubt concerning it."[11]

20 - *Yawm at-Talaaq* (The Day of Mutual Meeting)

Allah (سبحانه وتعالى) says:

﴿ رَفِيعُ ٱلدَّرَجَٰتِ ذُو ٱلْعَرْشِ يُلْقِى ٱلرُّوحَ مِنْ أَمْرِهِۦ عَلَىٰ مَن يَشَآءُ مِنْ
عِبَادِهِۦ لِيُنذِرَ يَوْمَ ٱلتَّلَاقِ ﴿١٥﴾ ﴾

﴿[He is Allah] Owner of High Ranks and Degrees, the Owner of the Throne. He sends the Revelation by His Command to any of His slaves He wills, that he [the

---

[10] *Tafseer Ibn Katheer*, 7/99.

[11] *Fatḥ al-Baari*, 11/395.

person who receives Revelation] may warn [men] of the Day of Mutual Meeting [i.e. the Day of Resurrection].﴾
(Qur'an 40: 15)

Ibn Katheer said: "Ibn 'Abbaas said: on that Day, Adam and the last of his children will meet. Ibn Zayd said: on that Day all people will meet. Qataadah, As-Suddi, Bilaal ibn Sa'd and Sufyaan ibn 'Uyaynah said: on that Day the people of heaven and earth will meet, and the Creator and His created beings will meet. Maymoon ibn Mahraan said: on that Day the oppressor and the one whom he oppressed will meet. It is also said that the Day of Mutual Meeting includes all of these meanings. It also includes the idea that everyone who did deeds will meet his deeds, both good and evil, as others suggested."[12]

21 - *Yawm at-Tanaad* (The Day When There will be Mutual Calling)

Allah (ﷻ) tells us that the believer among the people of Pharaoh said to his people:

﴿ وَيَٰقَوۡمِ إِنِّيٓ أَخَافُ عَلَيۡكُمۡ يَوۡمَ ٱلتَّنَادِ ﴿٣٢﴾ ﴾

﴾And, O' my people! Verily, I fear for you the Day when there will be mutual calling [between the people of Hell and of Paradise].﴾ *(Qur'an 40: 32)*

It is so called because there will be so much calling that Day. Each person will be called by name to be brought to account and rewarded or punished accordingly. The people of Paradise will call the people of Hell, and the people of Hell will call the people of Paradise, and the people of *Al-A'raaf*[13] will call both.

---

[12] *Tafseer Ibn Katheer,* 6/130.

[13] *Al-A'raaf* (the Heights): A wall between Paradise and Hell on which there are elevated places. See Qur'an (7: 46-48) (Translator).

22 - *Yawm at-Taghaabun* (The Day of Mutual Loss and Gain)

Allah (ﷻ) says:

﴿ يَوْمَ يَجْمَعُكُمْ لِيَوْمِ ٱلْجَمْعِ ذَٰلِكَ يَوْمُ ٱلتَّغَابُنِ ... ﴿٩﴾ ﴾

﴾[And remember] the Day when He will gather you [all] on the Day of Gathering, - that will be the Day of mutual loss and gain...﴿ *(Qur'an 64: 9)*

It is so called because the people of Paradise will get the better of the people of Hell; they will enter Paradise and take that which was promised to them, and they will inherit the *kuffaar's* (disbeliever's) share of Paradise.

These are the most famous names of the Day of Resurrection. Some scholars also list other names apart from those that we have mentioned. These names they have derived from what is mentioned in the texts. So they called it *Yawm aṣ-Sadr* (the Day of proceeding), based on the *aayah* (verse):

﴿ يَوْمَئِذٍ يَصْدُرُ ٱلنَّاسُ أَشْتَاتًا لِّيُرَوْا۟ أَعْمَٰلَهُمْ ﴿٦﴾ ﴾

﴾That Day mankind will proceed [*yaṣdur*] in scattered groups that they may be shown their deeds.﴿ *(Qur'an 99: 6)*

- and *Yawm al-Jidaal* (the Day of pleading), based on the *aayah*:

﴿ ۞ يَوْمَ تَأْتِى كُلُّ نَفْسٍ تُجَٰدِلُ عَن نَّفْسِهَا ... ﴿١١١﴾ ﴾

﴾[Remember] the Day when every person will come up pleading [*tujaadil*] for himself...﴿ *(Qur'an 16: 111)*

They listed names describing that Day in the same terms that Allah has described it. Among the names they mentioned are the following:

A Hard Day: A Mighty Day; the Day when all (the dwellers of the heavens and the earth) will be present; A Day, hard and distressful, that will make the faces look horrible (from extreme dislike of it); the Day after which there will be no night.

Other names that they have mentioned include:

The Day which will bring low and exalt: The Day of retribution; the Day of recompense; the Day when the Trumpet is blown; the Day of the (final) earthquake; the Day when the earth and the mountains will shake violently; the Day when the Trumpet is sounded; the Day of dispersal; the day when the earth will split; the Day when the contents of the graves are brought forth; the Day of regret; the Day of flight.

And other names include:

The Day when all the secrets will be examined: The Day when no person shall have power (to do) anything for another; the Day when they will be pushed down by force to the Fire of Hell, with a horrible, forceful pushing; the Day when the eyes will stare in horror; the Day when their excuses will be of no profit to the *Ẓaalimoon* (wrong-doers); the Day when they shall not speak; the Day whereon neither wealth nor children will avail; the Day when not a single fact will be hidden from Allah; the Day from Allah which none can avert; the Day on which there will be neither mutual bargaining nor befriending; the Day of which there is no doubt.

Some scholars add other names. Qurṭubi said: "There is no reason not to call it by names other than those which have been mentioned, based on the circumstances that will prevail on that Day, such as crowding, constriction, humiliation, helplessness, the appointed Day, and so on."[14]

---

[14] *At-Tadhkirah*, 233.

The reason why there are so many names

Qurṭubi said: "Everything that is of great status has many attributes and many names. This is the way in which the Arabs express the importance of a thing. Do you not see that because the sword is so important to them and is held in such high esteem by them, that they gave it five hundred names? And there are other similar examples.

Because the Resurrection is so important and its terrors are so many, Allah (ﷻ) has given it many names in His Book, and has described it in many ways."[15]

[15] *At-Tadhkirah*, 214.

CHAPTER TWO
THE DESTRUCTION OF LIVING THINGS

1 - THE BLAST OF THE TRUMPET

This strange and wonderful universe in which we live, teeming with life and living things both visible and invisible, filled with constant motion that never stops or ceases, will remain like this until the Day comes on which Allah (ﷻ) will destroy all living things except what He wills:

﴿ كُلُّ مَنْ عَلَيْهَا فَانٍ ﴿٢٦﴾ ﴾

﴾Whatsoever is on it [the earth] will perish.﴿
(Qur'an 55: 26)

﴿ ... كُلُّ شَيْءٍ هَالِكٌ إِلَّا وَجْهَهُ ... ﴿٨٨﴾ ﴾

﴾...Everything will perish save His Face...﴿
(Qur'an 28: 88)

When that Day comes, the Trumpet will be blown, and this trumpet-blast will put an end to life on earth and in the heavens.

﴿ وَنُفِخَ فِي الصُّورِ فَصَعِقَ مَن فِي السَّمَاوَاتِ وَمَن فِي الْأَرْضِ إِلَّا مَن شَاءَ اللَّهُ ... ﴿٦٨﴾ ﴾

﴾And the Trumpet will be blown, and all who are in the heavens and all who are on the earth will swoon away, except him whom Allah wills...﴿ *(Qur'an 39: 68)*

This will be a huge and destructive blast which a man will hear and will not be able to make any bequest or return to his family and friends:

﴿ مَا يَنظُرُونَ إِلَّا صَيْحَةً وَٰحِدَةً تَأْخُذُهُمْ وَهُمْ يَخِصِّمُونَ ﴿٤٩﴾ فَلَا يَسْتَطِيعُونَ تَوْصِيَةً وَلَآ إِلَىٰٓ أَهْلِهِمْ يَرْجِعُونَ ﴿٥٠﴾ ﴾

﴾They await only but a single *Ṣayḥah* [shout] which will seize them while they are disputing! Then they will not be able to make bequest, nor they will return to their family.﴿ *(Qur'an 36: 49-50)*

According to the hadith:

"Then the Trumpet will be blown, and no one will hear it but he will tilt his head. And he said, the first one to hear it will be a man who will be repairing a trough for his camels.

The Prophet (ﷺ) said,

'He will fall unconscious and the people will fall unconscious.'"[1]

The Messenger (ﷺ) spoke of how quickly people will die when the Hour comes. He said:

"The Hour will certainly come, whilst two men will be spreading out a garment between them, but they will not be able to sell it or fold it up; and the Hour will come when a man will milk his she-camel and will take the milk away, but he will not be able to drink it; and the Hour will come before a man who will repair his trough and will be able to bring his animals to drink from it; and the Hour will come when a man will raise a morsel of food to his mouth but he will not be able to eat it."[2]

---

[1] Muslim, *Kitaab al-Fitan, Baab Khurooj ad-Dajjaal*, 4/2259, hadith no. 2940.

[2] Bukhari, *Kitaab al-Fitan, Baab... taṣaddaqu*; *Fatḥ al-Baari*, 13/82, from Abu Hurayrah. It is also narrated in *Kitaab ar-Riqaaq, Fatḥ al-Baari*, 11/352.

2 - *AṢ-ṢOOR* - THE TRUMPET WHICH WILL BE BLOWN

Aṣ-Ṣoor in Arabic means a horn. The Messenger (ﷺ) was asked about the *ṣoor*, he explained it in terms of the words that the Arabs know. In *Sunan at-Tirmidhi, Sunan Abi Dawood, Sunan ibn Ḥibbaan, Musnad Aḥmad* and *Mustadrak al-Ḥaakim* it is narrated that 'Abdullah ibn 'Amr ibn al-'Aaṣ said: "A Bedouin came to the Prophet (ﷺ) and said, 'What is *aṣ-ṣoor*?' He said,

> '*Aṣ-Ṣoor* is a horn which is blown into.'"[3]

- Al-Ḥaakim said: its *isnaad* is *ṣaḥeeḥ*, and Adh-Dhahabi agreed with him. Tirmidhi said: it is a *ṣaḥeeḥ ḥasan* hadith.

It is said that Al-Ḥasan al-Baṣri read *aṣ-ṣoor* as *aṣ-ṣuwar*, which is the plural of *ṣoorah* (meaning image, form), and interpreted it as meaning when the bodies are blown into so that the souls return to them.

It is narrated from Abu 'Ubaydah and Al-Kalbi that *aṣ-ṣoor* was the plural of *ṣoorah.*

They said: Blowing into *ṣoor* means blowing into the bodies, for the souls to return to them. But what they said is mistaken for a number of reasons:

1) The version of the Qur'an recitation attributed to Al-Ḥasan al-Baṣri has not been attributed with any authority to any of the Imams whose recitation can be accepted as proof.

2) The plural of *ṣoorah* is *ṣuwar*, not *ṣoor* as claimed by Abu 'Ubaydah and Al-Kalbi. Allah (ﷻ) says:

﴿... وَصَوَّرَكُمْ فَأَحْسَنَ صُوَرَكُمْ ... ﴿٦٤﴾﴾

[3] *Silsilat al-Aḥaadeeth aṣ-Ṣaḥeeḥah*, 3/68, hadith no. 1080.

﴾...And has given you shape and made your shapes good [looking] [*aḥsana ṣuwarakum*]...﴿ *(Qur'an 40: 64)*

It has not been reported that any of the prominent reciters recited this as *aḥsana ṣoorakum*.

3) The words which they mentioned are not plurals; they are collective nouns, and the difference between these words and their singular is the addition of the *ta' marbootah*.

4) This view is contrary to the view of *Ahl as-Sunnah wal-Jamaa'ah*; what *Ahl as-Sunnah wal-Jamaa'ah* believe is that *aṣ-ṣoor* is a horn which will be blown into.

5) Again this view is contrary to the explanation of the Messenger (ﷺ), who explained it as meaning a horn, and it goes against many *aḥaadeeth* which indicate the same meaning.

6) Allah (سبحانه وتعالى) says:

﴿ وَنُفِخَ فِى ٱلصُّورِ فَصَعِقَ مَن فِى ٱلسَّمَٰوَٰتِ وَمَن فِى ٱلْأَرْضِ إِلَّا مَن شَآءَ ٱللَّهُ ۖ ثُمَّ نُفِخَ فِيهِ أُخْرَىٰ فَإِذَا هُمْ قِيَامٌ يَنظُرُونَ ﴿٦٨﴾ ﴾

﴾And the Trumpet will be blown, and all who are in the heavens and all who are on the earth will swoon away, except him whom Allah wills. Then it will be blown a second time, and behold they will be standing, looking on [waiting].﴿ *(Qur'an 39: 68)*

Allah (سبحانه وتعالى) tells us that the Trumpet will be blown twice. Had it meant blowing into *aṣ-ṣuwar*, meaning bodies (as opposed to *aṣ-ṣoor*, meaning Trumpet), it would not be correct to say, "Then it will be blown a second time," because at the resurrection, the souls will be blown into the bodies only once.[4]

---

[4] For more information on this issue, see *Tadhkirat al-Qurṭubi*, 182, 185; *Fatḥ al-Baari*, 11/367; *Lisaan al-'Arab*, 2/493.

With regard to the comments made by some of the scholars, that the Trumpet is made of rubies or of light, we know of no *ṣaḥeeḥ* hadith concerning that. And Allah knows best.

3 - THE ONE WHO WILL BLOW THE TRUMPET

Ibn Ḥajar al-'Asqallaani said: "It is well known that the one who will blow the Trumpet is Israafeel (عليه السلام) (may peace be upon him). Al-Ḥaleemi narrated that there is scholarly consensus on this. It is clearly stated in the hadith of Wahb ibn Munabbih, the hadith of Abu Sa'eed narrated by Al-Bayhaqi, the hadith of Abu Hurayrah narrated by Ibn Mardawayh, and the lengthy hadith about the Trumpet."[5]

The Messenger (ﷺ) has told us that the one who will blow the Trumpet is ever prepared to do so since the time Allah created him. In *Mustadrak al-Ḥaakim* it is narrated that Abu Hurayrah (رضي الله عنه) (may Allah be pleased with him) said: The Messenger of Allah (ﷺ) said:

> "Since the time when the one who will blow the Trumpet was appointed, his eyes are ever ready, looking towards the Throne, fearing lest the command be issued before he blinks, as if his eyes are two brilliant stars."

- Al-Ḥaakim said, its *isnaad* is *ṣaḥeeḥ*, and Adh-Dhahabi agreed with him.[6]

At this time, when the Hour has drawn so close, Israafeel is more prepared and is ready to blow the Trumpet anytime. It is narrated by Ibn al-Mubaarak in *Az-Zuhd*, Tirmidhi in *As-Sunan*, Abu Na'eem in *Al-Ḥilyah*, Abu Ya'laa in *Al-Musnad*, Ibn Ḥibbaan in *Aṣ-Ṣaḥeeḥ* and Al-Ḥaakim in *Al-Mustadrak*, that Abu Sa'eed al-Khudri stated that the Messenger of Allah (ﷺ) said:

---

[5] *Fatḥ al-Baari*, 11/368.

[6] *Silsilat al-Aḥaadeeth aṣ-Ṣaḥeeḥah*, 3/65, hadith no. 1078.

> "How could I relax when the bearer of the Trumpet has put the Trumpet to his lips and tilted his forehead, and is listening out, waiting for the command to blow the Trumpet?" The Muslims asked, "What should we say, O' Messenger of Allah?" He said, "Say, *Ḥasbunallah wa ni'am al-wakeel, tawakkalnaa 'alallahi Rabbinaa* (Allah is Sufficient for us and He is the best Disposer of affairs; we put our trust in Allah, our Lord)."

- Tirmidhi said, (it is) a *ḥasan* hadith. *Shaykh* Naaṣir mentioned its narrators among the *Ṣaḥaabah*, its *isnaad* and corroborating reports in *Silsilat al-Aḥaadeeth aṣ-Ṣaḥeeḥah*, which indicates that it is *ṣaḥeeḥ*.[7]

4 - THE DAY WHEN THE TRUMPET WILL BE BLOWN

The Hour will begin on a Friday. In Muslim it is narrated that Abu Hurayrah (ﷺ) said that the Messenger of Allah (ﷺ) said:

> "The best day on which the sun rises is Friday. On this day Adam was created, he entered Paradise on Friday, this day he was expelled from Paradise, and the Hour will only come on a Friday."[8]

According to another hadith, the Messenger (ﷺ) said that the Hour will come on Friday, and on Friday the people will be resurrected too. It is narrated that Aws ibn Aws said that the Messenger of Allah (ﷺ) said:

> "The best of your days is Friday. Adam was created on Friday, and this day he died, the Trumpet will be blown and all of the creation will swoon on Friday. So send

---

[7] *Silsilat al-Aḥaadeeth aṣ-Ṣaḥeeḥah*, 3/66, hadith no. 1079.

[8] *Mishkaat al-Maṣaabeeḥ*, 1/427, hadith no. 1356.

> more prayers upon me on Fridays, for your prayers will be presented to me."- This is narrated by Abu Dawood, An-Nasaa'i, Ibn Maajah, Ad- Daarimi and Al-Bayhaqi in *Ad-Da'waat al-Kabeer.*[9]

In *Musnad aṭ-Ṭabaraani al-Awsaṭ* and *Al-Ḥilyah* by Abu Na'eem, it is reported that Anas stated that the Messenger of Allah (ﷺ) said:

> "The days were shown to me, and among them Friday was shown to me. It looked like a white mirror in the middle of which is a black spot. I asked, 'What is this?' It was said, 'The Hour.'"[10]

Because the Hour will come on this day, every Friday all creatures are filled with fear, apart from humans and jinn. In *Muwaṭṭa'* of Imam Maalik, *Sunan Abi Dawood, Sunan at-Tirmidhi, Sunan an-Nasaa'i* and *Musnad Aḥmad*, it is narrated that Abu Hurayrah (رضي الله عنه) said that the Messenger of Allah (ﷺ) said:

> "The best day on which the sun rises is Friday. On this day Adam was created, on this day he came down (from Paradise), it was Friday when his repentance was accepted and this day he died. The Hour will occur on Friday. There is no creature which is not waiting every Friday, from the moment the sun rises, fearing the Hour - apart from jinn and men."[11]

---

[9] *Mishkaat al-Maṣaabeeḥ*, 1/430, hadith no. 1361; the editor of *Al-Mishkaat* said concerning its *isnaad* as recorded by Abu Dawood, it is *ṣaḥeeḥ*. It is classed as *ṣaḥeeḥ* by the *jamaa'ah* (bulk of the majority).

[10] *Shaykh* Naaṣir referred to this hadith in *Ṣaḥeeḥ al-Jaami'*, 4/31, hadith no. 3895, and noted its *isnaad* in *Silsilat al-Aḥaadeeth aṣ-Ṣaḥeeḥah*, 4/568, hadith no. 1930.

[11] *Mishkaat al-Maṣaabeeḥ*, 1/428, hadith no. 1359. The editor of *Al-Mishkaat* attributed it to Al-Muwaṭṭa' and Tirmidhi. Tirmidhi said, it is *ḥasan ṣaḥeeḥ*.

5 - HOW MANY TIMES WILL THE TRUMPET BE BLOWN?

What is apparent is that the angel Israafeel will blow the Trumpet two times: the first will cause all creatures to fall unconscious, and the second will bring about the Resurrection. Allah (سبحانه وتعالى) says:

﴿ وَنُفِخَ فِي ٱلصُّورِ فَصَعِقَ مَن فِي ٱلسَّمَٰوَٰتِ وَمَن فِي ٱلْأَرْضِ إِلَّا مَن شَآءَ
ٱللَّهُۖ ثُمَّ نُفِخَ فِيهِ أُخْرَىٰ فَإِذَا هُمْ قِيَامٌ يَنظُرُونَ ﴿٦٨﴾ ﴾

﴿And the Trumpet will be blown, and all who are in the heavens and all who are on the earth will swoon away, except him whom Allah wills. Then it will be blown a second time, and behold they will be standing, looking on [waiting].﴾ *(Qur'an 39: 68)*

The Qur'an calls the first blast of the Trumpet *Ar-Raajifah*, and the second *Ar-Raadifah*. Allah (سبحانه وتعالى) says:

﴿ يَوْمَ تَرْجُفُ ٱلرَّاجِفَةُ ﴿٦﴾ تَتْبَعُهَا ٱلرَّادِفَةُ ﴿٧﴾ ﴾

﴿On the Day [when the first blowing of the Trumpet is blown], the earth and the mountains will shake violently [and everybody will die]. The second blowing of the Trumpet follows it [and everybody will be resurrected].﴾ *(Qur'an 79: 6-7)*

Elsewhere the first blast is called *Aṣ-Ṣayḥah*, and the idea of blowing into the Trumpet is clearly mentioned in the second case. Allah (سبحانه وتعالى) says:

﴿ مَا يَنظُرُونَ إِلَّا صَيْحَةً وَٰحِدَةً تَأْخُذُهُمْ وَهُمْ يَخِصِّمُونَ ﴿٤٩﴾ فَلَا
يَسْتَطِيعُونَ تَوْصِيَةً وَلَآ إِلَىٰٓ أَهْلِهِمْ يَرْجِعُونَ ﴿٥٠﴾ وَنُفِخَ فِي ٱلصُّورِ فَإِذَا
هُم مِّنَ ٱلْأَجْدَاثِ إِلَىٰ رَبِّهِمْ يَنسِلُونَ ﴿٥١﴾ ﴾

﴿They await only but a single *Ṣayḥah* [shout] which will

> seize them while they are disputing! Then they will not be able to make bequest, nor they will return to their family. And the Trumpet will be blown [i.e. the second blowing] and behold from the graves they will come out quickly to their Lord.﴿ *(Qur'an 36: 49-51)*

The *aḥaadeeth* of the Prophet (ﷺ) clearly mention the two Trumpet-blasts. In Bukhari and Muslim, it is narrated that Abu Hurayrah (رضي الله عنه) said, "The Prophet (ﷺ) said: 'What is between the two Trumpet-blasts is forty.'

They said, 'O' Abu Hurayrah, forty days?' I refused to answer. They said, 'Forty months?' I refused to answer. They said, 'Forty years?' I refused to answer."[12]

In Muslim it is narrated from 'Abdullah ibn 'Amr ibn al-'Aaṣ that he heard the Messenger of Allah (ﷺ) say:

> "Then the Trumpet will be blown, and no one will hear it but will tilt his head. The first one to hear it will be a man who will be fixing the trough for his camels. He will fall unconscious, and the people will fall unconscious. Then Allah will send - or he said, send down - rain, like dew (*ṭill*) or shade (*ẓill*) (Nu'maan,[13] a narrator, was uncertain), which will cause the bodies of the people to grow. Then the Trumpet will be blown a second time, and they will be standing, looking on (waiting)."[14]

Al-Bayhaqi narrated with a *Qawiy isnaad* (dependable chain of narrators) from Ibn Mas'ood a *mawqoof* report which says: "Then the

---

[12] Bukhari in his *Ṣaḥeeḥ, Kitaab at-Tafseer, Tafseer Soorah az-Zumar*; *Fatḥ al-Baari*, 11/551. Also narrated by Muslim in his *Ṣaḥeeḥ*, 4/2270, hadith no. 2955.

[13] Nu'maan ibn Saalim, one of the narrators of this hadith.

[14] Muslim, 4/2258, hadith no. 2940.

angel of the Trumpet will stand between the heavens and the earth, and will blow (the Trumpet), which is a horn. Then no creature will be left in the heavens or on earth, but will die, apart from whomever your Lord wills. Then between the two Trumpet-blasts there will be a period as long as Allah wills."[15]

Aws ibn Aws al-Thaqafi narrated that the Messenger (ﷺ) said:

> "The best of your days is Friday. On this day the *ṣa'iqah* (when all creatures fall unconscious) will happen, and on this day the Trumpet will be sounded."[16]

This is also narrated by Abu Dawood, Nasaa'i and Aḥmad, and classed as *ṣaḥeeḥ* by Ibn Khuzaymah, Ibn Ḥibbaan and Al-Ḥaakim.[17]

What is indicated by the *aayaat* (verses) and *aḥaadeeth* which we have quoted here is viewed as most correct by a number of scholars, including Qurṭubi[18] and Ibn Ḥajar al-'Asqallaani.[19]

Another group of scholars are of the view that there will be three blasts of the Trumpet, namely the blast which strikes terror into all, the blast which causes all to fall unconscious, and the blast which signals the Resurrection.

Among the scholars who shared this view are Ibn al-'Arabi,[20] Ibn Taymiyah,[21] Ibn Katheer [22] and As-Safaareeni.[23] The evidence quoted by those who favour this view is the fact that Allah (ﷻ)

---

[15] *Fatḥ al-Baari*, 11/370.
[16] Ibid.
[17] Ibid.
[18] *At-Tadhkirah* Pp. 183, 184.
[19] *Fatḥ al-Baari*, 11/369.
[20] *Fataawa Shaykh al-Islam*, 4/260.
[21] *Fatḥ al-Baari*, 11/369; *Tadhkirat al-Qurṭubi*, Pp. 184.
[22] *An-Nihaayah* by Ibn Katheer, 1/253.
[23] *Lawaami' al-Anwaar al-Bahiyah*, 2/161.

mentions the Trumpet-blast which will strike terror into all in the *aayah* (verse):

﴿ وَيَوْمَ يُنفَخُ فِي ٱلصُّورِ فَفَزِعَ مَن فِي ٱلسَّمَٰوَٰتِ وَمَن فِي ٱلْأَرْضِ إِلَّا مَن شَآءَ ٱللَّهُ ... ﴿٨٧﴾ ﴾

﴾And [remember] the Day on which the Trumpet will be blown and all who are in the heavens and all who are on the earth, will be terrified except him whom Allah will [exempt]...﴿ *(Qur'an 27: 87)*

They also cite some *aḥaadeeth* which state that there will be three Trumpet-blasts, such as the hadith about the Trumpet, which is a lengthy hadith narrated by Aṭ-Ṭabari, in which it says:

> "Then there will be three blasts of the Trumpet, the blast which will strike terror, the blast which will cause all to fall unconscious, and the blast which will bring about the Resurrection to (meet) the Lord of the Worlds."[24]

The *aayah* they quoted that mentions the blast which will strike terror, does not clearly state that this is a third Trumpet-blast. What Allah says in this *aayah* about the blast which will strike terror into everyone in the heavens and on earth when the Trumpet is blown does not necessarily imply that this is a separate blast; the first Trumpet-blast will terrify all living beings before they fall unconscious, and the second Trumpet-blast will terrify all people when they are resurrected.

Ibn Ḥajar (may Allah have mercy on him) said: "The fact that these are two concepts does not mean that they cannot both happen as the result of the first Trumpet-blast."[25] And in *Tadhkirat al-Qurṭubi* it says: "The Trumpet blast which will strike terror is the blast which

---

[24] *Fatḥ al-Baari*, 11/369.
[25] Ibid, 11/369.

will cause all to fall unconscious, because the two things are both implied, i.e., they will be so terrified that they will die from it."[26]

The hadith about the Trumpet is *ḍa'eef* (weak) and faulty, as the eminent scholar of hadith, Ibn Ḥajar al-'Asqallaani (may Allah have mercy on him) said. It is also narrated from Al-Bayqahi that it is *ḍa'eef.*[27]

Ibn Ḥazm thought that the number of Trumpet-blasts on the Day of Resurrection would be four: "The first blast would cause everything to die; the second would bring them back to life, so that everyone who is dead will be resurrected and come forth from their graves; the third would fill them with terror and cause them to fall unconscious, but will not cause anyone to die; and the fourth would rouse them from that unconsciousness."[28]

After narrating Ibn Ḥazm's comments, Ibn Ḥajar said: "What he says about the two being four is not clear; there will be only two blasts. The differences in the case of each Trumpet-blast will have to do with those who hear it. In the first case, everyone who is alive will die, and those who are exempted by Allah and do not die will fall unconscious. In the second case, all those who died will come back to life, and those who fell unconscious will wake up. And Allah knows best."[29]

6 - THOSE WHO WILL NOT FALL UNCONSCIOUS WHEN THE TRUMPET IS BLOWN

Allah (ﷻ) tells us that some of those who are in the heavens and on earth will not swoon when everyone else in the heavens and on earth does so.

---

[26] *At-Tadhkirah*, Pp. 184.
[27] *Fatḥ al-Baari*, 11/369.
[28] Ibid, 6/446.
[29] Ibid.

﴿ وَنُفِخَ فِى ٱلصُّورِ فَصَعِقَ مَن فِى ٱلسَّمَٰوَٰتِ وَمَن فِى ٱلْأَرْضِ إِلَّا مَن شَآءَ ٱللَّهُ ۖ ثُمَّ نُفِخَ فِيهِ أُخْرَىٰ فَإِذَا هُمْ قِيَامٌ يَنظُرُونَ ﴿٦٨﴾ ﴾

﴾And the Trumpet will be blown, and all who are in the heavens and all who are on the earth will swoon away, except him whom Allah wills. Then it will be blown a second time, and behold they will be standing, looking on [waiting].﴿ *(Qur'an 39: 68)*

The scholars differed as to who exactly is referred to in the phrase, "except him whom Allah wills."

1) Ibn Ḥazm was of the view that this refers to all the angels, because he believed that the angels are souls, not souls in bodies, so they will never die.[30]

The view that the angels will not die cannot be accepted without questioning. The angels are part of the creation of Allah; they are slaves who are subjugated to their Lord. He created them, and He is Able to cause them to die and to bring them back to life. It is narrated authentically with more than one *isnaad* and from more than one of the *Ṣaḥaabah* that the Prophet (ﷺ) said:

> "When Allah speaks words of Revelation, the angels are overcome with something like swooning." According to another report: "When the angels hear His words, they fall unconscious."

In this hadith, he told us that they fall unconscious. If it is possible for them to fall unconscious, then it is also possible for them to die.[31]

2) Muqaatil and others were of the view that those who will be exempted are Jibra'eel, Mikaa'eel, Israafeel and the Angel of

---

[30] *Fatḥ al-Baari*, 6/371.

[31] *Majmoo' al-Fataawa Shaykh al-Islam*, 4/260.

Death.[32] Some scholars also included the bearers of the Throne.[33] The soundness of this view depends on the *aḥaadeeth* which they narrated. The scholars of hadith did not regard these reports as *ṣaḥeeḥ* (sound).[34]

3) Imam Aḥmad ibn Ḥanbal (may Allah have mercy on him) was of the view that this referred to those who are in Paradise, *Al-Ḥoor al-'Iyn* and immortal boys (cf. 56:17). Abu Isḥaaq ibn Shaaqilaa among the Ḥanbalis and Aḍ-Ḍaḥḥaak ibn Mazaaḥim also included the gatekeepers of Paradise and Hell, and the snakes and scorpions that are in Hell.[35]

Ibn Taymiyah (may Allah have mercy on him) said: "This exemption includes the *Ḥoor al- 'Iyn* who are in Paradise, for there is no death in Paradise."[36]

4) Abu'l-'Abbaas al-Qurṭubi, the author of *Al-Mufhim ila Sharḥ Muslim*, thought that what was meant was all the dead, because they have no feelings, so they cannot fall unconscious.[37]

What Abu'l-'Abbaas said is correct if we interpret *As-Sa'q* (falling unconscious or swooning) as meaning death, for man will die only once. Allah (ﷻ) says:

﴿ لَا يَذُوقُونَ فِيهَا ٱلْمَوْتَ إِلَّا ٱلْمَوْتَةَ ٱلْأُولَىٰ ... ﴿٥٦﴾ ﴾

﴿They will never taste death therein except the first death [of this world]...﴾ *(Qur'an 44: 56)*

---

[32] *Ar-Rooḥ* by Ibn al-Qayyim, Pp. 50; *Fatḥ al-Baari*, 6/371.

[33] *Fatḥ al-Baari*, 6/371.

[34] Ibid.

[35] *Ar-Rooḥ* by Ibn al-Qayyim, Pp. 50; *Fatḥ al-Baari*, 6/371.

[36] *Majmoo' al-Fataawa Shaykh al-Islam*, 4/261.

[37] *Fatḥ al-Baari*, 6/370.

In his book *Ar-Rooḥ*, Ibn al-Qayyim discusses how scholars differed concerning the death of souls when the Trumpet is blown.

What Ibn al-Qayyim thought was correct that the death of souls refers to when they leave their bodies. He refuted the view of those who say that the souls will die and vanish, because the texts indicate that the souls will remain in *Al-Barzakh*, either to be punished or to enjoy blessings.[38]

But if we interpret *Aṣ-Ṣa'q* referring to swooning or falling unconscious, then the souls will swoon and thus they are not included among those who are exempted by Allah. A man may see or hear something that terrifies him, so he falls unconscious, as happened to Moosa (Moses) (ﷺ) when he saw the mountain vanish from where it was:

﴿ ...لِلْجَبَلِ جَعَلَهُۥ دَكًّا وَخَرَّ مُوسَىٰ صَعِقًا... ﴿١٤٣﴾ ﴾

﴿...He made it collapse to dust, and Moosa [Moses] fell down unconscious...﴾ *(Qur'an 7: 143)*

This meaning is clear in some texts. According to the hadith of Abu Hurayrah narrated by Bukhari, the Messenger of Allah (ﷺ) said:

> "Do not prefer me over Moosa (Moses), for the people will fall unconscious on the Day of Resurrection; I will be the first to regain consciousness, and Moosa will be there, holding on to the side of the Throne. I do not know whether Moosa will be one of those who will fell unconscious and then wake up before me, or whether he will be one of those whom Allah exempted (from falling unconscious)."[39]

[38] *Ar-Rooḥ* by Ibn al-Qayyim, Pp. 49.

[39] Bukhari, *Kitaab Aḥaadeeth al-Anbiya, Baab Wafaat Moosa*; *Fatḥ al-Baari*, 6/441.

Bukhari also narrated it from Abu Hurayrah (ﷺ) with the wording:

> "I will be the first one to raise his head after the final Trumpet-blast, and I will see Moosa hanging on to the Throne, and I do not know whether he was like that before, or after the Trumpet-blast."[40]

In a third place it is narrated with the wording:

> "The people will fall unconscious on the Day of Resurrection, and I will be the first one to wake up. Then I will see Moosa holding on to one of the pillars of the Throne, and I do not know if he will be one of those who awoke before me, or if he is one of those who are exempted by Allah."[41]

This hadith clearly states that the dead will swoon, and if the Messenger of Allah (ﷺ), who is the leader of the Messengers, will swoon, then it is more likely that others will do so too.

Some scholars said that those who will fall unconscious or swoon are the *shuhadaa'* (martyrs), to the exclusion of others among the dead; other scholars also included the Prophets among this group.

The reason why this will be limited only to the *shuhadaa'* and Prophets, as the *shaykh* of Qurṭubi, Aḥmad ibn 'Umar, said: "is because after the *shuhadaa'* are killed, they are alive with their Lord, and they have provision, rejoicing in what Allah has bestowed upon them (cf. Qur'an 3:170). This is also the attribute of those who are alive in this world. If this is the situation of the *shuhadaa'*, then the Prophets are even more entitled to be in such a condition. Moreover, it is narrated in a *ṣaḥeeḥ* report from the Prophet (ﷺ) that the earth does not consume the bodies of the Prophets, and that the Prophet

---

[40] Bukhari, *Kitaab at-Tafseer, Tafseer Soorah az-Zumar*; *Fatḥ al-Baari*, 8/551.

[41] Ibid, *Kitaab ar-Riqaaq, Baab an-Nafkh fi'ṣ-Ṣoor*; *Fatḥ al-Baari*, 11/367.

(ﷺ) met with the Prophets - particularly Moosa (Moses) - on the night of the *Israa'* in *Bayt al-Maqdis* (Jerusalem) and in the heavens. The Prophet (ﷺ) has told us that Allah restores his soul to him so that he may return the greeting of *salaam* to all those who send *salaams* upon him. These and other reports combine to offer definitive proof that the death of the Prophets is merely their absence from us so that we cannot meet them, even though they exist and are alive. If we accept that they are alive, then when the Trumpet is blown with the blast that will cause everyone to fall unconscious, everyone in the heavens and on earth will fall unconscious, except for those whom Allah wills."[42]

Al-Bayhaqi thought that the *shuhadaa'* and Prophets will fall unconscious or swoon. He said concerning the swooning of the Prophets: "In my view, they are alive with their Lord like the *shuhadaa'*. When the first Trumpet-blast is sounded, they will fall unconscious, but that will not be a death in the true sense of the word; it will merely be a loss of consciousness. The Prophet (ﷺ) referred to the possibility that Moosa (Moses) may be one of those who are exempted by Allah, but if he is among them he will not lose consciousness at that time, because of what happened to him when the mountain crumbled."[43]

Based on this understanding, the Prophets and *shuhadaa'* will be among those who fall unconscious, and they are not included in the exception (mentioned in the *aayah*). It is narrated from Ibn 'Abbaas, Abu Hurayrah and Sa'eed ibn Jubayr that the Prophets and *shuhadaa'* will be among those who are exempted by Allah.[44] Ibn Ḥajar attributed this view to Al-Bayhaqi.[45] If it is that they will be

---

42 *At-Tadhkirah*, Pp. 169.

43 *Fatḥ al-Baari*, 11/371.

44 *Ar-Rooḥ* by Ibn al-Qayyim, Pp. 50.

45 *Fatḥ al-Baari*, 11/371.

exempted from death at that time, then this is true; if it is meant that they will be exempted from falling unconscious which will happen to all the dead, as indicated by the hadith of Moosa, then this is not the case.

Some scholars said that it is better for the Muslim to refrain from specifying who will be exempted by Allah, because there is no *ṣaḥeeḥ* report which lists them.

Qurṭubi, the author of *At-Tadhkirah*, said: "Our *Shaykh* Abu'l-'Abbaas said: the correct view is that there is no *ṣaheeḥ* report to specify who is referred to this exception. All the view mentioned above are possible."[46]

Ibn Taymiyah said: "This exemption refers to all those who are in Paradise, *Al-Ḥoor al-'Iyn*, because there is no death in Paradise, and it refers to others, but we cannot be certain of all those who will be exempted by Allah, because this is a general statement. The Prophet (ﷺ) refrained from making a definite comment as to whether Moosa (Moses) is one of those who will be exempted by Allah or not. Because the Prophet (ﷺ) was not told of all those who will be exempted by Allah, it is not possible for us to know any of that for certain. This is like the knowledge of when the Hour will come, or the names of all the Prophets, and other matters which Allah has not informed us of, for this is knowledge which cannot be known without a report. And Allah knows best."[47]

Qurṭubi narrated that Al-Ḥaleemi did not accept that the bearers of the Throne, Jibreel, Mikaa'eel and the Angel of Death, the immortal boys and *Al-Ḥoor al-'Iyn* in Paradise, or Moosa (Moses) would be among those who will be exempted. He explained his reasons for

---

[46] *At-Tadhkirah*, Pp. 167.

[47] *Majmoo' al-Fataawa Shaykh al-Islam*, 4/261.

rejecting this idea as follows: "The bearers of the Throne are not among the inhabitants of the heavens and the earth, because the Throne is above all the heavens, so how could its bearers be in the heavens? Jibreel, Mikaa'eel and the Angel of Death are among the angels gathered in ranks around the Throne, glorifying Allah. If the Throne is above the heavens, those who are gathered in ranks around it cannot be in the heavens. The same applies to the second group, because the immortal boys and *Al-Ḥoor al-'Iyn* are in Paradise, and even though parts of Paradise are above others, all of it is above the heavens and beneath the Throne. It is the only world that has been created to endure forever, so there is no doubt that it is excluded from that which Allah has created to pass away. There is no evidence to support the idea that Moosa will be exempted, because he has already died in reality, so he will not die when the Trumpet is blown for the second time."[48]

He refuted the view of those who said that the ones who will be exempted are the dead, "because the exemption applies only to those who could be included. As regards those who cannot be included, it makes no sense to exclude them. Those who die before the Trumpet is sounded will not be subject to this swooning, so there is no sense in excluding them."[49]

His view is that the swooning or loss of consciousness that will befall Moosa is not the swooning which will cause the people's death; rather it is the swooning that will befall the people in the arena of judgement after they have been resurrected, according to one of the two possibilities that he suggested.

Qurṭubi narrated that this was the view of his *shaykh*, Aḥmad ibn 'Umar. Qurṭubi said: "Our *shaykh*, Aḥmad ibn 'Umar, said: the

---

[48] *At-Tadhkirah*, Pp. 168.
[49] Ibid.

apparent meaning of the hadith of the Prophet (ﷺ) indicates that that will happen after the second Trumpet-blast, the blast which will signal the Resurrection. The text of the Qur'an implies that this exemption will take place after the Trumpet-blast which will cause everyone to fall unconscious. Because of this, some of the scholars suggested that it is possible that Moosa (عليه السلام) was one of the Prophets who did not die, but this is incorrect, because of what is mentioned above about his death. Al-Qaaḍi 'Iyaaḍ said: it is possible that what is meant by this swooning is the terror which will come after the Resurrection, when the heavens and earth will be split asunder ... and Allah knows best."[50]

Ibn al-Qayyim (may Allah have mercy on him) was certain that the swooning of which the Messenger (ﷺ) spoke was the swooning which will come after the Resurrection, referred to in the *aayah*:

﴿ فَذَرْهُمْ حَتَّىٰ يُلَٰقُوا۟ يَوْمَهُمُ ٱلَّذِى فِيهِ يُصْعَقُونَ ﴿٤٥﴾ ﴾

﴾So leave them alone till they meet their Day, in which they will sink into a fainting [with horror].﴿

(Qur'an 52: 45)[51]

And Allah knows best.

[50] *At-Tadhkirah*, Pp. 168.

[51] *Ar-Rooḥ*, Pp. 52.

CHAPTER THREE
THE RESURRECTION

1 - DEFINITION OF *AL-BA'TH WAN-NUSHOOR* (THE RESURRECTION)

The meaning of *al-ba'th* is the restoration of the body and bringing it back to life on the Day of Resurrection. *An-Nushoor* is a synonym of *al-ba'th*; it is said in Arabic, *nashara al-mayyit nushooran*, to refer to when the dead comes to life again after dying and Allah brings him back to life and resurrects him. When Allah (ﷻ) wills to bring His slaves back to life, He will command Israafeel to blow the Trumpet and the souls will return to the bodies, and the people will rise to meet the Lord of the Worlds.

﴿ وَنُفِخَ فِي ٱلصُّورِ فَصَعِقَ مَن فِي ٱلسَّمَٰوَٰتِ وَمَن فِي ٱلْأَرْضِ إِلَّا مَن شَآءَ ٱللَّهُ ثُمَّ نُفِخَ فِيهِ أُخْرَىٰ فَإِذَا هُمْ قِيَامٌ يَنظُرُونَ ﴿٦٨﴾ ﴾

﴾And the Trumpet will be blown, and all who are in the heavens and all who are on the earth will swoon away, except him whom Allah wills. Then it will be blown a second time, and behold they will be standing, looking on [waiting].﴿ *(Qur'an 39: 68)*

Allah (ﷻ) tells us of the strange and wondrous scenes (of that Day):

﴿ وَنُفِخَ فِي ٱلصُّورِ فَإِذَا هُم مِّنَ ٱلْأَجْدَاثِ إِلَىٰ رَبِّهِمْ يَنسِلُونَ ﴿٥١﴾ قَالُوا۟ يَٰوَيْلَنَا مَنۢ بَعَثَنَا مِن مَّرْقَدِنَا ۜ هَٰذَا مَا وَعَدَ ٱلرَّحْمَٰنُ وَصَدَقَ ٱلْمُرْسَلُونَ ﴿٥٢﴾ إِن كَانَتْ إِلَّا صَيْحَةً وَٰحِدَةً فَإِذَا هُمْ جَمِيعٌ لَّدَيْنَا مُحْضَرُونَ ﴿٥٣﴾ ﴾

﴾And the Trumpet will be blown [i.e. the second blowing] and behold from the graves they will come out

> quickly to their Lord. They will say: 'Woe to us! Who has raised us up from our place of sleep.' [It will be said to them]: 'This is what the Most Gracious [Allah] had promised, and the Messengers spoke truth!' It will be but a single *Sayḥah* [shout], so behold they will all be brought up before Us!" *(Qur'an 36: 51-53)*

There are *ahaadeeth* which state that the second Trumpet-blast will be preceded by the falling of water from the sky, which will cause the bodies of people to grow. In *Saheeḥ Muslim* it is narrated from 'Abdullah ibn 'Amr that the Messenger of Allah (ﷺ) said:

> "Then the Trumpet will be blown, and no one will hear it but tilt his head. The first one to hear it will be a man who will be fixing his camel's drinking-trough. He will fall unconscious, and all the people will fall unconscious. Then Allaah will send - or send down - rain like dew (*ṭill*) or a shadow (*ẓill*) (Nu'maan - one of the narrators of this hadith - was the one who was not sure), from which the bodies of the people will grow. Then the Trumpet will be blown again and they will be standing, looking on (waiting)."[1]

The way the bodies will grow from the ground after Allah sends down that water which will cause them to grow will be like the way plants grow from the earth when there is rain in this world. Hence, in His Book, Allah frequently likens the Resurrection to the revival of the earth with vegetation after rainfalls. Allah (ﷻ) says:

﴿ وَهُوَ ٱلَّذِى يُرْسِلُ ٱلرِّيَٰحَ بُشْرًۢا بَيْنَ يَدَىْ رَحْمَتِهِۦ ۖ حَتَّىٰٓ إِذَآ أَقَلَّتْ سَحَابًا ثِقَالًا سُقْنَٰهُ لِبَلَدٍ مَّيِّتٍ فَأَنزَلْنَا بِهِ ٱلْمَآءَ فَأَخْرَجْنَا بِهِۦ مِن كُلِّ ٱلثَّمَرَٰتِ ۚ كَذَٰلِكَ نُخْرِجُ ٱلْمَوْتَىٰ لَعَلَّكُمْ تَذَكَّرُونَ ﴿٥٧﴾ ﴾

[1] Muslim, 4/2259, hadith no. 2940.

﴿And it is He Who sends the winds as heralds of glad tidings, going before His Mercy [rain]. Till when they have carried a heavy-laden cloud, We drive it to a land that is dead, then We cause water [rain] to descend thereon. Then We produce every kind of fruit therewith. Similarly, We shall raise up the dead, so that you may remember or take heed.﴾ *(Qur'an 7: 57)*

Elsewhere, He (ﷻ) says:

﴿ وَٱللَّهُ ٱلَّذِىٓ أَرْسَلَ ٱلرِّيَٰحَ فَتُثِيرُ سَحَابًا فَسُقْنَٰهُ إِلَىٰ بَلَدٍ مَّيِّتٍ فَأَحْيَيْنَا بِهِ
ٱلْأَرْضَ بَعْدَ مَوْتِهَا ۚ كَذَٰلِكَ ٱلنُّشُورُ ﴿٩﴾ ﴾

﴿And it is Allah Who sends the winds, so that they raise up the clouds, and We drive them to a dead land, and revive therewith the earth after its death. As such [will be] the Resurrection!﴾ *(Qur'an 35: 9)*

Note that in these verses, Allah says, ﴿Similarly, We shall raise up the dead﴾ and ﴿As such [will be] the Resurrection.﴾ They point to the similarity between the restoration of people's bodies by means of them growing from the earth after the water comes down just before the Trumpet is blown, and the springing forth of vegetation after rain falls from the sky. We know that plants come from small seeds which lie dormant in the earth, then rain falls upon them and life stirs within them and they send down roots into the earth and send up shoots towards the sky, then they become fully-formed, green plants.

On the Last Day, humans will be formed from a small bone. When the water reaches this bone, it will grow like herbs. This bone is the coccyx (tailbone) which is a round bone at the base of the spine. In Bukhari and Muslim, it is narrated from Abu Hurayrah (رضي الله عنه) that the Messenger of Allah (ﷺ) said:

"Between the two Trumpet-blasts there will be forty, then water will come down from the sky, and they will grow like herbs. There is no part of man that does not disintegrate (after he dies), except for one bone, which is the coccyx. From this he will be created anew on the Day of Resurrection."

Muslim has another report about the coccyx:

"In man there is a bone which will not be consumed by the earth, and from it he will be created anew on the Day of Resurrection." They asked, "Which bone is that, O' Messenger of Allah?" He said, "The coccyx."

According to a report narrated by Muslim, *Al-Muwaṭṭa'*, Abu Dawood and Nasaa'i, the Messenger of Allah (ﷺ) said:

"All of the children of Adam will be consumed by the earth apart from the coccyx, from which he was created and will be created anew."[2]

The *ṣaḥeeḥ* (sound and authentic) texts indicate that the bodies of the Prophets will not decay or disappear as happens to the bodies of others. According to a hadith narrated by Abu Dawood and classed as *ṣaḥeeḥ* by Ibn Khuzaymah and others, "Allah has forbidden the earth to consume the bodies of the Prophets."[3]

2 - THE RESURRECTION WILL BE A NEW CREATION

Allah (ﷻ) will restore the souls of His slaves, but they will be created anew, different from the way they were in the life of this world. One feature of this new creation will be that they will not die, no matter what trials befall them.

---

[2] *Jaami' al-Uṣool*, 10/421, hadith no. 7941.

[3] *Fatḥ al-Baari*, 6/488.

﴿... وَيَأْتِيهِ ٱلْمَوْتُ مِن كُلِّ مَكَانٍ وَمَا هُوَ بِمَيِّتٍ ... ﴿١٧﴾﴾

﴾...And death will come to him from every side, yet he will not die...﴿ *(Qur'an 14: 17)*

According to a hadith narrated by Al-Ḥaakim with a *ṣaḥeeḥ isnaad*, 'Amr ibn Maymoon al-Awdi said: "Mu'aadh ibn Jabal stood up among us and he said, 'O' Banu Awd, I am the messenger of the Messenger of Allah (ﷺ). You know that you will be resurrected to (meet) Allah, then (you will go) to Paradise or to Hell, where you will settle and never leave, you will abide forever and never die, in bodies that will never die.'" A similar report is narrated by Aṭ-Ṭabaraani in *Al-Kabeer and Al-Awsaṭ*.[4]

For example, people will be able to see things that they could not see before. They will see the angels and the jinn, and other things which only Allah knows. Similarly, the people of Paradise will not spit, defecate or urinate.

This does not mean that those who are resurrected on the Day of Judgement will be an entirely different creation than they were in this world. Ibn Taymiyah (may Allah have mercy on him) said: "The two creations are two things of the same category, they are similar in one way and different in another."[5]

3 - THE FIRST PERSON FOR WHOM THE EARTH WILL BE SPLIT OPEN

The first person for whom the earth will be split open will be our Prophet Muhammad (ﷺ). In *Ṣaḥeeḥ Muslim* it is narrated that Abu

---

[4] *Silsilat al-Aḥaadeeth aṣ-Ṣaḥeeḥah*, 4/231, hadith no. 1668.

[5] *Majmoo' al-Fataawa Shaykh al-Islam*, 17/253. Ibn Taymiyah spoke at length about the matter which we have referred to here. For more information, please see the reference given here.

Hurayrah (ﷺ) said that the Messenger of Allah (ﷺ) said:

> "I will be the leader of the children of Adam on the Day of Resurrection, and the first one for whom the grave will be split open, the first one to intercede and the first one whose intercession will be accepted..."[6]

Bukhari and Muslim narrated that Abu Hurayrah said: "A man from among the Muslims and a man from among the Jews had an argument. The Muslim said, 'By the One Who chose Muhammad above all of creation,' and the Jew said, 'By the One Who chose Moosa (Moses) above all of creation.' At that point, the Muslim raised his hand and slapped the Jew. The Jew went to the Messenger of Allah (ﷺ) and told him what had taken place between him and the Muslim.

The Prophet (ﷺ) said,

> 'Do not prefer me over Moosa (Moses), for the people will fall unconscious, and I will be the first one to wake up, and I will see Moosa holding on to one of the pillars of the Throne. I do not know whether he will be one of those who fell unconscious and then woke up, or one of those who are exempted by Allah.'"

According to another report narrated by Bukhari and Muslim:

> "...The Trumpet will be blown, and everyone in the heavens and on earth will fall unconscious, except for those whom Allah wills. Then the Trumpet will be blown a second time and I will be the first one to be resurrected, and I will see Moosa (Moses) holding on to the Throne. I do not know whether he will be excused

---

[6] Muslim, *Kitaab al-Faḍaa'il*, *Baab Faḍl Nasab an-Nabi*, 4/1782, hadith no.2278.

because he fell unconscious at the Mount, or he will be resurrected before me."[7]

4 - ALL CREATED BEINGS WILL BE GATHERED TOGETHER IN ONE HUGE PLACE

Allah (ﷻ) calls the Day of Judgement the Day of Gathering, because Allah will gather all His slaves together.

﴿... ذَٰلِكَ يَوْمٌ مَّجْمُوعٌ لَّهُ ٱلنَّاسُ وَذَٰلِكَ يَوْمٌ مَّشْهُودٌ ﴿١٠٣﴾﴾

﴾...That is a Day whereon mankind will be gathered together, and that is a Day when all [the dwellers of the heavens and the earth] will be present.﴿ *(Qur'an 11: 103)*

In that gathering, the first and the last will all be included:

﴿قُلْ إِنَّ ٱلْأَوَّلِينَ وَٱلْآخِرِينَ ﴿٤٩﴾ لَمَجْمُوعُونَ إِلَىٰ مِيقَٰتِ يَوْمٍ مَّعْلُومٍ ﴿٥٠﴾﴾

﴾Say [O' Muhammad]: '[Yes] verily, those of old, and those of later times. All will surely be gathered together for appointed Meeting of a known Day.﴿

(Qur'an 56: 49-50)

The will of Allah encompasses all His slaves, and nothing is impossible for Allah. Although His slaves will die, Allah is Able to bring them back, even if they die in the farthest reaches of space or in the depths of the earth, or are eaten by vultures and wild animals, or by the fish of the sea, or are buried in their graves in the earth. All of that is the same for Allah.

﴿... أَيْنَ مَا تَكُونُوا۟ يَأْتِ بِكُمُ ٱللَّهُ جَمِيعًا ۚ إِنَّ ٱللَّهَ عَلَىٰ كُلِّ شَىْءٍ قَدِيرٌ ﴿١٤٨﴾﴾

---

[7] *Jaami' al-Uṣool*, 8/513, hadith no. 6308.

﴿...Wheresoever you may be, Allah will bring you together [on the Day of Resurrection]. Truly, Allah is Able to do all things.﴾ *(Qur'an 2: 148)*

As Allah's power encompasses His slaves, He will bring them forth no matter where they are. His knowledge also encompasses them and He will not forget any of them. None of them will be left out or overlooked; He has counted them all and He knows their numbers.

﴿ إِن كُلُّ مَن فِي ٱلسَّمَٰوَٰتِ وَٱلۡأَرۡضِ إِلَّآ ءَاتِي ٱلرَّحۡمَٰنِ عَبۡدٗا ﴿٩٣﴾ لَّقَدۡ أَحۡصَىٰهُمۡ وَعَدَّهُمۡ عَدّٗا ﴿٩٤﴾ وَكُلُّهُمۡ ءَاتِيهِ يَوۡمَ ٱلۡقِيَٰمَةِ فَرۡدًا ﴿٩٥﴾ ﴾

﴿There is none in the heavens and the earth but comes unto the Most Gracious [Allah] as a slave. Verily, He knows each one of them, and has counted them a full counting. And everyone of them will come to Him alone [without any helper, or protector or defender].﴾
(Qur'an 19: 93-95)

﴿ ... وَحَشَرۡنَٰهُمۡ فَلَمۡ نُغَادِرۡ مِنۡهُمۡ أَحَدٗا ﴿٤٧﴾ ﴾

﴿...And we shall gather them all together so as to leave not one of them behind.﴾ *(Qur'an 18: 47)*

The general meaning of these texts indicates that all of creation will be gathered together, humans, jinn and angels; there is nothing wrong with the view of those who say that the animals will be gathered too.

The scholars differed as to whether the animals would be included in this gathering. Ibn Taymiyah was of the view that this would be the case.

Shaykh al-Islam Ibn Taymiyah (may Allah have mercy on him) said: "As for the animals, they will all be gathered to Allah, as is indicated in the Qur'an and Sunnah." Allah (ﷻ) says:

﴿ وَمَا مِن دَآبَّةٖ فِي ٱلۡأَرۡضِ وَلَا طَٰٓئِرٖ يَطِيرُ بِجَنَاحَيۡهِ إِلَّآ أُمَمٌ أَمۡثَالُكُمۚ مَّا فَرَّطۡنَا فِي ٱلۡكِتَٰبِ مِن شَيۡءٖۚ ثُمَّ إِلَىٰ رَبِّهِمۡ يُحۡشَرُونَ ﴿٣٨﴾ ﴾

﴾There is not a moving [living] creature on earth, nor a bird that flies with its two wings, but are communities like you. We have neglected nothing in the Book, then unto their Lord they [all] shall be gathered.﴿ *(Qur'an 6: 38)*

﴿ وَإِذَا ٱلۡوُحُوشُ حُشِرَتۡ ﴿٥﴾ ﴾

﴾And when the wild beasts shall be gathered together.﴿ *(Qur'an 81: 5)*

﴿ وَمِنۡ ءَايَٰتِهِۦ خَلۡقُ ٱلسَّمَٰوَٰتِ وَٱلۡأَرۡضِ وَمَا بَثَّ فِيهِمَا مِن دَآبَّةٖۚ وَهُوَ عَلَىٰ جَمۡعِهِمۡ إِذَا يَشَآءُ قَدِيرٞ ﴿٢٩﴾ ﴾

﴾And among His *Aayaat* [proofs, evidences, lessons, signs, etc.] is the creation of the heavens and the earth, and whatever moving [living] creatures He has dispersed in them both. And He is All-Potent over their assembling [i.e. resurrecting them on the Day of Resurrection after their death, and dispersion of their bodies] whenever He wills.﴿ *(Qur'an 42: 29)*

The word *idha* (translated here as "whenever") is used to refer to something which will undoubtedly come to pass.

Qurṭubi reported the disagreement among the scholars as to whether the animals would be assembled. He thought that the correct view was that this will happen, because of the *ṣaḥeeḥ* (sound) reports on this matter. Qurṭubi said: "The people differed as to whether the animals will be assembled and will settle scores among one another. It is narrated from Ibn 'Abbaas that the gathering of the animals is their death. This was also the view of Aḍ-Ḍaḥḥaak. According to another report, it is narrated from Ibn 'Abbaas that the animals will be gathered and resurrected. This was the view of Abu Dharr, Abu Hurayrah, 'Amr ibn al-'Aaṣ, Al-Ḥasan al-Baṣri and others. This is the correct view, because Allah says (ﷻ):

﴿ وَإِذَا ٱلْوُحُوشُ حُشِرَتْ ﴿٥﴾ ﴾

﴾And when the wild beasts shall be gathered together.﴿
(Qur'an 81: 5)

And:

﴿ ... ثُمَّ إِلَىٰ رَبِّهِمْ يُحْشَرُونَ ﴿٣٨﴾ ﴾

﴾...Then unto their Lord they [all] shall be gathered.﴿
(Qur'an 6: 38)

Abu Hurayrah said: Allah (ﷻ) will gather all of creation on the Day of Resurrection, animals, birds, everything. The justice of Allah will reach the extent that animals without horns will have the vengeance against animals with horns, then it will be said, 'Be dust.' This is like what Allah says about the *kuffaar* (disbelievers):

﴿ ... وَيَقُولُ ٱلْكَافِرُ يَٰلَيْتَنِى كُنتُ تُرَٰبًۢا ﴿٤٠﴾ ﴾

﴾...And the disbeliever will say: 'Woe to me! Would that I were dust!'﴿ *(Qur'an 78: 40)*.[8]

5 - DESCRIPTION OF THE GATHERING OF MANKIND

Mankind will be gathered barefoot, naked and uncircumcised. Bukhari and Muslim narrated from Ibn 'Abbaas that the Prophet (ﷺ) said:

---

[8] *At-Tadhkirah*, Pp. 273.

"You will be gathered barefoot, naked and uncircumcised."

Then he (ﷺ) recited:

﴿... كَمَا بَدَأْنَآ أَوَّلَ خَلْقٍ نُّعِيدُهُۥ وَعْدًا عَلَيْنَآ إِنَّا كُنَّا فَٰعِلِينَ ﴿١٠٤﴾﴾

﴾...As We began the first creation, We shall repeat it. [It is] a promise binding upon Us. Truly, We shall do it.﴿ *(Qur'an 21: 104)*[9]

When 'Aa'ishah heard the Messenger of Allah (ﷺ) saying:

"Mankind will be gathered on the Day of Resurrection, barefoot, naked and uncircumcised," she said, "O' Messenger of Allah, men and women together, looking at one another?" He said, "O' 'Aa'ishah, it will be too distressing for them to be looking at one another."[10]

In some texts it is reported that each person will be resurrected in the clothes in which he died. Abu Dawood, Ibn Ḥibbaan and Al-Ḥaakim narrated that when Abu Sa'eed al-Khudri was dying, he called for a new garment and put it on, then he said, "I heard the Messenger of Allah (ﷺ) say,

'The dead person will be resurrected in the clothes in which he dies.'"

Al-Ḥaakim said, it is *ṣaḥeeḥ* according to the conditions of the two *Shaykhs* (Bukhari and Muslim). Adh-Dhahabi agreed with him. *Shaykh* Naaṣiruddeen al-Albaani said: it is as they said.[11]

---

9 *Mishkaat al-Maṣaabeeḥ*, 3/75, hadith no. 5535.

10 Ibid, 3/75, hadith no. 5536.

11 *Silasilat al-Aḥaadeeth aṣ-Ṣaḥeeḥah*, 4/234, hadith no. 1671.

Al-Bayhaqi reconciled between this hadith and the previous one in three ways:

Firstly: The clothes will wear out after they are resurrected from their graves, so that when they reach the place of gathering they will be naked, then they will be clothed with the garments of Paradise.

Secondly: When the Prophets are clothed, followed by the *Ṣiddeeqeen* (lovers of truth), then others according to their ranks, each person will be clothed in garments of the same type as those in which he died. Then when they enter Paradise, they will be clothed in garments of Paradise.

Thirdly: What is meant by garments here is one's deeds, i.e., they will be resurrected doing the same actions as they were doing when they died, whether good or bad.

Allah (ﷻ) says:

﴿ ... وَلِبَاسُ ٱلتَّقْوَىٰ ذَٰلِكَ خَيْرٌ ... ﴿٢٦﴾ ﴾

﴿...And the raiment of righteousness, that is better...﴾
(Qur'an 7: 26)

And:

﴿ وَثِيَابَكَ فَطَهِّرْ ﴿٤﴾ ﴾

﴿And purify your garments!﴾ *(Qur'an 74: 4)*

In support of this final point, Al-Bayhaqi quoted the hadith of Al-A'mash, narrated from Abu Sufyaan, from Jaabir, who said: "The Messenger of Allah (ﷺ) said:

'Each person will be resurrected in the state in which he died.'"[12]

---

[12] *An-Nihaayah* by Ibn Katheer, 1/288.

This hadith of Jaabir is narrated by Muslim in his *Ṣaḥeeḥ*.[13] It cannot be understood from this that each person will be resurrected in the clothes in which he was shrouded or in the clothes he was wearing, when he died. Rather, he will be resurrected in the state in which he died, either *eeman* (belief, faith) or *kufr* (disbelief), certainty or doubt. And he will be resurrected doing whatever action he was doing when he died. This is indicated by the report narrated by Muslim in his *Ṣaḥeeḥ* from 'Abdullah ibn 'Umar, who said: "I heard the Messenger of Allah (ﷺ) say,

> 'When Allah wants to punish a people, the punishment befalls whoever is among them, then they will be resurrected according to their deeds.'"[14]

Whoever dies in the state of *iḥraam* will be raised on the Day of Resurrection reciting the *Talbiyah*. In Bukhari, Muslim and *Musnad Aḥmad* it is narrated that 'Abdullah ibn 'Abbaas said that a man was with the Prophet (ﷺ), and his camel threw him off and he broke his neck. He was in *iḥraam*, and he died. The Messenger of Allah (ﷺ) said:

> "Wash him with water and lotus flowers, and shroud him in his two garments; do not anoint him with perfume or cover his head, for on the Day of Resurrection he will be raised reciting the *Talbiyah*."[15]

The *shaheed* (martyr) will be raised on the Day of Resurrection with his wounds bleeding red and with the scent of musk.

Hence it is *mustaḥabb* to encourage the dying person to say *Laa ilaaha ill-Allah* (there is no god except Allah), so that he may die

---

[13] Muslim, 4/2206, hadith no. 2878.

[14] Ibid, 2/2206, hadith no. 2879.

[15] *Mishkaat al-Maṣaabeeḥ*, 1/520, hadith no. 1637.

believing in *Tawḥeed*, and may be resurrected speaking these good words.

6 - THE CLOTHING OF MANKIND ON THE DAY OF RESURRECTION

We have mentioned above that on the Day of Resurrection, Allah will gather His slaves barefoot, naked and uncircumcised, as stated in *ṣaḥeeḥ aḥaadeeth*. Then He will clothe His slaves. The righteous will be clothed in noble garments, and the evildoers will be clothed in trousers of tar and a shield of scabs, and other awful garments.

The first one among the slaves of Allah to be clothed will be the Prophet of Allah Ibraaheem (Abraham) (ﷺ), the Close Friend of the Most Merciful (*Khaleel ar-Raḥmaan*). In Bukhari it is narrated from Ibn 'Abbaas that the Prophet (ﷺ) said:

> "The first of creation to be clothed on the Day of Resurrection will be *Ibraaheem al-Khaleel.*"[16]

Ibn Ḥajar said: "Al-Bayhaqi narrated a similar hadith via Ibn 'Abbaas, and added:

> 'The first one to be clothed on the Day of Resurrection will be Ibraaheem, who will be clothed in a garment from Paradise. A chair will be brought and placed to the right of the Throne, then I will be brought and clothed in a garment from Paradise, the like of which has never been seen.'"[17]

---

[16] Bukhari, *Kitaab ar-Riqaaq, Baab al-Ḥashr*, 11/377; also narrated in *Kitaab al-Anbiyaa'* - see *Fatḥ al-Baari*, 6/387.

[17] *Fatḥ al-Baari*, 11/384.

The scholars mentioned that the reason why Ibraaheem (عليه السلام) will be given priority over others in the matter of being clothed on the Day of Resurrection is that there was no one among the earlier or later generations who feared Allah more than he did. So he will be clothed so as to reassure him and give him peace of mind. It may also be - as is stated in the hadith - because he was the first person to wear trousers when he prayed, as an extra covering and to be more modest. He did what he was commanded to do, so he will be rewarded for that by being the first one to be covered on the Day of Resurrection. It may be that those who threw him into the fire removed his clothes in front of those present, as is done with one who is to be killed, thus he will be rewarded by being the first one to be clothed on the Day of Resurrection, to be witnessed by all people. This is the best explanation of why he will be the first to be clothed."[18]

---

[18] *At-Tadhkirah*, Pp. 209.

The scholars mentioned that the reasons why Ibraaheem (ﷺ) will be given priority over others in the matter of being clothed on the Day of Resurrection is that there was no one among the earlier or later generations who feared Allah more than he did. So he will be clothed so as to reassure him and give him peace of mind. It may also be – as is stated in the hadith – because he was the first person to wear trousers when he prayed, as an extra covering and to be more modest. He did what he was commanded to do, so he will be rewarded for that by being the first one to be covered on the Day of Resurrection. It may be that those who threw him into the fire removed his clothes in front of those present, as is done with one who is to be killed, thus he will be rewarded by being the first one to be clothed on the Day of Resurrection, to be witnessed by all people. This is the best explanation of why he will be the first to be clothed."[18]

[18] Al-Tadhkirah, p. 209

CHAPTER FOUR
THE LAND OF GATHERING

The land on which mankind will be gathered on the Day of Resurrection is other than this earth of ours. Allah (ﷻ)says:

﴿ يَوْمَ تُبَدَّلُ ٱلْأَرْضُ غَيْرَ ٱلْأَرْضِ وَٱلسَّمَٰوَٰتُ ۖ وَبَرَزُوا۟ لِلَّهِ ٱلْوَٰحِدِ ٱلْقَهَّارِ ﴿٤٨﴾ ﴾

> ﴾On the Day when the earth will be changed to another earth and so will be the heavens, and they [all creatures] will appear before Allah, the One, the Irresistible.﴿
>
> *(Qur'an 14: 48)*

The Messenger (ﷺ) has told us about how this new earth, on which the gathering will take place, will be. In Bukhari and Muslim, it is narrated that Sahl ibn Sa'd said: "I heard the Messenger of Allah (ﷺ) say:

> 'On the Day of Resurrection, mankind will be gathered on an earth that is reddish white, like a fine loaf of bread (made from pure fine flour).'

Sahl or someone else said, "That land will have no landmarks for anybody (to make use of)."[1]

Al-Khaṭṭaabi said: *'afra* (translated above as "reddish") means dull white. 'Iyaaḍ said: *'afra* is white which has a hint of red. Ibn Faaris said: *'afra* means pure white.[2]

---

[1] Bukhari in *Kitaab ar-Riqaaq, Baab Yaqbuḍ Allah al-Arḍ*; *Fatḥ al-Baari*, 11/372. Muslim, *Kitaab Ṣifaat al-Munaafiqeen, Baab al-Ba'th wan-Nushoor*, 4/215, hadith no. 2790. This version is narrated by Bukhari.

[2] *Fatḥ al-Baari*, 11/375.

Naqiy (translated above as "fine flour") means flour that is free from any contamination or husks.[3]

Ma'lam (translated as landmarks) means anything which may serve to show the way, such as a mountain or rock, or things such as signposts which are erected by people to show the way, or to mark boundaries.

Many texts have been narrated from a number of the *Ṣaḥaabah* explaining the hadith we have quoted here, which was narrated by the authors of the two *Ṣaḥeeḥs* (Bukhari and Muslim). 'Abd ibn Ḥumayd and Aṭ-Ṭabari narrated in their *Tafseers*, and Al-Bayhaqi narrated in *Shu'ab al-'Eemaan*, via 'Amr ibn Maymoon from 'Abdullah ibn Mas'ood, concerning the *aayah*, ﴿On the Day when the earth will be changed to another earth...﴾ *(Qur'an 14: 48)*, that 'Abdullah ibn Mas'ood said: This earth will be changed to another, like silver on which blood has never been shed and on which no sin has ever been committed. The men (of its *isnaad*) are the men of *ṣaḥeeḥ*, although it is *mawqoof*. Al-Bayhaqi narrated it with a different *isnaad*, as a *marfoo'* report. He said: the *mawqoof* version is more *ṣaḥeeḥ*.[4]

It is also reported by Aṭ-Ṭabari and Al-Ḥaakim from 'Aaṣim ibn Zurr ibn Ḥubaysh from Ibn Mas'ood, with the wording, "A white earth like an ingot of silver." The men of its *isnaad* are also *thiqaat*.[5]

'Abd ibn Ḥumayd narrated it from Al-Ḥakam ibn Abaan from 'Ikrimah, who said: "We heard that this earth will be rolled up, and alongside there will be another earth to which the people will be gathered." In the lengthy hadith about the Trumpet it says: "This earth will be changed to another earth and the heavens will also be

---

[3] *Fatḥ al-Baari*, 11/375.

[4] Ibid.

[5] Ibid.

changed, and Allah will smooth it out and flatten it, and spread it out like a carpet of 'Ukaaz, in which you will see nothing crooked or curved. Then Allah will issue a single command, and they will be standing on this new earth, in places like those in which they were standing before; whatever was inside it will be inside it, and whatever was on its surface will be on its surface.[6]

Some scholars said that what will be changed is the features of the earth only. For example, in the *mawqoof* hadith of 'Abdullah ibn 'Amr it says: "When the Day of Resurrection comes, the earth will be spread out like a carpet, and all creatures will be gathered." And Jaabir narrated in a *marfoo'* report: "The earth will be spread out like a carpet, then the son of Adam will have nothing of it except the place where his feet are standing." The men of its *isnaad* are *thiqaat*.[7]

And Ibn 'Abbaas said in his commentary on the *aayah*, ﴿On the Day when the earth will be changed to another earth...﴾ *(Qur'an 14: 48)*: "Some things will be added to it and some will be taken away, and its hills, mountains, valleys and trees will disappear, and it will be spread out like an 'Ukaaẓi carpet."[8]

The time when the earth will be changed to another earth and so will be the heavens

The Messenger (ﷺ) told us of the time when this change will happen. It will be the time when the people will be passing over *aṣ-ṣiraaṭ*, or shortly before that. In Muslim it is narrated that 'Aa'ishah said: "I asked the Messenger of Allah (ﷺ) about the *aayah*, ﴿On the Day when the earth will be changed to another earth and so will be the heavens...﴾ *(Qur'an 14: 48)* - where will the people be, O' Messenger

---

[6] *Fatḥ al-Baari*, 11/375.

[7] Ibid, 11/376.

[8] Ibid, 11/376.

of Allah?" He said,

"On the *Siraat.*"[9]

It is also narrated in Muslim from Thawbaan that one of the Jewish rabbis asked the Messenger of Allah (ﷺ), "Where will the people be on the Day of Resurrection when the earth is changed to another earth and so will be the heavens?" The Messenger of Allah (ﷺ) said,

"They will be in darkness just before the bridge."[10]

- What is meant by the bridge is *as-siraat.*

---

[9] Muslim, *Kitaab Şifaat al-Munaafiqeen, Baab al-Ba'th wan-Nushoor*, 4/2150, hadith no. 2791.

[10] Ibid, *Kitaab al-Ḥayḍ, Baab Bayaan Şifat Maniy ar-Rajal wal-Mar'ah*, 1/252, hadith no, 315.

CHAPTER FIVE

THOSE WHO DENY THE RESURRECTION, AND THE PROOF THAT IT WILL COME TO PASS

1 - THOSE WHO DENY THE RESURRECTION

Many people, in the past and the present, deny the Resurrection. Some of those who do believe in it have concepts which differ from those which were taught by the Messengers.

The Qur'an mentions what the disbelievers said, and it condemns them as *kaafir* and issues a strong warning to them. Allah (ﷻ) says:

﴿ ۞ وَإِن تَعْجَبْ فَعَجَبٌ قَوْلُهُمْ أَءِذَا كُنَّا تُرَٰبًا أَءِنَّا لَفِى خَلْقٍ جَدِيدٍ ۗ أُو۟لَٰٓئِكَ ٱلَّذِينَ كَفَرُوا۟ بِرَبِّهِمْ ۖ وَأُو۟لَٰٓئِكَ ٱلْأَغْلَٰلُ فِىٓ أَعْنَاقِهِمْ ۖ وَأُو۟لَٰٓئِكَ أَصْحَٰبُ ٱلنَّارِ ۖ هُمْ فِيهَا خَٰلِدُونَ ﴿٥﴾ ﴾

﴿And if you [O' Muhammad] wonder [at these polytheists who deny your message of Islamic Monotheism and have taken besides Allah others for worship who can neither harm nor benefit], then wondrous is their saying: 'When we are dust, shall we indeed then be [raised] in a new creation?' They are those who disbelieved in their Lord! They are those who will have iron chains tying their hands to their necks. They will be dwellers of the Fire to abide therein.﴾

(Qur'an 13: 5)

﴿ وَقَالُوٓا۟ إِنْ هِىَ إِلَّا حَيَاتُنَا ٱلدُّنْيَا وَمَا نَحْنُ بِمَبْعُوثِينَ ﴿٢٩﴾ وَلَوْ تَرَىٰٓ إِذْ وُقِفُوا۟ عَلَىٰ رَبِّهِمْ ۚ قَالَ أَلَيْسَ هَٰذَا بِٱلْحَقِّ ۚ قَالُوا۟ بَلَىٰ وَرَبِّنَا ۚ قَالَ فَذُوقُوا۟ ٱلْعَذَابَ بِمَا كُنتُمْ تَكْفُرُونَ ﴿٣٠﴾ ﴾

﴾And they said: 'There is no [other life] but our [present] life of this world, and never shall we be resurrected [on the Day of Resurrection].' If you could but see when they will be held [brought and made to stand] in front of their Lord! He will say: 'Is not this [Resurrection and the taking of the accounts] the truth?' They will say: 'Yes, by our Lord!' He will then say: 'So taste you the torment because you used not to believe.'﴿ *(Qur'an 6: 29-30)*

﴿ وَقَالُوٓاْ أَءِذَا كُنَّا عِظَٰمًا وَرُفَٰتًا أَءِنَّا لَمَبۡعُوثُونَ خَلۡقًا جَدِيدًا ﴿٤٩﴾ ۞ قُلۡ
كُونُواْ حِجَارَةً أَوۡ حَدِيدًا ﴿٥٠﴾ أَوۡ خَلۡقًا مِّمَّا يَكۡبُرُ فِي صُدُورِكُمۡۚ
فَسَيَقُولُونَ مَن يُعِيدُنَاۖ قُلِ ٱلَّذِي فَطَرَكُمۡ أَوَّلَ مَرَّةٍۚ ... ﴿٥١﴾ ﴾

﴾And they say: 'When we are bones and fragments [destroyed], should we really be resurrected [to be] a new creation?' Say [O' Muhammad]: 'Be you stones or iron, or some created thing that is yet greater [or harder] in your breasts [thoughts to be resurrected, even then you shall be resurrected].' Then, they will say: 'Who shall bring us back [to life]?' Say: 'He Who created you first!'...﴿ *(Qur'an 17: 49-51)*

And there are many similar texts.

Shaykh al-Islam Ibn Taymiyah discussed the different kinds of people who deny the Resurrection, Jews, Christians, Sabaeans, philosophers and the hypocrites of this ummah. He said: "Those who disbelieve among the Jews and Christians deny that people will eat, drink and get married in Paradise. They claim that the people of Paradise will only enjoy nice singing and pure souls, but despite this they say that the bodies will be resurrected with the souls and will be blessed or tormented.

Some groups of the *kuffaar* and others among the Sabaeans and philosophers and those who followed them say that only the souls will be gathered, and that the delights (of Paradise) and torments (of Hell) will only affect the soul. Other groups of *kuffaar*, *mushrikeen* etc., deny the Resurrection altogether, they do not believe in the Resurrection of either the soul or the body. But Allah (ﷻ) has explained in His Book and on the lips of His Messenger that both the soul and the body will be resurrected, and He refuted the false claims of the *kaafireen* and those who deny any part of that and explained the matter in the most eloquent terms.

As for the *munaafiqeen* (hypocrites) of this ummah, who do not believe the words of the Qur'an and Sunnah, but switch words around and say that these are examples presented to help us understand the spiritual resurrection, they are like the *Baaṭini Qaraamiṭah* whose ideas are a combination of Magian (Zoroastrian) and Sabaean ideas, and like the followers of the Sabaean philosophers who claim to be Muslims, and a group of others like them, such as some writers, doctors (physicians), scholars of *'ilm al-kalaam* (scholasticism), and Sufis, such as the author of *Ikhwaan aṣ-Ṣafaa* and others, or hypocrites. All of these are *kaafir* who should be executed by the consensus of the believers."[1]

Elsewhere, he (may Allah have mercy on him) said: "The *Baaṭini* philosophers explain what has been promised to people in the Hereafter as being an analogy to explain their ideas about what goes through after death, of pleasure or pain. They do not believe that these are real events which will cause pleasure or pain."[2]

In essence, what they are saying is that Allah and His Messenger (ﷺ) were not telling the truth when They (Allah and His Messenger)

[1] Adapted from *Majmoo' al-Fataawa Shaykh al-Islam*, 4/313.

[2] *Majmoo' al-Fataawa*, 13/238.

informed us of what will happen in the Resurrection. Hence *Shaykh al-Islam* Ibn Taymiyah called this kind of philosophers, who go against what the Muslims believe concerning the Resurrection, *Ahl at-Takhyeel* (people of imagination). According to him such a group includes those philosophers and the people who follow their path - such as scholars of *'ilm al-kalaam*, Sufis and those who claim to have knowledge. They say that what the Messenger (ﷺ) mentioned about believing in Allah and the Last Day is only metaphorical, to give the masses an impression about these things; it does not point to the reality (the whole truth), it is not true (and exact) guidance and it does not explain the facts."[3]

We may divide those who deny the Resurrection into three categories:

1) Atheists who deny the existence of the Creator. These include many of the naturalist philosophers and, in our time, communists. These people deny that the universe was brought into being by a Creator. Thus they deny both the first and second creation, and they deny that the Creator exists at all.

It is not worth engaging in debate with these people about the issue of the Resurrection. We should discuss with them the existence and oneness of the Creator first, then bring them proof of the resurrection, because belief in the resurrection is a branch of belief in Allah.

2) Those who acknowledge the existence of the Creator, but do not believe in the resurrection. These include the Arabs of whom Allah (سبحانه وتعالى) said:

﴿ وَلَئِن سَأَلْتَهُم مَّنْ خَلَقَ السَّمَٰوَٰتِ وَالْأَرْضَ لَيَقُولُنَّ اللَّهُ ... ﴿٢٥﴾ ﴾

﴾And if you [O' Muhammad] ask them: 'Who has

[3] *Majmoo' al-Fataawa Shaykh al-Islam*, 5/31.

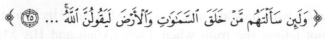

created the heavens and the earth,' they will certainly say: 'Allah.'...﴾ *(Qur'an 31: 25)*

﴿ وَقَالَ ٱلَّذِينَ كَفَرُوٓاْ أَءِذَا كُنَّا تُرَٰبًا وَءَابَآؤُنَآ أَئِنَّا لَمُخْرَجُونَ ﴿٦٧﴾ لَقَدْ وُعِدْنَا هَٰذَا نَحْنُ وَءَابَآؤُنَا مِن قَبْلُ إِنْ هَٰذَآ إِلَّآ أَسَٰطِيرُ ٱلْأَوَّلِينَ ﴿٦٨﴾ ﴾

﴿And those who disbelieve say: 'When we have become dust - we and our fathers - shall we really be brought forth [again]? Indeed we were promised this - we and our forefathers before [us], verily, these are nothing but tales of ancients.'﴾ *(Qur'an 27: 67-68)*

These people claim to believe in Allah, but they say that Allah's power is not able to bring them back to life after they die. These are the people for whom Allah coins parables and gives evidence to show that He is Able to bring about the resurrection and that nothing is beyond His power. Among these people is a group of Jews known as the Sadducees, who claimed that they believed only in the Torah of Moses; they do not believe in the resurrection or in Paradise or Hell.

3) Those who believe in the resurrection, but not in the way it is described in the Divinely-revealed scriptures.

2 - EVIDENCE OF THE RESURRECTION

The Qur'an and Sunnah indicate that we should believe in the resurrection. The entire Qur'an, from beginning to end, is filled with references to the Last Day and details of what will happen then, proving it with sound reports and analogies given to reinforce the lesson and guidance. The Qur'an also mentions proof of the resurrection, to refute those who deny it and to show that they are lying.

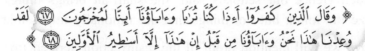

Sound *fiṭrah* also points to the resurrection. There is no validity in the claims of the misguided that it is irrational to believe in the resurrection. It is not irrational at all. The Prophets did not bring any irrational ideas, even though they might bring things that make one wonder. Hence our scholars said: the shari‘ah brings things that amaze the mind, but not things that are rationally impossible.

Below, we will mention proof of the resurrection derived from the Qur'an.

1) The All-Knowing, All-Aware, tells us that the resurrection will take place

The greatest proof that the resurrection will happen is that Allah, the All-High, has told us of that. Whoever believes in Allah and believes in His Messenger whom He sent and His Book which He revealed, has no choice but to believe in what He has told us about the resurrection, the reckoning, reward and punishment, and Paradise and Hell.

Allah (ﷻ) tells us about it in various ways, so that the idea may be implanted more firmly in our hearts.

1) In some places, He tells us that that Day will most certainly come, by using the Arabic particle *in* or *inna*, or *laam* (all of which may be translated as "verily"). For example, He (ﷻ) says:

﴿ إِنَّ ٱلسَّاعَةَ ءَاتِيَةٌ أَكَادُ أُخْفِيهَا ... ﴿١٥﴾ ﴾

﴾Verily, the Hour is coming and I am almost hiding it...﴿ *(Qur'an 20: 15)*

﴿ ... وَإِنَّ ٱلسَّاعَةَ لَآتِيَةٌ فَٱصْفَحِ ٱلصَّفْحَ ٱلْجَمِيلَ ﴿٨٥﴾ ﴾

﴾...And the Hour is surely, coming, so overlook [O' Muhammad], their faults with gracious forgiveness.﴿ *(Qur'an 15: 85)*

﴿ إِنَّ مَا تُوعَدُونَ لَآتٍ ... ﴿١٣٤﴾ ﴾

﴾Surely, that which you are promised, will verily, come to pass...﴿ *(Qur'an 6: 134)*

﴿ إِنَّمَا تُوعَدُونَ لَوَاقِعٌ ﴿٧﴾ ﴾

﴾Surely, what you are promised must come to pass.﴿ *(Qur'an 77: 7)*

2) Elsewhere, Allah swears that it will come to pass. For example, He (ﷻ) says:

﴿ ٱللَّهُ لَآ إِلَٰهَ إِلَّا هُوَ لَيَجْمَعَنَّكُمْ إِلَىٰ يَوْمِ ٱلْقِيَٰمَةِ لَا رَيْبَ فِيهِ... ﴿٨٧﴾ ﴾

﴾Allah! *Laa ilaaha illa Huwa* [none has the right to be worshipped but He]. Surely, He will gather you together on the Day of Resurrection about which there is no doubt...﴿ *(Qur'an 4: 87)*

And He (ﷻ) swears that He will bring that to pass for whomsover He wills among His creation, as He says:

﴿ وَٱلذَّٰرِيَٰتِ ذَرْوًا ﴿١﴾ فَٱلْحَٰمِلَٰتِ وِقْرًا ﴿٢﴾ فَٱلْجَٰرِيَٰتِ يُسْرًا ﴿٣﴾ فَٱلْمُقَسِّمَٰتِ أَمْرًا ﴿٤﴾ إِنَّمَا تُوعَدُونَ لَصَادِقٌ ﴿٥﴾ وَإِنَّ ٱلدِّينَ لَوَٰقِعٌ ﴿٦﴾ ﴾

﴾By [the winds] that scatter dust; And [the clouds] that bear heavy weight of water; And [the ships] that float with ease and gentleness; And those [angels] who distribute [provisions, rain, and other blessings] by [Allah's] Command, Verily, that which you are promised [i.e. Resurrection in the Hereafter and receiving the reward or punishment of good or bad deeds] is surely true. And verily, the Recompense is sure to happen.﴿ *(Qur'an 51: 1-6)*

﴿ وَٱلطُّورِ ۝١ وَكِتَٰبٍ مَّسْطُورٍ ۝٢ فِى رَقٍّ مَّنشُورٍ ۝٣ وَٱلْبَيْتِ ٱلْمَعْمُورِ
۝٤ وَٱلسَّقْفِ ٱلْمَرْفُوعِ ۝٥ وَٱلْبَحْرِ ٱلْمَسْجُورِ ۝٦ إِنَّ عَذَابَ رَبِّكَ لَوَٰقِعٌ
۝٧ مَّا لَهُۥ مِن دَافِعٍ ۝٨ ﴾

﴿By the *Toor* [Mount], and by the Book Inscribed in parchment unrolled. And by *Al-Bayt al-Ma'moor* [the house over the heavens parallel to the Ka'bah at Makkah, continuously visited by the angels]. And by the roof raised high [i.e. the heaven]. And by the sea kept filled [or it will be fire kindled on the Day of Resurrection]. Verily, the Torment of your Lord will surely come to pass. There is none that can avert it.﴾ *(Qur'an 52: 1-8)*

3) In some places, Allah, the All-Glorious, All-High, commands His Messenger to swear that the resurrection will indeed happen; this is in the context of refuting those who deny it. For example, Allah (ﷻ) says:

﴿ وَقَالَ ٱلَّذِينَ كَفَرُوا۟ لَا تَأْتِينَا ٱلسَّاعَةُ ۖ قُلْ بَلَىٰ وَرَبِّى لَتَأْتِيَنَّكُمْ ... ۝٣ ﴾

﴿Those who disbelieve say: 'The Hour will not come to us.' Say: 'Yes, by my Lord, the All-Knower of the Unseen, it will come to you...'﴾ *(Qur'an 34: 3)*

﴿ ۞ وَيَسْتَنۢبِـُٔونَكَ أَحَقٌّ هُوَ ۖ قُلْ إِى وَرَبِّىٓ إِنَّهُۥ لَحَقٌّ ... ۝٥٣ ﴾

﴿And they ask you [O' Muhammad] to inform them [saying]: 'Is it true [i.e. the torment and the establishment of the Hour - the Day of Resurrection]?' Say: 'Yes! By my Lord! It is the very truth!...'﴾ *(Qur'an 10: 53)*

﴿ زَعَمَ ٱلَّذِينَ كَفَرُوٓا۟ أَن لَّن يُبْعَثُوا۟ ۚ قُلْ بَلَىٰ وَرَبِّى لَتُبْعَثُنَّ ثُمَّ لَتُنَبَّؤُنَّ بِمَا عَمِلْتُمْ ۚ ... ﴿٧﴾ ﴾

﴾The disbelievers pretend that they will never be resurrected [for the Account]. Say [O' Muhammad]: 'Yes! By my Lord, you will certainly be resurrected, then you will be informed of [and recompensed for] what you did...'﴿ *(Qur'an 64: 7)*

4) Elsewhere, Allah (ﷻ) condemns those who deny the resurrection, as when He says:

﴿ ... قَدْ خَسِرَ ٱلَّذِينَ كَذَّبُوا۟ بِلِقَآءِ ٱللَّهِ وَمَا كَانُوا۟ مُهْتَدِينَ ﴿٤٥﴾ ﴾

﴾...Ruined indeed will be those who denied the Meeting with Allah and were not guided.﴿ *(Qur'an 10: 45)*

﴿ ... أَلَآ إِنَّ ٱلَّذِينَ يُمَارُونَ فِى ٱلسَّاعَةِ لَفِى ضَلَـٰلٍۭ بَعِيدٍ ﴿١٨﴾ ﴾

﴾...Verily, those who dispute concerning the Hour are certainly in error far away.﴿ *(Qur'an 42: 18)*

﴿ بَلِ ٱدَّٰرَكَ عِلْمُهُمْ فِى ٱلْـَٔاخِرَةِ ۚ بَلْ هُمْ فِى شَكٍّ مِّنْهَا ۖ بَلْ هُم مِّنْهَا عَمُونَ ﴿٦٦﴾ ﴾

﴾Nay, they have no knowledge of the Hereafter. Nay, they are in doubt about it. Nay, they are in complete blindness about it.﴿ *(Qur'an 27: 66)*

5) Sometimes, He (ﷻ) praises those who believe in the Resurrection:

﴿ ...وَٱلرَّٰسِخُونَ فِى ٱلْعِلْمِ يَقُولُونَ ءَامَنَّا بِهِۦ كُلٌّ مِّنْ عِندِ رَبِّنَا ۗ وَمَا يَذَّكَّرُ إِلَّآ أُو۟لُوا۟ ٱلْأَلْبَـٰبِ ﴿٧﴾ رَبَّنَا لَا تُزِغْ قُلُوبَنَا بَعْدَ إِذْ هَدَيْتَنَا وَهَبْ لَنَا مِن لَّدُنكَ رَحْمَةً ۚ إِنَّكَ أَنتَ ٱلْوَهَّابُ ﴿٨﴾ رَبَّنَآ إِنَّكَ جَامِعُ ٱلنَّاسِ لِيَوْمٍ لَّا رَيْبَ فِيهِ ۚ إِنَّ ٱللَّهَ لَا يُخْلِفُ ٱلْمِيعَادَ ﴿٩﴾ ﴾

﴿...And those who are firmly grounded in knowledge say: 'We believe in it; the whole of it [clear and unclear Verses] are from our Lord.' And none receive admonition except men of understanding. [*Tafseer aṭ-Ṭabari*] [They say]: 'Our Lord! Let not our hearts deviate [from the truth] after You have guided us, and grant us mercy from You. Truly, You are the Bestower. Our Lord! Verily, it is You Who will gather mankind together on the Day about which there is no doubt. Verily, Allah never breaks His Promise.'﴾

(Qur'an 3: 7-9)

﴿ الٓمٓ ﴿١﴾ ذَٰلِكَ ٱلْكِتَٰبُ لَا رَيْبَ فِيهِ هُدًى لِّلْمُتَّقِينَ ﴿٢﴾ ٱلَّذِينَ
يُؤْمِنُونَ بِٱلْغَيْبِ وَيُقِيمُونَ ٱلصَّلَوٰةَ وَمِمَّا رَزَقْنَٰهُمْ يُنفِقُونَ ﴿٣﴾
وَٱلَّذِينَ يُؤْمِنُونَ بِمَآ أُنزِلَ إِلَيْكَ وَمَآ أُنزِلَ مِن قَبْلِكَ وَبِٱلْءَاخِرَةِ هُمْ
يُوقِنُونَ ﴿٤﴾ أُو۟لَٰٓئِكَ عَلَىٰ هُدًى مِّن رَّبِّهِمْ ۖ وَأُو۟لَٰٓئِكَ هُمُ ٱلْمُفْلِحُونَ ﴿٥﴾

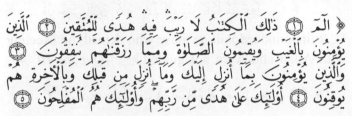

﴿*Alif-Laam-Meem*. [These letters are one of the miracles of the Qur'an and none but Allah (Alone) knows their meanings.] This is the Book [the Qur'an], whereof there is no doubt, a guidance to those who are *Al-Muttaqoon* [the pious believers of Islamic Monotheism who fear Allah much (abstain from all kinds of sins and evil deeds which He has forbidden) and love Allah much (perform all kinds of good deeds which He has ordained)]. Who believe in the *Ghayb* and perform *Aṣ-Ṣalaah* [*Iqaamat-aṣ-Ṣalaah*], and spend out of what we have provided for them [i.e. give Zakah, spend on themselves, their parents, their children, their wives, and also give charity to the poor and also in Allah's Cause - Jihad]. And who believe in [the Qur'an and the Sunnah] which has been sent down [revealed] to you [Muhammad] and in that which were sent down before you [the *Tawraat* (Torah) and the *Injeel* (Gospel)] and they believe with certainty in the Hereafter [Resurrection, recompense of their good and bad deeds, Paradise and Hell]. They are on [true] guidance from their Lord, and they are the successful.﴿ *(Qur'an 2: 1-5)*

﴾ ۞ لَّيْسَ ٱلْبِرَّ أَن تُوَلُّوا۟ وُجُوهَكُمْ قِبَلَ ٱلْمَشْرِقِ وَٱلْمَغْرِبِ وَلَٰكِنَّ ٱلْبِرَّ مَنْ ءَامَنَ بِٱللَّهِ وَٱلْيَوْمِ ٱلْءَاخِرِ وَٱلْمَلَٰٓئِكَةِ وَٱلْكِتَٰبِ وَٱلنَّبِيِّـۧنَ ... ﴿١٧٧﴾ ﴿

﴾It is not *Al-Birr* [piety, righteousness, and each and every act of obedience to Allah] that you turn your faces towards east and [or] west [in prayers]; but *Al-Birr* is [the quality of] the one who believes in Allah, the Last Day, the Angels, the Book, the Prophets...﴿ *(Qur'an 2: 277)*

6) Sometimes, He tells us that this is a true promise, something which will surely come to pass, an appointed time concerning which there is no doubt:

﴾ ... ذَٰلِكَ يَوْمٌ مَّجْمُوعٌ لَّهُ ٱلنَّاسُ وَذَٰلِكَ يَوْمٌ مَّشْهُودٌ ﴿١٠٣﴾ وَمَا نُؤَخِّرُهُۥٓ إِلَّا لِأَجَلٍ مَّعْدُودٍ ﴿١٠٤﴾ ﴿

﴾...That is a Day whereon mankind will be gathered together, and that is a Day when all [the dwellers of the heavens and the earth] will be present. And We delay it only for a term [already] fixed.﴿ *(Qur'an 11: 103-104)*

﴾ يَٰٓأَيُّهَا ٱلنَّاسُ ٱتَّقُوا۟ رَبَّكُمْ وَٱخْشَوْا۟ يَوْمًا لَّا يَجْزِى وَالِدٌ عَن وَلَدِهِۦ وَلَا مَوْلُودٌ هُوَ جَازٍ عَن وَالِدِهِۦ شَيْـًٔا ۚ إِنَّ وَعْدَ ٱللَّهِ حَقٌّ ... ﴿٣٣﴾ ﴿

﴾O' mankind! Be afraid of your Lord [by keeping your duty to Him and avoiding all evil], and fear a Day when no father can avail aught for his son, nor a son avail aught for his father. Verily, the Promise of Allah is true...﴿ *(Qur'an 31: 33)*

﴾ وَيَقُولُونَ مَتَىٰ هَٰذَا ٱلْوَعْدُ إِن كُنتُمْ صَٰدِقِينَ ۝٢٩ قُل لَّكُم مِّيعَادُ يَوْمٍ لَّا تَسْتَـْٔخِرُونَ عَنْهُ سَاعَةً وَلَا تَسْتَقْدِمُونَ ۝٣٠ ﴿

﴾And they say: 'When is this promise [i.e. the Day of Resurrection] if you are truthful?' Say [O' Muhammad]: 'The appointment to you is for a Day, which you cannot put back for an hour [or a moment] nor put forward.'﴿ *(Qur'an 34: 29-30)*

﴾ فَذَرْهُمْ يَخُوضُوا۟ وَيَلْعَبُوا۟ حَتَّىٰ يُلَٰقُوا۟ يَوْمَهُمُ ٱلَّذِى يُوعَدُونَ ۝٨٣ ﴿

﴾So leave them [alone] to speak nonsense and play until they meet the Day of theirs which they have been promised.﴿ *(Qur'an 43: 83)*

﴾ إِنَّمَا تُوعَدُونَ لَصَادِقٌ ۝٥ ﴿

﴾Verily, that which you are promised [i.e. Resurrection in the Hereafter and receiving the reward or punishment of good or bad deeds] is surely true.﴿ *(Qur'an 51: 5)*

7) And Allah tells us that it is coming and is near, such as when He (سبحانه وتعالى) says:

﴾ إِنَّهُمْ يَرَوْنَهُۥ بَعِيدًا ۝٦ وَنَرَىٰهُ قَرِيبًا ۝٧ ﴿

﴾Verily, they see it [the torment] afar off. But We see it [quite] near.﴿ *(Qur'an 70: 6-7)*

﴾ أَتَىٰٓ أَمْرُ ٱللَّهِ فَلَا تَسْتَعْجِلُوهُ ... ۝١ ﴿

﴾The Event [the Hour or the punishment of disbelievers

and polytheists or the Islamic laws or commandments] ordained by Allah will come to pass, so seek not to hasten it...﴿ *(Qur'an 16: 1)*

﴾ ٱقْتَرَبَتِ ٱلسَّاعَةُ وَٱنشَقَّ ٱلْقَمَرُ ﴿١﴾ ﴿

﴾The Hour has drawn near, and the moon has been cleft asunder.﴿ *(Qur'an 54: 1)*

8) Elsewhere, Allah praises Himself for bringing His creation back to life after they die, and He condemns the false gods whom the *mushrikeen* worship for their lack of power to create and recreate. For example, He (ﷻ) says:

﴾ وَٱتَّخَذُوا۟ مِن دُونِهِۦٓ ءَالِهَةً لَّا يَخْلُقُونَ شَيْـًٔا وَهُمْ يُخْلَقُونَ وَلَا يَمْلِكُونَ لِأَنفُسِهِمْ ضَرًّا وَلَا نَفْعًا وَلَا يَمْلِكُونَ مَوْتًا وَلَا حَيَوٰةً وَلَا نُشُورًا ﴿٣﴾ ﴿

﴾Yet they have taken besides Him other *aalihah* [gods] who created nothing but are themselves created, and possess neither harm nor benefit for themselves, and possess no power [of causing] death, nor [of giving] life, nor of raising the dead.﴿ *(Qur'an 25: 3)*

﴾ أَمَّن يَبْدَؤُا۟ ٱلْخَلْقَ ثُمَّ يُعِيدُهُۥ وَمَن يَرْزُقُكُم مِّنَ ٱلسَّمَآءِ وَٱلْأَرْضِ ۗ أَءِلَـٰهٌ مَّعَ ٱللَّهِ ۚ قُلْ هَاتُوا۟ بُرْهَـٰنَكُمْ إِن كُنتُمْ صَـٰدِقِينَ ﴿٦٤﴾ ﴿

﴾Is not He [better than your so-called gods] Who originates creation, and shall thereafter repeat it, and Who provides for you from heaven and earth? Is there any *ilaah* [god] with Allah? Say: Bring forth your proofs, if you are truthful.﴿ *(Qur'an 27: 64)*

9) Allah explains that this act of creation and resurrection, which His slaves are unable to do and is impossible for them, is easy for Him:

﴿ مَّا خَلْقُكُمْ وَلَا بَعْثُكُمْ إِلَّا كَنَفْسٍ وَاحِدَةٍ ... ﴿٢٨﴾ ﴾

﴿The creation of you all and the resurrection of you all are only as [the creation and resurrection of] a single person...﴾ *(Qur'an 31: 28)*

﴿ أَيَحْسَبُ ٱلْإِنسَٰنُ أَلَّن نَّجْمَعَ عِظَامَهُۥ ﴿٣﴾ بَلَىٰ قَٰدِرِينَ عَلَىٰٓ أَن نُّسَوِّىَ بَنَانَهُۥ ﴿٤﴾ ﴾

﴿Does man [a disbeliever] think that We shall not assemble his bones? Yes, We are Able to put together in perfect order the tips of his fingers.﴾ *(Qur'an 75: 3-4)*

2) Using the first creation as evidence for the second creation

The Qur'an uses the first creation as evidence for the second creation. Every day we see new life coming into being: children are born, birds hatch out from their eggs, animals give birth to their young, fish fill the seas and rivers. Man sees all of that with his own eyes, then he denies that something like that could happen again after Allah has caused this life to perish.

Those who seek proof of the resurrection after death ignore the fact that their own creation is the greatest proof. The One Who is Able to create them is Able to recreate them. How often the Qur'an offers proof of the final resurrection by referring to the first creation, and it reminds of this fact to those who think that it is unlikely to happen:

﴿ وَيَقُولُ ٱلْإِنسَٰنُ أَءِذَا مَا مِتُّ لَسَوْفَ أُخْرَجُ حَيًّا ﴿٦٦﴾ أَوَلَا يَذْكُرُ ٱلْإِنسَٰنُ أَنَّا خَلَقْنَٰهُ مِن قَبْلُ وَلَمْ يَكُ شَيْـًٔا ﴿٦٧﴾ ﴾

﴿And man [the disbeliever] says: 'When I am dead, shall I then be raised up alive?' Does not man remember that We created him before, while he was nothing?﴾ *(Qur'an 19: 66-67)*

The Qur'an reminds us elsewhere of the initial creation of man: Allah created our father Adam from dust, and the One Who is Able to make dust into a living human being is not incapable of recreating him as a living human being after he has died. He also reminds us of how He creates us, the descendents of Adam, from semen of worthless water *(cf. Qur'an 32: 8)*, which He changes into a *nutfah* (mixed drops of male and female sexual discharge), then the *nutfah* becomes an *'alaqah* (a clot), then it turns into a *muḍghah* (a lump of chewed flesh)... until the soul is breathed into it, and it becomes a human being. The One Who is Able to create in this manner which is known to us, is Able to bring it back into being and to bring the dead back to life.

﴿ يَٰٓأَيُّهَا ٱلنَّاسُ إِن كُنتُمۡ فِي رَيۡبٖ مِّنَ ٱلۡبَعۡثِ فَإِنَّا خَلَقۡنَٰكُم مِّن تُرَابٖ
ثُمَّ مِن نُّطۡفَةٖ ثُمَّ مِنۡ عَلَقَةٖ ثُمَّ مِن مُّضۡغَةٖ مُّخَلَّقَةٖ وَغَيۡرِ مُخَلَّقَةٖ لِّنُبَيِّنَ
لَكُمۡۚ وَنُقِرُّ فِي ٱلۡأَرۡحَامِ مَا نَشَآءُ إِلَىٰٓ أَجَلٖ مُّسَمّٗى ثُمَّ نُخۡرِجُكُمۡ طِفۡلٗا
ثُمَّ لِتَبۡلُغُوٓاْ أَشُدَّكُمۡۖ وَمِنكُم مَّن يُتَوَفَّىٰ وَمِنكُم مَّن يُرَدُّ إِلَىٰٓ
أَرۡذَلِ ٱلۡعُمُرِ لِكَيۡلَا يَعۡلَمَ مِنۢ بَعۡدِ عِلۡمٖ شَيۡـٔٗاۚ وَتَرَى ٱلۡأَرۡضَ هَامِدَةٗ
فَإِذَآ أَنزَلۡنَا عَلَيۡهَا ٱلۡمَآءَ ٱهۡتَزَّتۡ وَرَبَتۡ وَأَنۢبَتَتۡ مِن كُلِّ زَوۡجِۢ بَهِيجٖ
٥ ذَٰلِكَ بِأَنَّ ٱللَّهَ هُوَ ٱلۡحَقُّ وَأَنَّهُۥ يُحۡيِ ٱلۡمَوۡتَىٰ وَأَنَّهُۥ عَلَىٰ كُلِّ شَيۡءٖ قَدِيرٞ
٦ وَأَنَّ ٱلسَّاعَةَ ءَاتِيَةٞ لَّا رَيۡبَ فِيهَا وَأَنَّ ٱللَّهَ يَبۡعَثُ مَن فِي ٱلۡقُبُورِ
٧ ﴾

﴿O' mankind! If you are in doubt about the Resurrection, then verily, We have created you [i.e. Adam] from dust, then from a *Nutfah* [mixed drops of male and female sexual discharge, i.e. the offspring of Adam], then from a clot [a piece of thick coagulated blood] then from a little lump of flesh - some formed and some unformed [as in the case of miscarriage] - that We may make [it] clear to you [i.e. to show you Our Power and Ability to do what We will]. And We cause whom We will to remain in the wombs for an appointed term, then We bring you out as infants, then [give you growth] that you may reach your age of full strength. And among you there is he who dies [young], and among you there is he who is brought back to the miserable old age, so that he knows nothing after having known. And you see the earth barren, but when We send down water [rain] on it, it is stirred [to life], and it swells and puts forth every lovely kind [of growth]. That is because Allah: He is the Truth, and it is He Who gives life to the dead, and it is He Who is Able to do all things. And surely, the Hour is coming, there is no doubt about it; and certainly, Allah will resurrect those who are in the graves.》

(Qur'an 22: 5-7)

Allah (ﷻ) has commanded His slaves to travel through the earth, and to look at how creation began, so that they will realize that He is Able to re-create.

﴿ أَوَلَمْ يَرَوْا۟ كَيْفَ يُبْدِئُ ٱللَّهُ ٱلْخَلْقَ ثُمَّ يُعِيدُهُۥٓ ۚ إِنَّ ذَٰلِكَ عَلَى ٱللَّهِ يَسِيرٌ ﴿١٩﴾ قُلْ سِيرُوا۟ فِى ٱلْأَرْضِ فَٱنظُرُوا۟ كَيْفَ بَدَأَ ٱلْخَلْقَ ۚ ثُمَّ ٱللَّهُ يُنشِئُ ٱلنَّشْأَةَ ٱلْءَاخِرَةَ ۚ إِنَّ ٱللَّهَ عَلَىٰ كُلِّ شَىْءٍ قَدِيرٌ ﴿٢٠﴾

《See they not how Allah originates the creation, then repeats it. Verily, that is easy for Allah. Say: 'Travel in the land and see how [Allah] originated the creation, and then Allah will bring forth the creation of the Hereafter [i.e. resurrection after death]. Verily, Allah is Able to do all things.》 *(Qur'an 29: 19-20)*

﴿ وَهُوَ ٱلَّذِى يَبْدَؤُا۟ ٱلْخَلْقَ ثُمَّ يُعِيدُهُۥ وَهُوَ أَهْوَنُ عَلَيْهِ ۚ وَلَهُ ٱلْمَثَلُ ٱلْأَعْلَىٰ فِى ٱلسَّمَٰوَٰتِ وَٱلْأَرْضِ ۚ وَهُوَ ٱلْعَزِيزُ ٱلْحَكِيمُ ﴿٢٧﴾ ﴾

﴾And He it is Who originates the creation, then He will repeat it [after it has been perished]; and this is easier for Him. His is the highest description [i.e. none has the right to be worshipped but He, and there is nothing comparable unto Him] in the heavens and in the earth. And He is the All-Mighty, the All-Wise.﴿

(Qur'an 30: 27)

3) The One Who is able to create a greater thing is able to create lesser things

It is a fault in human thinking to accuse someone who is able to carry a heavy load of being unable to carry a lighter one. A similar case is when a person tells a tough, strong man, "You cannot wrestle this puny, weak man." Whoever is capable of building a palace is not incapable of building a small house.

And Allah's is the Supreme Example *(cf. Qur'an 30: 27)*. Among the things He has created are things which are greater than man. How can it be said to the One Who created the heavens and the earth that He is not able to create lesser things? Allah (ﷻ) says:

﴿ ... وَقَالُوٓاْ أَءِذَا كُنَّا عِظَٰمًا وَرُفَٰتًا أَءِنَّا لَمَبۡعُوثُونَ خَلۡقًا جَدِيدًا ﴿٩٨﴾ ۞
أَوَلَمۡ يَرَوۡاْ أَنَّ ٱللَّهَ ٱلَّذِي خَلَقَ ٱلسَّمَٰوَٰتِ وَٱلۡأَرۡضَ قَادِرٌ عَلَىٰٓ أَن يَخۡلُقَ
مِثۡلَهُمۡ وَجَعَلَ لَهُمۡ أَجَلًا لَّا رَيۡبَ فِيهِ فَأَبَى ٱلظَّٰلِمُونَ إِلَّا كُفُورًا ﴿٩٩﴾ ﴾

﴾...And [they] said: 'When we are bones and fragments, shall we really be raised up as a new creation?' See they not that Allah, Who created the heavens and the earth, is Able to create the like of them. And He has decreed for them an appointed term, whereof there is no doubt. But the *Ẓaalimoon* [polytheists and wrongdoers] refuse [the truth - the message of Islamic Monotheism, and accept nothing] but disbelief.﴿ *(Qur'an 17: 98-99)*

﴿ أَوَلَيْسَ ٱلَّذِى خَلَقَ ٱلسَّمَٰوَٰتِ وَٱلْأَرْضَ بِقَٰدِرٍ عَلَىٰٓ أَن يَخْلُقَ مِثْلَهُمۚ بَلَىٰ وَهُوَ ٱلْخَلَّٰقُ ٱلْعَلِيمُ ﴿٨١﴾ ﴾

﴿Is not He Who created the heavens and the earth, Able to create the like of them? Yes, indeed! He is the All-Knowing Supreme Creator.﴾ *(Qur'an 36: 81)*

﴿ أَوَلَمْ يَرَوْا۟ أَنَّ ٱللَّهَ ٱلَّذِى خَلَقَ ٱلسَّمَٰوَٰتِ وَٱلْأَرْضَ وَلَمْ يَعْىَ بِخَلْقِهِنَّ بِقَٰدِرٍ عَلَىٰٓ أَن يُحْۦِىَ ٱلْمَوْتَىٰۚ بَلَىٰٓ إِنَّهُۥ عَلَىٰ كُلِّ شَىْءٍ قَدِيرٌ ﴿٣٣﴾ ﴾

﴿Do they not see that Allah, Who created the heavens and the earth, and was not wearied by their creation, is Able to give life to the dead? Yes, He surely is Able to do all things.﴾ *(Qur'an 46: 33)*

﴿ لَخَلْقُ ٱلسَّمَٰوَٰتِ وَٱلْأَرْضِ أَكْبَرُ مِنْ خَلْقِ ٱلنَّاسِ ... ﴿٥٧﴾ ﴾

﴿The creation of the heavens and the earth is indeed greater than the creation of mankind...﴾ *(Qur'an 40: 57)*

Ibn Taymiyah said, after quoting these texts, "It is obvious to rational minds that the creation of the heavens and the earth is greater than the creation of something like the children of Adam, and the power involved is greater; and what is easier is more likely to be possible."[4]

The commentator on *At-Ṭaḥaawiyah* said: "Allah tells us that the One Who initiated the creation of the heavens and the earth, with their majestic proportions, can revive bones after they have turned to dust, and restore them to the way they were before."[5]

---

4 *Majmoo' al-Fataawa Shaykh al-Islam*, 3/299.

5 *Sharḥ al-'Aqeedah aṭ-Ṭaḥaawiyah*, Pp. 461.

4) His (Allah's) Ability to change His creation from one thing into another

Those who deny the Resurrection see how people die then turn into dust, and they think that it is impossible for them to be restored after that.

﴿ وَقَالُوٓاْ أَءِذَا ضَلَلۡنَا فِى ٱلۡأَرۡضِ أَءِنَّا لَفِى خَلۡقٖ جَدِيدِۭ ... ﴿١٠﴾ ﴾

﴿And they say: 'When we are [dead and become] lost in the earth, shall we indeed be created anew?...'﴾

(Qur'an 32: 10)

The word "lost" refers to the disintegration of their bodies, when they become mixed with the dust of the earth. The same word is used (in Arabic) to refer to ghee melting into food and becoming mixed with it.

In more than one place in the Qur'an, Allah explains that one aspect of His perfect *uloohiyah* (Divine Nature) and *ruboobiyah* (Divine Lordship) is His power to change His creation from one thing into another. Thus, He gives life and causes death, He creates and destroys, He brings forth the living from the dead and the dead from the living.

﴿ ۞ إِنَّ ٱللَّهَ فَالِقُ ٱلۡحَبِّ وَٱلنَّوَىٰۖ يُخۡرِجُ ٱلۡحَىَّ مِنَ ٱلۡمَيِّتِ وَمُخۡرِجُ ٱلۡمَيِّتِ
مِنَ ٱلۡحَىِّۚ ذَٰلِكُمُ ٱللَّهُۖ فَأَنَّىٰ تُؤۡفَكُونَ ﴿٩٥﴾ فَالِقُ ٱلۡإِصۡبَاحِ وَجَعَلَ ٱلَّيۡلَ سَكَنًا
وَٱلشَّمۡسَ وَٱلۡقَمَرَ حُسۡبَانًاۚ ذَٰلِكَ تَقۡدِيرُ ٱلۡعَزِيزِ ٱلۡعَلِيمِ ﴿٩٦﴾ ﴾

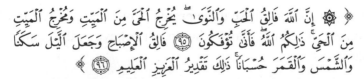

﴿Verily, it is Allah Who causes the seed grain and the fruit stone [like date stone] to split and sprout. He brings forth the living from the dead, and it is He Who brings forth the dead from the living. Such is Allah, then how are you deluded away from the truth? [He is the] Cleaver of the daybreak. He has appointed the night for resting, and the sun and the moon for reckoning. Such is the measuring of the All-Mighty, the All-Knowing.》

(Qur'an 6: 95-96)

From the dormant, lifeless seed comes forth fresh, green plants which flower and bear fruit, then this living plant produces dead seeds. From living birds comes forth dead eggs, and from the dead eggs come forth living, chirping birds, which fly in the vast reaches of the sky.

The way things change - death followed by life, then life followed by death - is a great sign pointing to the power of Allah, which makes hearts submit to His greatness and power.

﴿كَيْفَ تَكْفُرُونَ بِٱللَّهِ وَكُنتُمْ أَمْوَٰتًا فَأَحْيَٰكُمْ ۖ ثُمَّ يُمِيتُكُمْ ثُمَّ يُحْيِيكُمْ ثُمَّ إِلَيْهِ تُرْجَعُونَ ﴿٢٨﴾﴾

《How can you disbelieve in Allah? Seeing that you were dead and He gave you life. Then He will give you death, then again will bring you to life [on the Day of Resurrection] and then unto Him you will return.》

(Qur'an 2: 28)

These three proofs occur in one place in the Book of Allah

Allah (سبحانه وتعالى) mentions these three proofs in one place in His Book, in the context of refuting those who do not believe in the resurrection. He says:

﴿وَضَرَبَ لَنَا مَثَلًا وَنَسِيَ خَلْقَهُۥ ۖ قَالَ مَن يُحْيِ ٱلْعِظَٰمَ وَهِيَ رَمِيمٌ ﴿٧٨﴾ قُلْ يُحْيِيهَا ٱلَّذِىٓ أَنشَأَهَآ أَوَّلَ مَرَّةٍ ۖ وَهُوَ بِكُلِّ خَلْقٍ عَلِيمٌ ﴿٧٩﴾ ٱلَّذِى جَعَلَ لَكُم مِّنَ ٱلشَّجَرِ ٱلْأَخْضَرِ نَارًا فَإِذَآ أَنتُم مِّنْهُ تُوقِدُونَ ﴿٨٠﴾ أَوَلَيْسَ ٱلَّذِى خَلَقَ ٱلسَّمَٰوَٰتِ وَٱلْأَرْضَ بِقَٰدِرٍ عَلَىٰٓ أَن يَخْلُقَ مِثْلَهُم ۚ بَلَىٰ وَهُوَ ٱلْخَلَّٰقُ ٱلْعَلِيمُ ﴿٨١﴾ إِنَّمَآ أَمْرُهُۥٓ إِذَآ أَرَادَ شَيْـًٔا أَن يَقُولَ لَهُۥ كُن

فَيَكُونُ ﴿٨٢﴾ فَسُبْحَٰنَ ٱلَّذِى بِيَدِهِۦ مَلَكُوتُ كُلِّ شَىْءٍ وَإِلَيْهِ تُرْجَعُونَ ﴿٨٣﴾

﴾And he puts forth for Us a parable, and forgets his own creation. He says: 'Who will give life to these bones after they are rotten and have become dust?' Say [O' Muhammad]: 'He will give life to them Who created them for the first time! And He is the All-Knower of every creation!' He Who produces for you fire out of the green tree, when behold! you kindle therewith. Is not He Who created the heavens and the earth, Able to create the like of them? Yes, indeed! He is the All-Knowing Supreme Creator. Verily, His Command, when He intends a thing, is only that He says to it, 'Be!' and it is! So glorified be He and exalted above all that they associate with Him, and in Whose Hands is the dominion of all things, and to Him you shall be returned.﴿ *(Qur'an 36: 78-83)*

The one who had put forth this likeness was one of the disbelievers among the Arabs. The Sunnah mentions that this *kaafir* brought a dry bone which he then crumbled and blew away, then he said to the Messenger (ﷺ), "O Muhammad, are you claiming that Allah will resurrect this?" Then Allah revealed these verses, criticizing the *kaafir* for his ignorance and misguidance. ﴾And he puts forth for Us a parable, and forgets his own creation. He says: 'Who will give life to these bones after they are rotten and have become dust?'﴿ *(Qur'an 36: 78).*

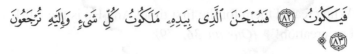

If he were really intelligent, he would not ask such a question, because the very fact that he exists answers this question. The text makes this quite clear, as is stated in a general sense at the beginning, where Allah (ﷻ) says: ﴾Say [O' Muhammad]: 'He will give life to them Who created them for the first time! And He is the All-Knower of every creation!'》 *(Qur'an 36: 79)*.

1) The initial creation is used as evidence that re-creation is possible. Every rational person will understand that the One Who is able to do the former is able to do the latter. If He were unable to do the latter, He would be even more unable to do the former.

Because creation implies that the Creator has power over His creation, and that He knows them in detail, Allah (ﷻ) says, 《...And He is the All-Knower of every creation!》 *(Qur'an 36: 79)*. He knows all the details of His first creation, its essence and form, and He knows His second creation equally well. If His knowledge and power are so perfect and complete, how can it be difficult for Him to revive bones that have turned to dust?[6]

2) Then Allah reinforced the idea with definitive and conclusive proof, which includes the answer to the question posed by the disbeliever: when the body disintegrates after death, bones become cold and dry, but the essence of life is such that it must be warm and moist, which proves the issue of resurrection and offers the proof and the answer all in one. Allah (ﷻ) says: 《He Who produces for you fire out of the green tree, when behold! you kindle therewith.》 *(Qur'an 36: 80)*

Allah (ﷻ) tells us that He brings forth this element, which is found in heat and dryness, from the green tree, which is filled with moisture and coldness. The One Who brings forth a thing from its opposite, and to Whom the essence and elements of His creation are subjugated, will not find any difficulty in that. He is the One Who will do what the disbelievers deny, which is reviving bodies that have turned to dust.

---

[6] *Sharḥ al-'Aqeedah aṭ-Ṭaḥaawiyah*, Pp. 46.

3) Then Allah confirms the matter by referring to something greater in order to prove something lesser. Every rational person knows that whoever is able to a do a great thing is able to do anything that is much less than that; whoever is able to carry a heavy weight is able to carry anything lighter than that. And Allah (ﷻ) says: ﴾Is not He Who created the heavens and the earth, Able to create the like of them?...﴿ *(Qur'an 36: 81).*

Allah tells us that the One Who initiated the creation of the heavens and the earth, with all their vastness and splendour, is more able to revive bones that have turned to dust and restore them to the way they were.[7]

4) Then Allah affirms this idea by explaining it in another way, which is that the way in which He does things is different from the way others do them. Others use tools and have to make an effort; they get tired and endure hardship. They cannot work independently; they need to have tools and helpers. But when Allah wants to create something, all He has to do is will it, and say to it, "Be!" then it exists just as He wills it. ﴾Verily, His Command, when He intends a thing, is only that He says to it, 'Be!' and it is!﴿ *(Qur'an 36: 82).*

Then Allah concludes this argument by telling us that the sovereignty of all things is in His hand, and He controls everything by His action and His words: ﴾So glorified be He and exalted above all that they associate with Him, and in Whose Hands is the dominion of all things, and to Him you shall be returned.﴿ *(Qur'an 36: 83)*[8]

5) The resurrection of some dead things in this life

Some human beings, at various times in history, have witnessed the revival of dead bodies and dry bones; they have even witnessed life

[7] *Sharḥ al-'Aqeedah aṭ-Ṭaḥaawiyah*, Pp. 460.
[8] Ibid, Pp. 461.

coming into inanimate objects. Allah has told us of some of these dazzling miracles. For example, the people of Moosa said to him:

﴿ ... لَن نُّؤْمِنَ لَكَ حَتَّىٰ نَرَى ٱللَّهَ جَهْرَةً ... ﴿٥٥﴾ ﴾

﴾...We shall never believe in you until we see Allah plainly...﴿ *(Qur'an 2: 55)*

So they were struck with a thunderbolt whilst they were looking on, then they were brought back from the dead.

﴿ ... فَأَخَذَتْكُمُ ٱلصَّـٰعِقَةُ وَأَنتُمْ تَنظُرُونَ ﴿٥٥﴾ ثُمَّ بَعَثْنَـٰكُم مِّنۢ بَعْدِ مَوْتِكُمْ لَعَلَّكُمْ تَشْكُرُونَ ﴿٥٦﴾ ﴾

﴾...But you were seized with a thunderbolt [lightning] while you were looking. Then We raised you up after your death, so that you might be grateful.﴿

(Qur'an 2: 55-56)

The Children of Israel killed a man, then each tribe accused another of killing him. So their Prophet commanded them to sacrifice a cow, and to strike the slain man with a piece of it. Then Allah brought him back to life whilst they were looking on, and he spoke of who had killed him.

﴿ فَقُلْنَا ٱضْرِبُوهُ بِبَعْضِهَا ۚ كَذَٰلِكَ يُحْىِ ٱللَّهُ ٱلْمَوْتَىٰ وَيُرِيكُمْ ءَايَـٰتِهِۦ لَعَلَّكُمْ تَعْقِلُونَ ﴿٧٣﴾ ﴾

﴾So We said: 'Strike him [the dead man] with a piece of it [the cow].' Thus Allah brings the dead to life and shows you His *Aayaat* [proofs, evidences, verses, lessons, signs, revelations, etc.] so that you may understand.﴿ *(Qur'an 2: 73)*

Allah has told us about the people who fled from their homes by the thousands; He caused them to die then He brought them back to life:

﴿ ۞ أَلَمْ تَرَ إِلَى ٱلَّذِينَ خَرَجُوا۟ مِن دِيَـٰرِهِمْ وَهُمْ أُلُوفٌ حَذَرَ ٱلْمَوْتِ فَقَالَ لَهُمُ ٱللَّهُ مُوتُوا۟ ثُمَّ أَحْيَـٰهُمْ ۚ إِنَّ ٱللَّهَ لَذُو فَضْلٍ عَلَى ٱلنَّاسِ وَلَـٰكِنَّ أَكْثَرَ ٱلنَّاسِ لَا يَشْكُرُونَ ﴿٢٤٣﴾ ﴾

﴿Did you [O' Muhammad] not think of those who went forth from their homes in thousands, fearing death? Allah said to them, 'Die.' And then He restored them to life. Truly, Allah is full of bounty to mankind, but most men thank not.﴾ *(Qur'an 2: 243)*

And He (ﷻ) tells us of a man who passed by a town which was dilapidated, and he wondered how Allah could bring it back to life after it had died. So Allah caused him to die for a hundred years, then He revived him. When he was asked how long he had stayed (dead), he thought that it had been only one day or part of a day. After reviving the man, Allah brought his donkey back to life whilst he was looking on, and he saw how the power of Allah restores His creation: first the bones come together, then they are clothed with flesh, then the soul is breathed into it. The food that the man had had with him before he died had remained fresh all this long time, it had not rotted or gone mouldy. This was another sign that pointed to the great power of Allah (ﷻ):

﴿ أَوْ كَٱلَّذِى مَرَّ عَلَىٰ قَرْيَةٍ وَهِىَ خَاوِيَةٌ عَلَىٰ عُرُوشِهَا قَالَ أَنَّىٰ يُحْىِۦ هَـٰذِهِ ٱللَّهُ بَعْدَ مَوْتِهَا ۖ فَأَمَاتَهُ ٱللَّهُ مِا۟ئَةَ عَامٍ ثُمَّ بَعَثَهُۥ ۖ قَالَ كَمْ لَبِثْتَ ۖ قَالَ لَبِثْتُ يَوْمًا أَوْ بَعْضَ يَوْمٍ ۖ قَالَ بَل لَّبِثْتَ مِا۟ئَةَ عَامٍ فَٱنظُرْ إِلَىٰ طَعَامِكَ وَشَرَابِكَ لَمْ يَتَسَنَّهْ ۖ وَٱنظُرْ إِلَىٰ حِمَارِكَ وَلِنَجْعَلَكَ ءَايَةً لِّلنَّاسِ ۖ وَٱنظُرْ إِلَى ٱلْعِظَامِ كَيْفَ نُنشِزُهَا ثُمَّ نَكْسُوهَا لَحْمًا ۚ فَلَمَّا تَبَيَّنَ لَهُۥ قَالَ أَعْلَمُ أَنَّ ٱللَّهَ عَلَىٰ كُلِّ شَىْءٍ قَدِيرٌ ﴿٢٥٩﴾ ﴾

﴿Or like the one who passed by a town and it had tumbled over its roofs. He said: 'O'! How will Allah ever bring it to life after its death?' So Allah caused him to die for a hundred years, then raised him up [again]. He said: 'How long did you remain [dead]?' He [the man] said: '[Perhaps] I remained [dead] a day or part of a day.' He said: 'Nay, you have remained [dead] for a hundred years, look at your food and your drink, they show no change; and look at your donkey! And thus We have made of you a sign for the people. Look at the bones, how We bring them together and clothe them with flesh.' When this was clearly shown to him, he said, 'I know [now] that Allah is Able to do all things.'﴿

(Qur'an 2: 259)

Ibraaheem (Abraham) (عليه السلام) prayed to his Lord to show him how He revived the dead; this is what Allah tells us about:

﴿وَإِذْ قَالَ إِبْرَٰهِـۧمُ رَبِّ أَرِنِى كَيْفَ تُحْىِ ٱلْمَوْتَىٰ ۖ قَالَ أَوَلَمْ تُؤْمِن ۖ قَالَ
بَلَىٰ وَلَـٰكِن لِّيَطْمَئِنَّ قَلْبِى ۖ قَالَ فَخُذْ أَرْبَعَةً مِّنَ ٱلطَّيْرِ فَصُرْهُنَّ إِلَيْكَ ثُمَّ
ٱجْعَلْ عَلَىٰ كُلِّ جَبَلٍ مِّنْهُنَّ جُزْءًا ثُمَّ ٱدْعُهُنَّ يَأْتِينَكَ سَعْيًا ۚ وَٱعْلَمْ أَنَّ ٱللَّهَ
عَزِيزٌ حَكِيمٌ ٢٦٠﴾

﴾And [remember] when Ibraaheem said, 'My Lord! Show me how You give life to the dead.' He [Allah] said: 'Do you not believe?' He [Ibraaheem] said: 'Yes [I believe], but to be stronger in Faith.' He said: 'Take four birds, then cause them to incline towards you [then slaughter them, cut them into pieces], and then put a portion of them on every hill, and call them, they will come to you in haste. And know that Allah is All-Mighty, All-Wise.'﴿ *(Qur'an 2: 260)*

Allah commanded him to take four birds and slaughter them, then to scatter them in pieces on a number of mountains; then he was to call them to come together. Each part of them came and fell into place, and when they were reassembled, Allah breathed life into them, and they flew up, soaring in the air.

'Eesa (Jesus) (عليه السلام) moulded clay into the shapes of birds, then he breathed into them and they became real birds, by Allah's leave. He used to bring the dead back to life by Allah's leave, and he said to his people:

﴿ وَرَسُولًا إِلَىٰ بَنِىٓ إِسْرَٰٓءِيلَ أَنِّى قَدْ جِئْتُكُم بِـَٔايَةٍ مِّن رَّبِّكُمْ ۖ أَنِّىٓ أَخْلُقُ لَكُم مِّنَ ٱلطِّينِ كَهَيْـَٔةِ ٱلطَّيْرِ فَأَنفُخُ فِيهِ فَيَكُونُ طَيْرًۢا بِإِذْنِ ٱللَّهِ ۖ وَأُبْرِئُ ٱلْأَكْمَهَ وَٱلْأَبْرَصَ وَأُحْىِ ٱلْمَوْتَىٰ بِإِذْنِ ٱللَّهِ ۖ ... ﴿٤٩﴾ ﴾

﴿A Messenger to the Children of Israel [saying]: 'I have come to you with a sign from your Lord, that I design for you out of clay, a figure like that of a bird, and breathe into it, and it becomes a bird by Allah's Leave; and I heal him who was born blind, and the leper, and I bring the dead to life by Allah's Leave...'﴾ *(Qur'an 3: 49)*

Allah (سبحانه وتعالى) covered up the sense of hearing of the People of the Cave (i.e., caused them to sleep) for three hundred and nine years, then they got up from their sleep after this long period of time:

﴿ ثُمَّ بَعَثْنَٰهُمْ لِنَعْلَمَ أَىُّ ٱلْحِزْبَيْنِ أَحْصَىٰ لِمَا لَبِثُوٓا۟ أَمَدًا ﴿١٢﴾ ﴾

﴿Then We raised them up [from their sleep], that We might test which of the two parties was best at calculating the time period that they had tarried.﴾ *(Qur'an 18: 12)*

﴿ وَكَذَٰلِكَ بَعَثْنَٰهُمْ لِيَتَسَآءَلُوا۟ بَيْنَهُمْ ۚ قَالَ قَآئِلٌ مِّنْهُمْ كَمْ لَبِثْتُمْ ۖ قَالُوا۟ لَبِثْنَا يَوْمًا أَوْ بَعْضَ يَوْمٍ ۚ قَالُوا۟ رَبُّكُمْ أَعْلَمُ بِمَا لَبِثْتُمْ ... ﴿١٩﴾ ﴾

﴿Likewise, We awakened them [from their long deep

sleep] that they might question one another. A speaker from among them said: 'How long have you stayed [here]?' They said: 'We have stayed [perhaps] a day or part of a day.' They said: 'Your Lord [Alone] knows best how long you have stayed [here]...》 *(Qur'an 18: 19)*

﴿ وَلَبِثُوا۟ فِى كَهْفِهِمْ ثَلَٰثَ مِا۟ئَةٍ سِنِينَ وَٱزْدَادُوا۟ تِسْعًا ﴿٢٥﴾ ﴾

《And they stayed in their Cave three hundred [solar] years, adding nine [for lunar years].》 *(Qur'an 18: 25)*

The greatest sign given to Moosa (Moses) (ﷺ) was an inanimate stick which he threw down onto the ground and it turned - by the power of Allah - into a snake:

﴿ فَأَلْقَىٰ عَصَاهُ فَإِذَا هِىَ ثُعْبَانٌ مُّبِينٌ ﴿٣٢﴾ ﴾

《So [Moosa (Moses)] threw his stick, and behold!, it was a serpent, manifest.》 *(Qur'an 26: 32)*

When the sorcerers threw down their ropes and sticks, Moosa threw down his stick and it swallowed those sticks and ropes, despite their great number.

﴿ فَأَلْقَىٰ مُوسَىٰ عَصَاهُ فَإِذَا هِىَ تَلْقَفُ مَا يَأْفِكُونَ ﴿٤٥﴾ ﴾

《Then Moosa [Moses] threw his stick, and behold!, it swallowed up all that they falsely showed!》 *(Qur'an 26: 45)*

6) The parable of the revival of the earth with vegetation

Allah (ﷻ) coins a parable of the resurrection of dead bodies and dry bones, by likening it to His reviving the earth with vegetation after it has been dead. He says:

﴿ فَٱنظُرْ إِلَىٰٓ ءَاثَٰرِ رَحْمَتِ ٱللَّهِ كَيْفَ يُحْىِ ٱلْأَرْضَ بَعْدَ مَوْتِهَآ ۚ إِنَّ ذَٰلِكَ لَمُحْىِ ٱلْمَوْتَىٰ ۖ وَهُوَ عَلَىٰ كُلِّ شَىْءٍ قَدِيرٌ ﴿٥٠﴾ ﴾

﴾Look then at the effects [results] of Allah's Mercy, how He revives the earth after its death. Verily, that [Allah] [Who revived the earth after its death] shall indeed raise the dead [on the Day of Resurrection], and He is Able to do all things.﴿ *(Qur'an 30: 50)*

وَٱللَّهُ ٱلَّذِىٓ أَرْسَلَ ٱلرِّيَٰحَ فَتُثِيرُ سَحَابًا فَسُقْنَٰهُ إِلَىٰ بَلَدٍ مَّيِّتٍ فَأَحْيَيْنَا بِهِ ٱلْأَرْضَ بَعْدَ مَوْتِهَا ۚ كَذَٰلِكَ ٱلنُّشُورُ ﴿٩﴾

﴾And it is Allah Who sends the winds, so that they raise up the clouds, and We drive them to a dead land, and revive therewith the earth after its death. As such [will be] the Resurrection!!﴿ *(Qur'an 35: 9)*

﴿ وَمِنْ ءَايَٰتِهِۦٓ أَنَّكَ تَرَى ٱلْأَرْضَ خَٰشِعَةً فَإِذَآ أَنزَلْنَا عَلَيْهَا ٱلْمَآءَ ٱهْتَزَّتْ وَرَبَتْ ۚ إِنَّ ٱلَّذِىٓ أَحْيَاهَا لَمُحْىِ ٱلْمَوْتَىٰٓ ۚ إِنَّهُۥ عَلَىٰ كُلِّ شَىْءٍ قَدِيرٌ ﴿٣٩﴾ ﴾

﴾And among His Signs [is this], that you see the earth barren, but when We send down water [rain] to it, it is stirred to life and growth [of vegetations]. Verily, He Who gives it life, surely is Able to give life to the dead [on the Day of Resurrection]. Indeed He is Able to do all things.﴿ *(Qur'an 41: 39)*

﴿ وَٱلَّذِى نَزَّلَ مِنَ ٱلسَّمَآءِ مَآءًۢ بِقَدَرٍ فَأَنشَرْنَا بِهِۦ بَلْدَةً مَّيْتًا ۚ كَذَٰلِكَ تُخْرَجُونَ ﴿١١﴾ ﴾

﴾And Who sends down water [rain] from the sky in due measure, then We revive a dead land therewith, and even so you will be brought forth [from the graves].﴿

(Qur'an 43: 11)

7) The wisdom of Allah dictates that His slaves will be resurrected to be brought to account and requited

The wisdom and justice of Allah dictate that Allah will resurrect His slaves to requite them for what they did before. Allah created His creatures to worship Him, and He sent Messengers and revealed books to show them the way in which they are to worship Him. Among His slaves are those who are steadfast in their worship of Allah and who exert themselves and spend their wealth for the sake of Allah. And there are others who refuse to worship Him properly, and they do evil and commit sins. Is it right then, that after that, the righteous and evil should both die and Allah not reward those who did good and punish those who did evil?

﴿ أَفَنَجْعَلُ ٱلْمُسْلِمِينَ كَٱلْمُجْرِمِينَ ﴿٣٥﴾ مَا لَكُمْ كَيْفَ تَحْكُمُونَ ﴿٣٦﴾ أَمْ لَكُمْ كِتَٰبٌ فِيهِ تَدْرُسُونَ ﴿٣٧﴾ إِنَّ لَكُمْ فِيهِ لَمَا تَخَيَّرُونَ ﴿٣٨﴾ ﴾

﴿Shall We then treat the Muslims [believers of Islamic Monotheism, doers of righteous deeds] like the *Mujrimoon* [criminals, polytheists and disbelievers]? What is the matter with you? How judge you? Or have you a Book wherein you learn, That you shall therein have all that you choose?﴾ *(Qur'an 68: 35-38)*

The misguided disbelievers are the ones who think that the universe was created in vain and for no reason, and that there is no difference between the destiny of the righteous believer and that of the disbelieving evil-doer, the destiny of the pious and the destiny of the sinner.

﴿ وَمَا خَلَقْنَا ٱلسَّمَآءَ وَٱلْأَرْضَ وَمَا بَيْنَهُمَا بَٰطِلًا ذَٰلِكَ ظَنُّ ٱلَّذِينَ كَفَرُوا۟ فَوَيْلٌ لِّلَّذِينَ كَفَرُوا۟ مِنَ ٱلنَّارِ ﴿٢٧﴾ أَمْ نَجْعَلُ ٱلَّذِينَ ءَامَنُوا۟ وَعَمِلُوا۟ ٱلصَّٰلِحَٰتِ كَٱلْمُفْسِدِينَ فِى ٱلْأَرْضِ أَمْ نَجْعَلُ ٱلْمُتَّقِينَ كَٱلْفُجَّارِ ﴿٢٨﴾ ﴾

﴾And We created not the heaven and the earth and all that is between them without purpose! That is the consideration of those who disbelieve! Then woe to those who disbelieve [in Islamic Monotheism] from the Fire! Shall We treat those who believe [in the Oneness of Allah - Islamic Monotheism] and do righteous good deeds as *Mufsidoon* [those who associate partners in worship with Allah and commit crimes] on earth? Or shall We treat the *Muttaqoon* [the pious] as the *Fujjaar* [criminals, disbelievers, the wicked]?﴿

(Qur'an 38: 27-28)

CHAPTER SIX
THE RESURRECTION ACCORDING TO THE PROPHETS AND IN THE SCRIPTURES OF THE PEOPLE OF THE BOOK

1 - ALL THE PROPHETS SPOKE OF THE RESURRECTION

Belief in the Resurrection and in Paradise and Hell is one of the basic principles of faith which all the Prophets and their sincere followers have in common: they know of these things and believe in them. The Qur'an is the preserved and protected Book of Allah which has not been changed or distorted; it clearly indicates that all the Prophets taught their nations about the Resurrection, gave them the glad tidings of Paradise and warned them about Hell. Several things indicate this:

1) The Qur'an tells us that all the doomed people in Hell will affirm that their Messengers warned them of the Last Day:

﴿... كُلَّمَآ أُلْقِيَ فِيهَا فَوْجٌ سَأَلَهُمْ خَزَنَتُهَآ أَلَمْ يَأْتِكُمْ نَذِيرٌ ﴿٨﴾ قَالُوا۟ بَلَىٰ قَدْ جَآءَنَا نَذِيرٌ فَكَذَّبْنَا وَقُلْنَا مَا نَزَّلَ ٱللَّهُ مِن شَىْءٍ إِنْ أَنتُمْ إِلَّا فِى ضَلَٰلٍ كَبِيرٍ ﴿٩﴾ وَقَالُوا۟ لَوْ كُنَّا نَسْمَعُ أَوْ نَعْقِلُ مَا كُنَّا فِىٓ أَصْحَٰبِ ٱلسَّعِيرِ ﴿١٠﴾﴾

﴾...Every time a group is cast therein, its keeper will ask: 'Did no warner come to you?' They will say: 'Yes, indeed a warner did come to us, but we belied him and said: 'Allah never sent down anything [of Revelation]; you are only in great error.'' And they will say: 'Had we but listened to or used our intelligence, we would not have been among the dwellers of the blazing Fire.'﴿

(Qur'an 67: 8-10)

﴿ وَسِيقَ ٱلَّذِينَ كَفَرُوٓا۟ إِلَىٰ جَهَنَّمَ زُمَرًا ۖ حَتَّىٰٓ إِذَا جَآءُوهَا فُتِحَتْ أَبْوَٰبُهَا وَقَالَ لَهُمْ خَزَنَتُهَآ أَلَمْ يَأْتِكُمْ رُسُلٌ مِّنكُمْ يَتْلُونَ عَلَيْكُمْ ءَايَٰتِ رَبِّكُمْ وَيُنذِرُونَكُمْ لِقَآءَ يَوْمِكُمْ هَٰذَا ۚ قَالُوا۟ بَلَىٰ وَلَٰكِنْ حَقَّتْ كَلِمَةُ ٱلْعَذَابِ عَلَى ٱلْكَٰفِرِينَ ﴿٧١﴾ ﴾

﴾And those who disbelieved will be driven to Hell in groups till when they reach it, the gates thereof will be opened [suddenly like a prison at the arrival of the prisoners]. And its keepers will say: 'Did not the Messengers come to you from yourselves, reciting to you the Verses of your Lord, and warning you of the Meeting of this Day of yours?' They will say: 'Yes,' but the Word of torment has been justified against the disbelievers!﴿ *(Qur'an 39: 71)*

When the *kuffaar* are exposed to the Fire and are asked, they will all affirm that their Messengers warned them of this Day, but they rejected it and disbelieved.

What is stated in the *aayaat* (verses) quoted above is mentioned in more than one place in the Qur'an. Allah (ﷻ) tells us that His Wisdom and Justice dictate that He will not punish anyone whom the Message has not reached and against whom proof has not been established:

﴿ ... وَمَا كُنَّا مُعَذِّبِينَ حَتَّىٰ نَبْعَثَ رَسُولًا ﴿١٥﴾ ﴾

﴾...And We never punish until We have sent a Messenger [to give warning].﴿ *(Qur'an 17: 15)*

﴿ رُّسُلًا مُّبَشِّرِينَ وَمُنذِرِينَ لِئَلَّا يَكُونَ لِلنَّاسِ عَلَى ٱللَّهِ حُجَّةٌۢ بَعْدَ ٱلرُّسُلِ ... ﴿١٦٥﴾ ﴾

﴾Messengers as bearers of good news as well as of

warning in order that mankind should have no plea against Allah after the [coming of] Messengers...﴾
(Qur'an 4: 165)

For this reason, the Message has been sent to all of mankind:

﴿ ... وَإِن مِّنْ أُمَّةٍ إِلَّا خَلَا فِيهَا نَذِيرٌ ﴿٢٤﴾ ﴾

﴿...And there never was a nation but a warner had passed among them.﴾ *(Qur'an 35: 24)*

2) When Allah sent Adam down to this earth, He told him about the resurrection:

﴿ قَالَ ٱهْبِطُوا۟ بَعْضُكُمْ لِبَعْضٍ عَدُوٌّ ۖ وَلَكُمْ فِى ٱلْأَرْضِ مُسْتَقَرٌّ وَمَتَـٰعٌ إِلَىٰ حِينٍ ﴿٢٤﴾ قَالَ فِيهَا تَحْيَوْنَ وَفِيهَا تَمُوتُونَ وَمِنْهَا تُخْرَجُونَ ﴿٢٥﴾ ﴾

﴿[Allah] said: 'Get down, one of you an enemy to the other [i.e. Adam, Ḥawwa (Eve), and *Shayṭaan* (Satan)]. On earth will be a dwelling place for you and an enjoyment for a time.' He said: 'Therein you shall live, and therein you shall die, and from it you shall be brought out [i.e. resurrected].'﴾ *(Qur'an 7: 24-25)*

When Allah became angry with *Iblees* (Satan) and expelled him from His Mercy, he asked Him for a respite until the Day of Resurrection, and Allah granted his request:

﴿ قَالَ رَبِّ فَأَنظِرْنِىٓ إِلَىٰ يَوْمِ يُبْعَثُونَ ﴿٧٩﴾ قَالَ فَإِنَّكَ مِنَ ٱلْمُنظَرِينَ ﴿٨٠﴾ إِلَىٰ يَوْمِ ٱلْوَقْتِ ٱلْمَعْلُومِ ﴿٨١﴾ ﴾

﴿[*Iblees* (Satan)] said: 'My Lord! Give me then respite till the Day the [dead] are resurrected.' [Allah] said: 'Verily, you are of those allowed respite till the Day of the time appointed.'﴾ *(Qur'an 38: 79-81)*

3) The first of the Messengers was Nooḥ (Noah) (ﷺ), who warned his people of the Day of Resurrection and told them parables which pointed to its coming. He said to his people:

﴿وَٱللَّهُ أَنۢبَتَكُم مِّنَ ٱلۡأَرۡضِ نَبَاتٗا ۝١٧ ثُمَّ يُعِيدُكُمۡ فِيهَا وَيُخۡرِجُكُمۡ إِخۡرَاجٗا ۝١٨﴾

﴿And Allah has brought you forth from the [dust of] earth? [*Tafseer aṭ-Ṭabari*] Afterwards He will return you into it [the earth], and bring you forth [again on the Day of Resurrection]?﴾ *(Qur'an 71: 17-18)*

4) The father of the Prophets, the Close Friend of the Most Merciful [*Khaleel ar-Raḥmaan*, i.e., Ibraaheem (Abraham) (ﷺ)] often mentioned the Last Day. When he prayed to his Lord for Makkah and its people, he said:

﴿... رَبِّ ٱجۡعَلۡ هَٰذَا بَلَدًا ءَامِنٗا وَٱرۡزُقۡ أَهۡلَهُۥ مِنَ ٱلثَّمَرَٰتِ مَنۡ ءَامَنَ مِنۡهُم بِٱللَّهِ وَٱلۡيَوۡمِ ٱلۡأٓخِرِۚ قَالَ وَمَن كَفَرَ فَأُمَتِّعُهُۥ قَلِيلٗا ثُمَّ أَضۡطَرُّهُۥٓ إِلَىٰ عَذَابِ ٱلنَّارِۖ وَبِئۡسَ ٱلۡمَصِيرُ ۝١٢٦﴾

﴿...'My Lord, make this city [Makkah] a place of security and provide its people with fruits, such of them as believe in Allah and the Last Day.' He [Allah] answered: 'As for him who disbelieves, I shall leave him in contentment for a while, then I shall compel him to the torment of the Fire, and worst indeed is that destination!'﴾ *(Qur'an 2: 126)*

In his *du'aa'* for himself, his father and the believers, he said:

﴿رَبَّنَا ٱغۡفِرۡ لِي وَلِوَٰلِدَيَّ وَلِلۡمُؤۡمِنِينَ يَوۡمَ يَقُومُ ٱلۡحِسَابُ ۝٤١﴾

﴿Our Lord! Forgive me and my parents, and [all] the believers on the Day when the reckoning will be established.﴾ *(Qur'an 14: 41)*

When he disputed with his people about the objects of their worship, he explained to them that his Lord was more worthy and deserving of worship, because He provides food and drink, and He gives life and causes death, and He heals the sick and will forgive sins on the Day of Judgement:

﴿ وَٱلَّذِى هُوَ يُطْعِمُنِى وَيَسْقِينِ ﴿٧٩﴾ وَإِذَا مَرِضْتُ فَهُوَ يَشْفِينِ ﴿٨٠﴾
وَٱلَّذِى يُمِيتُنِى ثُمَّ يُحْيِينِ ﴿٨١﴾ وَٱلَّذِىٓ أَطْمَعُ أَن يَغْفِرَ لِى خَطِيٓـَٔتِى يَوْمَ
ٱلدِّينِ ﴿٨٢﴾ ﴾

﴿And it is He Who feeds me and gives me to drink. And when I am ill, it is He Who cures me. And Who will cause me to die, and then will bring me to life [again]. And Who, I hope, will forgive me my faults on the Day of Recompense [the Day of Resurrection].﴾

(Qur'an 26: 79-82)

Then he prayed to his Lord, asking Him to grant him admittance to Paradise, and not to disgrace him on the Day of Resurrection:

﴿ وَٱجْعَلْنِى مِن وَرَثَةِ جَنَّةِ ٱلنَّعِيمِ ﴿٨٥﴾ وَٱغْفِرْ لِأَبِىٓ إِنَّهُۥ كَانَ مِنَ ٱلضَّآلِّينَ
﴿٨٦﴾ وَلَا تُخْزِنِى يَوْمَ يُبْعَثُونَ ﴿٨٧﴾ يَوْمَ لَا يَنفَعُ مَالٌ وَلَا بَنُونَ ﴿٨٨﴾ إِلَّا مَنْ أَتَى
ٱللَّهَ بِقَلْبٍ سَلِيمٍ ﴿٨٩﴾ ﴾

﴿And make me one of the inheritors of the Paradise of Delight. And forgive my father, verily, he is of the erring. And disgrace me not on the Day when [all the creatures] will be resurrected. The Day whereon neither wealth nor sons will avail, Except him who brings to Allah a clean heart [clean from *Shirk* (polytheism) and *Nifaaq* (hypocrisy)].﴾ *(Qur'an 26: 85-89)*

5) When Allah (ﷻ) conversed with Moosa (Moses) (ﷺ), He said:

﴿ إِنَّنِيٓ أَنَا ٱللَّهُ لَآ إِلَٰهَ إِلَّآ أَنَا۠ فَٱعْبُدْنِي وَأَقِمِ ٱلصَّلَوٰةَ لِذِكْرِيٓ ﴿١٤﴾ إِنَّ
ٱلسَّاعَةَ ءَاتِيَةٌ أَكَادُ أُخْفِيهَا لِتُجْزَىٰ كُلُّ نَفْسٍۭ بِمَا تَسْعَىٰ ﴿١٥﴾ فَلَا يَصُدَّنَّكَ
عَنْهَا مَن لَّا يُؤْمِنُ بِهَا وَٱتَّبَعَ هَوَىٰهُ فَتَرْدَىٰ ﴿١٦﴾ ﴾

﴾Verily, I am Allah! *Laa ilaaha illa Ana* [none has the right to be worshipped but I], so worship Me, and perform *Aṣ-Ṣalaah* [*Iqaamat-aṣ-Ṣalaah*] for My remembrance. Verily, the Hour is coming and I am almost hiding it that every person may be rewarded for that which he strives. Therefore, let not the one who believes not therein [i.e. in the Day of Resurrection, Reckoning, Paradise and Hell], but follows his own lusts, divert you therefrom, lest you perish.﴿

(Qur'an 20: 14-16)

And concerning the debate of Moosa (Moses) with Pharaoh (Fir'awn), Allah (ﷻ) said:

﴿ ۞ مِنْهَا خَلَقْنَٰكُمْ وَفِيهَا نُعِيدُكُمْ وَمِنْهَا نُخْرِجُكُمْ تَارَةً أُخْرَىٰ ﴿٥٥﴾ ﴾

﴾Thereof [the earth] We created you, and into it We shall return you, and from it We shall bring you out once again.﴿ *(Qur'an 20: 55)*

6) Prophet Hood (Hud) (ﷺ) warned his people of the meeting with their Lord, but they disbelieved:

﴿ وَقَالَ ٱلْمَلَأُ مِن قَوْمِهِ ٱلَّذِينَ كَفَرُوا۟ وَكَذَّبُوا۟ بِلِقَآءِ ٱلْـَٔاخِرَةِ وَأَتْرَفْنَٰهُمْ فِى
ٱلْحَيَوٰةِ ٱلدُّنْيَا مَا هَٰذَآ إِلَّا بَشَرٌ مِّثْلُكُمْ يَأْكُلُ مِمَّا تَأْكُلُونَ مِنْهُ وَيَشْرَبُ مِمَّا
تَشْرَبُونَ ﴿٣٣﴾ وَلَئِنْ أَطَعْتُم بَشَرًا مِّثْلَكُمْ إِنَّكُمْ إِذًا لَّخَٰسِرُونَ ﴿٣٤﴾ أَيَعِدُكُمْ
أَنَّكُمْ إِذَا مِتُّمْ وَكُنتُمْ تُرَابًا وَعِظَٰمًا أَنَّكُم مُّخْرَجُونَ ﴿٣٥﴾ ۞ هَيْهَاتَ هَيْهَاتَ

لِمَا تُوعَدُونَ ﴿٣٦﴾ إِنْ هِىَ إِلَّا حَيَاتُنَا ٱلدُّنْيَا نَمُوتُ وَنَحْيَا وَمَا نَحْنُ بِمَبْعُوثِينَ ﴿٣٧﴾

﴾And the chiefs of his people who disbelieved and denied the Meeting in the Hereafter, and whom We had given the luxuries and comforts of this life, said: 'He is no more than a human being like you, he eats of that which you eat, and drinks of what you drink. If you were to obey a human being like yourselves, then verily, you indeed would be losers. Does he promise you that when you have died and have become dust and bones, you shall come out alive [resurrected]? Far, very far is that which you are promised! There is nothing but our life of this world! We die and we live! And we are not going to be resurrected!'﴿ *(Qur'an 23: 33-37)*

7) Prophet Shu'ayb (عليه السلام) said to his people:

﴿ ... يَٰقَوْمِ ٱعْبُدُوا۟ ٱللَّهَ وَٱرْجُوا۟ ٱلْيَوْمَ ٱلْءَاخِرَ وَلَا تَعْثَوْا۟ فِى ٱلْأَرْضِ مُفْسِدِينَ ﴿٣٦﴾ ﴾

﴾...O' my people! Worship Allah [Alone] and hope for [the reward of good deeds by worshipping Allah Alone, on] the last Day [i.e. the Day of Resurrection], and commit no mischief on the earth as *Mufsidoon* [those who commit great crimes, oppressors, tyrants, mischief-makers, corrupters].﴿ *(Qur'an 29: 36)*

8) When Yoosuf (عليه السلام) prayed to his Lord, he said:

﴿ ۞ رَبِّ قَدْ ءَاتَيْتَنِى مِنَ ٱلْمُلْكِ وَعَلَّمْتَنِى مِن تَأْوِيلِ ٱلْأَحَادِيثِ ۚ فَاطِرَ ٱلسَّمَٰوَٰتِ وَٱلْأَرْضِ أَنتَ وَلِىِّۦ فِى ٱلدُّنْيَا وَٱلْءَاخِرَةِ ۖ تَوَفَّنِى مُسْلِمًا وَأَلْحِقْنِى بِٱلصَّٰلِحِينَ ﴿١٠١﴾ ﴾

﴿My Lord! You have indeed bestowed on me of the sovereignty, and taught me something of the interpretation of dreams - the [Only] Creator of the heavens and the earth! You are my *Wali* [Protector, Helper, Supporter, Guardian, God, Lord] in this world and in the Hereafter. Cause me to die as a Muslim [the one submitting to Your Will], and join me with the righteous.﴾ *(Qur'an 12: 101)*

9) Some of the followers of the Messengers, whose words are mentioned in the Qur'an, acknowledged the Resurrection, and the good news of Paradise and the warning of Hell. When *Dhul-Qarnayn* reached the setting-place of the sun and found it setting in a spring of black muddy (or hot) water, he found people there, and Allah (ﷻ) said to him:

﴿... يَٰذَا ٱلْقَرْنَيْنِ إِمَّآ أَن تُعَذِّبَ وَإِمَّآ أَن تَتَّخِذَ فِيهِمْ حُسْنًا ﴿٨٦﴾ قَالَ أَمَّا مَن ظَلَمَ فَسَوْفَ نُعَذِّبُهُۥ ثُمَّ يُرَدُّ إِلَىٰ رَبِّهِۦ فَيُعَذِّبُهُۥ عَذَابًا نُّكْرًا ﴿٨٧﴾ وَأَمَّا مَنْ ءَامَنَ وَعَمِلَ صَٰلِحًا فَلَهُۥ جَزَآءً ٱلْحُسْنَىٰ ۖ وَسَنَقُولُ لَهُۥ مِنْ أَمْرِنَا يُسْرًا ﴿٨٨﴾﴾

﴿...'O' *Dhul-Qarnayn*! Either you punish them, or treat them with kindness.' He said: 'As for him [a disbeliever in the Oneness of Allah] who does wrong, we shall punish him, and then he will be brought back unto his Lord, Who will punish him with a terrible torment [Hell]. But as for him who believes [in Allah's Oneness] and works righteousness, he shall have the best reward, [Paradise], and we [*Dhul-Qarnayn*] shall speak unto him mild words [as instructions].'﴾ *(Qur'an 18: 86-88)*

The believer from the family of Pharaoh believed with certainty in the resurrection; his knowledge of it was no different from our own. He issued a clear and detailed warning of that Day to his people and told them:

﴿ وَيَٰقَوۡمِ إِنِّيٓ أَخَافُ عَلَيۡكُمۡ يَوۡمَ ٱلتَّنَادِ ٣٢ يَوۡمَ تُوَلُّونَ مُدۡبِرِينَ مَا لَكُم مِّنَ
ٱللَّهِ مِنۡ عَاصِمٖۗ وَمَن يُضۡلِلِ ٱللَّهُ فَمَا لَهُۥ مِنۡ هَادٖ ٣٣ ﴾

﴾And, O' my people! Verily, I fear for you the Day when there will be mutual calling [between the people of Hell and of Paradise]. A Day when you will turn your backs and flee having no protector from Allah. And whomsoever Allah sends astray, for him there is no guide.﴿ *(Qur'an 40: 32-33)*

And he said:

﴿ يَٰقَوۡمِ إِنَّمَا هَٰذِهِ ٱلۡحَيَوٰةُ ٱلدُّنۡيَا مَتَٰعٞ وَإِنَّ ٱلۡأٓخِرَةَ هِيَ دَارُ ٱلۡقَرَارِ
٣٩ مَنۡ عَمِلَ سَيِّئَةٗ فَلَا يُجۡزَىٰٓ إِلَّا مِثۡلَهَاۖ وَمَنۡ عَمِلَ صَٰلِحٗا مِّن
ذَكَرٍ أَوۡ أُنثَىٰ وَهُوَ مُؤۡمِنٞ فَأُوْلَٰٓئِكَ يَدۡخُلُونَ ٱلۡجَنَّةَ يُرۡزَقُونَ فِيهَا
بِغَيۡرِ حِسَابٖ ٤٠ ۞ وَيَٰقَوۡمِ مَا لِيٓ أَدۡعُوكُمۡ إِلَى ٱلنَّجَوٰةِ وَتَدۡعُونَنِيٓ
إِلَى ٱلنَّارِ ٤١ ﴾

﴾O' my people! Truly, this life of the world is nothing but a [quick passing] enjoyment, and verily, the Hereafter that is the home that will remain forever. Whosoever does an evil deed, will not be requited except the like thereof; and whosoever does a righteous deed, whether male or female and is a true believer [in the Oneness of Allah], such will enter Paradise, where they will be provided therein [with all things in abundance] without limit. And O' my people! How is it that I call you to salvation while you call me to the Fire!﴿

(Qur'an 40: 39-41)

And he said:

﴿ لَا جَرَمَ أَنَّمَا تَدۡعُونَنِيٓ إِلَيۡهِ لَيۡسَ لَهُۥ دَعۡوَةٞ فِي ٱلدُّنۡيَا وَلَا فِي ٱلۡأٓخِرَةِ
وَأَنَّ مَرَدَّنَآ إِلَى ٱللَّهِ وَأَنَّ ٱلۡمُسۡرِفِينَ هُمۡ أَصۡحَٰبُ ٱلنَّارِ ٤٣ ﴾

﴾No doubt you call me to [worship] one who cannot grant [me] my request [or respond to my invocation] in this world or in the Hereafter. And our return will be to Allah, and *Al-Musrifoon* [i.e. polytheists and arrogant, those who commit great sins, the transgressors of Allah's set limits], they shall be the dwellers of the Fire!﴿

(Qur'an 40: 43)

When the sorcerers of Pharaoh saw the clear sign brought by Moosa (Moses), they fell down in prostration, and prostrated as believers. Pharaoh threatened them with a painful torment, but they turned to Allah their Lord, and paid no attention to [Pharaoh's] threats. They answered him by saying:

﴿إِنَّآ ءَامَنَّا بِرَبِّنَا لِيَغْفِرَ لَنَا خَطَٰيَٰنَا وَمَآ أَكْرَهْتَنَا عَلَيْهِ مِنَ ٱلسِّحْرِ ۗ وَٱللَّهُ خَيْرٌ
وَأَبْقَىٰٓ (٧٣) إِنَّهُۥ مَن يَأْتِ رَبَّهُۥ مُجْرِمًا فَإِنَّ لَهُۥ جَهَنَّمَ لَا يَمُوتُ فِيهَا وَلَا يَحْيَىٰ
(٧٤) وَمَن يَأْتِهِۦ مُؤْمِنًا قَدْ عَمِلَ ٱلصَّٰلِحَٰتِ فَأُو۟لَٰٓئِكَ لَهُمُ ٱلدَّرَجَٰتُ ٱلْعُلَىٰ
(٧٥) جَنَّٰتُ عَدْنٍ تَجْرِى مِن تَحْتِهَا ٱلْأَنْهَٰرُ خَٰلِدِينَ فِيهَا ۚ وَذَٰلِكَ جَزَآءُ مَن تَزَكَّىٰ
(٧٦)﴾

﴾Verily, we have believed in our Lord, that He may forgive us our faults, and the magic to which you did compel us. And Allah is better as regards reward in comparison to your [Fir'awn's (Pharaoh)] reward, and more lasting [as regards punishment in comparison to your punishment]. Verily, whoever comes to his Lord as a *Mujrim* [criminal, polytheist, sinner, disbeliever in the Oneness of Allah and His Messengers], then surely, for him is Hell, wherein he will neither die nor live. But whoever comes to Him [Allah] as a believer [in the Oneness of Allah], and has done righteous good deeds, for such are the high ranks [in the Hereafter], 'Adn

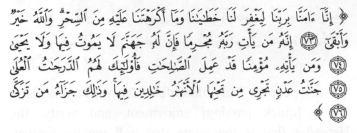

[Eden] Paradise [everlasting Gardens], under which rivers flow, wherein they will abide forever: such is the reward of those who purify themselves [by abstaining from all kinds of sins and evil deeds which Allah has forbidden and by doing all that Allah has ordained].﴾

(Qur'an 20: 73-76)

2 - A LOOK AT THE TEXTS ABOUT THE LAST DAY IN THE SCRIPTURES OF THE PEOPLE OF THE BOOK

No doubt the heavenly books which Allah (ﷻ) revealed were filled with mention of the Last Day, warning of that Day and giving glad tidings of what Allah has prepared for the believers in Gardens of Everlasting Delight, and warning of the Fire of Hell and the terrors of the Resurrection. But these scriptures have been subjected to a great deal of distortion, and many of their texts which speak of the Last Day have been lost.

1) In the Torah (Pentateuch) which is attributed to Moosa (Moses) we find only one passage which clearly mentions the Last Day. This is in the Samaritan Torah, where it is stated very clearly. However, in the Hebrew Torah the phrase in question has two possible meanings. In Deuteronomy 32: 34-35 in the Samaritan Torah it says:

"Is this not gathered with me and stored in my vaults, until the day of vengeance and requital, the time when their feet will slip."

In the Hebrew Torah, this passage reads:

"Have I not kept this in reserve and sealed it in my vaults? It is mine to avenge; I will repay. In due time their foot will slip."[1]

The Samaritan text indicates that the judgement will occur on the Day of Resurrection which is called the "day of vengeance and

---

[1] Translation taken from the New International Version of the Bible. (Translator)

requital." But the Hebrew text could refer to vengeance in this world, or it could refer to the Hereafter. Hence the Sadducees, a Jewish sect who believed only in the Hebrew Torah of Moses, did not believe in the resurrection, because there is no evidence (in the Hebrew Torah) pointing to the resurrection.

Other books of the Prophets in the Old Testament contain some texts which clearly mention the resurrection; this also applies to the New Testament.

2) In the Book of Daniel it says:

"Multitudes who sleep in the dust of the earth will awake: some to everlasting life, others to shame and everlasting contempt."[2]

3) In the Book of Psalms, mention is made of the gathering of people into the Fire of Hell:

"Like sheep they are driven to the Fire, and death will feed on them. The upright will rule over them in the morning; their forms will decay and the Pit (of Hell) will be their abode."[3]

4) In the Gospel of Luke, there is a reference to the torment of the grave:

"... The rich man also died and was buried. In hell, where he was in torment, he looked up..."[4]

Thus the immoral person who is buried will find himself in torment and will see his place in the Fire of Hell.

5) In the Gospel of Matthew, it says:

---

[2] Daniel 12:2 - New International Version. (Translator)

[3] A similar passage is to be found in Psalm 49:14. (Translator)

[4] Luke 16:22-23 - New International Version. (Translator)

"If your hand or your foot causes you to sin, cut it off and throw it away. It is better for you to enter life maimed or crippled than to have two hands or two feet and be thrown into eternal fire."[5]

One of the scriptures that speaks the most about Paradise and Hell is the Gospel of Barnabas, which says that the people of Paradise will eat and drink, but they will not urinate or defecate, because there is nothing unclean or impure in their food and drink. But the Christians reject this Gospel which has emerged recently, in our own times.

Some Jews believed in the Resurrection; they were known as the scribes. There was another group which was called the Sadducees, who did not believe in the resurrection or in eternal life in either Paradise or Hell. The Gospel of Matthew mentions that a group of those who did not believe in the resurrection came to Jesus and debated with him about the resurrection:

"That same day, the Sadducees, who say there is no resurrection, came to him..."[6]

And Jesus answered the question of one of his disciples who asked him, "Will these bodies of ours go to Paradise?" Jesus (peace be upon him) said: "Beware, O' Peter!, lest you become a Sadducee, for the Sadduccees say that the body will not be resurrected and that there are no angels; for that reason their bodies and their souls will be forbidden to enter Paradise."

The Christians believe that what will be blessed or tormented on the Day of Resurrection is the soul only. Some so-called Muslims, such as philosophers and misguided *baatini* sects said the same thing.

[5] Matthew 18:8 - New International Version. (Translator)
[6] Matthew 22:23 - New International Version. (Translator)

"If your hand or your foot causes you to sin cut it off and throw it away. It is better for you to enter life maimed or crippled than to have two hands or two feet and be thrown into eternal fire."[1]

One of the scriptures that speaks the most about Paradise and Hell is the Gospel of Barnabas, which says that the people of Paradise will eat and drink, but they will not urinate or defecate, because there is nothing unclean or impure in their food and drink. But the Christians reject this Gospel which has emerged recently in our own times.

Some Jews believed in the Resurrection; they were known as the scribes. There was another group which was called the Sadducees, who did not believe in the resurrection or in eternal life in either Paradise or Hell. The Gospel of Matthew mentions that a group of those who did not believe in the resurrection came to Jesus and debated with him about the resurrection:

"That same day, the Sadducees, who say there is no resurrection, came to him..."[2]

And Jesus answered the question of one of his disciples who asked him, "Will these bodies of ours go to Paradise?" Jesus (peace be upon him) said: "Beware, O' Peter, lest you become a Sadducee, for the Sadducees say that the body will not be resurrected and that there are no angels; for that reason their bodies and their souls will be forbidden to enter Paradise."

The Christians believe that what will be blessed or tormented on the Day of Resurrection is the soul only. Some so-called Muslims, such as philosophers and misguided *baatini* sects said the same thing

[1] Matthew 18:8 - New International Version. (Translated)
[2] Matthew 22:23 - New International Version. (Translated)

CHAPTER SEVEN
THE TERRORS OF THE DAY OF RESURRECTION

1 - EVIDENCE OF THE ENORMITY OF THE TERRORS OF THAT DAY

The Day of Resurrection will be a Day of tremendous import and immense horror, the like of which mankind will never have seen. Several things point to the enormity of its terrors:

1) Allah (ﷻ) described that Day as being great. His description of it as such is sufficient for us to know that it is more serious than we can ever imagine.

﴿ أَلَا يَظُنُّ أُولَٰٓئِكَ أَنَّهُم مَّبْعُوثُونَ ۝٤ لِيَوْمٍ عَظِيمٍ ۝٥ يَوْمَ يَقُومُ ٱلنَّاسُ لِرَبِّ ٱلْعَٰلَمِينَ ۝٦ ﴾

﴿Think they not that they will be resurrected [for reckoning], On a Great Day, the Day when [all] mankind will stand before the Lord of the *'Aalameen* [mankind, jinn and all that exists]?﴾ *(Qur'an 83: 4-6)*

Elsewhere, Allah, the Almighty, All-Powerful, describes it as being heavy, and as being hard:

﴿ إِنَّ هَٰٓؤُلَآءِ يُحِبُّونَ ٱلْعَاجِلَةَ وَيَذَرُونَ وَرَآءَهُمْ يَوْمًا ثَقِيلًا ۝٢٧ ﴾

﴿Verily, these [disbelievers] love the present life of this world, and put behind them a heavy Day [that will be hard].﴾ *(Qur'an 76: 27)*

﴿ فَذَٰلِكَ يَوْمَئِذٍ يَوْمٌ عَسِيرٌ ۝٩ عَلَى ٱلْكَٰفِرِينَ غَيْرُ يَسِيرٍ ۝١٠ ﴾

﴾Truly, that Day will be a Hard Day - Far from easy for the disbelievers.﴿ *(Qur'an 74: 9-10)*

2) The fear and terror which will befall mankind on that Day will be so great that the mother who would readily sacrifice herself for her infant will, on that Day, be heedless of him. Pregnant women will miscarry, and people will be like drunkards who have lost their senses.

﴿ يَٰٓأَيُّهَا ٱلنَّاسُ ٱتَّقُوا۟ رَبَّكُمْ ۚ إِنَّ زَلْزَلَةَ ٱلسَّاعَةِ شَىْءٌ عَظِيمٌ ﴿١﴾ يَوْمَ تَرَوْنَهَا تَذْهَلُ كُلُّ مُرْضِعَةٍ عَمَّآ أَرْضَعَتْ وَتَضَعُ كُلُّ ذَاتِ حَمْلٍ حَمْلَهَا وَتَرَى ٱلنَّاسَ سُكَٰرَىٰ وَمَا هُم بِسُكَٰرَىٰ وَلَٰكِنَّ عَذَابَ ٱللَّهِ شَدِيدٌ ﴿٢﴾ ﴾

﴾O' mankind! Fear your Lord and be dutiful to Him! Verily, the earthquake of the Hour [of Judgement] is a terrible thing. The Day you shall see it, every nursing mother will forget her nursling, and every pregnant one will drop her load, and you shall see mankind as in a drunken state, yet they will not be drunken, but severe will be the Torment of Allah.﴿ *(Qur'an 22: 1-2)*

Because of the intensity of the terror, on that Day eyes will be not blinking and not looking to the right or the left. Because of their great fear, their hearts will be empty, not comprehending anything at all.

﴿ وَلَا تَحْسَبَنَّ ٱللَّهَ غَٰفِلًا عَمَّا يَعْمَلُ ٱلظَّٰلِمُونَ ۚ إِنَّمَا يُؤَخِّرُهُمْ لِيَوْمٍ تَشْخَصُ فِيهِ ٱلْأَبْصَٰرُ ﴿٤٢﴾ مُهْطِعِينَ مُقْنِعِى رُءُوسِهِمْ لَا يَرْتَدُّ إِلَيْهِمْ طَرْفُهُمْ ۖ وَأَفْـِٔدَتُهُمْ هَوَآءٌ ﴿٤٣﴾ ﴾

﴾Consider not that Allah is unaware of that which the *Zaalimoon* [polytheists, wrongdoers] do, but He gives them respite up to a Day when the eyes will stare in horror. [They will be] hastening forward with necks

outstretched, their heads raised up [towards the sky], their gaze returning not towards them and their hearts empty [from thinking because of extreme fear].》
(Qur'an 14: 42-43)

Because of their extreme terror, the hearts of the evildoers will rise to their throats, but they will not come out, neither will they settle back in their places:

﴿ وَأَنذِرْهُمْ يَوْمَ ٱلْـَٔازِفَةِ إِذِ ٱلْقُلُوبُ لَدَى ٱلْحَنَاجِرِ كَـٰظِمِينَ ... ﴿١٨﴾ ﴾

《And warn them [O' Muhammad] of the Day that is drawing near [i.e. the Day of Resurrection], when the hearts will be choking the throats, and they can neither return them [hearts] to their chests nor can they throw them out...》 *(Qur'an 40: 18)*

Elsewhere, Allah (ﷻ) describes what will happen to people's hearts and eyes on that Day:

﴿ ... يَخَافُونَ يَوْمًا تَتَقَلَّبُ فِيهِ ٱلْقُلُوبُ وَٱلْأَبْصَـٰرُ ﴿٣٧﴾ ﴾

《...They fear a Day when hearts and eyes will be overturned [out of the horror of the torment of the Day of Resurrection].》 *(Qur'an 24: 37)*

﴿ قُلُوبٌ يَوْمَئِذٍ وَاجِفَةٌ ﴿٨﴾ أَبْصَـٰرُهَا خَـٰشِعَةٌ ﴿٩﴾ ﴾

《[Some] hearts that Day will shake with fear and anxiety. Their eyes will be downcast.》 *(Qur'an 79: 8-9)*

It suffices to know that the hair of the child who has never committed sin will turn grey because of the intense horror of what he is seeing:

﴿ فَكَيْفَ تَتَّقُونَ إِن كَفَرْتُمْ يَوْمًا يَجْعَلُ ٱلْوِلْدَٰنَ شِيبًا ﴿١٧﴾ ٱلسَّمَآءُ مُنفَطِرٌۢ
بِهِۦ ۚ كَانَ وَعْدُهُۥ مَفْعُولًا ﴿١٨﴾ ﴾

﴾Then how can you avoid the punishment, if you disbelieve, on a Day [i.e. the Day of Resurrection] that will make the children grey-headed? Whereon the heaven will be cleft asunder? His Promise is certainly to be accomplished.﴿ *(Qur'an 73: 17-18)*

3) Blood ties (bonds of kinship) will be severed on the Day of Resurrection, as Allah (ﷻ) says:

﴿ فَإِذَا نُفِخَ فِى ٱلصُّورِ فَلَآ أَنسَابَ بَيْنَهُمْ يَوْمَئِذٍ وَلَا يَتَسَآءَلُونَ ﴿١٠١﴾ ﴾

﴾Then, when the Trumpet is blown, there will be no kinship among them that Day, nor will they ask of one another.﴿ *(Qur'an 23: 101)*

On that Day, each person will care only about himself, and will not think of anyone else. Indeed, a man will run from those who are dearest to him, from his brother, his mother, his father, his wife and his sons:

﴿ فَإِذَا جَآءَتِ ٱلصَّآخَّةُ ﴿٣٣﴾ يَوْمَ يَفِرُّ ٱلْمَرْءُ مِنْ أَخِيهِ ﴿٣٤﴾ وَأُمِّهِۦ وَأَبِيهِ ﴿٣٥﴾
وَصَٰحِبَتِهِۦ وَبَنِيهِ ﴿٣٦﴾ لِكُلِّ ٱمْرِئٍ مِّنْهُمْ يَوْمَئِذٍ شَأْنٌ يُغْنِيهِ ﴿٣٧﴾ ﴾

﴾Then when there comes *Aṣ-Ṣaakhkhah* [the second blowing of the Trumpet on the Day of Resurrection] - That Day shall a man flee from his brother, and from his mother and his father, and from his wife and his children. Every man that Day will have enough to make him careless of others.﴿ *(Qur'an 80: 33-37)*

Elsewhere, Allah (ﷻ) says:

﴿ يَٰٓأَيُّهَا ٱلنَّاسُ ٱتَّقُوا۟ رَبَّكُمْ وَٱخْشَوْا۟ يَوْمًا لَّا يَجْزِى وَالِدٌ عَن وَلَدِهِۦ وَلَا
مَوْلُودٌ هُوَ جَازٍ عَن وَالِدِهِۦ شَيْـًٔا ۚ إِنَّ وَعْدَ ٱللَّهِ حَقٌّ ... ﴿٣٣﴾ ﴾

﴾O' mankind! Be afraid of your Lord [by keeping your duty to Him and avoiding all evil], and fear a Day when no father can avail aught for his son, nor a son avail aught for his father. Verily, the Promise of Allah is true...﴿ *(Qur'an 31: 33)*

﴿ وَٱتَّقُواْ يَوْمًا لَّا تَجْزِى نَفْسٌ عَن نَّفْسٍ شَيْـًٔا وَلَا يُقْبَلُ مِنْهَا شَفَٰعَةٌ وَلَا يُؤْخَذُ مِنْهَا عَدْلٌ وَلَا هُمْ يُنصَرُونَ ﴿٤٨﴾ ﴾

﴾And fear a Day [of Judgement] when a person shall not avail another, nor will intercession be accepted from him nor will compensation be taken from him nor will they be helped.﴿ *(Qur'an 2: 48)*

4) On the Day of Resurrection, the *kuffaar* (disbelievers) will be prepared to give up everything to save themselves from the punishment. If they possessed everything on earth, they would try to ransom themselves with it.

﴿ وَلَوْ أَنَّ لِكُلِّ نَفْسٍ ظَلَمَتْ مَا فِى ٱلْأَرْضِ لَٱفْتَدَتْ بِهِۦ ... ﴿٥٤﴾ ﴾

﴾And if every person who had wronged [by disbelieving in Allah and by worshipping others besides Allah] possessed all that is on the earth and sought to ransom himself therewith [it will not be accepted]...﴿ *(Qur'an 10: 54)*

Even if they had as many times as what is on earth, they would not be able to ransom themselves with it:

﴿ ... وَٱلَّذِينَ لَمْ يَسْتَجِيبُواْ لَهُۥ لَوْ أَنَّ لَهُم مَّا فِى ٱلْأَرْضِ جَمِيعًا وَمِثْلَهُۥ مَعَهُۥ لَٱفْتَدَوْاْ بِهِۦٓ ۚ أُوْلَٰٓئِكَ لَهُمْ سُوٓءُ ٱلْحِسَابِ ... ﴿١٨﴾ ﴾

﴾...But those who answered not His Call [disbelieved in the Oneness of Allah and followed not His Messenger

Muhammad], if they had all that is in the earth together with its like, they would offer it in order to save themselves [from the torment, but it will be in vain]. For them there will be the terrible reckoning...﴿

(Qur'an 13: 18)

He will be prepared to sacrifice what he has, even if it were an earthful of gold, if that were possible, but Allah will not accept it from him:

﴿ إِنَّ ٱلَّذِينَ كَفَرُوا۟ وَمَاتُوا۟ وَهُمْ كُفَّارٌ فَلَن يُقْبَلَ مِنْ أَحَدِهِم مِّلْءُ ٱلْأَرْضِ ذَهَبًا وَلَوِ ٱفْتَدَىٰ بِهِۦٓ أُو۟لَـٰٓئِكَ لَهُمْ عَذَابٌ أَلِيمٌ وَمَا لَهُم مِّن نَّـٰصِرِينَ ﴿٩١﴾ ﴾

﴾Verily, those who disbelieved, and died while they were disbelievers, the [whole] earth full of gold will not be accepted from anyone of them even if they offered it as a ransom. For them is a painful torment and they will have no helpers.﴿ *(Qur'an 3: 91)*

In *Ṣaḥeeḥ al-Bukhari* it is narrated from Anas ibn Maalik (رضي الله عنه) that the Prophet (ﷺ) used to say:

"The *kaafir* will be brought forth on the Day of Resurrection and it will be said to him, 'Do you think that if you had an earthful of gold that you would be able to ransom yourself with it?' He will say, 'Yes.' It will be said to him, 'I used to ask you for less than that.'"[1]

On that Day, things will be so bad for the *kaafir* that he will wish that he could send the most beloved of people to him to the Fire, in order to save himself from the torment:

---

[1] Bukhari, *Kitaab ar-Riqaaq, Baab man nooqisha al-ḥisaab 'udhiba*; *Fatḥ al-Baari*, 11/400.

﴿... يَوَدُّ ٱلْمُجْرِمُ لَوْ يَفْتَدِى مِنْ عَذَابِ يَوْمِئِذٍۭ بِبَنِيهِ ﴿١١﴾ وَصَـٰحِبَتِهِۦ وَأَخِيهِ ﴿١٢﴾ وَفَصِيلَتِهِ ٱلَّتِى تُـْٔوِيهِ ﴿١٣﴾ وَمَن فِى ٱلْأَرْضِ جَمِيعًا ثُمَّ يُنجِيهِ ﴿١٤﴾ كَلَّآ ۖ إِنَّهَا لَظَىٰ ﴿١٥﴾﴾

﴾...The *Mujrim*, [criminal, sinner, disbeliever] would desire to ransom himself from the punishment of that Day by his children. And his wife and his brother, and his kindred who sheltered him, and all that are in the earth, so that it might save him. By no means! Verily, it will be the fire of Hell.﴿ *(Qur'an 70: 11-15)*

5) Another indication of how terrible that Day will be is the fact that it will be so long.

Allah (ﷻ) says:

﴿ تَعْرُجُ ٱلْمَلَـٰٓئِكَةُ وَٱلرُّوحُ إِلَيْهِ فِى يَوْمٍ كَانَ مِقْدَارُهُۥ خَمْسِينَ أَلْفَ سَنَةٍ ﴿٤﴾ فَٱصْبِرْ صَبْرًا جَمِيلًا ﴿٥﴾ إِنَّهُمْ يَرَوْنَهُۥ بَعِيدًا ﴿٦﴾ وَنَرَىٰهُ قَرِيبًا ﴿٧﴾ ﴾

﴾The angels and the *Rooḥ* [Jibreel (Gabriel)] ascend to Him in a Day the measure whereof is fifty thousand years. So be patient [O' Muhammad], with a good patience. Verily, they see it [the torment] afar off. But We see it [quite] near.﴿ *(Qur'an 70: 4-7)*

The context of the *aayaat* (verses) clearly indicates that what is referred to here is the Day of Resurrection. It is reported with a *ṣaḥeeḥ isnaad* from Ibn 'Abbaas (رضي الله عنه) that this does indeed refer to the Day of Resurrection. This was also the view of Al-Ḥasan, Aḍ-Ḍaḥḥaak and Ibn Zayd.[2] Because that Day will be so long, on the Day of Resurrection, people will think that they only stayed in this world for a part of a day, as Allah (ﷻ) says:

---

[2] *An-Nihaayah* by Ibn Katheer, 1/323.

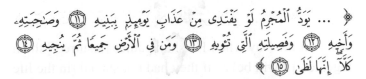

﴿ وَيَوْمَ يَحْشُرُهُمْ كَأَن لَّمْ يَلْبَثُوٓاْ إِلَّا سَاعَةً مِّنَ ٱلنَّهَارِ ... ﴿٤٥﴾ ﴾

﴿And on the Day when He shall gather [resurrect] them together, [it will be] as if they had not stayed [in the life of this world and graves] but an hour of a day...﴾ *(Qur'an 10: 45)*

Ibn Katheer said, in his *tafseer* of this *aayah* (verse): "Allah is reminding mankind of the Hour and when they will be gathered from their graves. 'And on the Day when He shall gather [resurrect] them together' - this is like the *aayaat* (verses):

﴿ كَأَنَّهُمْ يَوْمَ يَرَوْنَهَا لَمْ يَلْبَثُوٓاْ إِلَّا عَشِيَّةً أَوْ ضُحَىٰهَا ﴿٤٦﴾ ﴾

﴿The Day they see it, [it will be] as if they had not tarried [in this world] except an afternoon or a morning.﴾ *(Qur'an 79: 46)*

﴿ نَّحْنُ أَعْلَمُ بِمَا يَقُولُونَ إِذْ يَقُولُ أَمْثَلُهُمْ طَرِيقَةً إِن لَّبِثْتُمْ إِلَّا يَوْمًا ﴿١٠٤﴾ ﴾

﴿We know very well what they will say, when the best among them in knowledge and wisdom will say: 'You stayed no longer than a day!'﴾ *(Qur'an 20: 104)*

﴿ وَيَوْمَ تَقُومُ ٱلسَّاعَةُ يُقْسِمُ ٱلْمُجْرِمُونَ مَا لَبِثُواْ غَيْرَ سَاعَةٍ ... ﴿٥٥﴾ ﴾

﴿And on the Day that the Hour will be established, the *Mujrimoon* [criminals, disbelievers, polytheists, sinners] will swear that they stayed not but an hour...﴾ *(Qur'an 30: 55)*

This indicates how short the life of this world is in comparison with the Hereafter, as Allah (سبحانه وتعالى) says:

﴿ قَالَ كَمْ لَبِثْتُمْ فِي ٱلْأَرْضِ عَدَدَ سِنِينَ ﴿١١٢﴾ قَالُوا۟ لَبِثْنَا يَوْمًا أَوْ بَعْضَ يَوْمٍ فَسْـَٔلِ ٱلْعَآدِّينَ ﴿١١٣﴾ قَٰلَ إِن لَّبِثْتُمْ إِلَّا قَلِيلًا ۖ لَّوْ أَنَّكُمْ كُنتُمْ تَعْلَمُونَ ﴿١١٤﴾ ﴾

﴿He [Allah] will say: 'What number of years did you stay on earth?' They will say: 'We stayed a day or part of a day. Ask of those who keep account.' He [Allah] will say: 'You stayed not but a little, if you had only known!'﴾ *(Qur'an 23: 112-114)*"[3]

2 - SOME OF THE FEATURES OF THE HORRORS OF THE RESURRECTION

The Qur'an speaks of the horrors of that Day, which will shock people and leave them staring in terror, when they will be shaken to the core of their being.

One of the greatest of these horrors will be the total destruction of this earth with its mountains, and the heaven with its stars, sun and moon.

Our Lord tells us that this earth will be shaken and turned to powder, that the mountains will be made to pass away and will be blown away, the seas will become as blazing fire or will overflow, the sky will be rent asunder and will shake with a dreadful shaking, the sun will be wound round and will disappear, the moon will be eclipsed, the stars will fall and their light will be extinguished, and the entire system (of the universe) will collapse.

I will mention some of the texts which describe these terrible events, then I will mention what will happen to each of these great things (the earth, sun, etc) on that Day.

---

[3] *Tafseer Ibn Katheer,* 3/505.

1) The grasping of the earth and the rolling up of the heavens

Allah will grasp the earth in His Hand on the Day of Resurrection, and will roll up the heavens in His Right Hand, as He says:

﴿ وَمَا قَدَرُوا۟ ٱللَّهَ حَقَّ قَدْرِهِۦ وَٱلْأَرْضُ جَمِيعًا قَبْضَتُهُۥ يَوْمَ ٱلْقِيَـٰمَةِ وَٱلسَّمَـٰوَٰتُ مَطْوِيَّـٰتٌۢ بِيَمِينِهِۦ ۚ سُبْحَـٰنَهُۥ وَتَعَـٰلَىٰ عَمَّا يُشْرِكُونَ ﴿٦٧﴾ ﴾

﴾They made not a just estimate of Allah such as is due to Him. And on the Day of Resurrection the whole of the earth will be grasped by His Hand and the heavens will be rolled up in His Right Hand. Glorified be He, and High be He above all that they associate as partners with Him!﴿ *(Qur'an 39: 67)*

Elsewhere, Allah (ﷻ) tells us how He will roll up the heavens:

﴿ يَوْمَ نَطْوِى ٱلسَّمَآءَ كَطَىِّ ٱلسِّجِلِّ لِلْكُتُبِ ۚ كَمَا بَدَأْنَآ أَوَّلَ خَلْقٍ نُّعِيدُهُۥ ۚ وَعْدًا عَلَيْنَآ ۚ إِنَّا كُنَّا فَـٰعِلِينَ ﴿١٠٤﴾ ﴾

﴾And [remember] the Day when We shall roll up the heaven like a scroll rolled up for books. As We began the first creation, We shall repeat it. [It is] a promise binding upon Us. Truly, We shall do it.﴿ *(Qur'an 21: 104)*

Ibn Katheer said: "The correct view, narrated from Ibn 'Abbaas, is that the word *sijill* (scroll) means a scroll. This was the view of 'Ali ibn Abi Ṭalḥah, and of Al-'Awfi who narrated it from him. This is also stated by Mujaahid, Qataadah and others, and the view is favoured by Ibn Jareer, because this meaning is known in the (Arabic) language. Thus the meaning of this phrase is, the Day when the heavens will be rolled up like the scroll of a book, and as the scroll contains the writing, so too the heavens will be contained."[4]

---

[4] *Tafseer Ibn Katheer*, 4/602.

There are *ṣaḥeeḥ aḥaadeeth* which indicate the same as is indicated by these Qur'anic texts, but they also point to an additional idea, which is what Allah will say after seizing the earth and rolling up the heavens. According to a hadith whose authenticity is agreed upon by Bukhari and Muslim, Abu Hurayrah said that the Messenger of Allah (ﷺ) said:

> "Allah will seize the earth on the Day of Resurrection and will roll up the heavens in His Right Hand, then He will say: 'I am the King, where are the kings of the earth?'"[5]

According to a report in Muslim narrated from 'Abdullah ibn 'Umar, the Messenger of Allah (ﷺ) said:

> "Allah will roll up the heavens on the Day of Resurrection, then He will hold them in His Right Hand, and will say: 'I am the King. Where are the tyrants? Where are the arrogant ones?' Then He will roll up the earth in His Left Hand - according to one report, He will take hold of them with His other Hand - and will say, 'I am the King. Where are the tyrants? Where are the arrogant ones?'"[6]

Bukhari narrated from 'Abdullah ibn Mas'ood that a Jew came to the Prophet (ﷺ) and said, "O' Muhammad! Allah holds the heavens on one finger, the earth on another finger, the mountains on another finger, the trees on another finger, and created beings on another finger, then He says, 'I am the King.'" The Messenger of Allah (ﷺ) smiled so broadly that his eyeteeth could be seen, then he recited,

---

[5] *Mishkaat al-Maṣaabeeḥ*, 3/53, hadith no. 5522.

[6] Ibid, hadith no. 5523.

﴿ وَمَا قَدَرُوا۟ ٱللَّهَ حَقَّ قَدْرِهِۦ وَٱلْأَرْضُ جَمِيعًا قَبْضَتُهُۥ يَوْمَ ٱلْقِيَـٰمَةِ وَٱلسَّمَـٰوَٰتُ مَطْوِيَّـٰتٌۢ بِيَمِينِهِۦ ۚ سُبْحَـٰنَهُۥ وَتَعَـٰلَىٰ عَمَّا يُشْرِكُونَ ﴿٦٧﴾ ﴾

﴾They made not a just estimate of Allah such as is due to Him. And on the Day of Resurrection the whole of the earth will be grasped by His Hand and the heavens will be rolled up in His Right Hand. Glorified be He, and High be He above all that they associate as partners with Him!﴿ *(Qur'an 39: 67)*

This seizing of the earth and rolling up of the heavens will happen after Allah causes all creatures to die. It is said that a caller will cry out after all creatures have been gathered on an earth, white like silver, on which no sin has ever been committed. This was the view favoured by Abu Ja'far al-Nahhaas, who said: "This view is narrated with a *saheeh isnaad* from Ibn Mas'ood, and it is not something which could be worked out by analogy or interpretation [i.e., he must have heard it from the Prophet (ﷺ)]."

Qurtubi said: "The first view is more apparent, because the point demonstrated here is that Allah Alone has sovereignty, when there will no longer any others making any such claims, when every king and his kingdom will be disappeared, when every arrogant tyrant and his dominion will have vanished, and their claims would have disappeared with them. This is the more correct view."[7]

2) The crushing of the earth and the blowing away of the mountains

Our Lord tells us that on the Day of Judgement, when the Trumpet is blown, this stable earth of ours, with its strong and heavy mountains, will be crushed with a single crushing:

---

[7] Bukhari, *Kitaab at-Tawheed, Baab Qawl Allah ta'aala "Lima khalaqtu bi yadayy"*; *Fath al-Baari*, 13/393.

﴿فَإِذَا نُفِخَ فِي ٱلصُّورِ نَفۡخَةٞ وَٰحِدَةٞ ١٣ وَحُمِلَتِ ٱلۡأَرۡضُ وَٱلۡجِبَالُ فَدُكَّتَا دَكَّةٗ
وَٰحِدَةٗ ١٤ فَيَوۡمَئِذٖ وَقَعَتِ ٱلۡوَاقِعَةُ ١٥﴾

﴾Then when the Trumpet will be blown with one blowing [the first one]. And the earth and the mountains shall be removed from their places, and crushed with a single crushing. Then on that Day shall the [Great] Event befall.﴿ *(Qur'an 69: 13-15)*

﴿كَلَّآ إِذَا دُكَّتِ ٱلۡأَرۡضُ دَكّٗا دَكّٗا ٢١﴾

﴾Nay! When the earth is ground to powder.﴿
(Qur'an 89: 21)

At that time, these firm and solid mountains will be turned into fine sand, as Allah (سبحانه وتعالى) says:

﴿يَوۡمَ تَرۡجُفُ ٱلۡأَرۡضُ وَٱلۡجِبَالُ وَكَانَتِ ٱلۡجِبَالُ كَثِيبٗا مَّهِيلًا ١٤﴾

﴾On the Day when the earth and the mountains will be in violent shake, and the mountains will be a heap of sand poured out.﴿ *(Qur'an 73: 14)*

- i.e., after being solid rock, they will become like a heap of sand poured out, which describes the kind of sand where, if some is removed, the rest pours down. Words derived from the same root are used to describe what happens when a pile of sand collapses and the top of it falls to the bottom.

Elsewhere, Allah (سبحانه وتعالى) tells us that the mountains will become like wool, as He says:

﴿وَتَكُونُ ٱلۡجِبَالُ كَٱلۡعِهۡنِ ٩﴾

﴾And the mountains will be like flakes of wool.﴿
(Qur'an 70: 9)

In another text, He (ﷻ) likens them to carded wool:

﴿ بِأَنَّ رَبَّكَ أَوْحَىٰ لَهَا ۝٥ ﴾

﴿And the mountains will be like carded wool.﴾ *(Qur'an 101: 5)*

Then Allah will move these mountains from their places, and will flatten out the earth and there will no any peaks or troughs. The Qur'an describes the destruction of the mountains in various ways:

﴿ وَإِذَا ٱلْجِبَالُ سُيِّرَتْ ۝٣ ﴾

﴿And when the mountains shall be made to pass away.﴾ *(Qur'an 81: 3)*

﴿ وَسُيِّرَتِ ٱلْجِبَالُ فَكَانَتْ سَرَابًا ۝٢٠ ﴾

﴿And the mountains shall be moved away from their places and they will be as if they were a mirage.﴾ *(Qur'an 78: 20)*

﴿ وَإِذَا ٱلْجِبَالُ نُسِفَتْ ۝١٠ ﴾

﴿And when the mountains are blown away.﴾ *(Qur'an 77: 10)*

Then Allah explains what will happen to the earth after the mountains have been made to pass away and have been blown away:

﴿ وَيَوْمَ نُسَيِّرُ ٱلْجِبَالَ وَتَرَى ٱلْأَرْضَ بَارِزَةً ... ۝٤٧ ﴾

﴿And [remember] the Day We shall cause the mountains to pass away [like clouds of dust], and you will see the earth as a levelled plain...﴾ *(Qur'an 18: 47)*

i.e., it will be flat, with no peaks or troughs, as Allah (ﷻ) says:

﴿ وَيَسْـَٔلُونَكَ عَنِ ٱلْجِبَالِ فَقُلْ يَنسِفُهَا رَبِّى نَسْفًا ﴿١٠٥﴾ فَيَذَرُهَا قَاعًا صَفْصَفًا ﴿١٠٦﴾ لَّا تَرَىٰ فِيهَا عِوَجًا وَلَآ أَمْتًا ﴿١٠٧﴾ ﴾

﴿And they ask you concerning the mountains: say, 'My Lord will blast them and scatter them as particles of dust. Then He shall leave them as a level smooth plain. You will see therein nothing crooked or curved.'﴾

(Qur'an 20: 105-107)

3) The bursting forth and overflowing of the sea

These seas which cover the greater part of our planet, in which such great numbers of creatures live and on the surface of which ships come and go, will on that Day burst forth. In modern times, we have learned of the great horror which is unleashed by the explosion of atoms which are smaller than water molecules, so how will it be then when the molecules of water in these vast oceans explode, when the seas turn to blazing fire? You can imagine how these huge seas will be when they become inflammable, how they will look with flames reaching up to the sky.

Allah (ﷻ) says:

﴿ وَإِذَا ٱلْبِحَارُ فُجِّرَتْ ﴿٣﴾ ﴾

﴿And when the seas are burst forth [got dried up].﴾

(Qur'an 82: 3)

﴿ وَإِذَا ٱلْبِحَارُ سُجِّرَتْ ﴿٦﴾ ﴾

﴿And when the seas are become as blazing Fire or shall overflow.﴾ *(Qur'an 81: 6)*

The *mufassireen* of the past thought that this referred to the sea overflowing and breaking its barriers, so that the fresh water would be mixed with the salt water, and it would become one body of water.[8] But what we have mentioned is more obvious and closer to the meaning, because the idea of exploding fits the idea of busting forth. And Allah knows best.

4) The shaking and splitting of the sky

Our beautiful blue sky, which lifts our spirits when we look at it, will be terribly shaken:

﴿ يَوْمَ تَمُورُ ٱلسَّمَآءُ مَوْرًا ﴿٩﴾ ﴾

﴿On the Day when the heaven will shake with a dreadful shaking.﴾ *(Qur'an 52: 9)*

Then it will be rent asunder,

﴿ إِذَا ٱلسَّمَآءُ ٱنفَطَرَتْ ﴿١﴾ ﴾

﴿When the heaven is cleft asunder.﴾ *(Qur'an 82: 1)*

﴿ إِذَا ٱلسَّمَآءُ ٱنشَقَّتْ ﴿١﴾ وَأَذِنَتْ لِرَبِّهَا وَحُقَّتْ ﴿٢﴾ ﴾

﴿When the heaven is split asunder and listens and obeys its Lord, - and it must do so.﴾ *(Qur'an 84: 1-2)*

At that time it will become weak and torn up, like a great palace, solidly built with string pillars, when it is shaken by an earthquake, so you see how, after being strong, it becomes broken, weak and cracked.

﴿ وَٱنشَقَّتِ ٱلسَّمَآءُ فَهِىَ يَوْمَئِذٍ وَاهِيَةٌ ﴿١٦﴾ ﴾

﴿And the heaven will be rent asunder, for that Day it [the heaven] will be frail and torn up.﴾ *(Qur'an 69: 16)*

---

[8] *Tafseer al-Aaloosi*, 30/63.

The colour of this beautiful blue sky will also change. On that Day the sky will start to take on different colours, like dyes - red and yellow and green, and then blue, as Allah (ﷻ) says:

﴿ فَإِذَا ٱنشَقَّتِ ٱلسَّمَآءُ فَكَانَتْ وَرْدَةً كَٱلدِّهَانِ ۝٣٧ ﴾

﴾Then when the heaven is rent asunder, and it becomes rosy or red like red oil, or red hide.﴿ *(Qur'an 55: 37)*

It is narrated from Ibn 'Abbaas that on that Day, the sky will be like a bay mare which - as Al-Baghawi said - is yellow in the spring and red in the winter; when it becomes very cold, its colour changes. Al-Ḥasan al-Baṣri said that the phrase *wardah kad-dihaan* (translated here as rosy or red like red oil, or red hide) means that it will be of several colours.[9]

5) The rolling up of the sun, the eclipse of the moon and the falling of the stars

This sun which we see shining every day, that fills our world with light and gives us light and energy which we cannot do without in order to see and move, and which is needed by every living creature and every plant that grows, will be collected and rolled up, and its light will vanish, as Allah (ﷻ) says:

﴿ إِذَا ٱلشَّمْسُ كُوِّرَتْ ۝١ ﴾

﴾When the sun *kuwwirat* [wound round and lost its light and is overthrown].﴿ *(Qur'an 81: 1)*

Takweer in Arabic refers to the action of gathering something up together, such as wrapping a turban or folding a garment up. When parts of the sun are gathered up and wound round with others, its light will vanish and it will be cast aside.

---

[9] *Tafseer Ibn Katheer*, 6/494.

This moon, which appears at the beginning of the month as a crescent, then it waxes until it becomes a full moon, shining splendidly, of whose beauty has always been enchanted by poets, and it keeps travellers company on their long journeys at night, will be eclipsed and its light will vanish.

﴿ فَإِذَا بَرِقَ ٱلْبَصَرُ ﴿٧﴾ وَخَسَفَ ٱلْقَمَرُ ﴿٨﴾ ﴾

﴿So, when the sight shall be dazed, And the moon will be eclipsed.﴾ *(Qur'an 75: 7-8)*

These stars which are sprinkled across the blue dome of the sky, will come to an end and they will fall and be scattered:

﴿ وَإِذَا ٱلْكَوَاكِبُ ٱنتَثَرَتْ ﴿٢﴾ ﴾

﴿When the stars have fallen and been scattered.﴾ *(Qur'an 82: 2)*

﴿ وَإِذَا ٱلنُّجُومُ ٱنكَدَرَتْ ﴿٢﴾ ﴾

﴿And when the stars shall fall.﴾ *(Qur'an 81: 2)*

The words translated here as "fallen" and "scattered" come from roots which indicate "being poured out".[10]

6) Qurṭubi's *tafseer* of the texts which describe the horrors of the Day of Resurrection

Qurṭubi said: Tirmidhi narrated that Ibn 'Umar (رضي الله عنه) said: "The Messenger of Allah (ﷺ) said:

'Whoever wants to visualize the Day of Resurrection, let him recite:

[10] *Tafseer Ibn Katheer*, 7/221.

﴿ إِذَا ٱلشَّمْسُ كُوِّرَتْ ۝١ ﴾

﴿When the sun *kuwwirat* [wound round and lost its light and is overthrown].﴾ *(Qur'an 81: 1)*

﴿ إِذَا ٱلسَّمَآءُ ٱنفَطَرَتْ ۝١ ﴾

﴿When the heaven is cleft asunder.﴾ *(Qur'an 82: 1)*

﴿ إِذَا ٱلسَّمَآءُ ٱنشَقَّتْ ۝١ ﴾

﴿When the heaven is split asunder.﴾ *(Qur'an 84: 1).*'"

- He (Tirmidhi) said, this is a *ḥasan* hadith.[11]

These three *Soorahs* deal specifically with the Day of Resurrection, as they describe how the sky will be split and cleft asunder, how the sun will be wound round and how the stars and planets will fall and be scattered, and other terrors which will happen on that Day. And people will come forth from their graves to either prisons (in Hell) or palaces (in Paradise), after their records have been examined and they have been taken by their right or left hands, or seized from behind, as will be explained below. Allah (ﷻ) says:

﴿ إِذَا ٱلسَّمَآءُ ٱنشَقَّتْ ۝١ ﴾

﴿When the heaven is split asunder.﴾ *(Qur'an 84: 1)*

﴿ إِذَا ٱلسَّمَآءُ ٱنفَطَرَتْ ۝١ ﴾

﴿When the heaven is cleft asunder.﴾ *(Qur'an 82: 1)*

﴿ وَيَوْمَ تَشَقَّقُ ٱلسَّمَآءُ بِٱلْغَمَٰمِ ... ۝٢٥ ﴾

﴿And [remember] the Day when the heaven shall be rent

[11] A *ṣaḥeeḥ* hadith narrated by Tirmidhi, Al-Ḥaakim and Aḥmad. See *Ṣaḥeeḥ al-Jaami'*, 3/301, hadith no. 6191.

asunder with clouds...› *(Qur'an 25: 25)*

So you will see it broken and cracked, as Allah (ﷻ) says:

﴿ وَفُتِحَتِ ٱلسَّمَآءُ فَكَانَتْ أَبْوَٰبًا ﴿١٩﴾ ﴾

‹And the heaven shall be opened, and it will become as gates.› *(Qur'an 78: 19)*

The clouds will serve as a cover between the heaven and the earth. Or it is said that the Arabic *ba'* (in the phrase *bi'l-ghamaam*, translated here as "with clouds") means *'an* (i.e., from) i.e., it will be split to reveal white clouds. And it is said that it will split because of what reaches it of the heat of Hell. That is when there will be no more water, and there will be fire everywhere. At first the sky will turn red, like red oil, or red hide, and it will split because Allah will decree to bring this world to an end. And it is said that the sky will turn into different colours. It will turn yellow, then red, or red, then yellow, just as a foal tends to be yellowish in the spring, and as the days get warmer it becomes more reddish, then brownish. This is the view of Al-Ḥaleemi.

Concerning the *aayah*: ‹When the sun *kuwwirat* [wound round and lost its light and is overthrown].› *(Qur'an 81: 1)*

Ibn 'Abbaas (رضي الله عنه) said: this *takweer* (being wound round) means that it will be incorporated into the Throne. It is said that it refers to losing its brightness. This is the view of Al-Ḥasan and Qataadah; this is also narrated from Ibn 'Abbaas and Mujaahid. Abu 'Ubaydah said: it will be wound round like a turban, until it loses its light. Al-Rabee' ibn Khaytham said: *kuwwirat* means it will be cast aside - this is from the same root as the word *takawwara* which means to drop. I say, the root meaning of *takweer* is gathering together; the same word is used to describe wrapping a turban around the head. Then the sun's light will be extinguished and it will be cast aside. And Allah knows best.

The *aayah*: ❨And when the stars shall fall.❩ *(Qur'an 81: 2)* means, when they are scattered. It is said that they will fall from the hands of the angels, because they will die. There is a report which says that they are suspended between heaven and earth by chains in the hands of the angels. Ibn 'Abbaas (&) said: *ankadarat* (translated here as "shall fall") means, they will change. The root meaning of *ankadarat* is pouring out. So they will fall into the flaming seas, and become fire like them, and there will be no more water.

The *aayah*: ❨And when the mountains shall be made to pass away.❩ *(Qur'an 81: 3)* is like the *aayah*,

$$\text{﴿} \; \text{(٤٧)} \; ... \; \text{وَيَوْمَ نُسَيِّرُ ٱلْجِبَالَ} \; \text{﴾}$$

❨And [remember] the Day We shall cause the mountains
to pass away [like clouds of dust]...❩ *(Qur'an 18: 47)*

- i.e., they will no longer be like rocks, but will be like a heap of sand poured out, and they will be like wool; they will become floating dust particles and mirages, like a mirage which is really nothing.

It is said that after the mountains have been destroyed, they will be like wool due to the heat of Hell, just as the sky will become like the boiling filth of oil *(cf. Qur'an 70: 8)* because of its heat. Al-Ḥaleemi said: This - and Allah knows best - is because the water of the earth formed a barrier between the heaven and the earth. When this barrier is removed, the resulting increase in the heat of Hell will have an effect on both the heaven and the earth, as mentioned.

The *aayah*:

$$\text{﴿} \; \text{(٤)} \; \text{وَإِذَا ٱلْعِشَارُ عُطِّلَتْ} \; \text{﴾}$$

❨And when the pregnant she-camels will be neglected.❩
(Qur'an 81: 4)

- means that they will be ignored by their owners, and will not be milked because the people will be too preoccupied with their own concerns. The word *'ishaar* (translated here as "pregnant she-camels") is used to describe a camel that is ten months pregnant; the camel is so-called until it gives birth and after it has given birth. The reason why *'ishaar* are mentioned is because these camels are the most precious to the Arabs. But Allah tells us that they will be neglected on the Day of Resurrection. What this means is that when the people rise from their graves, and they see one another and the animals who are also gathered, including these *'ishaar* which were the most precious things they possessed, they will not care about them and will not pay any attention to them. It may mean that the neglecting of their she-camels refers to Allah abolishing all the possessions that people owned in this world, for people will see these camels but will have no way of getting them. It is also suggested that *'ishaar* refers to clouds, which will no longer contain any water, so no rain will fall. It is also suggested that *'ishaar* means houses, which will be abandoned and no one will live in them any longer, or that it means land which is neglected and not cultivated. The first view is the most well-known and is the view of most scholars.

The *aayah*:

﴿ وَإِذَا ٱلْوُحُوشُ حُشِرَتْ ۝٥ ﴾

﴿And when the wild beasts shall be gathered together.﴾ *(Qur'an 81: 5)*

- means, when they will be brought together. The *aayah*:

﴿ وَإِذَا ٱلْبِحَارُ سُجِّرَتْ ۝٦ ﴾

﴿And when the seas shall become as blazing Fire or shall overflow.﴾ *(Qur'an 81: 6)*

- means, when they catch fire. This is narrated by Aḍ-Ḍaḥḥaak from Ibn 'Abbaas (رضي الله عنه). Qataadah said, their water will be absorbed into the earth and disappear. Al-Ḥasan and Aḍ-Ḍaḥḥaak said: they will overflow. Ibn Abi Zamanayn said: *sujjirat* (translated here as "shall become as blazing Fire or shall overflow") means that they will become filled, then they will overflow until one becomes joined to another, and they will be all one thing. This is the meaning of what is said by Al-Ḥasan. And it is said that the sun will be rolled up and thrown into the sea, so the sea will heat up and turn into fire. Al-Ḥaleemi said: it may be that, for those who interpret *tasjeer* as meaning being overfilled, most of the sea on that Day will be fire, because the sun is many times greater than the earth, so when it is rolled up and thrown into the sea, it will turn into fire and it will become more full.

The *aayah*:

﴿ وَإِذَا ٱلنُّفُوسُ زُوِّجَتْ ۝٧ ﴾

﴿And when the souls shall be joined with their bodies.﴾ *(Qur'an 81: 7)*[12]

- Al-Ḥasan interpreted this as meaning that every sect will join with others of its kind, Jews with Jews, Christians with Christians, Magians with Magians. All those who worshipped anything other than Allah will join one another. Hypocrites will join hypocrites and believers will join believers. 'Ikrimah said: this means that they (the souls) will be joined to their bodies, i.e., they will be restored to them. It is also said that the misguided person will be joined with the one

[12] The original Arabic of this *aayah* is more general in meaning and may convey several meanings, such as those quoted from the *salaf* in the subsequent paragraph, which differ from the meaning chosen by the translators of the Qur'an. (Translator)

who misled him, whether a *shayṭaan* (Satan) or a human, or that the believers will be joined with *Al-Ḥoor al-'Iyn*, and the *kuffaar* will be joined with the *shayaaṭeen*.

The *aayah*:

﴿ وَإِذَا ٱلْمَوْءُۥدَةُ سُئِلَتْ ﴿٨﴾ ﴾

﴾And when the female [infant] buried alive [as the pagan Arabs used to do] shall be questioned.﴿

(Qur'an 81: 8)

- This refers to girls, who were buried alive during the *Jaahiliyyah* for two reasons. The first reason was that they believed the angels to be daughters of Allah, so they attached girls to Him. The second reason was that they feared poverty. The female infant will be questioned as a rebuke to the one who killed her, just as a child who has been beaten may be asked, "Why were you beaten? What wrong did you do?" Al-Ḥasan said: Allah means to rebuke the one who killed her, because she was killed when she had committed no sin. Some of them recited it as "when the female (infant) buried alive asks", i.e., the girl will be hanging onto her father, asking him, 'For what sin did you kill me?' Some said that the meaning of the phrase "[she] shall be questioned" is that questions will be asked about her, as in the *aayah*:

﴿ ... إِنَّ ٱلْعَهْدَ كَانَ مَسْـُٔولًا ﴿٣٤﴾ ﴾

﴾...Verily, the covenant will be questioned about.﴿

(Qur'an 17:34)

The *aayah*:

﴿ وَإِذَا ٱلصُّحُفُ نُشِرَتْ ﴿١٠﴾ ﴾

﴾And when the written pages of deeds [good and bad] of every person shall be laid open.﴿ *(Qur'an 81: 10)*

- means, for the purpose of reckoning, which will surely come to pass.

The *aayah*:

﴿ وَإِذَا ٱلسَّمَآءُ كُشِطَتْ ﴿١١﴾ ﴾

﴾And when the heaven shall be stripped off and taken away from its place.﴿ *(Qur'an 81: 11)*

It is said that this means, rolled up, as Allah (ﷻ) says:

﴿ يَوْمَ نَطْوِى ٱلسَّمَآءَ كَطَىِّ ٱلسِّجِلِّ لِلْكُتُبِ ... ﴿١٠٤﴾ ﴾

﴾And [remember] the Day when We shall roll up the heaven like a scroll rolled up for books...﴿ *(Qur'an 21: 104)*

- i.e., like when a scroll is rolled up over its contents. The word *kushiṭat* (stripped off) is the same word used to describe removing a roof, so the meaning is ripping it off and rolling it up. And Allah knows best. It was also suggested that *As-Sijill* was the (name of) the scribe of the Prophet (ﷺ), but there is no one among the *Ṣaḥaabah* who is known by the name *As-Sajill*.

The *aayah*:

﴿ وَإِذَا ٱلْجَحِيمُ سُعِّرَتْ ﴿١٢﴾ ﴾

﴾And when Hell-fire shall be kindled to fierce ablaze.﴿ *(Qur'an 81: 12)*

- means, when it is stoked up.

The *aayah*:

﴿ وَإِذَا ٱلْجَنَّةُ أُزْلِفَتْ ﴿١٣﴾ ﴾

﴾And when Paradise shall be brought near.﴿ *(Qur'an 81: 13)*

- means when it is brought close to its people.

And the *aayah*:

﴿ عَلِمَتْ نَفْسٌ مَّآ أَحْضَرَتْ ﴿١٤﴾ ﴾

﴾[Then] every person will know what he has brought [of good and evil].﴿ *(Qur'an 81: 14)*

- means, what his deeds are. This is like the *aayah*:

﴿ عَلِمَتْ نَفْسٌ مَّا قَدَّمَتْ وَأَخَّرَتْ ﴿٥﴾ ﴾

﴾[Then] a person will know what he has sent forward and [what he has] left behind [of good or bad deeds].﴿ *(Qur'an 82: 5)*

7) Al-Muḥaasibi depicts the terrors of that Day

Al-Haarith al-Muhaasibi (may Allah have mercy on him) described the terrors which will happen on that Day:

"When the number of dead is complete, and the heavens and earth have become empty, devoid of inhabitants, and they become still after they have been in motion, there will be nothing to be heard and there will be no one to be seen. Then the Compeller, the Most High will remain as He has always been, Eternal, One, Unique in His Might and Majesty. Then your soul will be startled by the cry of the caller, calling all of creation as well as you to stand before Allah with utter humility and submission. Imagine how this call will sound to you, what effect it will have on you when you realize that you are being called to stand before the Sovereign, the Most High. So your heart will sink and your hair will turn grey in response to this call, because it will be one call to appear before the Owner of Majesty and Honour, of Might and Pride. Whilst you will be filled with terror at the voice, you will hear the earth opening up above your head, so you will leap up, covered with dust from head to toe, standing on your feet in the gloom of your grave, staring in the direction of this call. All created beings will have gotten up when you did, covered with the dust of the earth in which they have been disintegrating for so long.

Imagine when they all start moving about in terror, all of them equally filled with fear. Imagine yourself, naked and humiliated, alone with your fear, grief and distress in the crowd of created beings, all of them naked, barefoot and silent. You can hear nothing but the sound of their footsteps and the voice of the caller. Everyone will be turning towards Him, and you will be one of them, turning towards his voice, running with fear and humility until you reach the place of gathering, crowded with all the nations of jinn and humans, naked and barefoot. All sovereignty will have been taken away from the kings of the earth, and they will be humbled and brought low; they will be the most humiliated of all those present, and the lowest in status, after they had been so proud and arrogant towards the slaves of Allah on earth.

Then the animals will be brought forth from the fields and mountaintops, hanging their heads in humiliation on the Day of Resurrection, individually after being powerful and vicious and proud. They will be humbled on the Day of Resurrection without having done anything wrong or committed any sin. Imagine how humiliated they will be on this great Day, the Day of Resurrection.

After being so powerful and savage, the wild animals will come hanging their heads in humility on the Day of Resurrection, until they stand humbly behind mankind, submitting themselves to the Sovereign, the Compeller. And the *shayaaṭeen* (devils) will come, after being so stubborn and rebellious, fearing the judgement of Allah. Glory be to the One who will gather them all after such a long trial, with all their different types and natures, despite their mutually unsociable characters. The resurrection will humble them all and bring them all together.

Then when the number of inhabitants of the earth will be completed - humans, jinn, devils, wild animals, cattle and other beasts - and they all will be gathered together in the place of reckoning, the stars will fall from above them and the sun and moon will be extinguished, and the earth will become dark because its light will be snuffed out. Whilst you and all other creatures will be in that state, the first heaven, despite its great size, will start to rotate above your heads, and you will see the horror of that with your own eyes. Then it will split, even though its thickness is as the distance of a five hundred-year journey, and how terrible its cracking will sound in your ears. Then it will be torn apart with the greatest horror that will come on the Day of Resurrection, with the angels standing on its sides, i.e., on the edges of its split. Imagine how terrible it will be when the heaven is rent asunder despite its immense size, then its Lord will cause it to melt like molten silver mixed with yellow because of the terror of that Day, as Allah (ﷻ) says:

﴿فَإِذَا ٱنشَقَّتِ ٱلسَّمَآءُ فَكَانَتْ وَرْدَةً كَٱلدِّهَانِ ﴿٣٧﴾﴾

﴾Then when the heaven is rent asunder, and it becomes rosy or red like red oil, or red hide.﴿ *(Qur'an 55: 37)*

﴿يَوْمَ تَكُونُ ٱلسَّمَآءُ كَٱلْمُهْلِ ﴿٨﴾ وَتَكُونُ ٱلْجِبَالُ كَٱلْعِهْنِ ﴿٩﴾﴾

﴾The Day that the sky will be like the boiling filth of oil [or molten copper or silver or lead]. And the mountains will be like flakes of wool.﴿ *(Qur'an 70: 8-9).*"

When the angels of the first heaven are standing on its edges, they will come down and be gathered on the earth for the reckoning, and they will come down from the edges with their immense bodies and their great status and their voices raised in glorification of the

Sovereign, the Most High (Allah), Who sent them down to be gathered on the earth in humiliation, to be questioned before Him.

Imagine them descending from the clouds with their huge size and terrifying voices. Imagine your terror and the terror that all creatures will feel, lest these angels are instructed to seize them. Imagine when people will ask them, is our Lord among you? The angels will be terrified at this question, glorifying their Sovereign and declaring Him to be far above being among them. They will call out in loud voices, declaring Him to be far above what the people of this earth imagine: "Glory be to our Lord! He is not among us but He is coming." Then they will take their positions surrounding the other created beings, with their heads lowered in humility. Imagine them, covering themselves with their wings and lowering their heads in humility despite their immense size, submitting themselves before their Lord. This is how it will be in each of the seven heavens, with the inhabitants of each heaven, with their huge numbers and immense size, surrounding the created beings in ranks.

Then when all the inhabitants of the seven heavens and the earth have come, the sun's heat will be multiplied by a factor of ten years, and it will be brought near until it is only the distance of a bow or two bows from their heads, and there will be no shade for anyone apart from the shade of the Throne of the Lord of the Worlds. There will be some who will be shaded by the shade of the Throne, and others who will be exposed to the heat of the sun. They will be melted and will suffer extreme distress because of its heat. Then the nations will be crowded together, pushing and shoving one another, with their throats parched with thirst and the heat of the sun combined with the body heat and hot breath of their fellow-creatures. Sweat will come pouring out of them until it covers the face of the earth and their own bodies, according to their status before Allah, whether they are blessed (destined for Paradise) or doomed (destined for Hell). For some of them, it will reach their heels, for others their ankles, or their earlobes. Some will be almost covered in their sweat, and some will be covered to a lesser extent.

It is narrated that 'Abdullah ibn 'Umar said: "The Messenger of Allah (ﷺ) said:

> 'On the day of Resurrection, a man (and on one occasion he said, a *kaafir*) will be standing in an ocean of his own sweat, halfway up his ears, because he has been standing for so long.'"

It is narrated from 'Abdullah, who attributed it to the Prophet (ﷺ), that,

> "Sweat will reach the mouth of the *kaafir* like reins on the Day of Resurrection, because that Day will be so long ('Ali said: because of the length of their standing), until he will say, 'O Lord, grant me respite even if it is in the Fire.'"

You know that you will be among them. Imagine yourself filled with distress, with sweat coming up to your head and the terror that you will feel. Imagine your chest being constricted with the sweat and fear and terror, and the people around you waiting for judgement to be passed in order to know whether their abode will be in Paradise or Hell, until you and the created beings around you reach the utmost level of exhaustion and can no longer speak or pay any attention to their own affairs.

It is narrated that Qataadah or Ka'b said: On the Day when people will rise to meet the Lord of the Worlds, they will stand for three hundred years. I heard Al-Ḥasan say: what do you think of people who will stand on their feet, waiting to meet Allah, for fifty thousand years, during which time they will not eat or drink anything? Then when their throats are parched with thirst and their stomachs are burning with hunger, they will be taken to the Fire, where they will be given to drink from a boiling spring whose heat would reach an extreme degree. When their exhaustion would reach the point that they could bear it no longer, they will speak to one another, looking for one who is close to his Lord so that he can intercede for them and ask that they be given a respite from standing and waiting to see whether they will be taken to Paradise or to Hell. They will turn to Adam and Nooḥ (Noah), then to Ibraaheem (Abraham), then Moosa (Moses) and 'Eesa (Jesus), but all of them will say to them, 'My Lord is angry today, He has never been so angry before and will not be so angry again.' All of them will refer to how angry their Lord is, and will be concerned only with their own selves. Each of them will say, 'myself, myself'. They will all be too concerned with their own selves to intercede with their Lord for them. This is what Allah (ﷻ) says:

﴿ يَوْمَ تَأْتِي كُلُّ نَفْسٍ تُجَٰدِلُ عَن نَّفْسِهَا ... ﴿١١١﴾ ﴾

﴿[Remember] the Day when every person will come up pleading for himself...﴾ *(Qur'an 16: 111)*

Imagine the voices of mankind as they are all calling out, each one of them caring only for himself, crying out "myself, myself!" All you will hear are the words, "myself, myself!" How terrifying it will be, and you will be one of them, caring only for yourself and that you might be saved from the wrath and punishment of your Lord. What do you think of a Day when they will call upon Adam, and Allah's Friend Ibraaheem (Abraham), and Moosa (Moses) to whom He spoke directly, and 'Eesa (Jesus) who was a spirit and a word from Him. Even though their status before Allah is so noble and great, each one of them will cry out, "myself, myself!" out of fear of the intense anger of their Lord. Where will you be with your fear and your grief and your concern solely for yourself on that Day? When everyone would be despaired of any intercession on their behalf, then the Prophet Muhammad (ﷺ) will come; they will ask him to intercede with their Lord and he will respond to their request. He will then stand before his Lord and seek permission, and permission will be granted to him. Then he will fall down prostrate before his Lord, and will praise Him as He deserves to be praised. You and all other creatures will hear that. Then his Lord will grant his request and will hasten on the judgement and examination of their affairs.[13]

[13] *Kitaab at-Tawahhum wal-Ahwaal*, Pp. 5.

CHAPTER EIGHT
STATE OF THE PEOPLE ON THE DAY OF RESURRECTION

PEOPLE'S POSITIONS (CASES) WILL VARY ON THE DAY OF RESURRECTION

The positions in which people will find themselves on the Day of Resurrection will vary clearly. Here we will discuss three: the *kaafir*, sinners among those who believed in *Tawḥeed* (Divine Unity), and those who would be righteous and pious.

1 - THE STATE OF THE *KUFFAAR*

1) Their humiliation, regret and despair

Anyone who ponders the texts of the Qur'an and Sunnah which describe the Day of Resurrection will see the immense horrors and great disasters that will befall the *kuffaar* - disbelievers - and evildoers on that great Day.

We will look here at some of the scenes which the Qur'an describes:

1) Allah (ﷻ) says, describing the state of the *kuffaar* when they emerge from their graves:

﴿يَوْمَ يَخْرُجُونَ مِنَ ٱلْأَجْدَاثِ سِرَاعًا كَأَنَّهُمْ إِلَىٰ نُصُبٍ يُوفِضُونَ ﴿٤٣﴾ خَٰشِعَةً أَبْصَٰرُهُمْ تَرْهَقُهُمْ ذِلَّةٌ ذَٰلِكَ ٱلْيَوْمُ ٱلَّذِى كَانُوا۟ يُوعَدُونَ ﴿٤٤﴾﴾

﴾The Day when they will come out of the graves quickly as racing to a goal, with their eyes lowered in fear and humility, ignominy covering them [all over]! That is the Day which they were promised!﴿ *(Qur'an 70: 43-44)*

This text describes how quickly they will come forth from their graves on that Day, rushing towards the source of the voice as if they are rushing towards the *anṣaab* (stone altars) which they used to worship in this world. But on that Day they will not be rushing with joy and exuberance as they used to do when they approached their *anṣaab*; on the contrary, they will be humble, with their eyes lowered and with their pride brought low, as Allah has warned them in this world.

2) Allah (ﷻ) says:

﴿فَتَوَلَّ عَنْهُمْ يَوْمَ يَدْعُ الدَّاعِ إِلَىٰ شَيْءٍ نُّكُرٍ ﴿٦﴾ خُشَّعًا أَبْصَارُهُمْ يَخْرُجُونَ مِنَ الْأَجْدَاثِ كَأَنَّهُمْ جَرَادٌ مُّنتَشِرٌ ﴿٧﴾ مُّهْطِعِينَ إِلَى الدَّاعِ يَقُولُ الْكَافِرُونَ هَٰذَا يَوْمٌ عَسِرٌ ﴿٨﴾﴾

﴾So [O' Muhammad] withdraw from them. The Day that the caller will call [them] to a terrible thing. They will come forth, with humbled eyes from [their] graves as if they were locusts spread abroad, hastening towards the caller. The disbelievers will say: 'This is a hard Day.'﴿ *(Qur'an 54: 6-8)*

This *aayah* also states that they will emerge humbly, with their eyes lowered, hastening towards the source of the voice which would be calling them. It explains the matter further by giving us a vivid picture of the resurrection and how they will be moving on that Day, emerging swiftly like a swarm of locusts. This text also informs us that the *kuffaar* will acknowledge how difficult their situation on that Day will be: "The disbelievers will say: 'This is a hard Day.'"

3) A third text informs us that the *kuffaar* will bewail their fate:

﴿وَنُفِخَ فِي الصُّورِ فَإِذَا هُم مِّنَ الْأَجْدَاثِ إِلَىٰ رَبِّهِمْ يَنسِلُونَ ﴿٥١﴾ قَالُوا يَا وَيْلَنَا مَن بَعَثَنَا مِن مَّرْقَدِنَا ... ﴿٥٢﴾﴾

﴿And the Trumpet will be blown [i.e. the second blowing] and behold from the graves they will come out quickly to their Lord. They will say: 'Woe to us! Who has raised us up from our place of sleep?...'﴾ *(Qur'an 36: 51-52)*

Abu Maḥkam al-Jisri, was a wise man, once some brothers met him, and when this *aayah* (verse) was recited he wept. He then said:

"The resurrection would make them lose their minds with terror. By Allah, if the people had really been in a state of sleep, as it appears from what they say, they would not bewail their fate when they would be resurrected. After that, at every stage where they will be questioned, they will experience a greater level of turmoil and horror. All the terror of the Hereafter is inescapable for them. They would be in their graves for so long, being tormented and punished, and they would not bewail when that would cease, except when they would be moved to a greater turmoil. If that would not be the case, these people would not regard as insignificant what they had gone through in the grave, or describe it as sleep.

The Qur'an indicates this:

﴿ فَإِذَا جَآءَتِ ٱلطَّآمَّةُ ٱلْكُبْرَىٰ ﴿٣٤﴾ ﴾

﴿But when there comes the greatest catastrophe [i.e., the Day of Recompense].﴾ *(Qur'an 79: 34).*"

- He then wept until his beard became wet.[1]

4) Another text gives further details of the state they will be in when they will be resurrected, and how their eyes will be staring in horror and their hearts will be filled with fear of the terror that surrounds them. Allah (ﷻ) says:

---

[1] *An-Nihaayah* by Ibn Katheer, 1/274.

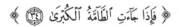

﴿ وَلَا تَحْسَبَنَّ ٱللَّهَ غَٰفِلًا عَمَّا يَعْمَلُ ٱلظَّٰلِمُونَ ۚ إِنَّمَا يُؤَخِّرُهُمْ لِيَوْمٍ
تَشْخَصُ فِيهِ ٱلْأَبْصَٰرُ ﴿٤٢﴾ مُهْطِعِينَ مُقْنِعِى رُءُوسِهِمْ لَا يَرْتَدُّ إِلَيْهِمْ
طَرْفُهُمْ ۖ وَأَفْـِٔدَتُهُمْ هَوَآءٌ ﴿٤٣﴾ ﴾

﴿Consider not that Allah is unaware of that which the *Zaalimoon* [polytheists, wrongdoers] do, but He gives them respite up to a Day when the eyes will stare in horror. [They will be] hastening forward with necks outstretched, their heads raised up [towards the sky], their gaze returning not towards them and their hearts empty [from thinking because of extreme fear].﴾

(Qur'an 14: 42-43)

Professor Sayyid Qutb (may Allah have mercy on him and reward him immensely) said in his commentary on these verses:

"The Messenger (ﷺ) did not think that Allah was unaware of the actions of the evildoers. But this may appear to be the case to some people, because they see the evildoers enjoying life, and they hear the warning of Allah but they do not see any punishment coming to them in this life. This phrase describes the time when they would be seized, after which it would not be postponed any further and there will be no escape. They would be seized on a terrifying Day when their eyes would stare in horror and they would be stunned with fear and paralyzed with terror.

Allah then describes how the people will crowd together in horror, rushing headlong, not paying any attention to anything, with their heads raised, not because they would want to do that but because they would compelled to do so, and they will be unable to move their heads. Their eyes will be staring unblinkingly at the horrors that they can see, and their hearts will be filled with fear, unable to understand or recall anything. This will be the Day after which Allah will not give them any further respite, as they will stand in that place and see with their own eyes the horror that is described in these four *aayaat* (verses); it will overwhelm them like a small bird caught in the talons of a sparrow hawk. Allah (ﷻ) says: ﴾Consider not that Allah is unaware of that which the *Ẓaalimoon* [polytheists, wrongdoers] do, but He gives them respite up to a Day when the eyes will stare in horror. [They will be] hastening forward with necks outstretched, their heads raised up [towards the sky], their gaze returning not towards them and their hearts empty [from thinking because of extreme fear].﴿ *(Qur'an 14: 42-43).*

Their speed will be that of the people who are running, with their eyes staring and their hearts filled with fear and devoid of any other thoughts... all of this points to the terror which will make their eyes stare in horror."[2]

5) The Qur'an describes the terror that will overwhelm the *kuffaar* on the Day when they will stand before Allah (ﷻ):

﴿ وَأَنذِرْهُمْ يَوْمَ ٱلْءَازِفَةِ إِذِ ٱلْقُلُوبُ لَدَى ٱلْحَنَاجِرِ كَٰظِمِينَ ۚ مَا لِلظَّٰلِمِينَ مِنْ حَمِيمٍ وَلَا شَفِيعٍ يُطَاعُ ﴿١٨﴾ ﴾

﴾And warn them [O' Muhammad] of the Day that is drawing near [i.e. the Day of Resurrection], when the hearts will be choking the throats, and they can neither return them [hearts] to their chests nor can they throw them out. There will be no friend, nor an intercessor for the *Ẓaalimoon* [polytheists and wrongdoers], who could be given heed to.﴿ *(Qur'an 40: 18)*

"The Day that is drawing near is the Day that is close at hand, which is the Day of Resurrection. The wording (*al-aa'zifah* - drawing near) portrays something that is edging nearer and approaching, which will

---

[2] *Fi Ẓilaal al-Qur'an*, 4/2111.

make them unable to breathe, as if their hearts will be distressed and will apply pressure to their throats, making them hold their breath and unable to express their pain and fear. This pressure will distress them, and will weigh heavily on their chests, but they will find no close friend to show them sympathy, and no intercessor whose word can be carried out to help them in this terrifying situation."[3]

6) According to the judgement of Allah, these people would be sinners who rebelled against their Creator and their God, arrogantly refusing to worship and obey Him. So they will be brought to the Lord and Creator bound together in fetters, wearing garments of pitch and with their faces covered with fire:

﴿ يَوْمَ تُبَدَّلُ ٱلْأَرْضُ غَيْرَ ٱلْأَرْضِ وَٱلسَّمَٰوَٰتُ ۖ وَبَرَزُوا۟ لِلَّهِ ٱلْوَٰحِدِ ٱلْقَهَّارِ ﴿٤٨﴾ وَتَرَى ٱلْمُجْرِمِينَ يَوْمَئِذٍ مُّقَرَّنِينَ فِى ٱلْأَصْفَادِ ﴿٤٩﴾ سَرَابِيلُهُم مِّن قَطِرَانٍ وَتَغْشَىٰ وُجُوهَهُمُ ٱلنَّارُ ﴿٥٠﴾ ﴾

﴾On the Day when the earth will be changed to another earth and so will be the heavens, and they [all creatures] will appear before Allah, the One, the Irresistible. And you will see the *Mujrimoon* [criminals, disbelievers in the Oneness of Allah Islamic Monotheism, polytheists] that Day *Muqarranoon* [bound together] in fetters. Their garments will be of pitch, and fire will cover their faces.﴿

(Qur'an 14: 48-50)

Aṭ-Ṭabari (may Allah have mercy on him) said in his commentary on this *aayah*:

"Those who disbelieved in Allah and were guilty of *shirk* will see with their own eyes the consequences of their *shirk* on that Day i.e., the Day when the earth will be changed to another earth and so will

---

[3] *Fi Ẓilaal al-Qur'an*, 6/3074.

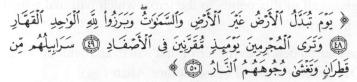

the heavens. 'Bound together in fetters', means, their hands and feet will be tied to their necks with chains."[4]

Saraabeel (garments) refers to shirts which they will wear. *Qiṭraan* (pitch) means the substance which is painted on camels when they suffer from mange. It is also suggested that *qiṭraan* refers to copper.

7) The sun will be brought close to the people's heads on that Day, until the distance between it and them will be no more than one mile. If it were not for the fact that they will be re-created in a form that will not die, it would melt them and cause them to evaporate, but after their death, they will not die again.

Their sweat will flow until it drenches the earth, then it will start to rise until it reaches a depth that will vary according to their actions. In Muslim it is narrated that Al-Miqdaad ibn al-Aswad said: "I heard the Messenger of Allah (ﷺ) say:

> 'On the Day of Resurrection, the sun will be brought so close to the people that it will be as close to them as one mile.'

Saleem ibn 'Aamir said: "By Allah, I do not know what was meant by the word *meel* [translated here as 'mile'], whether it refers to a measure of distance, or to the stick that is used to apply *koḥl* to the eyelids."

He said: "The people's sweat will vary according to the measure of their deeds. For some of them, their sweat will reach their ankles, for others it will reach their knees, or their waists, and for some it will reach their mouths, like reins."

And the Messenger of Allah (ﷺ) pointed to his mouth with his hand.[5]

---

[4] *Tafseer Ibn Jareer aṭ-Ṭabari*, 13/254.

[5] Muslim, *Kitaab al-Jannah, Baab fi Ṣifat al-Qiyaamah*, 4/2196, hadith no. 2864.

Bukhari and Muslim narrated from Ibn 'Umar from the Prophet (ﷺ):

﴿ يَوْمَ يَقُومُ ٱلنَّاسُ لِرَبِّ ٱلْعَٰلَمِينَ ۝٦ ﴾

﴾The Day when [all] mankind will stand before the Lord of the *'Aalameen* [mankind, jinn and all that exists].﴿

(Qur'an 83: 6)

He (ﷺ) said: "Some of them will stand with sweat reaching to half-way up their ears."[6]

Both Bukhari and Muslim narrated from Abu Hurayrah (رضي الله عنه) that the Messenger of Allah (ﷺ) said:

"The people will sweat on the Day of Resurrection until their sweat penetrates seventy cubits into the earth, then it will come up to their ears."[7]

8) When the *kuffaar* see the punishment and humiliation that befalls the disbelievers and polytheists, they will be filled with grief and regret. Because of the grief that the punishment will bring, Allah has called this Day *Yawm al-Ḥasrah* (the Day of grief and regrets):

﴿ وَأَنذِرْهُمْ يَوْمَ ٱلْحَسْرَةِ إِذْ قُضِىَ ٱلْأَمْرُ وَهُمْ فِى غَفْلَةٍ وَهُمْ لَا يُؤْمِنُونَ ۝٣٩ ﴾

﴾And warn them [O' Muhammad] of the Day of grief and regrets, when the case has been decided, while [now] they are in a state of carelessness, and they believe not.﴿

(Qur'an 19: 39)

Because of the intensity of the grief and regret that the *kuffaar* will feel for not having followed the Messenger who was sent to them,

---

[6] Bukhari: *Kitaab ar-Riqaaq, Baab Qawl Allah ta'aala, 'ala yaẓunnu oolaa'ika annhum mab'oothoon', Fatḥ al-Baari*, 11/392. Muslim: *Kitaab al-Jannah wa Ṣifat Na'eemihaa, Baab fi Ṣifat Yawm al-Qiyaamah*, 4/2862, hadith no. 2862.

[7] Ibid. This version is narrated by Bukhari.

and for following the enemies of the Messengers, they will bite on their hands:

﴿ وَيَوْمَ يَعَضُّ ٱلظَّالِمُ عَلَىٰ يَدَيْهِ يَقُولُ يَٰلَيْتَنِى ٱتَّخَذْتُ مَعَ ٱلرَّسُولِ سَبِيلًا ﴿٢٧﴾ يَٰوَيْلَتَىٰ لَيْتَنِى لَمْ أَتَّخِذْ فُلَانًا خَلِيلًا ﴿٢٨﴾ لَّقَدْ أَضَلَّنِى عَنِ ٱلذِّكْرِ بَعْدَ إِذْ جَآءَنِى ۗ وَكَانَ ٱلشَّيْطَٰنُ لِلْإِنسَٰنِ خَذُولًا ﴿٢٩﴾ ﴾

﴿And [remember] the Day when the *Ẓaalim* [wrongdoer, oppressor, polytheist] will bite at his hands, he will say: 'O'! Would that I had taken a path with the Messenger [Muhammad].﴾ Ah! Woe to me! Would that I had never taken so-and-so as a *Khaleel* [an intimate friend]! He indeed led me astray from the Reminder [this Qur'an] after it had come to me. And *Shayṭaan* [Satan] is to man ever a deserter in the hour of need.'﴾

(Qur'an 25: 27-29)

9) On that Day, the *kuffaar* will know for sure that their sins are not forgiven and that their excuses are not accepted. So they will despair of the mercy of Allah:

﴿ وَيَوْمَ تَقُومُ ٱلسَّاعَةُ يُبْلِسُ ٱلْمُجْرِمُونَ ﴿١٢﴾ ﴾

﴿And on the Day when the Hour will be established, the *Mujrimoon* [disbelievers, sinners, criminals, polytheists] will be plunged into destruction with [deep regrets, sorrows, and] despair.﴾ *(Qur'an 30: 12)*

10) On that Day, the *kuffaar* will wish that Allah would destroy them and turn them into dust:

﴿ يَوْمَئِذٍ يَوَدُّ ٱلَّذِينَ كَفَرُوا۟ وَعَصَوُا۟ ٱلرَّسُولَ لَوْ تُسَوَّىٰ بِهِمُ ٱلْأَرْضُ ...﴿٤٢﴾ ﴾

﴿On that day those who disbelieved and disobeyed the

Messenger [Muhammad] will wish that they were buried in the earth...﴾ *(Qur'an 4: 42)*

﴿... وَيَقُولُ ٱلْكَافِرُ يَـٰلَيْتَنِى كُنتُ تُرَٰبًا ﴿٤٠﴾ ﴾

﴿...And the disbeliever will say: 'Woe to me! Would that I were dust!'﴾ *(Qur'an, 78: 40)*

So what do you think of people for whom death is the ultimate wish!

2) The rejection of their deeds

The actions of the *kuffaar* are of two types. The first type includes actions which are evil and sinful, spreading corruption on earth, etc. These are all false and evil actions from which people can never hope for anything good or to earn any reward.

The Qur'an likens these actions to darkness, layers of darkness, one on top of the other:

﴿ أَوْ كَظُلُمَـٰتٍ فِى بَحْرٍ لُّجِّىٍّ يَغْشَىٰهُ مَوْجٌ مِّن فَوْقِهِۦ مَوْجٌ مِّن فَوْقِهِۦ سَحَابٌ ظُلُمَـٰتٌۢ بَعْضُهَا فَوْقَ بَعْضٍ إِذَآ أَخْرَجَ يَدَهُۥ لَمْ يَكَدْ يَرَىٰهَا وَمَن لَّمْ يَجْعَلِ ٱللَّهُ لَهُۥ نُورًا فَمَا لَهُۥ مِن نُّورٍ ﴿٤٠﴾ ﴾

﴿Or [the state of a disbeliever] is like the darkness in a vast deep sea, overwhelmed with waves topped by waves, topped by dark clouds, [layers of] darkness upon darkness: if a man stretches out his hand, he can hardly see it! And he for whom Allah has not appointed light, for him there is no light.﴾ *(Qur'an 24: 40)*

The second kind of actions are those which they think will earn them something from Allah, such as charity, freeing slaves, upholding ties of kinship, spending for good purposes. But Allah has coined likenesses of such actions in His Book.

In some places He likens them to mirages which a person thinks are water, but when he comes to them, hoping that he will be able to quench his thirst, he does not find anything:

﴿ وَٱلَّذِينَ كَفَرُوٓا۟ أَعْمَٰلُهُمْ كَسَرَابٍۭ بِقِيعَةٍ يَحْسَبُهُ ٱلظَّمْـَٔانُ مَآءً حَتَّىٰٓ إِذَا
جَآءَهُۥ لَمْ يَجِدْهُ شَيْـًٔا وَوَجَدَ ٱللَّهَ عِندَهُۥ فَوَفَّىٰهُ حِسَابَهُۥ ۗ وَٱللَّهُ سَرِيعُ
ٱلْحِسَابِ ﴿٣٩﴾ ﴾

﴾As for those who disbelieved, their deeds are like a mirage in a desert. The thirsty one thinks it to be water, until he comes up to it, he finds it to be nothing; but he finds Allah with him, Who will pay him his due [Hell]. And Allah is Swift in taking account.﴿ *(Qur'an 24: 39)*

Elsewhere, He likens them to a strong, cold wind that blows on the crops and fruits and destroys them:

﴿ مَثَلُ مَا يُنفِقُونَ فِى هَٰذِهِ ٱلْحَيَوٰةِ ٱلدُّنْيَا كَمَثَلِ رِيحٍ فِيهَا صِرٌّ أَصَابَتْ
حَرْثَ قَوْمٍ ظَلَمُوٓا۟ أَنفُسَهُمْ فَأَهْلَكَتْهُ ۚ وَمَا ظَلَمَهُمُ ٱللَّهُ وَلَٰكِنْ أَنفُسَهُمْ
يَظْلِمُونَ ﴿١١٧﴾ ﴾

﴾The likeness of what they spend in this world is the likeness of a wind which is extremely cold; it struck the harvest of a people who did wrong against themselves and destroyed it [i.e. the good deed of a person is only accepted if he is a monotheist and believes in all the Prophets of Allah, including Jesus and Muhammad]. Allah wronged them not, but they wronged themselves.﴿

(Qur'an 3: 117)

This intensely cold wind is *kufr* and *shirk*, which burns up their righteous deeds.

In a third place, Allah likens these deeds to sand which is scattered all over by the wind; how can a person gather it all up again after it has been scattered?

﴿مَّثَلُ ٱلَّذِينَ كَفَرُوا۟ بِرَبِّهِمْ ۖ أَعْمَـٰلُهُمْ كَرَمَادٍ ٱشْتَدَّتْ بِهِ ٱلرِّيحُ فِى يَوْمٍ عَاصِفٍ ۖ لَّا يَقْدِرُونَ مِمَّا كَسَبُوا۟ عَلَىٰ شَىْءٍ ۚ ذَٰلِكَ هُوَ ٱلضَّلَـٰلُ ٱلْبَعِيدُ ﴿١٨﴾﴾

﴿The parable of those who disbelieved in their Lord is that their works are as ashes, on which the wind blows furiously on a stormy day; they shall not be able to get aught of what they have earned. That is the straying, far away [from the Right Path].﴾ *(Qur'an 14: 18)*

Hence Allah (ﷻ) will make their deeds like scattered floating grains of dust:

﴿وَقَدِمْنَآ إِلَىٰ مَا عَمِلُوا۟ مِنْ عَمَلٍ فَجَعَلْنَـٰهُ هَبَآءً مَّنثُورًا ﴿٢٣﴾﴾

﴿And We shall turn to whatever deeds they [disbelievers, polytheists, sinners] did, and We shall make such deeds as scattered floating particles of dust.﴾ *(Qur'an 25: 23)*

This group, who think that they are following something good, will have a shock on the Day of Resurrection when they discover that their deeds are worthless. This group includes the devoted worshippers among the Jews and Christians, after the time of the Prophet (ﷺ). A group of them strive in worship and doing good deeds, and they think that this will benefit them before Allah. The same is also true of some of those who claim to be Muslims, but they associate others in worship with Allah for which He has not sent down any authority, and they worship things other than Allah. All of these people will not benefit at all from their good deeds, and those deeds will carry no weight before Allah on the Day of Resurrection:

﴿ قُلْ هَلْ نُنَبِّئُكُم بِٱلْأَخْسَرِينَ أَعْمَٰلًا ﴿١٠٣﴾ ٱلَّذِينَ ضَلَّ سَعْيُهُمْ فِى ٱلْحَيَوٰةِ ٱلدُّنْيَا وَهُمْ
يَحْسَبُونَ أَنَّهُمْ يُحْسِنُونَ صُنْعًا ﴿١٠٤﴾ أُو۟لَٰٓئِكَ ٱلَّذِينَ كَفَرُوا۟ بِـَٔايَٰتِ رَبِّهِمْ وَلِقَآئِهِۦ
فَحَبِطَتْ أَعْمَٰلُهُمْ فَلَا نُقِيمُ لَهُمْ يَوْمَ ٱلْقِيَٰمَةِ وَزْنًا ﴿١٠٥﴾ ذَٰلِكَ جَزَآؤُهُمْ جَهَنَّمُ بِمَا
كَفَرُوا۟ وَٱتَّخَذُوٓا۟ ءَايَٰتِى وَرُسُلِى هُزُوًا ﴿١٠٦﴾ ﴾

﴿Say [O' Muhammad]: Shall We tell you the greatest losers in respect of [their] deeds? Those whose efforts have been wasted in this life while they thought that they were acquiring good by their deeds. They are those who deny the *Aayaat* [proofs, evidences, verses, lessons, signs, revelations, etc.] of their Lord and the Meeting with Him [in the Hereafter]. So their works are in vain, and on the Day of Resurrection, We shall assign no weight for them. That shall be their recompense, Hell; because they disbelieved and took My *Aayaat* [proofs, evidences, verses, lessons, signs, revelations, etc.] and My Messengers by way of jest and mockery.﴾

(Qur'an 18: 103-106)

Muṣ'ab ibn Sa'd asked his father Sa'd ibn Abi Waqqaaṣ about those who will be the greatest losers with regard to their actions. He said: "They are the Jews and the Christians. The Jews rejected Muhammad (ﷺ), and the Christians rejected the idea of Paradise and said that there is no food or drink there."[8]

So the Jews and Christians will be amongst the greatest losers with regard to their actions, because many of them think that they are following the truth, and they strive in worship. But the fact of the matter is that they are losers, because they reject the final Messenger of Allah and His revealed Book, in addition to the fact that they reject much of that which was revealed to them from their Lord, and they

---

[8] Bukhari, *Kitaab at-Tafseer, Soorah* no. 18; *Fatḥ al-Baari*, 8/425.

believe in the distorted version of their religion.

These deeds which the *kuffaar* think will benefit them on the Day of Resurrection will carry no weight and have no value on that Day, because they are not based on any solid foundation:

﴿ وَمَن يَبْتَغِ غَيْرَ ٱلْإِسْلَـٰمِ دِينًا فَلَن يُقْبَلَ مِنْهُ وَهُوَ فِى ٱلْـَٔاخِرَةِ مِنَ ٱلْخَـٰسِرِينَ ﴿٨٥﴾ ﴾

﴿And whoever seeks a religion other than Islam, it will never be accepted of him, and in the Hereafter he will be one of the losers.﴾ *(Qur'an 3: 85)*

That basis is Islam. So long as a man is not a Muslim who affirms the Oneness of Allah (*Tawḥeed*), his good deeds will be rejected, and his efforts will carry the burden of sin and will not be appreciated. Muslim narrated in his *Ṣaḥeeḥ* that 'Aa'ishah said: "O' Messenger of Allah! During the *Jaahiliyah*, Ibn Jad'aan used to uphold the ties of kinship and feed the poor; will that benefit him at all?" He said,

"It will not be of any benefit to him, because he never said one day, 'O' Lord, forgive me my sins on the Day of Judgement.'"[9]

3) The dispute of the People of the Fire

When the *kuffaar* - disbelievers - the enemies of Allah, see with their own eyes the torment that Allah has prepared for them, and the horrors that surround them, they will hate themselves and will hate those who were their loved ones and close friends in this world. All love that was based on anything other than faith will turn to enmity. Allah (ﷻ) says:

---

[9] Muslim, *Kitaab al-Eemaan, Baab ahwan Ahl ad-Dunya 'adhaaban*, 1/196, hadith no. 214.

﴿ ٱلۡأَخِلَّآءُ يَوۡمَئِذِۭ بَعۡضُهُمۡ لِبَعۡضٍ عَدُوٌّ إِلَّا ٱلۡمُتَّقِينَ ٦٧ ﴾

﴿Friends on that Day will be foes one to another except *Al-Muttaqoon* [the pious].﴾ *(Qur'an 43: 67)*

At that point, the people of Hell will dispute with one another and argue with one another; worshippers will dispute with the objects of their worship, and followers will argue with their leaders, and the weak will argue with those who arrogantly oppressed them. A man will argue with his *qareen* (jinn companion), and a *kaafir* will even argue with his own limbs.

a) The dispute of the worshippers with the objects of their worship

﴿ وَبُرِّزَتِ ٱلۡجَحِيمُ لِلۡغَاوِينَ ٩١ وَقِيلَ لَهُمۡ أَيۡنَ مَا كُنتُمۡ تَعۡبُدُونَ ٩٢ مِن دُونِ
ٱللَّهِ هَلۡ يَنصُرُونَكُمۡ أَوۡ يَنتَصِرُونَ ٩٣ فَكُبۡكِبُواْ فِيهَا هُمۡ وَٱلۡغَاوُۥنَ ٩٤ وَجُنُودُ
إِبۡلِيسَ أَجۡمَعُونَ ٩٥ قَالُواْ وَهُمۡ فِيهَا يَخۡتَصِمُونَ ٩٦ تَٱللَّهِ إِن كُنَّا لَفِي ضَلَٰلٖ
مُّبِينٍ ٩٧ إِذۡ نُسَوِّيكُم بِرَبِّ ٱلۡعَٰلَمِينَ ٩٨ وَمَآ أَضَلَّنَآ إِلَّا ٱلۡمُجۡرِمُونَ
٩٩ ﴾

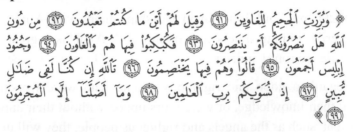

﴿And the [Hell] Fire will be placed in full view of the erring. And it will be said to them: 'Where are those [the false gods whom you used to set up as rivals with Allah] that you used to worship. Instead of Allah? Can they help you or [even] help themselves?' Then they will be thrown on their faces into the [Fire], they and the *Ghaawoon* [devils, and those who were in error]. And the whole hosts of *Iblees* [Satan] together. They will say while contending therein, By Allah, we were truly, in a manifest error, When we held you [false gods] as equals [in worship] with the Lord of the *'Aalameen* [mankind, jinn and all that exists]; And none has brought us into error except the *Mujrimoon* [*Iblees* (Satan) and those of human beings who commit crimes, murderers, polytheists, oppressors].﴾ *(Qur'an 26: 91-99)*

Here Allah tells us that they will address the gods whom they used to worship, and will admit that they were misguided when they worshipped them and regarded them as being equal to the Creator. Whoever raises a created being to the level of the Creator is doomed and is a loser, and everyone who worships some god other than Allah has put the Creator and the created being on the same level. This is the greatest wrongdoing, as Luqmaan said to his son when he was advising him:

﴿ ... يَـٰبُنَىَّ لَا تُشْرِكْ بِٱللَّهِ إِنَّ ٱلشِّرْكَ لَظُلْمٌ عَظِيمٌ ﴿١٣﴾ ﴾

﴾...O' my son! Join not in worship others with Allah. Verily, joining others in worship with Allah is a great *Zulm* [wrong] indeed.﴿ *(Qur'an 31: 13)*

With regard to good and righteous people who were worshipped without their knowledge, or were worshipped without their approval or consent, such as the angels and righteous people, they will disown their worshippers and show the claims of those worshippers to be lies and fabrications. For the angels did not ask to be worshipped and they were not pleased with it. The ones who asked for it were the jinn, in order that they might lead mankind astray and condemn them to Hell, so those misguided people were worshippers of the jinn, not of the angels.

﴿ وَيَوْمَ يَحْشُرُهُمْ جَمِيعًا ثُمَّ يَقُولُ لِلْمَلَـٰٓئِكَةِ أَهَـٰٓؤُلَآءِ إِيَّاكُمْ كَانُوا۟ يَعْبُدُونَ ﴿٤٠﴾ قَالُوا۟ سُبْحَـٰنَكَ أَنتَ وَلِيُّنَا مِن دُونِهِم ۖ بَلْ كَانُوا۟ يَعْبُدُونَ ٱلْجِنَّ ۖ أَكْثَرُهُم بِهِم مُّؤْمِنُونَ ﴿٤١﴾ ﴾

﴾And [remember] the Day when He will gather them all together, then He will say to the angels: 'Was it you that

> these people used to worship?' They [the angels] will say: 'Glorified be You! You are our *Wali* [Lord] instead of them. Nay, but they used to worship the jinn; most of them were believers in them.'﴿ *(Qur'an 34: 40-41)*

On the Day of Judgement, 'Eesa ibn Maryam (Jesus) (عليه السلام) will disown those who took him as god and worshipped him instead of Allah:

﴿ وَإِذْ قَالَ ٱللَّهُ يَٰعِيسَى ٱبْنَ مَرْيَمَ ءَأَنتَ قُلْتَ لِلنَّاسِ ٱتَّخِذُونِى وَأُمِّىَ
إِلَٰهَيْنِ مِن دُونِ ٱللَّهِ ۖ قَالَ سُبْحَٰنَكَ مَا يَكُونُ لِىٓ أَنْ أَقُولَ مَا لَيْسَ لِى بِحَقٍّ ۚ
إِن كُنتُ قُلْتُهُۥ فَقَدْ عَلِمْتَهُۥ ۚ تَعْلَمُ مَا فِى نَفْسِى وَلَآ أَعْلَمُ مَا فِى نَفْسِكَ ۚ إِنَّكَ
أَنتَ عَلَّٰمُ ٱلْغُيُوبِ ﴿١١٦﴾ مَا قُلْتُ لَهُمْ إِلَّا مَآ أَمَرْتَنِى بِهِۦٓ أَنِ ٱعْبُدُوا۟ ٱللَّهَ رَبِّى
وَرَبَّكُمْ ۚ ... ﴿١١٧﴾ ﴾

> ﴾And [remember] when Allah will say [on the Day of Resurrection]: 'O' 'Eesa [Jesus], son of Maryam [Mary]! Did you say unto men: 'Worship me and my mother as two gods besides Allah?' He will say: 'Glory be to You! It was not for me to say what I had no right [to say]. Had I said such a thing, You would surely have known it. You know what is in my inner-self though I do not know what is in Yours; truly, You, only You, are the All-Knower of all that is hidden [and unseen]. Never did I say to them aught except what You [Allah] did command me to say: 'Worship Allah, my Lord and your Lord."...﴿ *(Qur'an 5: 116-117)*

This will be the attitude of all those who were worshipped and taken as gods without their approval or consent. They will disown those who worshipped them, and will show their claims to be false, and will affirm their own submission to their Lord, Allah (سبحانه وتعالى):

﴿ وَإِذَا رَءَا ٱلَّذِينَ أَشْرَكُوا۟ شُرَكَآءَهُمْ قَالُوا۟ رَبَّنَا هَٰٓؤُلَآءِ شُرَكَآؤُنَا ٱلَّذِينَ كُنَّا نَدْعُوا۟ مِن دُونِكَ ۖ فَأَلْقَوْا۟ إِلَيْهِمُ ٱلْقَوْلَ إِنَّكُمْ لَكَٰذِبُونَ ﴿٨٦﴾ وَأَلْقَوْا۟ إِلَى ٱللَّهِ يَوْمَئِذٍ ٱلسَّلَمَ ۖ وَضَلَّ عَنْهُم مَّا كَانُوا۟ يَفْتَرُونَ ﴿٨٧﴾ ﴾

﴾And when those who associated partners with Allah see their [Allah's so-called] partners, they will say: 'Our Lord! These are our partners whom we used to invoke besides you.' But they will throw back their word at them [and say]: 'Surely, you indeed are liars!' And they will offer [their full] submission to Allah [Alone] on that Day, and their invented false deities [all that they used to invoke besides Allah, e.g. idols, saints, priests, monks, angels, jinn, Jibreel (Gabriel), Messengers] will vanish from them.﴿ *(Qur'an 16: 86-87)*

Elsewhere, Allah (ﷻ) says:

﴿ وَيَوْمَ نَحْشُرُهُمْ جَمِيعًا ثُمَّ نَقُولُ لِلَّذِينَ أَشْرَكُوا۟ مَكَانَكُمْ أَنتُمْ وَشُرَكَآؤُكُمْ ۚ فَزَيَّلْنَا بَيْنَهُمْ ۖ وَقَالَ شُرَكَآؤُهُم مَّا كُنتُمْ إِيَّانَا تَعْبُدُونَ ﴿٢٨﴾ فَكَفَىٰ بِٱللَّهِ شَهِيدًۢا بَيْنَنَا وَبَيْنَكُمْ إِن كُنَّا عَنْ عِبَادَتِكُمْ لَغَٰفِلِينَ ﴿٢٩﴾ هُنَالِكَ تَبْلُوا۟ كُلُّ نَفْسٍ مَّآ أَسْلَفَتْ ۚ وَرُدُّوٓا۟ إِلَى ٱللَّهِ مَوْلَىٰهُمُ ٱلْحَقِّ ۖ وَضَلَّ عَنْهُم مَّا كَانُوا۟ يَفْتَرُونَ ﴿٣٠﴾ ﴾

﴾And the Day whereon We shall gather them all together, then We shall say to those who did set partners in worship with Us: 'Stop at your place! You and your partners [whom you had worshipped in the worldly life].' Then We shall separate them, and their [Allah's so-called] partners shall say: 'It was not us that you used to worship. So sufficient is Allah as a witness between us and you that we indeed knew nothing of your worship of us.' There! Every person will know [exactly] what he had earned before and they will be brought back to Allah, their rightful *Mawla* [Lord], and their invented false deities will vanish from them.﴾

(Qur'an 10: 28-30)

b) The dispute of the followers with the leaders of misguidance

The dispute of the followers with the leaders of misguidance who propagated their misleading ideas and theories, and their principles that went against Islam, is mentioned elsewhere, where Allah (ﷻ) says:

﴿ فَإِنَّمَا هِيَ زَجْرَةٌ وَاحِدَةٌ فَإِذَا هُمْ يَنظُرُونَ ﴿١٩﴾ وَقَالُوا يَا وَيْلَنَا هَٰذَا يَوْمُ الدِّينِ
﴿٢٠﴾ هَٰذَا يَوْمُ الْفَصْلِ الَّذِي كُنتُم بِهِ تُكَذِّبُونَ ﴿٢١﴾ ۞ احْشُرُوا الَّذِينَ
ظَلَمُوا وَأَزْوَاجَهُمْ وَمَا كَانُوا يَعْبُدُونَ ﴿٢٢﴾ مِن دُونِ اللَّهِ فَاهْدُوهُمْ إِلَىٰ صِرَاطِ
الْجَحِيمِ ﴿٢٣﴾ وَقِفُوهُمْ ۖ إِنَّهُم مَّسْئُولُونَ ﴿٢٤﴾ مَا لَكُمْ لَا تَنَاصَرُونَ ﴿٢٥﴾ بَلْ هُمُ
الْيَوْمَ مُسْتَسْلِمُونَ ﴿٢٦﴾ وَأَقْبَلَ بَعْضُهُمْ عَلَىٰ بَعْضٍ يَتَسَاءَلُونَ ﴿٢٧﴾ قَالُوا إِنَّكُمْ كُنتُمْ
تَأْتُونَنَا عَنِ الْيَمِينِ ﴿٢٨﴾ قَالُوا بَل لَّمْ تَكُونُوا مُؤْمِنِينَ ﴿٢٩﴾ وَمَا كَانَ لَنَا عَلَيْكُم
مِّن سُلْطَانٍ ۖ بَلْ كُنتُمْ قَوْمًا طَاغِينَ ﴿٣٠﴾ فَحَقَّ عَلَيْنَا قَوْلُ رَبِّنَا ۖ إِنَّا لَذَائِقُونَ
﴿٣١﴾ فَأَغْوَيْنَاكُمْ إِنَّا كُنَّا غَاوِينَ ﴿٣٢﴾ فَإِنَّهُمْ يَوْمَئِذٍ فِي الْعَذَابِ مُشْتَرِكُونَ ﴿٣٣﴾
إِنَّا كَذَٰلِكَ نَفْعَلُ بِالْمُجْرِمِينَ ﴿٣٤﴾ إِنَّهُمْ كَانُوا إِذَا قِيلَ لَهُمْ لَا إِلَٰهَ إِلَّا اللَّهُ
يَسْتَكْبِرُونَ ﴿٣٥﴾ ﴾

﴿It will be a single *Zajrah* [shout (i.e. the second blowing of the Trumpet)], and behold, they will be staring! They will say: 'Woe to us! This is the Day of Recompense!' [It will be said]: 'This is the Day of Judgement which you used to deny.' [It will be said to the angels]: 'Assemble those who did wrong, together with their companions [from the devils] and what they used to worship, instead of Allah, and lead them on to the way of flaming Fire [Hell]; but stop them, verily, they are to be questioned.

What is the matter with you? Why do you not help one another [as you used to do in the world]?' Nay, but that Day they shall surrender. And they will turn to one another and question one another. They will say: 'It was you who used to come to us from the right side [i.e., from the right side of one of us and beautify for us every evil, enjoin on us polytheism, and stop us from the truth, i.e. Islamic Monotheism and from every good deed].' They will reply: 'Nay, you yourselves were not believers. And we had no authority over you. Nay! But you were *Ṭaaghoon* [transgressing] people [polytheists, and disbelievers]. So now the Word of our Lord has been justified against us, that we shall certainly [have to] taste [the torment]. So we led you astray because we were ourselves astray.' Then verily, that Day, they will [all] share in the torment. Certainly, that is how We deal with *Al-Mujrimoon* [polytheists, sinners, disbelievers, criminals, the disobedient to Allah]. Truly, when it was said to them: *Laa ilaaha ill-Allah* [none has the right to be worshipped but Allah], they puffed themselves up with pride [i.e. denied it]. ﴾ *(Qur'an 37: 19-35)*

What is mentioned in these verses is the way the people of Hell will blame one another on the Day of Resurrection. The followers will say to the leaders of misguidance, you are the ones who made falsehood attractive to us, and tempted us to go against the truth. As Allah (ﷻ) says:

﴿ ... وَٱلَّذِينَ كَفَرُوٓاْ أَوۡلِيَآؤُهُمُ ٱلطَّٰغُوتُ يُخۡرِجُونَهُم مِّنَ ٱلنُّورِ إِلَى ٱلظُّلُمَٰتِۗ ... ﴿٢٥٧﴾ ﴾

﴿...But as for those who disbelieve, their *Awliya* [supporters and helpers] are *Ṭaaghoot* [false deities and

false leaders], they bring them out from light into
darkness...❭ *(Qur'an 2: 257)*

But the leaders and thinkers will reject that and will say to them:
"You have to bear the consequences of your own actions; you chose
kufr, we had no power over you; it was your own transgression and
arrogance that brought you to this end."

c) The dispute of the weak with the leaders

Allah also mentions the dispute of the weak with the leaders such as
kings, governors and elders of tribes, who had power over people,
and the weak who supported their leaders and helped them in their
falsehood by means of their own selves and their wealth. Allah (ﷻ)
says:

﴿ وَبَرَزُواْ لِلَّهِ جَمِيعًا فَقَالَ ٱلضُّعَفَٰٓؤُاْ لِلَّذِينَ ٱسۡتَكۡبَرُوٓاْ إِنَّا كُنَّا لَكُمۡ تَبَعًا
فَهَلۡ أَنتُم مُّغۡنُونَ عَنَّا مِنۡ عَذَابِ ٱللَّهِ مِن شَيۡءٍۚ قَالُواْ لَوۡ هَدَىٰنَا ٱللَّهُ
لَهَدَيۡنَٰكُمۡۖ سَوَآءٌ عَلَيۡنَآ أَجَزِعۡنَآ أَمۡ صَبَرۡنَا مَا لَنَا مِن مَّحِيصٍ ۞ ﴾

❬And they all shall appear before Allah [on the Day of
Resurrection]; then the weak will say to those who were
arrogant [chiefs]: 'Verily, we were following you; can
you avail us anything against Allah's Torment?' They
will say: 'Had Allah guided us, we would have guided
you. It makes no difference to us [now] whether we rage,
or bear [these torments] with patience; there is no place
of refuge for us.'❭ *(Qur'an 14: 21)*

Let us listen to the *daa'iyah* and *mufassir* Prof. Sayyid Quṭb (may
Allah have mercy on him and give him a great reward) as he gives his
commentary on these verses, let us walk with him "*In the Shade of
the Qur'an*"...

"And they all shall appear before Allah" - they are the oppressors
who rejected the truth and their followers among the weak and

humiliated... and with them will be the *Shayṭaan* (Satan)... then those who believed in the Messengers and did righteous deeds... they will all be brought forth and exposed, although they are exposed to Allah all the time. But at this time they will know and will feel that they are exposed and there will be nothing to conceal them or cover them or protect them... They will be exposed when the arena will be filled and all covers will have been removed, and the discussion will begin. Then the weak will say to those who were arrogant (chiefs): 'Verily, we were following you; can you avail us anything against Allah's Torment?'... the weak are those who gave up one of the most special characteristics of the man who is dear to Allah when they gave up their personal freedom of thought and belief, and made themselves followers of the arrogant and false leaders, and they submitted themselves to Allah's slaves instead of to Allah, and preferred that to being slaves of Allah. Weakness is no excuse, in fact it is itself a crime. Allah does not want anyone to be weak, and He calls all people to His protection and to seek their pride in Him, for all pride is with Him. Allah does not want anyone to give up his share of freedom - which is the distinguishing feature of mankind, upon which human honour rests - whether willingly or unwillingly, by force. Physical force, no matter how severe it is, cannot enslave a man who wants to be free and who insists on maintaining his human dignity. All that this physical force can do is possess his body, torturing it, harming it, chaining it and detaining it. But his conscience, his spirit, his mind cannot be possessed or detained or humiliated by anybody, unless he himself wants to submit it to detention and humiliation.

Who is the one who has the power to make those weak people follow the arrogant in beliefs, in thought, in behaviour? Who is the one who has the power to make those weak people submit to anyone other than Allah, when it is Allah Alone Who is their Creator, their Provider and their Sustainer? No one. No one but their own weak selves. They are weak not because they have less physical strength than the false leaders, and not because they have less power or money or status... Far from it. All of these are external matters which cannot be counted as weakness in and of themselves or as being the cause of the weakness of the weak. They are weak because of the weakness in their souls and hearts, and because they are weak and lacking in pride in one of the most special characteristics of man.

The weak and oppressed are many, and the false leaders and oppressors are few. Who is it that makes so many submit to so few? What makes them submit? Their submission reflects weakness of spirit, a lack of ambition, a lack of dignity and a loss of that honour which Allah (ﷻ) bestowed upon mankind.

The false leaders cannot subjugate the masses without the will of these masses. They can always stand up to the tyrants if they want. Willpower is what these flocks are lacking!

Humiliation cannot occur unless a person has the potential to be humiliated... this potential is the only thing that the tyrants rely on. And here we see the humiliated in the Hereafter, in their weakness and submission to those who were arrogant, asking them:

﴿... إِنَّا كُنَّا لَكُمْ تَبَعًا فَهَلْ أَنتُم مُّغْنُونَ عَنَّا مِنْ عَذَابِ ٱللَّهِ مِن شَىْءٍ ... ﴿٢١﴾﴾

﴿...Verily, we were following you; can you avail us anything against Allah's Torment?...﴾ *(Qur'an 14: 21)*

We followed you, and we ended up in this appalling state!

Or perhaps when they have seen the punishment, they will want to rebuke the arrogant for their leadership which has led them to this punishment. The verse tells us what they will say and describes the humiliated tone in which they will say it.

Those who were arrogant will respond to this question by saying:

﴿... قَالُوا۟ لَوْ هَدَىٰنَا ٱللَّهُ لَهَدَيْنَٰكُمْ ۖ سَوَآءٌ عَلَيْنَآ أَجَزِعْنَآ أَمْ صَبَرْنَا مَا لَنَا مِن مَّحِيصٍ ﴿٢١﴾﴾

﴾...Had Allah guided us, we would have guided you. It makes no difference to us [now] whether we rage, or bear [these torments] with patience; there is no place of refuge for us.﴿ *(Qur'an 14: 21)*

This is a response which reflects their exasperation and stress: "Had Allah guided us, we would have guided you." Why are you blaming us when we and you are both on the same path, leading to the same fate? We were not guided ourselves and we led you astray. If Allah had guided us, we would have led you to guidance with us, just as we led you to misguidance when we were misguided. They will attribute their guidance and misguidance to Allah. At this time, they will acknowledge His power, which previously they used to deny and they used to treat the weak with contempt, not paying any attention to the Subduer, the Compeller. They will try to escape responsibility for their own misguidance and their misguiding others by referring the whole matter to Allah... But Allah does not enjoin misguidance, as He (ﷻ) says:

﴿... إِنَّ ٱللَّهَ لَا يَأْمُرُ بِٱلْفَحْشَآءِ ... ﴿٢٨﴾﴾

﴾...Allah never commands *Faaḥisha* [evil deeds]...﴿ *(Qur'an 7: 28)*

Then they will rebuke the weak in a subtle way, telling them that there is no point in either panicking or being patient, because the punishment has now been decided and neither patience nor panic will ward it off. The time when fear of the punishment may have been of benefit by making the misguided turn to guidance, or when being patient during adversity may have brought the mercy of Allah, has now passed. It is now too late, and there is no way out and no escape.

The matter has been decided, and there is now no room for argument or debate... And now we will see a strange sight. We see the *Shayṭaan* (Satan), the one who promoted misguidance and encouraged people to go astray... now we will see him speaking like a devilish preacher, trying to fool the weak and the arrogant alike, with words that may be harder for them to bear than the torment itself:

﴿وَقَالَ ٱلشَّيْطَٰنُ لَمَّا قُضِىَ ٱلْأَمْرُ إِنَّ ٱللَّهَ وَعَدَكُمْ وَعْدَ ٱلْحَقِّ وَوَعَدتُّكُمْ فَأَخْلَفْتُكُمْ ۖ وَمَا كَانَ لِىَ عَلَيْكُم مِّن سُلْطَٰنٍ إِلَّآ أَن دَعَوْتُكُمْ فَٱسْتَجَبْتُمْ لِى ۖ فَلَا تَلُومُونِى وَلُومُوٓا۟ أَنفُسَكُم ۖ مَّآ أَنَا۠ بِمُصْرِخِكُمْ وَمَآ أَنتُم بِمُصْرِخِىَّ ۖ إِنِّى كَفَرْتُ بِمَآ أَشْرَكْتُمُونِ مِن قَبْلُ ۗ إِنَّ ٱلظَّٰلِمِينَ لَهُمْ عَذَابٌ أَلِيمٌ ﴿٢٢﴾﴾

﴿And *Shayṭaan* [Satan] will say when the matter has been decided: 'Verily, Allah promised you a promise of truth. And I too promised you, but I betrayed you. I had no authority over you except that I called you, and you responded to me. So blame me not, but blame yourselves. I cannot help you, nor can you help me. I deny your former act in associating me [Satan] as a partner with Allah [by obeying me in the life of the world]. Verily, there is a painful torment for the *Ẓaalimoon* [polytheists and wrongdoers].'﴾ *(Qur'an 14: 22)*

How astounding this is! This really is the *Shayṭaan*, whose character is shown perfectly here, just as the character of the weak and the arrogant are shown perfectly in this discussion.

This is the *Shayṭaan* who whispers into people's hearts, encouraging them to commit sin and making *kufr* attractive to them, preventing them from hearing the call of truth... This is the one who tells them, whilst he is stabbing them, so that they cannot respond in kind - now that the matter is decided - this is what he is saying now, when it is too late: ﴾...Verily, Allah promised you a promise of truth. And I too promised you, but I betrayed you...﴿ *(Qur'an 14: 22).*

Then he will strike them a second blow, shaming them for responding to him when he had no power over them, except that they gave up their own power and forgot the ancient enmity that existed between them and the *Shayṭaan*, so they responded to his call of falsehood and ignored the call of Allah to the truth: ﴾...I had no authority over you except that I called you, and you responded to me...﴿ *(Qur'an 14: 22).*

Then he will rebuke them, and will call upon them to rebuke themselves. He will rebuke them for obeying him! ﴾...So blame me not, but blame yourselves...﴿ *(Qur'an 14: 22)*

Then he will abandon them and leave them to their fate, although he is the one who had made promises to them and given them hope, and he had insinuated to them the idea that no one would prevail over them. But now he will not want to respond to them when they scream out, and they will never help him if he screams out either. ﴾...I cannot help you, nor can you help me...﴿ *(Qur'an 14: 22)* And there is no tie of loyalty between us!

Then he will deny and reject their association of him with Allah: ﴾...I deny your former act in associating me [Satan] as a partner with Allah [by obeying me in the life of the world]...﴿ *(Qur'an 14:22).* And he will conclude his devilish speech with very harsh words addressed to his advocates and followers: ﴾...Verily, there is a painful torment for the *Ẓaalimoon* [polytheists and wrongdoers].﴿ *(Qur'an 14:22).*

How bad it will be for the *Shayṭaan*, and for them, because of their friend who called them to misguidance and they obeyed him, whilst the Messengers called them to Allah and they rejected them and shunned them.[10]

---

[10] *Fi Ẓilaal al-Qur'an* (In the Shade of the Qur'an), 4/2095.

Elsewhere, Allah mentions the dispute between the weak and their arrogant leaders, when He (ﷻ) says:

﴿وَإِذْ يَتَحَآجُّونَ فِى ٱلنَّارِ فَيَقُولُ ٱلضُّعَفَٰٓؤُا۟ لِلَّذِينَ ٱسْتَكْبَرُوٓا۟ إِنَّا كُنَّا لَكُمْ تَبَعًا فَهَلْ أَنتُم مُّغْنُونَ عَنَّا نَصِيبًا مِّنَ ٱلنَّارِ ﴿٤٧﴾ قَالَ ٱلَّذِينَ ٱسْتَكْبَرُوٓا۟ إِنَّا كُلٌّ فِيهَآ إِنَّ ٱللَّهَ قَدْ حَكَمَ بَيْنَ ٱلْعِبَادِ ﴿٤٨﴾﴾

﴿And, when they will dispute in the Fire, the weak will say to those who were arrogant: 'Verily, we followed you, can you then take from us some portion of the Fire?' Those who were arrogant will say: 'We are all [together] in this [Fire]! Verily, Allah has judged between [His] slaves!'﴾ *(Qur'an 40: 47-48)*

These verses follow a passage which describes Pharaoh's arrogance in slaughtering the children, his attempt to kill Moosa (Moses) (عليه السلام), and his debate with that believer who stood up to Pharaoh and refuted his false arguments. It described how the people's attitude was like a blind following, obeying all the wishes of the tyrant. So they started to slaughter, persecute and expel [the believers]. These people, who in this world were helpers of the evil oppressors will, on the Day of Resurrection, come to know just how terrible were the sins that they committed, they will say to their leaders like Pharaoh: ﴿...Verily, we followed you, can you then take from us some portion of the Fire?﴾ *(Qur'an 40: 47).*

But the leaders will not be able to do anything for themselves, or to help themselves, and they will say: ﴿...We are all [together] in this [Fire]! Verily, Allah has judged between [His] slaves!﴾ *(Qur'an 40: 48).*

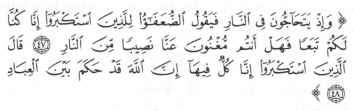

This attitude and stand guide us to the answer that enables us to face the false statement, repeated by some evildoers when they tell their followers: "Follow me, and I will bear your burden of sin if there is any sin on you." Although they will indeed bear a burden equivalent to that of their followers' sins, this does not mean that their followers will escape punishment.

﴿ وَقَالَ ٱلَّذِينَ كَفَرُوا۟ لِلَّذِينَ ءَامَنُوا۟ ٱتَّبِعُوا۟ سَبِيلَنَا وَلْنَحْمِلْ خَطَـٰيَـٰكُمْ
وَمَا هُم بِحَـٰمِلِينَ مِنْ خَطَـٰيَـٰهُم مِّن شَىْءٍ ۖ إِنَّهُمْ لَكَـٰذِبُونَ ﴿١٢﴾
وَلَيَحْمِلُنَّ أَثْقَالَهُمْ وَأَثْقَالًا مَّعَ أَثْقَالِهِمْ ۖ وَلَيُسْـَٔلُنَّ يَوْمَ ٱلْقِيَـٰمَةِ عَمَّا كَانُوا۟
يَفْتَرُونَ ﴿١٣﴾ ﴾

﴾And those who disbelieve say to those who believe: 'Follow our way and we will, verily, bear your sins.' Never will they bear anything of their sins. Surely, they are liars. And verily, they shall bear their own loads, and other loads besides their own; and verily, they shall be questioned on the Day of Resurrection about that which they used to fabricate.﴿ *(Qur'an 29: 12-13)*

Elsewhere, Allah (ﷻ) tells us how the weak will dispute with the arrogant:

﴿ ... وَلَوْ تَرَىٰٓ إِذِ ٱلظَّـٰلِمُونَ مَوْقُوفُونَ عِندَ رَبِّهِمْ يَرْجِعُ بَعْضُهُمْ إِلَىٰ
بَعْضٍ ٱلْقَوْلَ يَقُولُ ٱلَّذِينَ ٱسْتُضْعِفُوا۟ لِلَّذِينَ ٱسْتَكْبَرُوا۟ لَوْلَآ أَنتُمْ لَكُنَّا
مُؤْمِنِينَ ﴿٣١﴾ قَالَ ٱلَّذِينَ ٱسْتَكْبَرُوا۟ لِلَّذِينَ ٱسْتُضْعِفُوٓا۟ أَنَحْنُ صَدَدْنَـٰكُمْ عَنِ
ٱلْهُدَىٰ بَعْدَ إِذْ جَآءَكُم ۖ بَلْ كُنتُم مُّجْرِمِينَ ﴿٣٢﴾ وَقَالَ ٱلَّذِينَ ٱسْتُضْعِفُوا۟
لِلَّذِينَ ٱسْتَكْبَرُوا۟ بَلْ مَكْرُ ٱلَّيْلِ وَٱلنَّهَارِ إِذْ تَأْمُرُونَنَآ أَن نَّكْفُرَ بِٱللَّهِ
وَنَجْعَلَ لَهُۥٓ أَندَادًا ۚ وَأَسَرُّوا۟ ٱلنَّدَامَةَ لَمَّا رَأَوُا۟ ٱلْعَذَابَ وَجَعَلْنَا ٱلْأَغْلَـٰلَ فِىٓ
أَعْنَاقِ ٱلَّذِينَ كَفَرُوا۟ ۚ هَلْ يُجْزَوْنَ إِلَّا مَا كَانُوا۟ يَعْمَلُونَ ﴿٣٣﴾ ﴾

﴾...But if you could see when the *Ẓaalimoon* [polytheists and wrongdoers] will be made to stand before their Lord, how they will cast the [blaming] word one to another!

> Those who were deemed weak will say to those who were arrogant: 'Had it not been for you, we should certainly have been believers!' And those who were arrogant will say to those who were deemed weak: 'Did we keep you back from guidance after it had come to you? Nay, but you were *Mujrimoon* [polytheists, sinners, disbelievers, criminals].' Those who were deemed weak will say to those who were arrogant: 'Nay, but it was your plotting by night and day, when you ordered us to disbelieve in Allah and set up rivals to Him!' And each of them [parties] will conceal their own regrets [for disobeying Allah during this worldly life], when they behold the torment. And We shall put iron collars round the necks of those who disbelieved. Are they requited aught except what they used to do? ﴿
>
> *(Qur'an 34: 31-33)*

The weak followers will accuse their leaders, saying: you prevented us from believing; were it not for you, we would have been among those who followed that which was sent down to us from our Lord. But the arrogant will reject this accusation and will say to them, you are the evildoers, all that happened is that we called you and you responded; we had no power over you. The weak and misguided people will say: but you plotted against us by night and by day; you misguided us and led us astray from the path of truth; the conspiracies and conferences, the various kinds of media throughout the ages, which depicted truth as falsehood and falsehood as truth, and the ways in which the leaders promoted doubts and false ideas among the people - all of that led us astray and made us not believe in Allah, and made us associate others with Him. But the fact of the matter is that all of them are wrong, and they will have no excuse for their misguidance and *kufr*.

Allah (ﷻ) describes this dispute among the people of Hell when they enter the Fire, as He says:

﴿ هَٰذَاۚ وَإِنَّ لِلطَّٰغِينَ لَشَرَّ مَـَٔابٖ ﴿٥٥﴾ جَهَنَّمَ يَصۡلَوۡنَهَا فَبِئۡسَ ٱلۡمِهَادُ ﴿٥٦﴾
هَٰذَا فَلۡيَذُوقُوهُ حَمِيمٞ وَغَسَّاقٞ ﴿٥٧﴾ وَءَاخَرُ مِن شَكۡلِهِۦٓ أَزۡوَٰجٌ ﴿٥٨﴾ هَٰذَا فَوۡجٞ
مُّقۡتَحِمٞ مَّعَكُمۡۖ لَا مَرۡحَبَۢا بِهِمۡۚ إِنَّهُمۡ صَالُواْ ٱلنَّارِ ﴿٥٩﴾ قَالُواْ بَلۡ أَنتُمۡ لَا مَرۡحَبَۢا
بِكُمۡۖ أَنتُمۡ قَدَّمۡتُمُوهُ لَنَاۖ فَبِئۡسَ ٱلۡقَرَارُ ﴿٦٠﴾ قَالُواْ رَبَّنَا مَن قَدَّمَ لَنَا هَٰذَا فَزِدۡهُ
عَذَابٗا ضِعۡفٗا فِي ٱلنَّارِ ﴿٦١﴾ وَقَالُواْ مَا لَنَا لَا نَرَىٰ رِجَالٗا كُنَّا نَعُدُّهُم مِّنَ ٱلۡأَشۡرَارِ
﴿٦٢﴾ أَتَّخَذۡنَٰهُمۡ سِخۡرِيًّا أَمۡ زَاغَتۡ عَنۡهُمُ ٱلۡأَبۡصَٰرُ ﴿٦٣﴾ إِنَّ ذَٰلِكَ لَحَقّٞ تَخَاصُمُ
أَهۡلِ ٱلنَّارِ ﴿٦٤﴾ ﴾

﴾This is so! And for the *Ṭaaghoon* [transgressors, the disobedient to Allah and His Messenger - disbelievers in the Oneness of Allah, criminals] will be an evil final return [Fire]. Hell! Where they will burn, and worst [indeed] is that place to rest! This is so! Then let them taste it a boiling fluid and dirty wound discharges. And other [torments] of similar kind all together! This is a troop entering with you [in Hell], no welcome for them! Verily, they shall burn in the Fire! [The followers of the misleaders will say]: 'Nay, you [too]! No welcome for you! It is you [misleaders] who brought this upon us [because you misled us in the world], so evil is this place to stay in!' They will say: 'Our Lord! Whoever brought this upon us, add to him a double torment in the Fire!' And they will say: 'What is the matter with us that we see not men whom we used to count among the bad ones? Did we take them as an object of mockery, or have [our] eyes failed to perceive them? Verily, that is the very truth the mutual dispute of the people of the Fire!﴿

(Qur'an 38: 55-64)

These people who used to welcome and respect one another in this world, on that Day will start to say to one another: ﴿... no welcome for them! Verily, they shall burn in the Fire! [The followers of the misleaders will say]: 'Nay, you [too]! No welcome for you!...﴾ *(Qur'an 38: 59-60).*

Each party will hope that Allah will increase the torment and pain of those who were dear to them in this world. This dispute among the people of Hell will surely come to pass, and there is no doubt about it. This is what our Lord tells us.

d) The dispute between the *kaafir* and his devil-companion *(qareen)*

On that Day, there will be a dispute between the *kaafir* and his devil-companion (*qareen*). Allah (ﷻ) says:

﴿وَقَالَ قَرِينُهُۥ هَٰذَا مَا لَدَيَّ عَتِيدٌ (٢٣) أَلْقِيَا فِي جَهَنَّمَ كُلَّ كَفَّارٍ عَنِيدٍ (٢٤)
مَّنَّاعٍ لِّلْخَيْرِ مُعْتَدٍ مُّرِيبٍ (٢٥) ٱلَّذِي جَعَلَ مَعَ ٱللَّهِ إِلَٰهًا ءَاخَرَ فَأَلْقِيَاهُ فِي
ٱلْعَذَابِ ٱلشَّدِيدِ (٢٦) ۞ قَالَ قَرِينُهُۥ رَبَّنَا مَآ أَطْغَيْتُهُۥ وَلَٰكِن كَانَ فِي ضَلَٰلٍۭ بَعِيدٍ
(٢٧) قَالَ لَا تَخْتَصِمُوا۟ لَدَيَّ وَقَدْ قَدَّمْتُ إِلَيْكُم بِٱلْوَعِيدِ (٢٨) مَا يُبَدَّلُ ٱلْقَوْلُ لَدَيَّ
وَمَآ أَنَا۠ بِظَلَّٰمٍ لِّلْعَبِيدِ (٢٩)﴾

﴿And his companion [angel] will say: 'Here is [this Record] ready with me!' Allah will say to the angels: 'Both of you throw into Hell every stubborn disbeliever [in the Oneness of Allah, in His Messengers] - Hinderer of good, transgressor, doubter, Who set up another *ilaah* [god] with Allah. Then both of you cast him in the severe torment.' His companion [Satan-devil] will say: 'Our Lord! I did not push him to transgression, [in disbelief, oppression, and evil deeds], but he was himself in error far astray.' Allah will say: 'Dispute not in front of Me, I had already in advance sent you the threat. The Sentence that comes from Me cannot be changed, and I am not unjust to the slaves.'﴾ *(Qur'an 50: 23-29)*

e) The dispute of the *kaafir* with his own limbs

This dispute will reach its peak when a man argues with his own limbs:

﴿ وَيَوْمَ يُحْشَرُ أَعْدَاءُ اللَّهِ إِلَى النَّارِ فَهُمْ يُوزَعُونَ ﴿١٩﴾ حَتَّىٰ إِذَا مَا جَاءُوهَا شَهِدَ عَلَيْهِمْ سَمْعُهُمْ وَأَبْصَارُهُمْ وَجُلُودُهُم بِمَا كَانُوا يَعْمَلُونَ ﴿٢٠﴾ وَقَالُوا لِجُلُودِهِمْ لِمَ شَهِدتُّمْ عَلَيْنَا ۖ قَالُوا أَنطَقَنَا اللَّهُ الَّذِي أَنطَقَ كُلَّ شَيْءٍ وَهُوَ خَلَقَكُمْ أَوَّلَ مَرَّةٍ وَإِلَيْهِ تُرْجَعُونَ ﴿٢١﴾ ﴾

﴿And [remember] the Day that the enemies of Allah will be gathered to the Fire, then they will be driven [(to the Fire), former ones being withheld till their later ones will join them]. Till, when they reach it [Hell-fire], their hearing [ears] and their eyes and their skins will testify against them as to what they used to do. And they will say to their skins, 'Why do you testify against us?' They will say: 'Allah has caused us to speak.' He causes all things to speak, and He created you the first time, and to Him you are made to return.﴾ *(Qur'an 41: 19-21)*

This is what will happen in the case of the *kuffaar*, when they see with their own eyes the severe torment that Allah has prepared for them. They will resort to lies and denials, claiming that they were righteous people, and that the testimony of the angels, Messengers and righteous people who testified against them is false. At that point, Allah will place a seal over their mouths and their hands and feet will speak of what they used to do. Then they will say to their own limbs, "Away with you! It was for your sake that I was arguing!"[11]

---

[11] This phrase comes from a hadith narrated by Muslim and others. See *Tafseer Ibn Katheer*, 6/168.

Muslim, Tirmidhi, Ibn Mardawayh and Al-Bayhaqi narrated that Abu Sa'eed and Abu Hurayrah (may Allah be pleased with them both) stated: The Messenger of Allah (ﷺ) said:

> "The slave will meet his Lord, and Allah will say, 'Did I not honour you and make you a leader and give you a spouse, and subjugate horses and camels for your use, and let you become a leader?' He will say, 'Yes indeed, O' Lord.' (Allah) will say, 'Did you think that you would meet Me?' He will say, 'No.' (Allah) will say, 'I will forget you as you forgot Me.' Then a second slave will meet Him, and He will say something similar to him. Then a third slave will meet Him, and He will say something similar, but he (the third slave) will say, 'I believed in You and in Your Book and Your Messenger. I prayed, fasted and gave in charity.' He will praise himself as much as he can. Then (Allah) will say, 'Shall We not send Our witness against you?' and he will wonder who that witness could be. Then a seal will be placed over his mouth, and it will be said to his thigh, 'Speak!' So his thigh will speak, as will his mouth and his bones, of what he used to do, and thus he will be left with no excuse. That is the *munaafiq* (hypocrite), and that is the one with whom Allah will be angry."[12]

This debate that will take place between a person and his limbs and faculties is a strange and wondrous matter, which made the Messenger (ﷺ) smile. According to the hadith narrated by Muslim, Anas ibn Maalik said: we were with the Messenger of Allah (ﷺ) and he smiled. He (ﷺ) said:

---

[12] Muslim, 4/2280, hadith no. 2969.

"Do you know why I am smiling?' We said, 'Allah and His Messenger know best.' He said, "(It is) because of what the slave will say to his Lord. He will say, 'O' Lord, did You not promise not to be unjust?' Allah will say, 'Indeed, I did.' The man will say, 'I will only accept a witness from myself.' Allah will say, 'You yourself are sufficient as a witness against you this Day, and the honourable scribes (*kiraaman kaatibeen* - i.e., the recording angels) will suffice as witnesses.' Then a seal will be placed over his mouth, and it will be said to his limbs, 'Speak!' And they will speak of his actions. Then he will be allowed to speak again, and he will say (to his own limbs), 'Away with you! It was for your sake that I was fighting!'"'[13]

f) The dispute of the body with the soul

The body will dispute with the soul on the Day of Resurrection.

Ibn Katheer said: "Ibn Mandah narrated in his book *Ar-Rooḥ* that Ibn 'Abbaas (رضي الله عنه) said: the people will dispute on the Day of Resurrection to such an extent that the soul will dispute with the body. The soul will say to the body, you did such and such, and the body will say to the soul, you told me to do such and such, and you inspired me to do such and such.

Allah will send an angel to judge between them, and he will say to them, you are like a paralyzed man and a blind man who go into a garden. The paralyzed man tells the blind man, I can see some fruit over there, but I cannot reach it. The blind man says to him, climb on me and you can get it. So he will climb on him and get it. Which of them is the sinner? They will say, Both of them. So the angel will say to them, you have passed judgement against yourselves. In other

---

[13] Muslim, 4/2280, hadith no. 2969.

words, the body is like a vehicle for the soul, and the soul is like the passenger."[14]

g) In that situation they will hate themselves

﴿إِنَّ ٱلَّذِينَ كَفَرُوا۟ يُنَادَوْنَ لَمَقْتُ ٱللَّهِ أَكْبَرُ مِن مَّقْتِكُمْ أَنفُسَكُمْ إِذْ تُدْعَوْنَ إِلَى ٱلْإِيمَٰنِ فَتَكْفُرُونَ ﴿١٠﴾﴾

﴾Those who disbelieve will be addressed [at the time of entering the Fire]: 'Allah's aversion was greater towards you [in the worldly life when you used to reject the Faith] than your aversion towards one another [now in the fire of Hell, as you are now enemies to one another], when you were called to the Faith but you used to refuse.'﴿ *(Qur'an 40: 10)*

They will also hate those who were dear to them and were their close friends in this world. They will pray against them and ask for their punishment to be increased:

﴿يَوْمَ تُقَلَّبُ وُجُوهُهُمْ فِى ٱلنَّارِ يَقُولُونَ يَٰلَيْتَنَآ أَطَعْنَا ٱللَّهَ وَأَطَعْنَا ٱلرَّسُولَا۠ ﴿٦٦﴾ وَقَالُوا۟ رَبَّنَآ إِنَّآ أَطَعْنَا سَادَتَنَا وَكُبَرَآءَنَا فَأَضَلُّونَا ٱلسَّبِيلَا۠ ﴿٦٧﴾ رَبَّنَآ ءَاتِهِمْ ضِعْفَيْنِ مِنَ ٱلْعَذَابِ وَٱلْعَنْهُمْ لَعْنًا كَبِيرًا ﴿٦٨﴾﴾

﴾On the Day when their faces will be turned over in the Fire, they will say: 'Oh! would that we had obeyed Allah and obeyed the Messenger [Muhammad].' And they will say: 'Our Lord! Verily, we obeyed our chiefs and our great ones, and they misled us from the [Right] Way. Our Lord! Give them double torment and curse them with a mighty curse!'﴿ *(Qur'an 33: 66-68)*

---

[14] *Tafseer Ibn Katheer*, 6/92.

Because of their intense hatred of those who led them astray, they will ask Allah (ﷻ) to show them those who misguided them so that they might step on them:

﴿ وَقَالَ ٱلَّذِينَ كَفَرُوا۟ رَبَّنَآ أَرِنَا ٱلَّذَيْنِ أَضَلَّانَا مِنَ ٱلْجِنِّ وَٱلْإِنسِ نَجْعَلْهُمَا تَحْتَ أَقْدَامِنَا لِيَكُونَا مِنَ ٱلْأَسْفَلِينَ ﴿٢٩﴾ ﴾

﴿And those who disbelieve will say: 'Our Lord! Show us those among jinn and men who led us astray, that we may crush them under our feet so that they become the lowest.'﴾ *(Qur'an 41: 29)*

When they enter the Fire, they will raise their voices, cursing one another, then they will wish increased torment on one another:

﴿ ... كُلَّمَا دَخَلَتْ أُمَّةٌ لَّعَنَتْ أُخْتَهَا ۖ حَتَّىٰٓ إِذَا ٱدَّارَكُوا۟ فِيهَا جَمِيعًا قَالَتْ أُخْرَىٰهُمْ لِأُولَىٰهُمْ رَبَّنَا هَٰٓؤُلَآءِ أَضَلُّونَا فَـَٔاتِهِمْ عَذَابًا ضِعْفًا مِّنَ ٱلنَّارِ ۖ ... ﴿٣٨﴾ ﴾

﴿...Every time a new nation enters, it curses its sister nation [that went before] until they will be gathered all together in the Fire. The last of them will say to the first of them: 'Our Lord! These misled us, so give them a double torment of the Fire.'...﴾ *(Qur'an 7: 38)*

2 - THE STATE OF SINNERS WHO WERE BELIEVERS

Some of the believers may have committed sins which mean that they will be faced with horrors and difficulties. Here we will look at the cases of some sinners and the trials that will befall them on that Day.

1) Those who did not pay zakah

One of the greatest rights that Allah has over people is zakah, which is what is due from one's wealth. Those who do not pay zakah from their wealth will be punished by this wealth on that great Day. The texts tell us that their punishment may take various forms.

1) A man's wealth will appear to him in the form of a huge bald snake with two black spots above its eyes. It will seize him around his neck, saying, "I am your wealth, I am your treasure." In *Ṣaḥeeḥ Bukhari* it is narrated that Abu Hurayrah (رَضِيَ ٱللَّهُ عَنْهُ) stated: the Messenger of Allah (ﷺ) said:

> "Whoever is given wealth by Allah and he does not pay zakah on it, his wealth will appear to him on the Day of Resurrection like a huge bald snake with two black spots over its eyes. It will seize him on the Day of Resurrection and will say, 'I am your wealth, I am your treasure.'" Then he recited:
>
> ﴿ وَلَا يَحْسَبَنَّ ٱلَّذِينَ يَبْخَلُونَ بِمَآ ءَاتَىٰهُمُ ٱللَّهُ مِن فَضْلِهِۦ هُوَ خَيْرًا لَّهُم بَلْ هُوَ شَرٌّ لَّهُمْ سَيُطَوَّقُونَ مَا بَخِلُوا۟ بِهِۦ يَوْمَ ٱلْقِيَـٰمَةِ ... ﴿١٨٠﴾ ﴾
>
> ﴿And let not those who covetously withhold of that which Allah has bestowed on them of His Bounty [wealth] think that it is good for them [and so they do not pay the obligatory Zakah]. Nay, it will be worse for them; the things which they covetously withheld, shall be tied to their necks like a collar on the Day of Resurrection...﴾ *(Qur'an 3: 180)*[15]

2) The wealth on which zakah is withheld will be brought forth, and if it was gold and silver, it will be made into plates of fire with which its owner will be tormented. If the wealth was in the form of livestock, camels or cattle or sheep, they will be sent to torment their owner. Allah (سُبْحَانَهُ وَتَعَالَىٰ) says:

---

15 *Mishkaat al-Maṣaabeeḥ*, 1/559, hadith no. 1774.

﴿ ... وَٱلَّذِينَ يَكْنِزُونَ ٱلذَّهَبَ وَٱلْفِضَّةَ وَلَا يُنفِقُونَهَا فِى سَبِيلِ
ٱللَّهِ فَبَشِّرْهُم بِعَذَابٍ أَلِيمٍ ٣٤ يَوْمَ يُحْمَىٰ عَلَيْهَا فِى نَارِ جَهَنَّمَ
فَتُكْوَىٰ بِهَا جِبَاهُهُمْ وَجُنُوبُهُمْ وَظُهُورُهُمْ هَٰذَا مَا كَنَزْتُمْ
لِأَنفُسِكُمْ فَذُوقُوا۟ مَا كُنتُمْ تَكْنِزُونَ ٣٥ ﴾

﴿...And those who hoard up gold and silver [*Al-Kanz*: the money, the Zakah of which has not been paid] and spend them not in the way of Allah, announce unto them a painful torment. On the Day when that [*Al-Kanz*: money, gold and silver, the Zakah of which has not been paid] will be heated in the fire of Hell and with it will be branded their foreheads, their flanks, and their backs, [and it will be said unto them]: 'This is the treasure which you hoarded for yourselves. Now taste of what you used to hoard.'﴾ *(Qur'an 9: 34-35)*

In Muslim it is narrated that Abu Hurayrah ( ) said: the Messenger of Allah ( ) said:

"There is no one who owns gold or silver and does not pay what is due on them, but on the Day of Resurrection plates of Fire will be served to him. They will be heated in the Fire of Hell, then his sides, forehead and back will be branded with them. Every time they cool down, they will be heated again and put back on him, for a day which will be as long as fifty thousand years, until judgement is passed among mankind, and he will be shown his destiny, either Paradise or Hell.'

It was said, 'O' Messenger of Allah, what about camels?'

He said, 'There is no one who owns camels and does not pay what is due on them, (which includes) milking them on the day when they come to drink water, but on the

Day of Resurrection he will be thrown on his face in a spacious plain as wide as possible. Not a single little camel will be missing from them, but they will all step on him with their hooves and bite him with their mouths. When the first of them leaves him, the last will come, for a day which will be as long as fifty thousand years, until judgement is passed among mankind, and he will be shown his destiny, either Paradise or Hell.'

It was said, 'O' Messenger of Allah, what about cattle and sheep?'

He said, 'There is no one who owns cattle and sheep and does not pay what is due on them, but on the Day of Resurrection he will be thrown on his face in a spacious plain as wide as possible. Not a single animal will be missing from them, not even those with mutilated horns, missing horns or defective horns, but they will gore him with their horns and will all step on him with their hooves. When the first of them leaves him, the last will come, for a day which will be as long as fifty thousand years, until judgement is passed among mankind, and he will be shown his destiny, either Paradise or Hell.'"[16]

2) The arrogant

Arrogance is a major sin according to the laws of shari'ah. Allah hates the arrogant very much, and when He resurrects His slaves, He will gather the arrogant in a humiliating image. According to a hadith narrated by Tirmidhi from 'Amr ibn Shu'ayb from his father from his grandfather, the Messenger of Allah (ﷺ) said:

---

[16] Muslim: *Kitaab az-Zakah, Baab Ithm Maani' az-Zakah*, 2/680, hadith no. 987. The hadith is also to be found in the books of *Ṣaḥeeḥ* and *Sunan*, narrated from many of the *Ṣaḥaabah*. See *Jaami' al-Uṣool*, 4/554.

"The arrogant will be gathered like small ants in the form of men on the Day of Resurrection, overwhelmed by humiliation from all sides."[17]

Small ants are something to which people pay no attention; they step on them without even realizing.

As Allah hates the arrogant, so too He hates the names that they give to themselves out of pride and arrogance. These names, in which they used to rejoice when they heard them, are the most hated, despised and loathsome of names to Allah.

Bukhari, Muslim and Tirmidhi narrated from Abu Hurayrah (رضي الله عنه) that the Prophet (ﷺ) said:

> "The most insignificant name before Allah on the Day of Resurrection will be that of a man who was called *Malik al-Amlaak* (king of kings)." Muslim added, in one report, "There is no King except Allah, may He be glorified."

Muslim and Aḥmad narrated it from Abu Hurayrah with the wording:

> "The most hated and despised man before Allah on the Day of Resurrection will be a man who was called *Malik al-Amlaak* (king of kings); there is no King except Allah."[18]

Ibn Baṭṭaal said: if the name is one of the most humiliating of names, the person who is called by it will be one of the most humiliated of people.[19]

---

[17] *Mishkaat al-Maṣaabeeḥ*, 2/635, hadith no. 5112; its *isnaad* is *ḥasan* as the editor of *Al-Mishkaat* stated.

[18] *Silsilat al-Aḥaadeeth aṣ-Ṣaḥeeḥah*, 2/619, hadith no. 914.

[19] *Fatḥ al-Baari*, 10/589.

3) Sins for which Allah will not speak to a person or praise him

There are many texts which discourage sins by warning that on the Day of Resurrection, Allah will not speak to those who commit them, nor will He praise them, and theirs will be a painful torment.

Among these sinners are those who conceal what Allah has revealed of the Scripture. These are the rabbis and monks and scholars who conceal the knowledge that they have in order to please rulers or to serve some interest, or for the purpose of worldly gains, such as when the rabbis and monks concealed the knowledge that they had from their own books of the characteristics of the Messenger (ﷺ), and denied his Prophethood, even though they knew it as well as they knew their own sons.

Allah (سبحانه وتعالى) says concerning these people:

﴿إِنَّ ٱلَّذِينَ يَكۡتُمُونَ مَآ أَنزَلَ ٱللَّهُ مِنَ ٱلۡكِتَٰبِ وَيَشۡتَرُونَ بِهِۦ ثَمَنٗا قَلِيلًا أُوْلَٰٓئِكَ مَا يَأۡكُلُونَ فِي بُطُونِهِمۡ إِلَّا ٱلنَّارَ وَلَا يُكَلِّمُهُمُ ٱللَّهُ يَوۡمَ ٱلۡقِيَٰمَةِ وَلَا يُزَكِّيهِمۡ وَلَهُمۡ عَذَابٌ أَلِيمٌ ﴿١٧٤﴾ أُوْلَٰٓئِكَ ٱلَّذِينَ ٱشۡتَرَوُاْ ٱلضَّلَٰلَةَ بِٱلۡهُدَىٰ وَٱلۡعَذَابَ بِٱلۡمَغۡفِرَةِۚ فَمَآ أَصۡبَرَهُمۡ عَلَى ٱلنَّارِ ﴿١٧٥﴾﴾

﴾Verily, those who conceal what Allah has sent down of the Book, and purchase a small gain therewith [of worldly things], they eat into their bellies nothing but fire. Allah will not speak to them on the Day of Resurrection, nor purify them, and theirs will be a painful torment. Those are they who have purchased error at the price of guidance, and torment at the price of forgiveness. So how bold they are [for evil deeds which will push them] to the Fire.﴿ *(Qur'an 2: 174-175)*

Ibn Katheer said in his commentary on the *aayah*, ﴾Allah will not speak to them on the Day of Resurrection, nor purify them﴿: "That is because He will be angry with them, because they concealed what they knew, so they will deserve His anger. He will not look at them, or purify them, i.e., He will not praise them[20]; on the contrary, He will subject them to a painful torment."[21]

Abu Hurayrah (رضي الله عنه) narrated that the Messenger of Allah (ﷺ) said:

> "Whoever is asked about knowledge that he has but conceals will be bridled with reins of fire on the Day of Resurrection."

This is narrated and classed as *hasan* by Abu Dawood and Tirmidhi; it is also narrated by Ibn Maajah and by Ibn Ḥibbaan in his *Ṣaheeh*, and by Al-Bayhaqi. Al-Ḥaakim narrated something similar to it, and said that it is *ṣaḥeeḥ* according to the conditions of the two *shaykhs* (Bukhari and Muslim), although they did not narrate it. According to a version narrated by Ibn Maajah, he (ﷺ) said:

> "There is no man who has knowledge which he conceals but he will be brought forth on the Day of Resurrection bridled with reins of fire."[22]

Among those with whom Allah (سبحانه وتعالى) will be angry on the Day of Resurrection, and will neither speak to nor praise, and who will have a painful torment, are those who break the covenant that they had made with Allah and sell their faith for a worthless price, those who swear a false oath for some insignificant worldly gain. Allah says:

﴿ إِنَّ ٱلَّذِينَ يَشْتَرُونَ بِعَهْدِ ٱللَّهِ وَأَيْمَٰنِهِمْ ثَمَنًا قَلِيلًا أُو۟لَٰٓئِكَ لَا خَلَٰقَ لَهُمْ فِى ٱلْءَاخِرَةِ وَلَا يُكَلِّمُهُمُ ٱللَّهُ وَلَا يَنظُرُ إِلَيْهِمْ يَوْمَ ٱلْقِيَٰمَةِ وَلَا يُزَكِّيهِمْ وَلَهُمْ عَذَابٌ أَلِيمٌ ﴿٧٧﴾ ﴾

---

[20] The Arabic word *yuzakkeehim*, translated here as "purify them", may also mean "praise them", which is the meaning chosen here by Ibn Katheer. (Translator)

[21] *Tafseer Ibn Katheer*, 1/363.

[22] *At-Targheeb wa't-Tarheeb* by Al-Ḥaafiẓ al-Mundhiri, 1/97.

> ﴾Verily, those who purchase a small gain at the cost of Allah's Covenant and their oaths, they shall have no portion in the Hereafter [Paradise]. Neither will Allah speak to them nor look at them on the Day of Resurrection nor will He purify them, and they shall have a painful torment.﴿ *(Qur'an 3: 77)*

Ibn Katheer quoted many *aḥaadeeth* which have to do with this *aayah*, including the hadith narrated by Muslim and the authors of *Sunan*, and by Aḥmad, from Abu Dharr, who said: The Messenger of Allah (ﷺ) said:

> "There are three to whom Allah will not speak on the Day of Resurrection, and He will not look at them or praise them, and theirs will be a painful torment.' I said, 'O' Messenger of Allah, who are they? They are indeed lost and doomed.' The Messenger of Allah repeated that three times, then he said: '(They are) the one who lets his garment hang down below his ankles (*isbaal*); the one who sells his goods by means of false oaths; and the one who reminds others of his favours.'"

Bukhari and Muslim narrated on the authority of 'Abdullah that the Messenger of Allah (ﷺ) said:

> "Whoever swears an oath in which he is lying in order to take a Muslim's wealth unlawfully, will meet Allah when He is angry with him."

Bukhari narrated from 'Abdullah ibn Abi Awfaa that a man displayed some goods for sale in the market-place, and swore by Allah that he had been offered more than what a man was offering him, in order to persuade him to buy. Then this *aayah* (verse) was revealed: ﴾Verily, those who purchase a small gain at the cost of Allah's Covenant and their oaths...﴿ *(Qur'an 3: 77)*

Aḥmad, Abu Dawood and Tirmidhi narrated on the authority of Abu Hurayrah (رضي الله عنه) that the Messenger of Allah (ﷺ) said:

> "There are three to whom Allah will not speak on the Day of Resurrection, and He will not look at them or praise them, and theirs will be a painful torment: a man who denies his surplus water to the wayfarer; a man who swears an oath concerning his goods for sale after '*Aṣr*, i.e., swears a false oath; and a man who swears allegiance to a leader, and if he gives him something he remains loyal to him, otherwise he does not."

- Tirmidhi said: it is *ṣaḥeeḥ ḥasan* hadith.[23]

Bukhari narrated in his *Ṣaḥeeḥ* from Abu Hurayrah (رضي الله عنه) that the Prophet (ﷺ) said:

> "There are three to whom Allah will not speak on the Day of Resurrection, and He will not look at them: a man who swears an oath about his goods for sale, saying that he has been offered more for them than he is being offered, and he is lying; a man who swears a false oath after '*Aṣr* in order to take a Muslim's wealth wrongfully; and a man who withholds his surplus water. Allah will say on the Day of Resurrection: today I will deprive you of My bounty, just as you deprived others of the bounty of things that you did not make."[24]

Among the sins for which Allah warns that He will not speak to a person or look at him or praise him, in addition to those mentioned above, are: *zina* (adultery) on the part of an old man, lying on the part

---

[23] *Tafseer Ibn Katheer*, 2/60.

[24] Bukhari, *Kitaab at-Tawḥeed, Baab Qawl Allah, Wujuhun yawma'idhin naaḍirah, Fatḥ al-Baari*, 13/419.

of a king, arrogance on the part of a poor man, disobedience to one's parents, imitation of men by women, *diyaathah* (cuckoldry, lack of protective jealousy towards one's womenfolk), anal intercourse with one's wife, and letting one's garment drag along the ground out of pride.

In *Ṣaḥeeḥ Muslim* and *Sunan an-Nasaa'i* it is narrated that Abu Hurayrah (رضي الله عنه) related: The Messenger of Allah (ﷺ) said:

> "There are three to whom Allah will not speak on the Day of Resurrection, and He will not praise them or look at them, and theirs will be a painful torment: an old man who commits *zina* (adultery), a king who tells lies, and a poor man who is arrogant."[25]

In *Musnad Aḥmad*, *Sunan an-Nasaa'i* and *Mustadrak al-Ḥaakim*, it is narrated that 'Abdullah ibn 'Amr (رضي الله عنه) reported: The Messenger of Allah (ﷺ) said:

> "There are three at whom Allah will not look on the Day of Resurrection: the one who disobeys his parents, the woman who imitates men, and the *duyooth* (man who has no protective jealousy towards his womenfolk)."[26]

It is narrated from Abu Hurayrah (رضي الله عنه) that the Messenger of Allah (ﷺ) said:

> "The one who has intercourse with his wife in her back passage, Allah will not look at him (on the Day of Resurrection)." - He narrated it in *Sharḥ as-Sunnah*.[27]

---

[25] *Ṣaḥeeḥ al-Jaami' aṣ-Ṣagheer*, 3/73, hadith no. 3064.

[26] *Ṣaḥeeḥ al-Jaami' aṣ-Ṣagheer*, 3/74, hadith no. 3066.

[27] *Mishkaat as-Maṣabeeḥ*, 2/184, hadith no. 3194. The editor of *Al-Mishkaat* said: This is narrated by Nasaa'i in *Al-Kubra*, and it is a ṣaḥeeḥ hadith.

It is narrated by Bukhari and Muslim from Abu Hurayrah (ﷺ) that the Messenger of Allah (ﷺ) said:

> "On the Day of Resurrection, Allah will not look at the one who drags his garment out of pride."[28]

It is also narrated in *Saheeḥayn* (Bukhari and Muslim) from Ibn 'Umar that the Prophet (ﷺ) said:

> "Whoever drags his garment out of pride, Allah will not look at him on the Day of Resurrection."[29]

It is further narrated from Ibn 'Umar that the Prophet (ﷺ) said:

> "*Isbaal* (letting one's garment hang down below the ankles) may apply to the lower garment, the shirt and the turban. Whoever lets his garment drag out of pride, Allah will not look at him on the Day of Resurrection."

- This is narrated by Abu Dawood, Nasaa'i and Ibn Maajah.[30]

4) The rich who are living in the lap of luxury

Those who are content with the life of this world, and who enjoy a great deal of luxury, will have a hard time on the Day of Resurrection. The Messenger (ﷺ) has told us that the one who frequently has a full stomach in this world will feel hungry for a long time on the Day of Resurrection. In *Sunan at-Tirmidhi*, *Sunan ibn Maajah* and *Mustadrak al-Ḥaakim* it is narrated that the Messenger (ﷺ) said to one of his Companions:

---

[28] *Mishkaat al-Maṣaabeeḥ*, 2/472, hadith no. 4311.

[29] Ibid, 2/472, hadith no. 4312.

[30] Its *isnaad* is *ṣaḥeeḥ* as stated by the editor of *Mishkaat al-Maṣaabeeḥ*, 2/474, hadith no. 4332.

> "Withhold your burps from us, for those who are most satisfied in this world will be hungry for the longest time on the Day of Resurrection."[31]

And he told us that those who own a lot of wealth and worldly luxuries will have the least reward on the Day of Resurrection, unless they spent their wealth in good ways. Both Bukhari and Muslim narrated that Abu Dharr said:

> "Those who have the most will have the least on the Day of Resurrection, except for those upon whom Allah bestowed wealth, and they started giving it away left and right, front and back, and used it to do good."[32]

Paucity of *ḥasanaat* (good deeds) will delay their entry and cause others to go ahead of them, after they were foremost in this world. In *Sunan ibn Maajah* it is narrated that Abu Dharr said: The Messenger of Allah (ﷺ) said:

> "Those who have a lot will be the lowest in status on the Day of Resurrection, except those who said with their wealth, 'this way and that way' (i.e., spending in the way of Allah), and earned it from good sources.'"[33]

The Messenger (ﷺ) also told us that those who indulge heavily in worldly luxuries and wealth will not be able to overcome the obstacles and terrors of the Day of Resurrection. In *Shu'ab al-Eemaan* it is narrated that Umm ad-Darda' said: "I said to Abu'd-Darda', 'Why do you not ask as So and so has asked?' He said, 'I heard the Messenger of Allah (ﷺ) say, 'Ahead of you there is a very

---

[31] The *isnaad* of this hadith is quoted by *Shaykh* Naaṣiruddeen al-Albaani in *Silsilat al-Aḥaadeeth aṣ-Ṣaḥeeḥah*, hadith no. 343.

[32] *Ṣaḥeeḥ al-Jaami' aṣ-Ṣagheer*, 2/165, hadith no. 1950.

[33] *Silsilat al-Aḥaadeeth aṣ-Ṣaḥeeḥah*, 4/364, hadith no. 1766.

difficult obstacle which those who are burdened (with wealth and luxury) will not be able to overcome.'"[34]

5) Exposure of the betrayer

It is narrated on the authority of Ibn 'Umar that the Messenger of Allah (ﷺ) said:

> "When Allah gathers the first and the last on the Day of Resurrection, a banner will be raised for every betrayer, and it will be said, 'This is the betrayer of So and so the son of So and so.'"[35]

The betrayer is the one who makes a promise then does not fulfil it. The banner is a large flag which is not carried by anyone except the leader of the army at war, or the standard-bearer of an army, so that the people follow him.[36] So a banner will be erected for the betrayer, on which his betrayal will be written, and he will be exposed on the Day of Resurrection. This banner will be placed at his backside. Muslim narrated that Abu Sa'eed said: The Messenger of Allah (ﷺ) said:

> "For every betrayer a banner will be raised at his backside on the Day of Resurrection."[37]

The greater the act of betrayal, the higher the banner will be raised on that great Day. It is narrated that Abu Sa'eed related: The Messenger of Allah (ﷺ) said:

---

[34] *Mishkaat al-Maṣaabeeḥ*, 2/607, hadith no. 5204. In *Ṣaḥeeḥ al-Jaami'* it is also attributed to Al-Ḥaakim. See *Ṣaḥeeḥ al-Jaami'*, 2/178, hadith no. 1997.

[35] Muslim, 3/1359, hadith no. 1735. The hadith is also narrated by Bukhari, Abu Dawood, Tirmidhi and others.

[36] *Sharḥ an-Nawawi 'ala Muslim*, 11/42.

[37] Muslim, 3/1361, hadith no. 1738.

> "On the Day of Resurrection, for every betrayer a banner will be raised according to the extent of his betrayal, and no betrayal is greater than that of a ruler."[38]

Ruler here refers to leader or *khaleefah*; his betrayal is regarded as being so bad because it affects many people, and because the leader or ruler possesses power and authority, so he has no need to resort to betrayal.

Allah will make the punishment take this form because this is the way in which people will understand the punishment... The Arabs used to raise a banner beside betrayers in their gatherings and on the occasion of Ḥajj, and they paraded the offender with a description of his crime.[39]

6) *Al-Ghalool*: Stealing from war booty before it is distributed

Ghalool means stealing from the war booty, before it is distributed. This is a sin which involves some measure of selfishness and greed. Allah (ﷻ) has warned the one who steals from the war booty and has threatened to expose him before all creatures on the Day of Resurrection, by making him carry whatever he stole on that Day:

﴿ ... وَمَن يَغْلُلْ يَأْتِ بِمَا غَلَّ يَوْمَ ٱلْقِيَـٰمَةِ ۚ ثُمَّ تُوَفَّىٰ كُلُّ نَفْسٍ مَّا كَسَبَتْ وَهُمْ لَا يُظْلَمُونَ ﴿١٦١﴾ ﴾

> ﴾...And whosoever deceives his companions as regards the booty, he shall bring forth on the Day of Resurrection that which he took [illegally]. Then every person shall be paid in full what he has earned, and they shall not be dealt with unjustly.﴿ *(Qur'an 3: 161)*

Qurṭubi said in his commentary on this *aayah*: "i.e., he will be brought forth carrying it on his back and around his neck, tormented

---

[38] Ibid.

[39] *At-Tadhkirah* by Qurṭubi, 297.

by having to bear its weight and terrified by its noise, rebuked in the open for his betrayal in front of all creatures."[40]

Ghalool also includes the stealing of rulers, employees, workers and governors from the public coffers. The Messenger (ﷺ) explained how those who steal in this manner will carry the things that they stole on the Day of Resurrection. This is narrated in more than one hadith. It is narrated on the authority of Abu Hurayrah (رضي الله عنه) that,

> "The Messenger of Allah (ﷺ) stood among us one day, and mentioned *ghalool* and how serious this matter is. Then he said, 'I do not want to see any of you coming on the Day of Resurrection with a bellowing camel on his shoulders, saying, 'O' Messenger of Allah, help me,' and I will say to him, 'I cannot do anything for you, I conveyed the message to you."
> 'I do not want to see any of you coming on the Day of Resurrection with a neighing horse on his shoulders, saying, 'O' Messenger of Allah, help me,' and I will say to him, 'I cannot do anything for you, I conveyed the message to you."'
> 'I do not want to see any of you coming on the Day of Resurrection with a bleating sheep on his shoulders, saying, 'O' Messenger of Allah, help me,' and I will say to him, 'I cannot do anything for you, I conveyed the message to you."
> 'I do not want to see any of you coming on the Day of Resurrection with a screaming soul on his shoulders, saying, 'O' Messenger of Allah, help me,' and I will say to him, 'I cannot do anything for you, I conveyed the message to you."

---

40 *Tafseer al-Qurṭubi*, 4/256.

> 'I do not want to see any of you coming on the Day of Resurrection with a flapping banner on his head, saying, 'O' Messenger of Allah, help me,' and I will say to him, 'I cannot do anything for you, I conveyed the message to you."
>
> 'I do not want to see any of you coming on the Day of Resurrection with gold and silver on his shoulders, saying, 'O' Messenger of Allah, help me,' and I will say to him, 'I cannot do anything for you, I conveyed the message to you.""'

Agreed upon - this version is narrated by Muslim, and it is the most complete.[41]

Ṭabaraani narrated in *Al-Mu'jam al-Kabeer*, Al-Bayhaqi narrated in *As-Sunan* and Al-Ḥumaydi narrated in *Al-Musnad* that the Messenger (ﷺ) put 'Ubaadah ibn aṣ-Ṣaamit in charge of the *ṣadaqah* (zakah), then he told him:

> "Fear Allah, O' Abu'l-Waleed, lest you come on the Day of Judgement with a bellowing camel, carrying it on your shoulder, or a lowing cow, or a bleating sheep."[42]

In his *Tafseer*, Ibn Katheer quotes several frightening *aḥaadeeth* about *ghalool*, including *ghalool* on the part of workers who steal from the *ṣadaqah*. He quoted the hadith of Abu Ḥumayd as-Saa'adi who said,

> "The Messenger of Allah (ﷺ) put a man from Azd who was called Ibn al-Latbiyah in charge of the *sadaqah*, and he came and said, 'This is for you, and this was given to me as a gift.' The Messenger of Allah (ﷺ) stood up on

---

[41] *Mishkaat al-Maṣaabeeḥ*, 2/401, hadith no. 3995.

[42] *Silsilat al-Aḥaadeeth aṣ-Ṣaheeḥah*, 2/537, hadith no. 857. The hadith is *ṣaḥeeḥ*.

the minbar and said: 'What is the matter with a worker whom we sent out to do a task, and he says, 'This is for you and this is for me? Why does he not sit in the house of his mother and father, and see if anyone would bring him a gift? By the One in Whose hand is the soul of Muhammad, no one of you takes anything from it, but he will come with it on his shoulders on the Day of Resurrection, even if it is a bellowing camel, a lowing cow or a bleating sheep.'" - This is narrated by Bukhari and Muslim.[43]

7) One who seizes land by force

It is narrated that 'Abdullah ibn 'Umar said: The Prophet (ﷺ) said:

> "Whoever seizes any portion of land unlawfully will be swallowed up by it on the Day of Resurrection, and will sink to the seventh earth."[44]

8) One who is two-faced

The most evil of people on the Day of Resurrection will be the one who is fickle, who is not consistent in his attitude, but presents one face to some people and another face to others. Bukhari and Muslim narrated in their *Saheehs* that Abu Hurayrah (رضي الله عنه) said: The Messenger of Allah (ﷺ) said:

> "You will find the most evil of people on the Day of Resurrection, the one who is two-faced, who presents one face to one group of people and another face to another group."[45]

---

[43] *Tafseer Ibn Katheer*, 2/145.

[44] Bukhari: *Kitaab ar-Riqaaq, Baab Ithm man ẓalama shay'an min al-Arḍ, Fatḥ al-Baari*, 5/103.

[45] *Mishkaat al-Maṣaabeeḥ*, 2/578, hadith no. 4820.

It is narrated in some *aḥaadeeth* that this kind of person will have a tongue of fire on the Day of Resurrection. It is narrated by Abu Dawood (and the following version is by him), and by Bukhari in *Al-Adab al-Mufrad* and by Ad-Daarimi, Abu Ya'la and others, that 'Ammaar ibn Yaasir (ﷺ) said: The Messenger of Allah (ﷺ) said:

> "Whoever is two-faced in this world, will have a tongue of fire on the Day of Resurrection."[46]

9) The ruler who stays aloof from his people

Abu Dawood, Ibn Maajah and Al-Ḥaakim narrated with a *ṣaḥeeḥ isnaad* that Abu Maryam al-Azdi related that the Messenger of Allah (ﷺ) said:

> "Whoever is put in charge of any of the affairs of the Muslims and remains aloof from them and pays no attention to their needs and poverty, Allah will remain aloof from him on the Day of Resurrection, and will pay no attention to his needs and poverty."[47]

10) The one who begs when he has the means of being independent

The one who begs from people when he has the means of being independent will be resurrected with scratches on his face. Abu Dawood, Nasaa'i, Tirmidhi, Ad-Daarimi and others narrated that 'Abdullah ibn Mas'ood related: The Messenger of Allah (ﷺ) said:

> "Whoever begs from people when he has the means of being independent, his begging will appear on the Day of Resurrection as scratches on his face." He was asked,

---

[46] *Silsilat al-Aḥaadeeth aṣ-Ṣaḥeeḥah*, 2/584, hadith no. 892.

[47] *Ṣaḥeeḥ al-Jaami' aṣ-Ṣagheer*, 5/368, hadith no. 6471.

> "O' Messenger of Allah, what are the means of being independent?" He said: "Fifty dirhams, or the equivalent amount in gold."[48]

In *Musnad al-Imam Aḥmad*, it is narrated that 'Imraan ibn Ḥuṣayn said: The Messenger of Allah (ﷺ) said:

> "The begging of a rich person will appear as a disfigurement on his face on the Day of Resurrection."[49]

11) Spitting towards the *Qiblah*

The direction of the *Qiblah* is sacred and holy, hence a number of *aḥaadeeth* forbid facing the *Qiblah* or turning one's back towards it when urinating and defecating.

One of the things that the Prophet (ﷺ) forbade was spitting in the direction of the *Qiblah*. He told us that the one who does this will come on the Day of Resurrection with his spit on his face. Al-Bazzaar narrated in his *Musnad*, and Ibn Ḥibbaan and Ibn Khuzaymah narrated in their *Ṣaḥeeḥs*, that Ibn 'Umar said: "The one who spits towards the *Qiblah* will be raised on the Day of Resurrection with it (the spit) on his face."[50]

Abu Dawood narrated in his *Sunan*, and Ibn Ḥibbaan narrated in his *Ṣaḥeeḥ*, that Ḥudhayfah ibn al-Yamaan narrated that the Messenger of Allah (ﷺ) said:

> "Whoever spits towards the *Qiblah* will come on the Day of Resurrection with the spit between his eyes."

---

[48] *Silsilat al-Aḥaadeeth aṣ-Ṣaḥeeḥah*, hadith no. 499.

[49] *Ṣaḥeeḥ al-Jaami' aṣ-Ṣagheer*, 5/208, hadith no. 5747. The editor said: it is *ṣaḥeeḥ*.

[50] *Ṣaḥeeḥ al-Jaami' aṣ-Ṣagheer*, 3/33, hadith no. 2907. *Shaykh* Naaṣir said: it is *ṣaḥeeḥ*. See also the comments of *Shaykh* Naaṣiruddeen al-Albaani on this hadith in *Silsilat al-Aḥaadeeth aṣ-Ṣaḥeeḥah*, hadith no. 223.

- Its *isnaad* is *ṣaḥeeḥ.*[51]

12) One who lies about his dreams

The one who lies about his dreams will be punished on the Day of Resurrection by being told to tie together two grains of barley. The one who eavesdrops on people when they dislike that will be punished by having molten lead poured into his ears on the Day of Resurrection.

Bukhari narrated in his *Ṣaḥeeḥ* from Ibn 'Abbaas that the Prophet (ﷺ) said:

> "Whoever speaks of a dream that he did not see will be told to tie two grains of barley together, and he will never be able to do it. And whoever eavesdrops on people's conversations when they do not like that or they try to move away from him, will have molten lead poured into his ears on the Day of Resurrection."[52]

3 - THE STATE OF THE PIOUS

1) The people will be terrified on the Day of Resurrection, but the pious will not be terrified

One group of the slaves of Allah will not be terrified when the people are terrified, and they will not grieve when the people grieve. They are the *awliya'* (close friends) of the Most Merciful who believed in Allah and strove to obey and worship Allah in preparation for that Day, so Allah (ﷻ) will keep them safe on that Day. When they are resurrected from their graves, they will be met by the angels of the Most Merciful who will calm them down and reassure them.

---

[51] Ibid, hadith no. 222.

[52] Bukhari: *Kitaab Ta'beer ar-Ru'yaa, Baab man kadhaba fi ḥilmihi, Fatḥ al-Baari*, 12/427.

﴿ إِنَّ ٱلَّذِينَ سَبَقَتْ لَهُم مِّنَّا ٱلْحُسْنَىٰٓ أُو۟لَٰٓئِكَ عَنْهَا مُبْعَدُونَ ﴿١٠١﴾ لَا يَسْمَعُونَ حَسِيسَهَا ۖ وَهُمْ فِى مَا ٱشْتَهَتْ أَنفُسُهُمْ خَٰلِدُونَ ﴿١٠٢﴾ لَا يَحْزُنُهُمُ ٱلْفَزَعُ ٱلْأَكْبَرُ وَتَتَلَقَّىٰهُمُ ٱلْمَلَٰٓئِكَةُ هَٰذَا يَوْمُكُمُ ٱلَّذِى كُنتُمْ تُوعَدُونَ ﴿١٠٣﴾ ﴾

﴾Verily, those for whom the good has preceded from Us, they will be removed far therefrom [Hell] [e.g. 'Eesa (Jesus), son of Maryam; 'Uzayr (Ezra)]. They shall not hear the slightest sound of it [Hell], while they abide in that which their ownselves desire. The greatest terror [on the Day of Resurrection] will not grieve them, and the angels will meet them, [with the greeting]: 'This is your Day which you were promised.'﴿

(Qur'an 21: 101-103)

The "greatest terror" is that which will befall people when they are resurrected from their graves:

﴿ ... إِنَّمَا يُؤَخِّرُهُمْ لِيَوْمٍ تَشْخَصُ فِيهِ ٱلْأَبْصَٰرُ ﴿٤٢﴾ ﴾

﴾...But He gives them respite up to a Day when the eyes will stare in horror.﴿ *(Qur'an 14: 42)*

On that Day, the callers of the Most Merciful will call the close friends (*awliya'*) of the Most Merciful, reassuring them:

﴿ يَٰعِبَادِ لَا خَوْفٌ عَلَيْكُمُ ٱلْيَوْمَ وَلَآ أَنتُمْ تَحْزَنُونَ ﴿٦٨﴾ ٱلَّذِينَ ءَامَنُوا۟ بِـَٔايَٰتِنَا وَكَانُوا۟ مُسْلِمِينَ ﴿٦٩﴾ ﴾

﴾[It will be said to the true believers of Islamic Monotheism]: My worshippers! No fear shall be on you this Day, nor shall you grieve, [you] who believed in Our *Aayaat* [proofs, verses, lessons, signs, revelations, etc.] and were Muslims [i.e. who submit totally to Allah's

Will, and believe in the Oneness of Allah - Islamic Monotheism].﴿ *(Qur'an 43: 68-69)*

Elsewhere, Allah (ﷻ) says:

﴿ أَلَآ إِنَّ أَوْلِيَآءَ ٱللَّهِ لَا خَوْفٌ عَلَيْهِمْ وَلَا هُمْ يَحْزَنُونَ ﴿٦٢﴾
ٱلَّذِينَ ءَامَنُوا۟ وَكَانُوا۟ يَتَّقُونَ ﴿٦٣﴾ لَهُمُ ٱلْبُشْرَىٰ فِى ٱلْحَيَوٰةِ ٱلدُّنْيَا
وَفِى ٱلْءَاخِرَةِ ۚ لَا تَبْدِيلَ لِكَلِمَٰتِ ٱللَّهِ ۚ ذَٰلِكَ هُوَ ٱلْفَوْزُ ٱلْعَظِيمُ
﴿٦٤﴾ ﴾

﴾No doubt! Verily the *Awliya'* of Allah, no fear shall come upon them nor shall they greive. Those who believed, and used to fear Allah much [by abstaining from evil deeds and sins and by doing righteous deeds]. For them are glad tidings, in the life of the present world, and in the Hereafter.﴿ *(Qur'an 10: 62-64)*

The reason for this feeling of security which Allah will bestow upon His pious slaves will be that in this world their hearts were filled with fear of Allah, so they stood in prayer at night and fasted by day, and they made preparations for the Day when they would stand before Allah. Allah (ﷻ) tells us that they used to say:

﴿ إِنَّا نَخَافُ مِن رَّبِّنَا يَوْمًا عَبُوسًا قَمْطَرِيرًا ﴿١٠﴾ ﴾

﴾Verily we fear from our Lord a Day, hard and distressful, that will make the faces look horrible [from extreme dislike of it].﴿ *(Qur'an 76: 10)*

Whoever is like this, Allah (ﷻ) will protect him from the evils of that Day, and will keep him safe:

﴿ فَوَقَىٰهُمُ ٱللَّهُ شَرَّ ذَٰلِكَ ٱلْيَوْمِ وَلَقَّىٰهُمْ نَضْرَةً وَسُرُورًا ﴿١١﴾ وَجَزَىٰهُم بِمَا صَبَرُوا۟
جَنَّةً وَحَرِيرًا ﴿١٢﴾ ﴾

﴾So Allah saved them from the evil of that Day, and gave them *Naḍrah* [a light of beauty] and joy. And their recompense shall be Paradise, and silken garments, because they were patient.﴿ *(Qur'an 76: 11-12)*

According to a hadith narrated by Abu Na'eem in Al-Ḥilyah from Shaddaad ibn Aws, the Messenger of Allah (ﷺ) said:

"Allah says, By My Glory and Majesty, I will not give My slave two securities and two terrors. If he feels safe from Me in the world, I will cause him to feel afraid on the Day when I gather My slaves together, and if he fears Me in the world, I will make him feel safe on the Day when I gather My slaves together."[53]

The more sincere a person is towards his Lord, the more secure he will feel on the Day of Resurrection. The monotheists (people of *Tawḥeed*) whose faith was not contaminated with any element of *shirk* will have complete security on the Day of Resurrection. This is indicated by the answer given by Ibraaheem (Abraham) (عليه السلام) to his people, when they tried to scare him with their idols. He responded by saying:

﴿ وَكَيْفَ أَخَافُ مَآ أَشْرَكْتُمْ وَلَا تَخَافُونَ أَنَّكُمْ أَشْرَكْتُم بِٱللَّهِ مَا لَمْ يُنَزِّلْ بِهِۦ عَلَيْكُمْ سُلْطَٰنًا ۚ فَأَىُّ ٱلْفَرِيقَيْنِ أَحَقُّ بِٱلْأَمْنِ ۖ إِن كُنتُمْ تَعْلَمُونَ ﴿٨١﴾ ٱلَّذِينَ ءَامَنُوا۟ وَلَمْ يَلْبِسُوٓا۟ إِيمَٰنَهُم بِظُلْمٍ أُو۟لَٰٓئِكَ لَهُمُ ٱلْأَمْنُ وَهُم مُّهْتَدُونَ ﴿٨٢﴾ ﴾

﴾And how should I fear those whom you associate in worship with Allah [though they can neither benefit nor harm], while you fear not that you have joined in worship with Allah things for which He has not sent

[53] *Silsilat al-Aḥaadeeth aṣ-Ṣaḥeeḥah*, 2/377, hadith no. 742. Its *isnaad* is *ḥasan*.

> down to you any authority. [So] which of the two parties has more right to be in security? If you but know. It is those who believe [in the Oneness of Allah and worship none but Him Alone] and confuse not their Belief with *Ẓulm* [wrong, i.e. by worshipping others besides Allah], for them [only] there is security and they are the guided.﴾
>
> *(Qur'an 6: 81-82)*

2) Those whom Allah will shade with His shade

When the people are standing in that vast arena, beneath the harsh glare of the sun, tasting a torment which even the mighty mountains could not bear, a group of the best among them will be at peace in the shade of the Throne of the Most Merciful, and they will be spared the distress suffered by the rest of the people.

These will be the people of high ambition and sincere resolve, the characteristics represented by the *'aqeedah* (faith) of Islam with its sublime values, or they will be the people who did noble good deeds, which are of great importance in Islam.

Who are these people? Among them will be the just ruler, who had power and authority, but did not abuse that, rather he established justice among the people in accordance with the divinely revealed laws.

And among them will be the young man who grew up worshipping his Lord, restraining himself with the reins of *taqwa* and controlling his whims and desires, so he remained pure all his life.

And among them will be those who frequented the mosques of Allah, finding their rest in being close to the mosques and conversing with Allah; hardly have they left the mosque when they long to return to it.

And among them will be those who loved one another for the sake of Allah, tied together by the bonds of the brotherhood of faith, coming together in righteousness and piety, and parting after doing good deeds.

And among them will be those who shunned the temptation of women, who were prevented by their fear of Allah from falling into sin.

And among them will be the one who spent sincerely for the sake of Allah alone, hiding his charity even from himself.

And among them will be the one whose heart is filled with fear of Allah, so that he weeps for that reason when he is alone and there is no one else with him.

Bukhari and Muslim narrated in their *Saheehs* that Abu Hurayrah (ﷺ) related: The Messenger of Allah (ﷺ) said:

> "There are seven whom (Allah) will shade with His shade on the Day when there will be no shade except His: the just ruler; the young man who grows up worshipping his Lord; the man whose heart is attached to the mosque; two men who love one another for the sake of Allah, meeting and parting for that reason; a man who is invited (to sin) by a woman of high status and beauty, but he says, 'I fear Allah'; a man who gives in charity so secretly that his left hand does not know what his right hand gives; and a man who remembers Allah when he is alone, and his eyes fill with tears."[54]

Many texts indicate that Allah will shade those who love one another for His sake in the shade of His Throne on that Day. Among these reports is the hadith of Abu Hurayrah, narrated by Muslim, in which he said: The Messenger of Allah (ﷺ) said:

---

[54] Bukhari: *Kitaab al-Adhaan, Baab man jalasa fil-Masjid, Fath al-Baari*, 2/143. Also narrated by Muslim, 2/715, hadith no. 103. This version is narrated by Bukhari.

> "Allah will say on the Day of Resurrection, where are those who loved one another for My glory? Today I will shade them with My shade, on the Day when there will be no shade except Mine."[55]

In *Mu'jam aṭ-Ṭabaraani al-Kabeer*, *Musnad Aḥmad*, *Ṣaḥeeḥ ibn Ḥibbaan* and *Mustadrak al-Ḥaakim*, it is narrated that Mu'aadh said that the Messenger of Allah ﷺ said:

> "Those who love one another for the sake of Allah will be in the shade of the Throne."[56]

In the book *Al-Ikhwaan* by Ibn Abi'd-Dunya, it is narrated with a *ṣaḥeeḥ isnaad* from 'Ubaadah ibn aṣ-Ṣaamit that the Messenger of Allah (ﷺ) said:

> "Allah says: 'I grant My love to those who love one another (for My sake), and I will shade them with the shade of the Throne on the Day when there will no shade except My shade.'"[57]

The shade of the Throne will not be restricted only to the seven mentioned in the hadith. Many texts indicate that Allah will shade others too. Ibn Ḥajar al-'Asqallaani compiled a list of the characteristics of those whom Allah will shade, in a book entitled *Ma'rifat al-Khiṣaal al-Mooṣilah ila aẓ-Ẓilaal - Characteristics which will earn one the shade (of Allah).*[58]

Among these attributes is extending the time-limit for a debtor who is in difficulty, or waiving the debt altogether. In *Ṣaḥeeḥ Muslim* and

---

[55] Muslim, 4/1988, hadith no. 2566.

[56] *Ṣaḥeeḥ al-Jaami' aṣ-Ṣagheer*, 2/161, hadith no. 1933.

[57] Ibid, 4/116.

[58] *Fatḥ al-Baari*, 2/144.

Musnad Aḥmad it is narrated from Abu'l-Yusr that the Messenger of Allah (ﷺ) said:

> "Whoever extends the time-limit for a debtor who is in difficulty or waives the debt altogether, Allah will shade him with His shade."[59]

In *Musnad Aḥmad* and *Sunan ad-Daarimi* it is narrated with a *ṣaheeḥ isnaad* from Abu Qataadah that the Messenger of Allah (ﷺ) said:

> "Whoever shows leniency towards a debtor or writes off his debt, will be in the shade of the Throne on the Day of Resurrection."[60]

3) Those who strive to meet their brothers' needs

One of the greatest things that will relieve a person's distress on the Day of Resurrection is his efforts in this world to relieve the distress of those who are in distress, and to help those who are in need, and to make things easy for those who are in difficulty, and to overlook the mistakes of those who err. In Muslim it is narrated that Abu Hurayrah (رضي الله عنه) said: The Messenger of Allah ﷺ said:

> "Whoever relieves a believer of distress in this world, Allah will relieve him of some of the distress of the Day of Resurrection. Whoever makes things easy for those who are in difficulty, Allah will make things easy for him in this world and in the next. Whoever conceals (the faults of) a Muslim in this world, Allah will conceal him (his faults) in this world and in the Hereafter. Allah will help the slave so long as the slave helps his brother."[61]

---

[59] Muslim, 4/2302, hadith no. 3006.

[60] *Ṣaheeḥ al-Jaami' aṣ-Ṣagheer*, 4/364, hadith no. 1452.

[61] *Mishkaat al-Maṣaabeeḥ*, 1/71, hadith no. 204.

Bukhari narrated from 'Abdullah ibn 'Umar that the Messenger of Allah (ﷺ) said:

> "The Muslim is the brother of his fellow-Muslim; he should not mistreat him or let him down. Whoever meets the needs of his brother, Allah will meet his needs, and whoever relieves a Muslim of some distress, Allah will relieve him of some of the distress of the Day of Resurrection. Whoever conceals (the faults of) a Muslim, Allah will conceal him (his faults) in this world and the next."[62]

Ad-Deenoori narrated in *Al-Mujaalisah*, Al-Bayhaqi narrated in *Al-Shu'ab* and Aḍ-Ḍiyaa' narrated in *Al-Mukhtaarah* from Anas that the Prophet (ﷺ) said:

> "Whoever helps his brother in secret, Allah will help him in this world and the next."[63]

4) Those who show leniency to those who are in difficulty

Bukhari and Muslim narrated from Abu Hurayrah (رضي الله عنه) that the Prophet (ﷺ) said:

> "A man used to lend money to people, and he used to say to his servant, 'When you come to one who is in difficulty, let him off, perhaps Allah will let us off.' And when he met Allah, Allah let him off."[64]

Nasaa'i, Ibn Ḥibbaan and Al-Ḥaakim narrated with a *ṣaḥeeḥ isnaad* from Abu Hurayrah (رضي الله عنه) that the Prophet (ﷺ) said:

---

[62] Bukhari: *Kitaab al-Maẓaalim, Baab laa yaẓlim al-Muslim al-Muslim, Fatḥ al-Baari*, 5/97.

[63] *Silsilat al-Aḥaadeeth aṣ-Ṣaḥeeḥah*, 3/218, hadith no. 1217.

[64] *Mishkaat al-Maṣaabeeḥ*, 2/108, hadith no. 2899.

> "There was a man who never did anything good. However, he used to lend money to people, and would say to his messenger, 'Take what they can afford to pay you, and forget about what they cannot afford, and let them off. Perhaps Allah will let us off.' When he died, it was asked, 'Have you ever done anything good?' He said, 'No, but I had a slave and I used to lend money to people. When I sent him to collect the debts, I would tell him, 'Take what they can afford to pay you, and forget about what they cannot afford, and let them off. Perhaps Allah will let us off." Allah said: 'I will let you off.'"[65]

In *Mustadrak al-Ḥaakim* it is narrated with a *ṣaḥeeḥ isnaad* from Ḥudhayfah, 'Uqbah ibn 'Aamir and Abu Mas'ood that the Messenger of Allah (ﷺ) said:

> "Allah will bring forth one of His slaves to whom He had given wealth, and will say to him, 'What did you do in the world?' He will say, 'I did not do anything, O' Lord, but You gave me wealth, and I used to engage in trade with people. One of the ways in which I treated people was that I would be easy-going with those who could afford it and I would postpone payment for those who were in difficulty.' Allah will say, 'I should be more tolerant than you; let My slave off.'"[66]

5) Those who are just in their judgements, towards their families and in any matter which is entrusted to them

Those who are fair and just will be in a high position on the Day of Resurrection, seated on thrones of light on the Right Hand of the

---

[65] *Ṣaḥeeḥ al-Jaami' aṣ-Ṣagheer*, 2/204, hadith no. 2073.

[66] *Ṣaḥeeḥ al-Jaami' aṣ-Ṣagheer*, 1/92, hadith no. 124.

Most Merciful - and both His Hands are Right Hands. Muslim narrated that 'Abdullah ibn 'Amr (رضي الله عنه) related: The Messenger of Allah (ﷺ) said:

> "Those who are fair and just will be with Allah on thrones of light, on the Right Hand of the Most Merciful - and both His Hands are Right Hands - those who were just in their judgements, towards their families and in any matter which was entrusted to them."[67]

6) The *shuhada'* (martyrs) and the *muraabiṭoon* (guards stationed out on the borders of the Muslim state)

When the people will be filled with terror on the Day of Resurrection, the *shaheed* (martyr) will feel no fear. In *Sunan at-Tirmidhi* and *Sunan ibn Maajah* it is narrated that Al-Miqdaam ibn Ma'di Karb related: The Messenger of Allah (ﷺ) said:

> "Before Allah, the *shaheed* has six virtues: he is forgiven from the first drop of blood shed; he will be shown his place in Paradise; he will be protected from the torment of the grave; he will be safe from the greater terror (of the Day of Resurrection); a crown of dignity will be placed on his head, of which one ruby is better than this world and all that is in it; he will be married to seventy-two of *Al-Ḥoor al-'Iyn*; and he will intercede for seventy of his relatives."[68]

The pertinent point in this hadith is that the *shaheed* will be safe from the greater terror, the terror of the Day of Resurrection. Similar to the *shaheed* (martyr) is the *muraabiṭ*, who guards the borders of Islam for

---

[67] Muslim, 3/1458, hadith no. 1827.

[68] *Mishkaat al-Maṣaabeeh*, 2/358, hadith no. 3834. The editor of *Al-Mishkaat* said: its *isnaad* is *ṣaheeh*.

the sake of Allah. If he dies whilst he is guarding the borders of Islam, Allah will keep him safe from the greater terror. Ṭabaraani narrated with a *ṣaḥeeḥ isnaad* from Abu'd-Dardaa' that the Prophet (ﷺ) said:

> "Guarding the borders of Islam for a day is better than fasting for a lifetime. Whoever dies guarding the borders of Islam for the sake of Allah will be kept safe from the greater terror, his provision and breeze will be brought from Paradise, and the reward of the *muraabiṭ* will continue until Allah resurrects him."[69]

One of the ways in which Allah will honour the *shaheed* on the Day of Resurrection will be that He will raise him with his wounds flowing with blood. The colour will be of blood but it will smell like musk. Bukhari narrated from Abu Hurayrah (رضي الله عنه) that the Messenger of Allah (ﷺ) said:

> "By the One in Whose Hand is my soul, no one is wounded for the sake of Allah - and Allah knows best who is wounded for His sake - but he will come on the Day of Resurrection with his wounds flowing with blood. The colour will be of blood but smell like musk."[70]

Tirmidhi, Nasaa'i and Abu Dawood narrated with a *ṣaḥeeḥ isnaad* from Mu'aadh ibn Jabal that he heard the Messenger of Allah (ﷺ) say:

> "Whoever fights for the sake of Allah, even for the interval between two milkings of a camel, will be entitled to Paradise, and whoever is wounded or injured

---

[69] *Ṣaḥeeḥ al-Jaami' aṣ-Ṣagheer*, 3/171, hadith no. 3473.

[70] Bukhari: *Kitaab al-Jihaad, Baab man yujraḥ fi sabeel Allah, Fatḥ al-Baari*, 6/20.

for the sake of Allah, the injury will appear on the Day of Resurrection bleeding copiously, the colour of saffron and with the fragrance of musk."[71]

Ibn Ḥajar said: "The scholars said: 'The reason why he will be resurrected in this state is that it will be a testimony to his virtue, because he sacrificed himself in obeying Allah.'"[72]

7) Those who control their anger

There are many difficult situations in which a person is subjected to annoyance. These may be caused by a relative, a friend or someone to whom one has done a favour. Undoubtedly the annoyance, whether it is something that we hear, see or feel, is something that causes us pain in our hearts and provokes all kinds of feelings that may motivate us to confront them openly. Self-control in such situations is something that only the strongest can achieve.

Islam counts controlling anger as a noble Islamic characteristic, for which a person deserves to be honoured with Paradise as wide as the heavens and the earth, which has been prepared for the pious. Controlling anger is one of the foremost characteristics of the pious.

﴿ ۞ وَسَارِعُوٓا۟ إِلَىٰ مَغْفِرَةٍ مِّن رَّبِّكُمْ وَجَنَّةٍ عَرْضُهَا ٱلسَّمَٰوَٰتُ
وَٱلْأَرْضُ أُعِدَّتْ لِلْمُتَّقِينَ ﴿١٣٣﴾ ٱلَّذِينَ يُنفِقُونَ فِى ٱلسَّرَّآءِ وَٱلضَّرَّآءِ
وَٱلْكَٰظِمِينَ ٱلْغَيْظَ وَٱلْعَافِينَ عَنِ ٱلنَّاسِ ۗ وَٱللَّهُ يُحِبُّ ٱلْمُحْسِنِينَ ﴿١٣٤﴾ ﴾

﴾And march forth in the way [which leads to] forgiveness from your Lord, and for Paradise as wide as the heavens and the earth, prepared for *Al-Muttaqoon* [the pious]. Those who spend [in Allah's Cause] in prosperity and in adversity, who repress anger, and who

---

[71] *Mishkaat al-Maṣaabeeḥ*, 2/355, hadith no. 3825.
[72] *Fatḥ al-Baari*, 6/20.

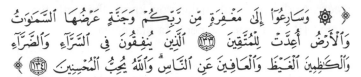

> pardon men; verily, Allah loves *Al-Muḥsinoon* [the good-doers].﴾ *(Qur'an 3: 133-134)*

On the Day of Resurrection, the Lord of Glory will call those who controlled their anger before all of creation, then He will let them choose whichever of *Al-Ḥoor al-'Iyn* they want. Tirmidhi and Abu Dawood narrated from Sahl ibn Mu'aadh ibn Jabal that his father said: The Messenger of Allah (ﷺ) said:

> "Whoever controls his anger when he is able to act upon it, Allah will call him before all of creation on the Day of Resurrection, and will let him choose whichever of *Al-Ḥoor al-'Iyn* he wants."[73]

8) Those who free Muslim slaves

Among the righteous deeds which will enable a person to overcome the difficult obstacles of the Day of Resurrection is freeing slaves. Allah (ﷻ) says:

﴿ فَلَا اقْتَحَمَ الْعَقَبَةَ ﴿١١﴾ وَمَا أَدْرَاكَ مَا الْعَقَبَةُ ﴿١٢﴾ فَكُّ رَقَبَةٍ ﴿١٣﴾ ﴾

> ﴾But he has made no effort to pass on the path that is steep. And what will make you know the path that is steep? [It is] freeing a neck [a slave, etc.].﴾ *(Qur'an 90: 11-13)*

In his *tafseer* of this *aayah*, Ibn Katheer quotes *aḥaadeeth* which explain these verses. Imam Aḥmad said: 'Ali ibn Ibraaheem told us, 'Abdullah, i.e., Ibn Sa'eed ibn Abi Hind told us, from Ismaa'eel ibn Abi Ḥakeem, the freed slave of Aal az-Zubayr, from Sa'eed ibn Mirjaanah, that he heard Abu Hurayrah say: The Messenger of Allah

---

[73] *Mishkaat al-Maṣaabeeḥ*, 2/631, hadith no. 5088. *Shaykh* Naṣir classed its *isnaad* as *ḥasan* in *Ṣaḥeeḥ al-Jaami'* (5/353, hadith no. 6398). He attributed it to Aḥmad and Ṭabaraani, see hadith no. 6394 in *Ṣaḥeeḥ al-Jaami'*.

(ﷺ) said:

> "Whoever frees a believing slave, Allah will free all of his limbs from the Fire because of that, so He will free an arm for an arm, a leg for a leg..."

'Ali ibn al-Ḥusayn said: "Did you hear this from Abu Hurayrah?" Sa'eed said, "Yes." 'Ali ibn al-Ḥusayn called for a slave of his, who was the best of his slaves, saying, "Call Maṭraf." When he (Maṭraf) came to him, he said, "Go, you are free for the sake of Allah." This is narrated by Bukhari, Muslim, Tirmidhi and Nasaa'i, through various *isnaads* from Sa'eed ibn Mirjaanah. According to Muslim, this slave who was set free by 'Ali ibn al-Ḥusayn Zayn al-'Aabideen had been bought for a price of ten thousand dirhams.

Qataadah said, narrating from Saalim ibn Abi al-Ja'd, from Mi'daan ibn Abi Ṭalḥah, that Abu Nujayḥ said: "I heard the Messenger of Allah (ﷺ) say:

> 'Any Muslim man who sets a Muslim man free, Allah will make that the ransom for his bones, bone for bone, saved from the Fire. Any Muslim woman who sets a Muslim woman free, Allah will make that the ransom for her bones, bone for bone, from the Fire."

- This is narrated by Ibn Jareer. This Abu Nujayḥ is 'Amr ibn 'Absah as-Sulami, may Allah be pleased with him.

Imam Aḥmad said: Ḥayawah ibn Shurayḥ told us, Baqiyah told us, Bajeer ibn Sa'd told me, from Khaalid ibn Mi'daan, from Katheer ibn Murrah, from 'Amr ibn 'Absah that he told them that the Prophet (ﷺ) said:

> "Whoever builds a mosque so that Allah will be remembered therein, Allah will build for him a house in Paradise. Whoever frees a Muslim person, that will be

> his ransom from Hell. Whoever turns grey (grows old) in Islam, that grey hair will be a light for him on the Day of Resurrection."

Aḥmad said: Al-Ḥakam ibn Naafi' told us, Jareer told us, from Saleem ibn 'Aamir, that Sharḥabeel ibn as-Samiṭ said to 'Amr ibn 'Absah, "Tell us a hadith to which nothing has been added and of which nothing has been forgotten." 'Amr said: I heard the Messenger of Allah (ﷺ) say:

> "Whoever frees a Muslim slave, that will be his ransom from Hell, limb for limb. Whoever turns grey in Islam, that grey hair will be a light for him on the Day of Resurrection. Whoever shoots an arrow and it reaches (the enemy), whether it hits the target or misses, it will be as if he set free a slave from among the children of Isma'eel." - Abu Dawood and Nasaa'i narrated part of this.

Aḥmad said: Haashim ibn al-Qaasim told us, Al-Faraj told us, Luqmaan told us, from Abu Umaamah from 'Amr ibn 'Absah as-Sulami, who said: "I said to him, 'Tell us a hadith you heard from the Messenger of Allah (ﷺ), in which nothing is missing and there is no confusion.' He said, 'I heard him say:

> 'Whoever has three children in Islam and they die before reaching the age of puberty, Allah will admit him to Paradise by virtue of His mercy towards them. Whoever turns grey in Islam being obedient towards Allah, his grey hair will be a light for him on the Day of Resurrection. Whoever shoots an arrow for the sake of Allah and it reaches the enemy, whether it strikes the target or not, it will be as if he freed a slave, and whoever frees a believing slave, for every limb of (the

> slave's) body, Allah will ransom his respective limbs from the Fire. Whoever spends a pair for the sake of Allah, then Allah will allow him to enter Paradise through whichever of its eight gates he wishes.'""

- These *isnaads* are *jayyid qawiy.* And to Allah be Praise.

Abu Dawood said: 'Eesa ibn Muhammad ar-Rama told us that Damurah told us, from Ibn Abi 'Ablah, from Al-'Areef ibn 'Ayaash ad-Daylami, who said: "We came to Waathilah ibn al-Asqa' and said to him, 'Tell us a hadith to which nothing has been added or taken away.' He got angry and said, 'Some of you recite Qur'an when you have the *Mushaf* hanging up in your homes and he adds to it and takes away from it (by mistake, i.e., no one can be so precise).' We said, 'All we want is a hadith that you heard from the Messenger of Allah (ﷺ).' He said: 'We came to the Messenger of Allah (ﷺ) bringing a companion of ours who was bound to go to Hell because he had committed murder. The Prophet (ﷺ) said,

> 'Free a slave on his behalf, and for every limb of (the slave's body), Allah will ransom his respective limbs from the Fire.'''

- This is narrated by Nasaa'i from the hadith of Ibraaheem ibn Abi 'Ablah, from Al-'Areef ibn 'Ayaash ad-Daylami, from Waathilah.

Aḥmad said: 'Abd aṣ-Ṣamad told us, Hishaam told us, from Qataadah, from Qays al-Judaami, from 'Uqbah ibn 'Aamir al-Juhani, that the Messenger of Allah (ﷺ) said:

> "Whoever frees a Muslim slave, that will be his ransom from the Fire."

And 'Abdul-Wahhaab al-Khaffaaf told us, from Sa'eed from Qataadah, who said: he mentioned to us that Qays al-Judaami narrated from 'Uqbah ibn 'Aamir that the Messenger of Allah (ﷺ) said:

> "Whoever sets free a believing slave, that will be his ransom from the Fire." - It has been reported only by Aḥmad with this *isnaad*.

Imam Aḥmad said: Yaḥyaa ibn Adam and Abu Aḥmad told us, 'Eesa ibn 'Abdur-Raḥmaan al-Bajali told us, from Banu Bajeelah, from Banu Sulaym, from Ṭalḥah ibn Muṣarrif, from 'Abdurl-Rahmaan ibn 'Awsajah, that Al-Baraa' ibn 'Aazib said: A Bedouin came to the Prophet (ﷺ) and said: "O' Messenger of Allah, tell me of an action that will earn me admittance to Paradise." He said,

> "You have asked in a few brief words about a matter that is very vast. *A'taq an-nasamah* and *Fukka ar-raqabah* [both phrases may be translated as 'set slaves free']." He said, "O' Messenger of Allah, are they not the same thing?" He said, "No, *a'taq an-nasamah* means doing it on your own and *fukka ar-raqabah* means helping others to set them free. And give in charity to relatives who mistreat you. If you cannot do that, then feed the hungry, give water to the thirsty, enjoin what is good and forbid what is evil. And if you cannot do that, then restrain your tongue and (speak nothing) but good."[74]

9) The virtue of the *muadh-dhins* (who calls to prayer)

Among those whose virtue will be made manifest on the Day of Resurrection will be the *muadh-dhins*. They will have the longest necks on that Day. Muslim narrated in his *Ṣaḥeeḥ* that Mu'aawiyah ibn Abi Sufyaan said: I heard the Messenger of Allah (ﷺ) say:

> "The *muadh-dhins* will have the longest necks of all the people on the Day of Resurrection."[75]

---

[74] *Tafseer Ibn Katheer*, 7/295.

[75] Muslim, 4/290, hadith no. 387.

A long neck is a sign of beauty, and it is befitting for them because of the work they do, conveying to the people with their voices the words of the *adhaan*, which is a declaration of *Tawḥeed* and the call to prayer.

On that Day, everyone and everything that heard his voice when he raised his voice for *adhaan* (prayer call) in this world will testify in favour of the *muadh-dhin*, Bukhari narrated that Abu Sa'eed al-Khudri said to 'Abdur-Raḥmaan ibn Ṣa'ṣa'ah:

> "I see that you love sheep and the open country. When you are with your sheep or in the open country and you call *adhaan* for the prayer, raise your voice in making the call, for no jinn, human or anything else hears the voice of the *muadh-dhin*, as far as it carries, but it will testify for him on the Day of Resurrection."[76]

10) Those who go grey (grow old) in Islam

Grey hair will be a light for its owner if he is Muslim on the Day of Resurrection, as is stated in the *ṣaḥeeḥ aḥaadeeth*. In *Sunan at-Tirmidhi* and *Sunan an-Nasaa'i* it is narrated from Ka'b ibn Murrah that the Messenger of Allah (ﷺ) said:

> "Whoever turns grey in Islam, his grey hair will be a light for him on the Day of Resurrection."[77]

In *Musnad Aḥmad* and the *Sunans* of Tirmidhi, Nasaa'i and Ibn Ḥibbaan it is narrated that 'Umar ibn 'Absah said: The Messenger of Allah (ﷺ) said:

---

[76] Bukhari: *Kitaab at-Tawḥeed, Baab Qawl an-Nabi*, *"Al-Maahir bil-Qur'an..."*; *Fatḥ al-Baari*, 13/518.

[77] *Ṣaḥeeḥ al-Jaami' aṣ-Ṣagheer*, 5/304, hadith no. 6183. *Shaykh* Naaṣir said that it is *ṣaḥeeḥ*.

> "Whoever turns grey for the sake of Allah, his grey hair will be a light for him on the Day of Resurrection."[78]

Al-Bayhaqi narrated in *Shu'ab al-Eemaan* with a *ḥasan isnaad* from 'Abdullah ibn 'Amr that he said: The Messenger of Allah (ﷺ) said:

> "Grey hair is the light of the Muslim. No man turns grey in Islam but for every grey hair he will have one *hasanah* and his status will be raised by one degree."[79]

- This hadith has corroborating evidence in the *marfoo'* hadith of Abu Hurayrah:

> "Do not pluck grey hair, for it will be a light on the Day of Resurrection. Whoever turns grey in Islam, for every grey hair he will have one *ḥasanah* and his status will be raised by one degree." - This is narrated by Ibn Ḥibbaan with a *ḥasan isnaad*.[80]

It is narrated by Ibn 'Adiy by Al-Bayhaqi in *Al-Shu'ab* that Faddaalah ibn 'Ubayd said: The Messenger of Allah (ﷺ) said:

> "Grey hair is a light on the face of the Muslim. Do you really want to take away your light?"[81]

11) The virtue of *wuḍoo'* (ritual cleansing)

Those who respond to the Messenger (ﷺ), establishing regular prayer and doing *wuḍoo'* as their Prophet commanded them, will be called on the Day of Resurrection with their faces and limbs shining with the traces of *wuḍoo'*. Bukhari narrated that Abu Hurayrah said: I

---

[78] *Ṣaḥeeḥ al-Jaami' aṣ-Ṣagheer*, 5/304, hadith no. 6184. The hadith is *ṣaḥeeḥ* as stated by the editor of the book.

[79] *Silsilat al-Aḥaadeeth aṣ-Ṣaheeḥah*, 3/247, hadith no. 1243.

[80] Ibid.

[81] Ibid, hadith no. 1244.

heard the Messenger of Allah (ﷺ) say:

> "On the Day of Resurrection, my ummah will be called *Al-Ghurr al-Muḥajjaloon* because of the traces of *wuḍoo'*."[82]

Ibn Ḥajar said: "*Ghurr* is the plural of *agharr*, i.e., one who has a *ghurrah* (white spot or blaze). The word ghurrah originally means a white blaze on the face of a horse, but it was then used to indicate beauty, fame and a good reputation. What is meant here is the light that will shine on the faces of the ummah of Muhammad (ﷺ). When they are called before all of creation, they will be called by this name, and this is how they will look.

Muḥajjaloon comes from the word *taḥjeel*, which refers to whiteness on three of a horse's feet. This word comes from *hijl* which means *khulhaal* (anklets). What is meant here is also light."[83]

This *ghurrah* (white blaze) and *taḥjeel* (white limbs) will be the adornment of the believer on the Day of Resurrection. In Muslim it is narrated that Abu Hurayrah said: The Messenger of Allah said: "The adornment of the believer will extend as far as his *wuḍoo'* reached."[84]

By this adornment of light, this ummah will be distinguished on the Day of Resurrection, and the Messenger (ﷺ) will know his ummah from the rest of mankind, with no difference between his Companions and others. In Muslim it is narrated from Abu Hurayrah that the Messenger of Allah (ﷺ) came to a graveyard and said:

> "*As-Salaamu 'alaykum*, O' dwelling of a believing people. *In sha Allah* we will soon join you. Would that

[82] Bukhari: *Kitaab al-Wuḍoo', Baab Faḍl al-Wuḍoo', Fatḥ al-Baari*, 1/235.

[83] *Fatḥ al-Baari*, 1/236.

[84] *Mishkaat al-Maṣaabeeḥ*, 1/96, hadith no. 291.

> we had seen our brothers." They said, "Are we not your brothers, O' Messenger of Allah?" He said, "You are my Companions. Our brothers are those who have not yet come." They said, "How will you recognize those of your ummah who have not yet come, O' Messenger of Allah?" He said, "Do you not see that if a man has a horse with a white blaze and white feet among other horses which do not have these markings, he will recognize his horse?" They said, "Of course, O' Messenger of Allah." He said, "They will come with their faces and limbs shining from *wuḍoo'*, and I will be there before them at the *hawḍ* (the cistern)."[85]

Aḥmad narrated with a *ṣaḥeeḥ isnaad* from Abu'd-Darda' that he said: The Messenger of Allah (ﷺ) said:

> "I will be the first one to be given permission to prostrate on the Day of Resurrection, and I will be the first one to be given permission to raise his head, and I will look at what is before me. I will look ahead of me, behind me, and to my right and left, and I will recognize my ummah from among the other nations." A man said, "O Messenger of Allah, how will you recognize your ummah from among the other nations from Nooḥ (Noah) to your ummah?" He said, "Their faces and limbs will be shining with the traces of *wuḍoo'*, and no one but they will be like that. And I will know them because they will be given their books (the record of their deeds) in their right hands, and I will know them because their children will be around them."[86]

---

[85] *Mishkaat al-Maṣaabeeḥ*, 1/98, hadith no. 298.

[86] *Mishkaat al-Maṣaabeeḥ*, 1/99, hadith no. 299.

CHAPTER NINE
ASH-SHAFAA'AH - INTERCESSION

When the distress of the people in that great gathering grows intense, they will search for a long time among those of high status for someone to intercede for them with their Lord, so that He may come to pass judgement and the people may be relieved of the distress and terrors of that gathering. They will ask their father Adam (عليه السلام) to undertake this great mission, and they will remind him of his virtue and how Allah honoured him, but he will refuse and will make excuses. He will mention how he disobeyed his Lord by eating from the tree from which Allah forbade him to eat, and he will refer them to Nooḥ (Noah) (عليه السلام), the first Messenger whom Allah sent to mankind, whom Allah called a grateful slave. But he will refuse and make excuses by referring to some of his shortcomings in his duties towards his Lord and Master. He will refer them to the Mighty Messengers who came after him, and each of them in turn will refer them to the one who came after him, until they come to the Last Messenger, Muhammad (ﷺ), to whom Allah forgave all his past and future sins, so he occupies a position for which the earlier and later generations will praise him, and his great and high status will thereby be made manifest. He will ask his Lord for permission, which will be granted, and he will praise and glorify Him, and ask Him with regard to his ummah, and his prayer will be answered. That is because Allah has granted each Prophet a prayer for his nation which will not be refused. Every Prophet hastened to offer that supplication in this world, but the Messenger (ﷺ) saved his prayer for that great gathering when his ummah will need his supplication. May Allah bless him and grant him peace, for he is kind and merciful towards his ummah, as his Lord described him. It is narrated in Bukhari and Muslim that Anas ibn Maalik (رضي الله عنه) said: The Messenger of Allah (ﷺ) said:

> "Every Prophet asked for something or every Prophet was granted one supplication for his nation, but I have postponed my supplication in order to intercede for my ummah on the Day of Resurrection."[1]

In *Ṣaheeḥ Muslim* it is narrated from Jaabir ibn 'Abdullah that the Prophet (ﷺ) said:

> "Every Prophet is granted one supplication for his nation, but I have postponed my supplication in order to intercede for my ummah on the Day of Resurrection."[2]

It is narrated in Bukhari and Muslim, and in *Sunan at-Tirmidhi*, from Abu Hurayrah (رضي الله عنه) that the Messenger of Allah (ﷺ) said:

> "Every Prophet has one supplication that is granted to him, and every Prophet hastened to make that supplication (in this world). But I have postponed my supplication in order to intercede for my ummah on the Day of Resurrection, and if Allah wills, it will include every one of my ummah who dies not associating anything in worship with Allah."[3]

Tirmidhi and Abu Dawood narrated that Anas ibn Maalik said: The Messenger of Allah (ﷺ) said:

> "My intercession will be for those among my ummah who committed major sins."[4]

---

[1] *Jaami' al-Uṣool*, 10/475, hadith no. 8009.
[2] Ibid, 10/475, hadith no. 8010.
[3] Ibid, 10/476, hadith no. 8011.
[4] Ibid, hadith no. 8012. Its *isnaad* is *ṣaḥeeḥ* as the editor stated.

1 - THE *AḤAADEETH* ABOUT INTERCESSION

There are many *ahaadeeth* which describe the great intercession, but it is sufficient here to quote those which Ibn al-Atheer compiled in *Jaami' al-Uṣool.*[5]

1) Bukhari and Muslim narrated in their *Ṣaḥeeḥs* that Ma'bad ibn Hilaal al-'Anzi said: "We set out to see Anas ibn Maalik, and we asked Thaabit to take us to meet him. We reached him when he was praying *Ḍuḥaa*, and Thaabit asked for permission for us to see him. We went in, and Thaabit sat down with him on his bed and said, 'O' Abu Ḥamzah, your brothers from Baṣrah are asking you to tell them the hadith about intercession.' He said: Muhammad (ﷺ) told us:

> "When the Day of Resurrection comes, the people will be milling around, then they will come to Adam (عليه السلام) and say: 'Intercede for your offspring.' He will say, 'I am not able for that, but you can go and ask Ibraaheem (Abraham) (عليه السلام), for he is the Close Friend of Allah (*Khaleel-Allah*).' So they will go to Ibraaheem, but he will say, 'I am not able for that, but you can go to Moosa (Moses) (عليه السلام), for he is the one who spoke with Allah (*Kaleem-Allah*).' So they will go to Moosa, but he will say, 'I am not able for that, but go to 'Eesa (Jesus) (عليه السلام), for he is the Spirit created by Allah and His Word.' So they will go to 'Eesa, but he will say, 'I am not able for it, but you can go to Muhammad.'
>
> So they will come to me and I will say, 'I am able for it.' Then I will go and seek permission from my Lord, and He will grant me permission. So I will stand before Him and praise Him in a manner that I could not do unless He

---

[5] *Jaami' al-Uṣool*, 10/477. We have also included the comments of the editor of *Jaami' al-Uṣool* on these *aḥaadeeth.*

> inspired me to do it. Then I will fall down prostrating before our Lord, and He will say, 'O' Muhammad, raise your head. Speak and you will be heard, ask and it will be given to you, intercede and your intercession will be accepted.' I will say, 'O' Lord, my ummah, my ummah.' He will say, 'Go, and whoever has in his heart faith equal to a grain of wheat or barley, bring him forth from it (the Fire).' So I will go and do that.
>
> Then I will come back to my Lord and praise Him in a similar manner. Then I will fall down prostrating before our Lord, and He will say, 'O' Muhammad, raise your head. Speak and you will be heard, ask and it will be given to you, intercede and your intercession will be accepted.' I will say, 'O' Lord, my ummah, my ummah.' He will say, 'Go, and whoever has in his heart faith equal to a grain of mustard seed, bring him forth from the Fire.' So I will go and do that.
>
> Then I will come back to my Lord and praise Him in a similar manner. Then I will fall down prostrating before our Lord, and He will say, 'O' Muhammad, raise your head. Speak and you will be heard, ask and it will be given to you, intercede and your intercession will be accepted.' I will say, 'O' Lord, my ummah, my ummah.' He will say, 'Go, and whoever has in his heart faith even less and less and less than that, bring him forth from the Fire.' So I will go and do that."

This is the hadith that Anas told us about. So we left him and when we had just passed by the graveyard we said, "Why don't we go to Al-Ḥasan and greet him whilst he is hiding in the house of Abu Khaleefah?" So we went to him and greeted him with *salaam*, and said, "O' Abu Sa'eed, we have come from your brother Abu Ḥamzah, and we have never heard anything like the hadith he told us about intercession." He said, "What was it?" So we told him the hadith. He said, "Then what?" We said, "He did not tell us anything more." He said, "He told us that twenty years ago, when he was young and strong. There is something that he did not tell you, and I do not know whether he forgot, or else he did not want to tell you lest you become complacent." We said to him, "Tell us." He smiled and said: ﴾Man is created of haste...﴿ *(Qur'an 21: 37)*. I would not have mentioned this to you if I did not want to tell you about it. He [the Prophet (ﷺ)] said:

> "Then I will go back to my Lord a fourth time, and will praise Him in a similar manner. Then I will fall down prostrating before our Lord, and He will say, 'O' Muhammad, raise your head. Speak and you will be heard, ask and it will be given to you, intercede and your intercession will be accepted.' I will say, 'O' Lord, grant me permission with regard to anyone who said *Laa ilaaha ill-Allah.*' He will say, 'That will not be granted to you, but by My Glory, Pride and Might, I will bring forth from it (the Fire) those who said *Laa ilaaha ill-Allah.*'"

- Then he bore witness that Al-Ḥasan had told them that and he had heard it from Anas ibn Maalik - I think he said, twenty years ago, when he was young and strong.

According to a report narrated by Qataadah, Anas said: the Messenger of Allah (ﷺ) said:

> "Allah will gather the people on the Day of Resurrection, and they will become distressed because of that - according to another report - they will be inspired - and they will say, 'Let us seek intercession with our Lord, so that He may grant us relief from this.' So they will go to Adam (عليه السلام) and say, 'You

are Adam, the father of mankind. Allah created you with His hand, and breathed into you of His spirit, and He commanded the angels to prostrate to you. Intercede for us with your Lord, so that He might relieve us of this distress.' He will say, 'I am not able to do that for you,' and he will mention the sin that he committed, and he will feel shy before his Lord because of that, (and he will say), 'But go to Nooḥ (Noah) (ﷺ), the first Messenger whom Allah sent to the people of the earth.'

So they will go to Nooḥ, and he will say, 'I am not able to do that for you,' and he will mention the sin that he committed, and he will feel shy before his Lord because of that, (and he will say), 'But go to Ibraaheem (Abraham) (ﷺ), whom Allah took as a close friend (*Khaleel*). So they will go to Ibraaheem, and he will say, 'I am not able to do that for you,' and he will mention the sin that he committed, and he will feel shy before his Lord because of that, (and he will say), 'But go to Moosa (Moses) (ﷺ), with whom Allah spoke and to whom He gave the *Tawraat*.' So they will go to Moosa, and he will say, 'I am not able to do that for you,' and he will mention the sin that he committed, and he will feel shy before his Lord because of that, (and he will say), 'But go to 'Eesa (Jesus) (ﷺ), the spirit created by Allah and His Word.' So they will go to 'Eesa, the spirit created by Allah and His Word, but he will say, 'I am not able to do that for you,' and he will mention the sin that he committed, and he will feel shy before his Lord because of that, (and he will say), 'But go to Muhammad, a slave for whom Allah forgave all his past and future sins.'

... So they will come to me, and I will ask my Lord for permission, which will be granted to me. As soon as I

> see Him, I will fall down prostrating. I will be left in that state for as long as Allah wills, then it will be said, 'O' Muhammad, stand up. Speak and you will be heard, ask and it will be given to you, intercede and your intercession will be accepted. I will praise my Lord in a manner that my Lord will teach me, then I will intercede. A limit will be set for me, and I will bring them forth from the Fire and bring them into Paradise. Then I will go back and fall down prostrating. I will be left in that state for as long as Allah wills, then it will be said, 'O' Muhammad, stand up. Speak and you will be heard, ask and it will be given to you, intercede and your intercession will be accepted. I will praise my Lord in a manner that my Lord will teach me, then I will intercede. A limit will be set for me, and I will bring them forth from the Fire and bring them into Paradise."

He (the narrator) said: I do not know whether it was the third or fourth time that he said:

> "I will say, 'O' Lord, there is no one left in the Fire but those whom the Qur'an has detained (i.e., those who the Qur'an says are doomed to abide therein for eternity), or those who are condemned to stay there forever." - This is narrated by Bukhari and Muslim.

Bukhari also narrated *ta'leeqan* from Qataadah from Anas that the Prophet (ﷺ) said:

> "The believers will be detained on the Day of Resurrection..." and he mentioned a similar report, at the end of which he said: "There is no one left in the Fire but those whom the Qur'an has detained, i.e., those who are condemned to stay there forever."

Then he recited the verse:

﴿... عَسَىٰٓ أَن يَبۡعَثَكَ رَبُّكَ مَقَامًا مَّحۡمُودًا ﴿٧٩﴾﴾

﴿...It may be that your Lord will raise you to *Maqaam Maḥmood* [a station of praise and glory, i.e., the honour of intercession on the Day of Resurrection].﴾ *(Qur'an 17: 79)*

He said: "This is the station of praise and glory which was promised to your Prophet (ﷺ)."

In another report he added: The Prophet (ﷺ) said:

"There will be brought forth from the Fire whoever said *Laa ilaaha ill-Allah* and had goodness in his heart equivalent to a grain of barley. Then there will be brought forth from the Fire whoever said *Laa ilaaha ill-Allah* and had goodness in his heart equivalent to a grain of wheat. Then there will be brought forth from the Fire whoever said *Laa ilaaha ill-Allah* and had goodness in his heart equivalent of a small ant."

Yazeed ibn Zuray' said: I met Shu'bah, and I told him this hadith. Then Shu'bah said: Qataadah told us this from Anas ibn Maalik from the Prophet (ﷺ), but instead of *dharrah* (small ant) he said *dhurah* (sorghum). Yazeed said: Abu Buṣtaam pronounced it differently. This is how it is narrated in the book of Muslim from the report of Yazeed from Shu'bah. Bukhari said: Abaan said something similar, narrating from Qataadah. There it says "*min eemaan* (of faith)" instead of "*min khayr* (of goodness)." In one report he added that the Prophet (ﷺ) said - according to the hadith which speaks of the believers asking for intercession -

"Then they will come to me, and I will ask for

> permission to speak to my Lord, and permission will be granted to me."

Bukhari narrated part of it from Ḥumayd from Anas, who said: I heard the Prophet (ﷺ) say:

> "When the Day of Resurrection comes, I will be granted intercession and I will say, 'Admit into Paradise (even) those who have faith equal to a mustard-seed in their hearts.' They will enter, then I will say, 'Enter Paradise (even) those who have the smallest amount of faith in their hearts.' Anas said: 'It is as if I am looking at the fingers of the Prophet (ﷺ).'"[6]

2) Bukhari, Muslim and Tirmidhi narrated that Abu Hurayrah (رضي الله عنه) said: "We were with the Prophet (ﷺ) at a meal to which we had been invited. He lifted the leg (of meat) up - which he used to like - and nibbled a piece from it, and he said,

> 'I will be the leader of mankind on the Day of Resurrection. Do you know why that is? Allah will gather the first and the last in one arena, and they will all be seen and they will all hear the call of the caller. The sun will be brought close to them, and the people will suffer unbearable distress and grief. The people will say, 'Do you not see the state you are in and how bad it is? Why don't you look for someone who will intercede for

---

[6] Bukhari: 13/395-397, in *At-Tawḥeed, Baab Kalaam ar-Rabb ta'aala Yawm al-Qiyaamah ma' al-Anbiya' wa ghayrihim*; and in *Baab Qawl Allah ta'aala* ﴾*Lima khalaqtu biyaday*﴿; and in *Baab Qawl Allah ta'aala* ﴾*Wa kallama Moosa takleeman*﴿; and in the *Tafseer* of *Soorah al-Baqarah, Baab Qawl Allah ta'aala* ﴾*Wa 'allama Aadam al-asmaa'a kullahaa*﴿; and in *Ar-Riqaaq, Baab Ṣifat al-Jannah wan-Naar*. Also narrated by Muslim, hadith no. 193, in *Al-Eemaan, Baab Adnaa Ahl al-Jannah manzilatan feehaa.*

you with your Lord? And the people will say to one another, 'Your father Adam (عليه السلام).'

So they will go to him and say, 'O' Adam, you are the father of mankind; Allah created you with His hand and breathed into you the soul (created by Allah for you); He commanded the angels to prostrate to you and He caused you to dwell in Paradise. Why do you not intercede for us with your Lord? Do you not see the state we are in and how bad it is?' He will say, 'My Lord is angry today in a way that He has never been before and never will be again. He forbade me (to eat) from the tree, and I disobeyed him. Myself, myself, myself. Go to someone else, go to Nooh (Noah) (عليه السلام).'

So they will go to Nooh and will say, 'O' Nooh, you were the first of the Messengers to the people of the earth, and Allah called you a grateful slave. Do you not see the state we are in and how bad it is? Why do you not intercede for us with your Lord?' He will say, 'My Lord is angry today in a way that He has never been before and never will be again. I had one supplication and I prayed against my people. Myself, myself, myself. Go to someone else, go to Ibraaheem (Abraham) (عليه السلام).'

So they will go to Ibraaheem and will say: 'You are the Prophet of Allah, His Close Friend (*Khaleel*) among the people of the earth. Intercede for us with your Lord. Do you not see the state we are in?' He will say to them: 'My Lord is angry today in a way that He has never been before and never will be again, and I told three lies - which he will mention - Myself, myself, myself. Go to someone else, go to Moosa (Moses) (عليه السلام).'

So they will go to Moosa and will say, 'You are the Messenger of Allah, and He favoured you above the people by sending you and by speaking to you. Intercede for us with your Lord. Do you not see the state we are in?' He will say to them: 'My Lord is angry today in a way that He has never been before and never will be again, and I killed a soul whom I had not been commanded to kill. Myself, myself, myself. Go to someone else, go to 'Eesa (Jesus) (ﷺ).'

So they will come to 'Eesa, and will say, 'O' 'Eesa, you are the Messenger of Allah and His Word which He bestowed on Maryam, and a spirit created by Him, and you spoke to the people in the cradle. Intercede for us with your Lord. Do you not see the state we are in?' 'Eesa will say to them: 'My Lord is angry today in a way that He has never been before and never will be again,' and he will not mention any sin. 'Myself, myself, myself. Go to someone else, go to Muhammad.'

So they will come to Muhammad (ﷺ) - according to one report, they will come to me - and will say, 'O' Muhammad, you are the Messenger of Allah and the Seal of the Prophets. Allah forgave you all your past and future sins. Intercede for us with your Lord. Do you not see the state we are in?' So I will set out and come beneath the Throne, where I will fall down prostrating to my Lord. Then Allah will inspire me to praise Him in a way that no one before me was ever inspired. Then it will be said, 'O' Muhammad, raise your head. Ask and you will be given, intercede and your intercession will be accepted.' So I will raise my head and say, 'My ummah, O' Lord, my ummah O' Lord, my ummah O' Lord.' It will be said, 'O' Muhammad, admit to Paradise those among your ummah who will not be brought to account, from the right-hand gate of the gates of

> Paradise.' They will have the right to enter through the same gates as other people. Then he said: 'By the One in Whose Hand is my soul, the distance between two of the gateposts of Paradise is like the distance between Makkah and Hajar - or like the distance between Makkah and Buṣrah."

In the book of Bukhari it says, "between Makkah and Ḥimyar." According to another report he said: "A platter of *thareed* and meat was placed before the Messenger of Allah (ﷺ). He picked up the leg - which was the part of the sheep meet he liked best - and took a small bite, then he said:

> 'I will be the leader of mankind on the Day of Resurrection.' Then he took another small bite and said, 'I will be the leader of mankind on the Day of Resurrection.' When he saw that his Companions were not asking any questions, he said: 'Why don't you ask me how?' They said, 'How will that be, O' Messenger of Allah?' He said, 'The people will be resurrected to meet the Lord of the Worlds...'"

And he quoted a similar hadith to that quoted above, but in the story of Ibraaheem (Abraham) he added:

> "And he mentioned what he said to the star, 'You are my lord'; and what he said of their gods, that this big one did it (broke the other idols); and when he said, 'I am sick.' And he said: 'By the One in Whose Hand is the soul of Muhammad, the distance between two of the gateposts of Paradise is like the distance between Makkah and Hajar, or Hajar and Makkah.'"

I (the narrator) do not know which of them he said. This is narrated by Bukhari, Muslim and Tirmidhi, but in the book of Muslim it says that each Prophet said "Myself, myself," twice. Al-Ḥumaydi mentioned what we have said. According to the report narrated by Tirmidhi, it says "Myself, myself, myself," three times in each case.[7]

Muslim narrated that Ḥudhayfah ibn al-Yamaan and Abu Hurayrah (may Allah be pleased with them both) said: The Messenger of Allah (ﷺ) said:

> "Allah will gather the people, and the believers will stand until Paradise is brought close to them. They will go to Adam (عليه السلام) and will say: 'O' our father, ask for Paradise to be opened for us.' He will say, 'Were you expelled from Paradise for anything other than the sin of your father? I am not the one to do that. Go to my son Ibraaheem (Abraham) (عليه السلام), the Close Friend of Allah.' But Ibraaheem will say, 'I am not the one to do that. I was the Friend of Allah from beyond and beyond; go to Moosa (Moses) (عليه السلام) with whom Allah spoke directly.' So they will go to Moosa, and he will say, 'I am not the one to do that, go to 'Eesa (Jesus) (عليه السلام), the Word of Allah and a spirit created by Him.' But 'Eesa will say, 'I am not the one to do that.' Then they will come to Muhammad (ﷺ). He will stand up, and permission will be granted to him, and trustworthiness and kinship will be sent and will stand on either side of *Aṣ-Ṣiraaṭ*, right and left. The first of you will cross it like (at the speed

---

[7] Bukhari, 6/264, 265 in *Al-Anbiya', Baab Qawl Allah ta'aala,* ﴿*Wa laqad arsalnaa Nooḥan ila qawmihi*﴾; *Baab Qawl Allah ta'aala* ﴿*Wa attakhadha Allah Ibraaheema khaleelan*﴾; in the *Tafseer* of *Soorah Bani Israa'eel, Baab* ﴿*Dhurriyat man ḥamalnaa ma' Nooḥ innahu kaana 'abdan shukooran.*﴾ Muslim, hadith no. 194, in *Al-Eemaan, Baab Adnaa Ahl al-Jannah manzilatan feehaa.* Tirmidhi, hadith no. 2436 in *Ṣifat al-Qiyaamah, Baab ma jaa'a fish-Shafaa'ah.*

of) lightning.' He (the narrator) said: 'May my father and mother be sacrificed for you, what thing is like lightning?' He said: 'Have you not seen lightning, how it goes and returns in the blink of an eye? Then (others will cross it) like the wind, or like birds and men running fast; they will move according to their deeds. Your Prophet will be standing on *Aṣ-Ṣiraaṭ*, saying, 'O' Lord, help him, help him,' until the deeds of the people will fail them, and a man will come who will only be able to move by crawling. On the edges of *Aṣ-Ṣiraaṭ* will be hooks ready to catch anyone whom they are commanded to catch. Some will be scratched by those hooks but will be saved, and others will be piled up in Hell. By the One in Whose Hand is the soul of Abu Hurayrah, it would take seventy years to plumb the depths of Hell."[8]

3) Tirmidhi narrated that Abu Sa'eed al-Khudri (ﷺ) said: The Messenger of Allah (ﷺ) said:

"I will be the leader of the sons of Adam on the Day of Resurrection, and I am not boasting. In my hand will be a banner of praise, and I am not boasting. There will be no Prophet that Day, from Adam onwards, who will not be under my banner. I will be the first one for whom the earth will be split open, and I am not boasting. The people will suffer three terrors, then they will go to Adam and say, 'You are our father Adam, intercede for us with your Lord.' He will say, 'I committed a sin, and was sent down to the earth. Go to Nooḥ (Noah) instead.' So they will go to Nooḥ, but he will say, 'I prayed against the people of the earth and they were destroyed.

---

[8] *Al-Eemaan*, hadith no. 195, *Baab Adnaa Ahl al-Jannah manzilatan feehaa.*

> Go to Ibraaheem instead.' So they will go to Ibraaheem (Abraham), but he will say, 'I told three lies.' Then the Messenger of Allah (ﷺ) said, 'They were not lies, they were arguments for the sake of the religion of Allah. (And Ibraaheem will say) 'Go to Moosa (Moses) instead.' So they will go to Moosa, and he will say, 'I killed a man, Go to 'Eesa (Jesus) instead.' So they will go to 'Eesa, but he will say, 'I was worshipped instead of Allah. Go to Muhammad (ﷺ) instead.' So they will come to me, and I will set out with them."

Ibn Jad'aan said: Anas said: it is as if I can see the Messenger of Allah (ﷺ).

> He said: 'I will take hold of the ring on the gate of Paradise and will knock. It will be said, 'Who is this?' It will be said in reply, 'Muhammad.' So they will open the gate and welcome me, and will say, 'Welcome.' I will fall down prostrating and my Lord will inspire me with words of praise. Then it will be said to me, 'Raise your head. Ask and you will be given, intercede and your intercession will be accepted, speak and your words will be heard.' That is the station of praise and glory of which Allah says, ﴾...It may be that your Lord will raise you to *Maqaam Maḥmood* [a station of praise and glory, i.e., the honour of intercession on the Day of Resurrection].﴿ *(Qur'an 17: 79)*.'"

Sufyaan said, "There is nothing from Anas except these words: 'I will take hold of the ring on the gate of Paradise and will knock.'" This is narrated by Tirmidhi.[9]

---

[9] Hadith no. 3147 in *At-Tafseer, Baab wa min Soorah Bani Israa'eel*. Tirmidhi said: this is a *ḥasan* hadith, and it is as he said.

2 - HOW THE *AḤAADEETH* ABOUT THE GREATER INTERCESSION ARE INTERPRETED

When reading these *ahaadeeth*, one sees that the believers will approach the Prophets, the last of whom is Muhammad (ﷺ), to save them from their terrible situation, but we see that when the Messenger (ﷺ) does intercede, it is for his own ummah. The commentator on *Aṭ-Ṭahaawiyah* said, after quoting some of the *aḥaadeeth* about intercession that we have quoted above: "What is strange indeed is that the scholars have mentioned this hadith with a number of *isnaads*, but they do not mention the first intercession, when the Lord will come to pass judgement, as is narrated in the hadith about the Trumpet, which is the point in this context, and is what is implied by the wording at the beginning of the hadith. When the people will seek intercession from Adam and the Prophets after him, it will be concerning judgement of the people, so that they might be relieved of waiting in that place, as is indicated by the contexts in all the reports. When they reach the point of recompense, they will seek intercession for the sinners among this ummah and for them to be brought forth from the Fire. It appears as if the aim of the *Salaf* (pious predecessors) in quoting only those parts of the hadith was to refute the *Khawaarij* and those among the *Mu'tazilah* who agreed with them concerning this matter, who denied that anyone would ever come forth from Hell after entering it, so they (the *Salaf*) limited themselves to quoting those parts of the hadith which contain a clear refutation of their innovated view which went against the *aḥaadeeth*."[10] Then he quoted the text of the hadith about the Trumpet.

Muhammad ibn Muhammad ibn 'Abi'l-'Izz al-Ḥanafi referred to a number of points:

---

[10] *Sharḥ aṭ-Ṭaḥaawiyah*, Pp. 255.

1) He confirmed that there is a problematic issue concerning these *aḥaadeeth*. Among those who referred to this issue was Ibn Ḥajar al-'Asqallaani, who quoted it from Ad-Daraawirdi, and said: "It is as if the narrator of this hadith did not put it in the right order. That is because at the beginning it mentions intercession for relief from the distress of waiting, and at the end it mentions intercession for bringing people forth from the Fire, i.e., that will happen after they have moved on from the place of waiting and crossed *Aṣ-Ṣiraaṭ*, and some of them would have fallen into the Fire. After that there will be intercession for bringing people forth from Hell."[11] After quoting the comments of Ad-Daraawirdi, Ibn Ḥajar said: "And this is a serious issue."[12]

2) The commentator on *Aṭ-Ṭaḥaawiyah* also commented on this issue, as we have quoted above, and stated that those who transmitted these (hadith) texts fell short in their transmission, and the reason for this was their intention to refute the *Khawaarij* who denied that anyone would be brought forth from Hell after having entered it. They claimed that everyone who enters Hell will abide there forever, and cited as evidence for this the hadith about the Trumpet in which it states that the Messenger (ﷺ) will intercede first for Allah to come and pass judgement between the people, then he will intercede a second time for admittance to Paradise. If the hadith about the Trumpet were *ṣaḥeeḥ*, this would resolve the issue, but it is a *da'eef* (weak) hadith, as has been explained by Shaykh Naaṣiruddeen al-Albaani in his comments on the *aḥaadeeth* in *Aṭ-Ṭaḥaawiyah*.

Perhaps what was stated by Al-Qaaḍi 'Iyaaḍ, and An-Nawawi, Ibn Ḥajar and others agreed with him, is more accurate and more effective in resolving the issue than what the commentator on *Aṭ-*

---

[11] *Fatḥ al-Baari*, 11/437.

[12] Ibid, 11/438.

Ṭaḥaawiyah said. Ibn Ḥajar said: Al-Qaaḍi 'Iyaaḍ - and An-Nawawi and others agreed with him - dealt with this issue by saying that it arose in the hadith of Ḥudhayfah which parallels the hadith of Abu Hurayrah, after the phrase "and they will come to Muhammad, so he will stand and permission will be granted to him - i.e., permission to intercede, and trustworthiness and kinship will be sent and will stand to either side of *Aṣ-Ṣiraaṭ*, right and left. The first of you will pass over it like lightning..." 'Iyaaḍ said: thus the issue is resolved, because the intercession which the people will seek will be for relief from the distress of waiting, then will come the intercession for bringing people forth from Hell. The hadith of Abu Hurayrah mentions the command to every nation to follow that which it used to worship. Then the hypocrites will be separated from the believers, then there will be intercession after the *Ṣiraaṭ* has been laid down and the people have crossed it. The command for every nation to follow that which it used to worship marks the beginning of the judgement and relief from the distress of waiting. He said: in this manner the texts of the *aḥaadeeth* may be reconciled, and the events mentioned therein come in the right order.[13]

Al-Ḥaafiẓ ibn Ḥajar clarified the matter further and narrated texts which indicate that some of the *aḥaadeeth* have been shortened somewhat. He said: "I say: it is as if some of the narrators memorized material that others did not. The rest of it is quoted later in the hadith in which it says, '...and a man will come who will only be able to move by crawling. On the edges of *Aṣ-Ṣiraaṭ* will be hooks ready to catch anyone whom they are commanded to catch. Some will be scratched by those hooks but will be saved, and others will be piled up in Hell.'" From this it appears that he [the Prophet (ﷺ)] will be the first one to intercede so that judgement may be passed among the

[13] *Fatḥ al-Baari*, 11/438.

people, and that the intercession for those who are to be brought forth from the Fire into which they have fallen will happen after that.

This is stated clearly in the hadith of Ibn 'Umar which is more concise than the hadith narrated by Anas and Abu Hurayrah. It is previously quoted in *Kitaab az-Zakah* from Ḥamzah ibn 'Abdullah ibn 'Umar from his father, with the wording, 'The sun will be brought close to them until their sweat reaches halfway up their ears. Whilst they are in that state they will seek the help of Adam, then Moosa, then Muhammad, to intercede so that judgement may be passed on mankind, so he will go and take hold of the ring on the gate, and on that Day Allah will raise him to a station of praise and glory, for which all the people in that gathering will praise him.'

And in the hadith of Ubayy ibn Ka'b narrated by Abu Ya'la, it says, 'Then I will praise Him with words for which He will be pleased with me, then I will be granted permission to speak. Then my ummah will cross the *Ṣiraaṭ* which will be suspended above Hell, for them to pass over it.'

In the hadith of Ibn 'Abbaas narrated by 'Abdullah ibn al-Ḥaarith and recorded by Aḥmad, it says: "And (Allah) will say, 'O' Muhammad, what do you want Me to do for your ummah?' I will say, 'O' Lord, hasten their reckoning.'"

According to a report narrated from Ibn 'Abbaas and recorded by Aḥmad and Abu Ya'la, it says: "And I will say, I am able for it, until Allah will grant permission to whomever He wills and is pleased with. When Allah wants to conclude the matter of His creation, a caller will cry out, 'Where are Muhammad and his ummah?'"

Aṭ-Ṭayyibi dicussed this issue in a different manner. He said: it could be that what is meant by the fire is the detention, distress and difficulty that the people will experience during the waiting, when the sun is brought close to their heads and they are touched by its heat and flames, which will make their sweat cover them up to their mouths, and it could be that their being brought forth from it means their being rescued from that state.

Ibn Ḥajar said: this is a far-fetched notion, unless it may be said that there are two occasions on which people will be brought forth, the first of which is in the hadith in that chapter, with its different *isnaads*, which refers to their being saved from the distress of waiting, and the second is in the hadith in the following chapter where it says, 'And He will say, Whoever used to worship anything, let him follow it,' after they have been saved from the waiting and the *Ṣiraaṭ* has been laid down and the command has been given to cross it. The second bringing forth will be for those who fall into the Fire whilst crossing it. Thus the two reports become one and are reconciled.'

Qurṭubi dealt with the root of this issue by noting that at the end of the hadith of Abu Zar'ah, narrated from Abu Hurayrah, after the Prophet (ﷺ) says, "I will say, 'O' Lord, my ummah, my ummah!', it says: 'And it will be said, Admit through the right-hand gate of Paradise those of your ummah who will not be brought to account or punished.' He said: this indicates that the Prophet (ﷺ) will intercede for the reckoning to be hastened on. When he is granted permission to admit those who are not to be brought to account, this implies that those who are to be brought to account will be detained for the purpose of the reckoning. In the lengthy hadith about the Trumpet narrated by Abu Ya'la it says: 'And I will say, 'You promised me intercession, and my intercession is for the people of Paradise to enter Paradise.' And Allah will say, 'I have accepted your intercession for them and I grant them permission to enter Paradise.'

I say: this is an indication that the waiting, the weighing of deeds in the Balance and the distribution of the records of deeds will happen at this stage (of the Hereafter), then the caller will cry out, 'Let each nation follow that which it used to worship.' So the *kuffaar* will fall into Hell, then the believers will be distinguished from the hypocrites by means of their prostration when the Shin is laid bare. Then permission will be granted for the *Ṣiraaṭ* to be laid out and for the people to cross it. The light of the hypocrites will be extinguished and they will fall into the Fire too, and the believers will cross it to Paradise. Some of the sinners will fall, and some of those who are saved will be detained at *Al-Qanṭarah* (a bridge between Paradise and Hell), then they will enter Paradise."[14]

I say, if this could be proven, that would resolve the matter. But Al-Kalbi is *ḍa'eef* (weak), moreover he did not give it an *isnaad*. In addition to that, this contradicts what is clearly stated in the *ṣaḥeeḥ aḥaadeeth*, that the believers' asking the Prophets one after another (for intercession) will only happen when they are waiting, before the believers enter Paradise. And Allah knows best.

3 - ACCEPTED AND REJECTED INTERCESSION: KINDS OF ACCEPTED INTERCESSION

The *aḥaadeeth* that we have quoted refer to two types of intercession that will happen on that Day.

1) The greater intercession, which is the station of praise and glory (*Al-Maqaam al-Maḥmood*). This is when the first and the last will approach the Messenger (ﷺ) to intercede with his Lord so that the people may find relief from the terrors of the gathering.

2) Intercession for the sinners among the monotheists (believers in *Tawḥeed*) who entered Hell (for their sins). This kind of intercession is discussed in greater detail in the chapter "Admittance to Paradise" in my book "Paradise and Hell."

---

[14] *Fatḥ al-Baari*, 11/438.

The other kinds of intercession will be mentioned in the *aḥaadeeth* which we shall quote here in brief:

First and second: The intercession of the Messenger (ﷺ) for people whose *ḥasanaat* (good deeds) and *sayi'aat* (bad deeds) are equal. He will intercede for them to be admitted to Paradise. There will be other people who have been ordered to Hell and he will intercede to save them from it.

Third: His intercession for those who have entered Paradise to be raised in status therein, above the level determined by the reward for their deeds.

Fourth: Intercession for people who will be admitted to Paradise without being brought to account. This may be understood from the hadith of 'Ukaashah ibn Muḥṣan, in which the Messenger (ﷺ) prayed that he might be made one of the seventy thousand who will enter Paradise without being brought to account. This hadith is narrated in *Ṣaḥeeḥayn* (Bukhari and Muslim).

Fifth: The intercession of the Messenger (ﷺ) for the reduction of the punishment of his uncle Abu Ṭaalib, when Allah will bring him out to a shallow part of the Fire which will cover his feet and cause his brain to boil.

Sixth: His intercession for permission for the believers to enter Paradise. This kind of intercession is discussed further in the book on Paradise.[15]

Intercession for sinners is not specific for the last Messenger (ﷺ). The Prophets, martyrs and scholars may all intercede. A man's deeds will also intercede for him. But our Messenger (ﷺ) will have the greatest share of this type of intercession. Others may also intercede

---

[15] *Sharḥ aṭ-Ṭaḥaawiyah*, 253.

for the status of the believers to be raised, but all other kinds of intercession will be only for the last Messenger (ﷺ).

These are the kinds of intercession that will happen on the Day of Resurrection. The kind of intercession that will be rejected is the kind known in this world, where a person may intercede even if the one with whom he is interceding is not willing to accept this intercession, but he is forced to accept that intercession because of their high status and power. This is the kind of intercession which the *mushrikeen* and Christians believe in with regard to their gods, and the innovators (people of bid'ah) among this ummah believe in with regard to their *shaykhs*. Allah has stated that those who believe in this are liars. No one will be able to intercede on that Day except with the permission of Allah, and none will intercede unless Allah is pleased with both the intercessor and the one for whom intercession is made. Allah (سبحانه وتعالى) says:

﴿...مَن ذَا ٱلَّذِى يَشْفَعُ عِندَهُۥٓ إِلَّا بِإِذْنِهِۦ ... ﴿٢٥٥﴾﴾

﴾...Who is he that can intercede with Him except with His Permission?...﴿ *(Qur'an 2: 255)*

﴿... وَلَا يَشْفَعُونَ إِلَّا لِمَنِ ٱرْتَضَىٰ ... ﴿٢٨﴾﴾

﴾...And they cannot intercede except for him with whom He is pleased...﴿ *(Qur'an 21: 28)*

Hence, because the father of Ibraaheem (Abraham) died as a *kaafir*, Allah will not accept the intercession of His Close Friend for him on that Day. Bukhari narrated in his *Ṣaḥeeḥ* from Abu Hurayrah (رضي الله عنه) that the Prophet (ﷺ) said:

"Ibraaheem will meet his father Aazar on the Day of Resurrection, and Aazar's face will be dark and covered with dust. Ibraaheem will say to him, 'Did I not tell you not to disobey me?' His father will say to him, 'This Day I will not disobey you.' Ibraaheem will say, 'O' Lord, You promised me that You would not disgrace me on the Day when (all the creatures) are resurrected. What disgrace is greater than the fact that my father is among those who are cast out from Your mercy?' Allah will say, 'I have forbidden Paradise to the *kaafireen*.' Then it will be said to Ibraaheem, 'What is beneath your feet?' He will look and there he will see a *bazeekh* (an animal) blood-stained, which will be caught by the legs and thrown in the (Hell) Fire."[16]

[16] *Mishkaat al-Maṣaabeeḥ*, 3/58.

CHAPTER TEN
THE RECKONING AND REQUITAL

INTRODUCTION

What is meant by the Reckoning and requital

What is meant by the Reckoning and requital is that Allah will make His slaves stand before Him, and He will remind them of the deeds that they did, the words that they said, the faith or *kufr* that they followed in this world, whether they followed the Straight Path or deviated from it, whether they were obedient or disobedient. He will tell them what rewards or punishments they deserve, and the slaves will be given their books (records of their deeds) in their right hands if they were righteous and in their left hands if they were evil.

The Reckoning includes what Allah will say to His slaves, what they will say to Him, the proof and evidence that will be established against them, the testimony of the witnesses and the weighing of their deeds.

Some of the Reckoning will be difficult, and some will be easy; some of it will involve honouring and some will involve rebuking; some will involve generosity and forgiveness, and the One Who is in charge of that is the Most Generous.

1 - THE SCENE OF THE RECKONING

Our Lord has described for us the scene of the Reckoning and requital on the Day of Reckoning. Allah (سُبْحَانَهُ وَتَعَالَى) says:

﴿ وَأَشْرَقَتِ ٱلْأَرْضُ بِنُورِ رَبِّهَا وَوُضِعَ ٱلْكِتَٰبُ وَجِاْىٓءَ بِٱلنَّبِيِّـۧنَ وَٱلشُّهَدَآءِ وَقُضِىَ بَيْنَهُم بِٱلْحَقِّ وَهُمْ لَا يُظْلَمُونَ ﴿٦٩﴾ ﴾

﴾And the earth will shine with the light of its Lord [Allah, when He will come to judge among men], and the Book will be placed [open], and the Prophets and the witnesses will be brought forward, and it will be judged between them with truth, and they will not be wronged.﴿

(Qur'an 39: 69)

Knowing that the Judge and Reckoner on that Day is the Most Wise and Most Just, the Sustainer of the heavens and the earth, is sufficient explanation of how great, majestic and frightening that scene will be. The shining referred to in the *aayah* will happen when the Majestic Sovereign (Allah) comes to pass judgement.

Allah (ﷻ) says:

﴿ هَلْ يَنظُرُونَ إِلَّآ أَن يَأْتِيَهُمُ ٱللَّهُ فِى ظُلَلٍ مِّنَ ٱلْغَمَامِ وَٱلْمَلَٰٓئِكَةُ وَقُضِىَ ٱلْأَمْرُ ۚ وَإِلَى ٱللَّهِ تُرْجَعُ ٱلْأُمُورُ ﴿٢١٠﴾ ﴾

﴾Do they then wait for anything other than that Allah should come to them in the shadows of the clouds and the angels? [Then] the case would be already judged. And to Allah return all matters [for decision].﴿

(Qur'an 2: 210)

Allah knows best the precise nature of this coming; we believe in it and know that it is true, and we do not take it for anything other than face value; we do not twist its meaning or reject it. The *aayah* (verse) also states that the angels will come. This is a majestic scene in which the angels of the Most Merciful will bring the books of deeds in which are recorded all the deeds, actions and words of mankind, to be used as evidence against His slaves. This is the book which leaves neither a small thing nor a big thing, but has recorded it with numbers:

﴿ وَوُضِعَ ٱلْكِتَٰبُ فَتَرَى ٱلْمُجْرِمِينَ مُشْفِقِينَ مِمَّا فِيهِ وَيَقُولُونَ يَٰوَيْلَتَنَا مَالِ هَٰذَا ٱلْكِتَٰبِ لَا يُغَادِرُ صَغِيرَةً وَلَا كَبِيرَةً إِلَّآ أَحْصَىٰهَا ۚ وَوَجَدُوا۟ مَا عَمِلُوا۟ حَاضِرًا ۗ وَلَا يَظْلِمُ رَبُّكَ أَحَدًا ﴿٤٩﴾ ﴾

﴾And the Book [one's Record] will be placed [in the right hand for a believer in the Oneness of Allah, and in the left hand for a disbeliever in the Oneness of Allah], and you will see the *Mujrimoon* [criminals, polytheists, sinners], fearful of that which is [recorded] therein. They will say: 'Woe to us! What sort of Book is this that leaves neither a small thing nor a big thing, but has recorded it with numbers!' And they will find all that they did, placed before them, and your Lord treats no one with injustice.﴿ *(Qur'an 18: 49)*

The Messengers will be brought forth in the arena of judgement and reckoning, and will be asked about the matter with which Allah entrusted them, namely the conveying of the Revelation of Allah to those to whom they were sent. And they will testify against their people concerning what they know about them.

On that great Day the witnesses will stand up and testify against the people, speaking of what they did. These witnesses are the angels who used to record everything that a person did. The Prophets and scholars will also testify against people, as will the earth, the sky, nights and days.

The people will be brought, for whom Allah will hold this court in order to bring them to account. They will stand in rows before the Lord of mankind:

﴿ وَعُرِضُوا۟ عَلَىٰ رَبِّكَ صَفًّا ... ﴿٤٨﴾ ﴾

﴾And they will be set before your Lord in [lines as] rows...﴿ *(Qur'an 18: 48)*

The sinners among them will be brought forth; these are the ones who rejected the Messengers and rebelled against their Lord, and were arrogant in the earth. They will be bound in fetters, wearing garments of pitch:

﴿ وَتَرَى ٱلْمُجْرِمِينَ يَوْمَئِذٍ مُّقَرَّنِينَ فِي ٱلْأَصْفَادِ ﴿٤٩﴾ سَرَابِيلُهُم مِّن قَطِرَانٍ وَتَغْشَىٰ وُجُوهَهُمُ ٱلنَّارُ ﴿٥٠﴾ لِيَجْزِيَ ٱللَّهُ كُلَّ نَفْسٍ مَّا كَسَبَتْ إِنَّ ٱللَّهَ سَرِيعُ ٱلْحِسَابِ ﴿٥١﴾ ﴾

﴾And you will see the *Mujrimoon* [criminals, disbelievers in the Oneness of Allah Islamic Monotheism, polytheists] that Day *Muqarranoon* [bound together] in fetters. Their garments will be of pitch, and fire will cover their faces. That Allah may requite each person according to what he has earned. Truly, Allah is Swift at reckoning.﴿

(Qur'an 14: 49-51)

Because of the intensity of the horrors, the nations will be brought to their knees when the people are called for the reckoning, because of the enormity of what they are witnessing and the state they are in.

﴿ وَتَرَىٰ كُلَّ أُمَّةٍ جَاثِيَةً كُلُّ أُمَّةٍ تُدْعَىٰ إِلَىٰ كِتَٰبِهَا ٱلْيَوْمَ تُجْزَوْنَ مَا كُنتُمْ تَعْمَلُونَ ﴿٢٨﴾ ﴾

﴾And you will see each nation humbled to their knees [kneeling], each nation will be called to its Record [of deeds]. This Day you shall be recompensed for what you used to do.﴿ *(Qur'an 45: 28)*

This is a great and majestic scene indeed. We ask Allah to save us by His grace, bounty and generosity.

2 - WILL THE *KUFFAAR* BE QUESTIONED? WHY WILL THEY BE QUESTIONED?

The scholars differed as to whether the *kuffaar* will be brought to account and questioned, or will be ordered straight to Hell without any questioning, because their deeds are all false and worthless, so there is no point in questioning them. If they are to be brought to account and questioned, what is the point of that reckoning and questioning?

Shaykh al-Islam Ibn Taymiyah said: "This issue was a subject of disagreement among the later scholars, the companions of Aḥmad and others. Among those who said that they would not be brought to account were Abu Bakr 'Abdul-'Azeez, Abu'l-Ḥasan at-Tameemi, Al-Qaaḍi Abu Ya'la and others. Among those who said that they would be brought to account were Abu Ḥafṣ al-Barmaki among the companions of Aḥmad, and Abu Sulaymaan ad-Dimashqi and Abu Ṭaalib."[1]

The correct view is that the *kuffaar* (disbelievers) will be brought to account and questioned, and their deeds will be weighed in the Balance. This is indicated by many texts, such as:

﴿ وَيَوْمَ يُنَادِيهِمْ فَيَقُولُ أَيْنَ شُرَكَآءِىَ ٱلَّذِينَ كُنتُمْ تَزْعُمُونَ ﴿٦٢﴾ ﴾

﴾And [remember] the Day when He will call to them and say: 'Where are My [so-called] partners whom you used to assert.'﴿ *(Qur'an 28: 62)*

﴿ وَيَوْمَ يُنَادِيهِمْ فَيَقُولُ مَاذَآ أَجَبْتُمُ ٱلْمُرْسَلِينَ ﴿٦٥﴾ ﴾

﴾And [remember] the Day [Allah] will call to them, and say: 'What answer gave you to the Messengers?'﴿ *(Qur'an 28: 65)*

---

[1] *Majmoo' al-Fataawa Shaykh al-Islam*, 4/305.

﴿ فَأَمَّا مَن ثَقُلَتْ مَوَٰزِينُهُۥ ۝٦ فَهُوَ فِى عِيشَةٍ رَّاضِيَةٍ ۝٧ وَأَمَّا مَنْ خَفَّتْ مَوَٰزِينُهُۥ ۝٨ فَأُمُّهُۥ هَاوِيَةٌ ۝٩ وَمَآ أَدْرَىٰكَ مَا هِيَهْ ۝١٠ نَارٌ حَامِيَةٌۢ ۝١١ ﴾

﴾Then as for him whose Balance [of good deeds] will be heavy, He will live a pleasant life [in Paradise]. But as for him whose Balance [of good deeds] will be light, He will have his home in *Haawiyah* [pit, i.e. Hell]. And what will make you know what it is? [It is] a fiercely blazing Fire!﴿ *(Qur'an 101: 6-11)*

﴿ وَمَنْ خَفَّتْ مَوَٰزِينُهُۥ فَأُو۟لَـٰٓئِكَ ٱلَّذِينَ خَسِرُوٓا۟ أَنفُسَهُمْ فِى جَهَنَّمَ خَـٰلِدُونَ ۝١٠٣ تَلْفَحُ وُجُوهَهُمُ ٱلنَّارُ وَهُمْ فِيهَا كَـٰلِحُونَ ۝١٠٤ أَلَمْ تَكُنْ ءَايَـٰتِى تُتْلَىٰ عَلَيْكُمْ فَكُنتُم بِهَا تُكَذِّبُونَ ۝١٠٥ ﴾

﴾And those whose scales [of good deeds] are light, they are those who lose their ownselves, in Hell will they abide. The Fire will burn their faces, and therein they will grin, with displaced lips [disfigured]. Were not My Verses [this Qur'an] recited to you, and then you used to deny them?﴿ *(Qur'an 23: 103-105)*

There is no doubt that these verses are speaking of the *kuffaar* and *mushrikeen* (the disbelievers and the polytheists).

1) With regard to why they will be brought to account and their deeds weighed in the Balance even though their deeds are worthless and will be rejected, this is for a number of reasons:

a) To establish proof against them, and to make manifest Allah's justice towards them. There is none to whom justification of actions is dearer than Allah. He is the One Who is absolutely Just. Hence He (ﷻ) will question them and bring them to account, and will examine their records which contain their deeds. The Balance will demonstrate how great are their *sayi'aat* (bad deeds) and how evil are their actions:

﴿ وَنَضَعُ ٱلْمَوَٰزِينَ ٱلْقِسْطَ لِيَوْمِ ٱلْقِيَٰمَةِ فَلَا تُظْلَمُ نَفْسٌ شَيْـًٔا ۖ وَإِن كَانَ مِثْقَالَ حَبَّةٍ مِّنْ خَرْدَلٍ أَتَيْنَا بِهَا ۗ وَكَفَىٰ بِنَا حَٰسِبِينَ ﴿٤٧﴾ ﴾

﴾And We shall set up Balances of justice on the Day of Resurrection, then none will be dealt with unjustly in anything. And if there be the weight of a mustard seed, We will bring it. And Sufficient are We to take account.﴿ *(Qur'an 21: 47)*

﴿ وَوُضِعَ ٱلْكِتَٰبُ فَتَرَى ٱلْمُجْرِمِينَ مُشْفِقِينَ مِمَّا فِيهِ وَيَقُولُونَ يَٰوَيْلَتَنَا مَالِ هَٰذَا ٱلْكِتَٰبِ لَا يُغَادِرُ صَغِيرَةً وَلَا كَبِيرَةً إِلَّآ أَحْصَىٰهَا ۚ وَوَجَدُوا۟ مَا عَمِلُوا۟ حَاضِرًا ۗ وَلَا يَظْلِمُ رَبُّكَ أَحَدًا ﴿٤٩﴾ ﴾

﴾And the Book [one's Record] will be placed [in the right hand for a believer in the Oneness of Allah, and in the left hand for a disbeliever in the Oneness of Allah], and you will see the *Mujrimoon* [criminals, polytheists, sinners], fearful of that which is [recorded] therein. They will say: 'Woe to us! What sort of Book is this that leaves neither a small thing nor a big thing, but has recorded it with numbers!' And they will find all that they did, placed before them, and your Lord treats no one with injustice.﴿ *(Qur'an 18: 49)*

Qurṭubi said: "The Creator will question His creatures in this world and in the Hereafter, in order to establish proof and demonstrate His Wisdom."[2]

---

[2] *At-Tadhkirah*, 225.

b) Allah (ﷻ) will bring them to account in order to rebuke them. *Shaykh al-Islam* said: "The Reckoning may mean showing the *kuffaar* their deeds and rebuking them accordingly, or it may mean weighing *ḥasanaat* (good deeds) against *sayi'aat* (bad deeds). If the first meaning is intended, then undoubtedly they will be brought to account in this sense. If the second meaning is intended, implying that the *kuffaar* may have good deeds to their credit for which they may deserve Paradise, then this is obviously mistaken."[3]

This rebuke is clearly mentioned in many texts, such as:

﴿ وَلَوْ تَرَىٰٓ إِذْ وُقِفُوا۟ عَلَىٰ رَبِّهِمْ ۚ قَالَ أَلَيْسَ هَـٰذَا بِٱلْحَقِّ ۚ قَالُوا۟ بَلَىٰ وَرَبِّنَا ۚ قَالَ فَذُوقُوا۟ ٱلْعَذَابَ بِمَا كُنتُمْ تَكْفُرُونَ ﴿٣٠﴾ ﴾

﴾If you could but see when they will be held [brought and made to stand] in front of their Lord! He will say: 'Is not this [Resurrection and the taking of the accounts] the truth?' They will say: 'Yes, by our Lord!' He will then say: 'So taste you the torment because you used not to believe.'﴿ *(Qur'an 6: 30)*

﴿ يَـٰمَعْشَرَ ٱلْجِنِّ وَٱلْإِنسِ أَلَمْ يَأْتِكُمْ رُسُلٌ مِّنكُمْ يَقُصُّونَ عَلَيْكُمْ ءَايَـٰتِى وَيُنذِرُونَكُمْ لِقَآءَ يَوْمِكُمْ هَـٰذَا ۚ قَالُوا۟ شَهِدْنَا عَلَىٰٓ أَنفُسِنَا ۖ وَغَرَّتْهُمُ ٱلْحَيَوٰةُ ٱلدُّنْيَا وَشَهِدُوا۟ عَلَىٰٓ أَنفُسِهِمْ أَنَّهُمْ كَانُوا۟ كَـٰفِرِينَ ﴿١٣٠﴾ ﴾

﴾O' you assembly of jinn and Mankind! 'Did not there come to you Messengers from amongst you, reciting unto you My Verses and warning you of the Meeting of this Day of yours?' They will say: 'We bear witness against ourselves.' It was the life of this world that deceived them. And they will bear witness against

---

[3] *Majmoo' al-Fataawa Shaykh al-Islam*, 4/305.

themselves that they were disbelievers.﴿

(Qur'an 6: 130)

﴾ وَبُرِّزَتِ ٱلْجَحِيمُ لِلْغَاوِينَ ﴿٩١﴾ وَقِيلَ لَهُمْ أَيْنَ مَا كُنتُمْ تَعْبُدُونَ ﴿٩٢﴾ ﴿

﴾And the [Hell] Fire will be placed in full view of the erring. And it will be said to them: 'Where are those [the false gods whom you used to set up as rivals with Allah] that you used to worship?'﴿ *(Qur'an 26: 91-92)*

﴾ وَقِيلَ ٱدْعُوا۟ شُرَكَآءَكُمْ فَدَعَوْهُمْ فَلَمْ يَسْتَجِيبُوا۟ لَهُمْ وَرَأَوُا۟ ٱلْعَذَابَ ۚ لَوْ أَنَّهُمْ كَانُوا۟ يَهْتَدُونَ ﴿٦٤﴾ ﴿

﴾And it will be said [to them]: 'Call upon your [so-called] partners [of Allah]', and they will call upon them, but they will give no answer to them, and they will see the torment. [They will then wish] if only they had been guided!﴿ *(Qur'an 28: 64)*

Ibn Katheer said: "As for the *kuffaar*, their deeds will be weighed even though they have no *ḥasanaat* which can benefit them and counterbalance their *kufr*, in order to demonstrate that they are doomed and to expose them before all of creation."[4]

c) The *kuffaar* are obliged to follow the basic principles of shari'ah just as they are obliged to follow its minor issues. They will be questioned about their shortcomings and transgressions in that regard. Qurṭubi said: "In the Qur'an there is evidence that the minor issues of shari'ah are addressed to them and they will be questioned about them, and brought to account for that, and they will be punished for not doing that, because Allah (ﷻ) says:

﴾ ... وَوَيْلٌ لِّلْمُشْرِكِينَ ﴿٦﴾ ٱلَّذِينَ لَا يُؤْتُونَ ٱلزَّكَوٰةَ ... ﴿٧﴾ ﴿

---

[4] *An-Nihaayah* by Ibn Katheer, 2/35.

﴿...And woe to *Al-Mushrikoon* [the polytheists, idolaters, disbelievers in the Oneness of Allah]. Those who give not the Zakah...﴾ *(Qur'an 41: 6-7)*

They are threatened because of their failure to pay zakah. And Allah tells us that it will be said to them:

﴿ مَا سَلَكَكُمْ فِي سَقَرَ ﴿٤٢﴾ قَالُوا لَمْ نَكُ مِنَ الْمُصَلِّينَ ﴿٤٣﴾ وَلَمْ نَكُ نُطْعِمُ الْمِسْكِينَ ﴿٤٤﴾ وَكُنَّا نَخُوضُ مَعَ الْخَائِضِينَ ﴿٤٥﴾ وَكُنَّا نُكَذِّبُ بِيَوْمِ الدِّينِ ﴿٤٦﴾ ﴾

﴿'What has caused you to enter Hell?' They will say: 'We were not of those who used to offer the *Ṣalaah* [prayers], Nor we used to feed *Al-Miskeen* [the poor]; And we used to talk falsehood [all that which Allah hated] with vain talkers. And we used to belie the Day of Recompense.'﴾ *(Qur'an 74: 42-46)*

Thus it is apparent that the commands to believe and establish regular prayer and pay zakah are addressed to the *mushrikeen* and they will be questioned about that and punished accordingly."[5]

d) The *kuffaar* vary in the degree of their *kufr* (disbelief) and sin, and they will be punished in Hell according to their degree of their sins. The Fire is composed of levels, one beneath another, just as Paradise is composed of degrees, one above another. The more intense a person's *kufr* and misguidance were, the more severe will be his torment. Some of the *kuffaar* will be in the lowest level of Hell, including the *munaafiqeen* (hypocrites):

﴿ إِنَّ الْمُنَافِقِينَ فِي الدَّرْكِ الْأَسْفَلِ مِنَ النَّارِ ... ﴿١٤٥﴾ ﴾

[5] *At-Tadhkirah*, Pp. 309.

﴾Verily, the hypocrites will be in the lowest depth [grade] of the Fire...﴿ *(Qur'an 4: 145)*

Shaykh al-Islam Ibn Taymiyah said:

"The punishment for the one who committed many evil deeds will be greater than the punishment for the one who committed few evil deeds. Whoever has any good deeds to his credit will have his punishment reduced, just as Abu Ṭaalib's torment is less than that of Abu Lahab... The Reckoning will be in order to make manifest the varying degrees of torment, not in order to admit them to Paradise."[6]

Qurṭubi mentions two scenarios for the weighing of people's deeds:

The first is that a person's *kufr* and evil deeds will be placed in one pan of the Balance, and the *kaafir* will find no good deed to place in the other pan, so the pan of evil deeds will weigh heavily because the other pan is empty.

The second is that the *kaafir's* good deeds, such as upholding the ties of kinship, giving charity and offering comfort to the distressed will be placed in the pan of good deeds, but the pan of evil deeds will weigh more heavily because of his *kufr* and *shirk*.[7]

The first scenario is the one which is correct, because *shirk* cancels out good deeds:

﴿ وَلَقَدْ أُوحِىَ إِلَيْكَ وَإِلَى ٱلَّذِينَ مِن قَبْلِكَ لَئِنْ أَشْرَكْتَ لَيَحْبَطَنَّ عَمَلُكَ وَلَتَكُونَنَّ مِنَ ٱلْخَـٰسِرِينَ ﴿٦٥﴾ ﴾

﴾If you join others in worship with Allah, [then] surely, [all] your deeds will be in vain.﴿ *(Qur'an 39: 65)*

---

[6] *Majmoo' al-Fataawa Shaykh al-Islam*, 4/305.

[7] *At-Tadhkirah*, Pp. 312.

﴿... وَمَن يَرْتَدِدْ مِنكُمْ عَن دِينِهِۦ فَيَمُتْ وَهُوَ كَافِرٌ فَأُوْلَٰٓئِكَ حَبِطَتْ أَعْمَٰلُهُمْ فِى ٱلدُّنْيَا وَٱلْءَاخِرَةِ ۖ وَأُوْلَٰٓئِكَ أَصْحَٰبُ ٱلنَّارِ ۖ هُمْ فِيهَا خَٰلِدُونَ ﴿٢١٧﴾﴾

﴿...And whosoever of you turns back from his religion and dies as a disbeliever, then his deeds will be lost in this life and in the Hereafter, and they will be the dwellers of the Fire. They will abide therein forever.﴾

(Qur'an 2: 217)

And according to the hadith: "Allah does not accept any deed except that which is done purely and sincerely for Him, seeking His pleasure."[8]

2) Because it is reported in a *ṣaḥeeḥ* hadith that the Messenger (ﷺ) said that the *kaafir* is fed by virtue of his good deeds in this world, so on the Day of Resurrection he will come with no *ḥasanaat*. In Muslim and Musnad Aḥmad it is narrated that the Messenger of Allah (ﷺ) said:

> "Allah does not deal unjustly with the believer with regard to his *ḥasanaat*. He gives him things in return for it in this world (according to one report, he rewards him for it with provision in this world), and will reward him for it in the Hereafter. But as for the *kaafir*, he will be granted provision by virtue of his good deeds that he did for the sake of Allah in this world, so that when he reaches the Hereafter he will have no *ḥasanaat* for which he might be rewarded."[9]

---

[8] Nasaa'i in *Al-Jihaad* from Abu Umaamah. See *Silsilat al-Aḥaadeeth aṣ-Ṣaḥeeḥah*, hadith no. 521.

[9] *Silsilat al-Aḥaadeeth aṣ-Ṣaḥeeḥah*, 1/82, hadith no. 53.

Understanding the texts which indicate that the *kuffaar* will not be questioned

It might be said: "You state above that the *kuffaar* will be questioned, and they will speak and offer their excuses, so what do you say about the texts which indicate the opposite, such as the *aayaat* (verses) -

﴿... وَلَا يُسْـَٔلُ عَن ذُنُوبِهِمُ ٱلْمُجْرِمُونَ ۝٧٨﴾

﴿...But the *Mujrimoon* [criminals, disbelievers, polytheists, sinners] will not be questioned of their sins [because Allah knows them well, so they will be punished without being called to account.﴾

(Qur'an 28: 78)

﴿فَيَوْمَئِذٍ لَّا يُسْـَٔلُ عَن ذَنۢبِهِۦٓ إِنسٌ وَلَا جَآنٌّ ۝٣٩﴾

﴿So on that Day no question will be asked of man or jinni as to his sin.﴾ *(Qur'an 55: 39)*

﴿هَٰذَا يَوْمُ لَا يَنطِقُونَ ۝٣٥ وَلَا يُؤْذَنُ لَهُمْ فَيَعْتَذِرُونَ ۝٣٦﴾

﴿That will be a Day when they shall not speak [during some part of it], And they will not be permitted to put forth any excuse.﴾ *(Qur'an 77: 35-36)*

- and other similar verses?

We say: there is no contradiction between these verses and the others. The scholars have reconciled between them on a number of points:

a) The *kuffaar* (disbelievers) will not be asked any questions that might bring them some comfort, rather they will be asked questions that will rebuke them, why did you do such and such?[10] Allah will

[10] *At-Tadhkirah*, Pp. 286.

not speak to them in a manner that they would like, rather He will say to them words of reprimand.[11]

b) They will not be asked questions aimed at finding something out, for Allah (ﷻ) knows all of their deeds. Rather they will be asked questions aimed at confirming what is already known. It will be said to them, 'Why did you do such and such?' Al-Ḥasan and Qataadah said: 'They will not be asked about their sins, because Allah has kept a record of them and the angels have recorded them.'[12]

c) They will be questioned at different stages during the Day of Resurrection. Qurṭubi said: "The Resurrection will be in stages, in some of which there will be questioning and in others there will be no questioning."[13]

As-Safaareeni said: "It is said, they will be questioned in some stages and not others. This is narrated by 'Ikrimah from Ibn 'Abbaas (رضي الله عنه)... People will be in various states on the Day of Resurrection, and the *aayaat* are to be interpreted in the light of these various stages. Therefore Imam Aḥmad said in *Al-Ajoobah al-Qur'aniyah*: 'When people are first resurrected, they will stay for the equivalent of sixty years without speaking, and they will not be permitted to make excuses. Then they will be granted permission to speak, so they will speak. This is what Allah (ﷻ) says:

﴿... رَبَّنَآ أَبۡصَرۡنَا وَسَمِعۡنَا فَٱرۡجِعۡنَا نَعۡمَلۡ صَٰلِحًا إِنَّا مُوقِنُونَ ۝١٢﴾

> ﴾...[They will say] Our Lord! We have now seen and heard, so send us back [to the world], that we will do righteous good deeds.﴿ *(Qur'an 32: 12)*.'[14]

---

[11] Ibid, 287.

[12] *Lawaami' al-Anwaar al-Bahiyyah*, 2/174.

[13] *At-Tadhkirah*, Pp. 286.

[14] *Lawaami' al-Anwaar al-Bahiyyah*, 2/174.

When they are granted permission to speak, they will speak and dispute. This is what Allah (ﷻ) says:

﴿ ثُمَّ إِنَّكُمْ يَوْمَ ٱلْقِيَـٰمَةِ عِندَ رَبِّكُمْ تَخْتَصِمُونَ ﴿٣١﴾ ﴾

﴾Then, on the Day of Resurrection, you will be disputing before your Lord.﴿ *(Qur'an 39: 31)*

- at the time of the Reckoning and settling scores. Then it will be said to them:

﴿ قَالَ لَا تَخْتَصِمُوا۟ لَدَىَّ وَقَدْ قَدَّمْتُ إِلَيْكُم بِٱلْوَعِيدِ ﴿٢٨﴾ ﴾

﴾Allah will say: 'Dispute not in front of Me, I had already in advance sent you the threat.'﴿ *(Qur'an 50: 28)*

- i.e., in this world. At that point, the punishment will be inevitable."[15]

d) Qurṭubi said: "The meaning of the *aayah* (verse):

﴿ ... وَلَا يُسْـَٔلُ عَن ذُنُوبِهِمُ ٱلْمُجْرِمُونَ ﴿٧٨﴾ ﴾

﴾...But the *Mujrimoon* [criminals, disbelievers, polytheists, sinners] will not be questioned of their sins [because Allah knows them well, so they will be punished without being called to account].﴿ *(Qur'an 28: 78)*

- is not that they will be asked questions to distinguish the believers from the *kaafirs*, for the angels will have no need to ask anyone on the Day of Resurrection, 'What is your religion? What you used to do in the world?' so that a person might tell them whether he is a believer or a *kaafir*. But the believers will have shining faces and a composed

[15] *Lawaami' al-Anwaar al-Bahiyyah*, 2/174.

manner, whilst the *mushrikeen* will have black faces and will be distressed. So when the angels will be instructed to drive the sinners to Hell, it will be sufficient for them to look at their faces in order to differentiate and know about their (Hell dwellers) respective religions..."[16]

3 - THE PRINCIPLES ACCORDING TO WHICH THE PEOPLE WILL BE BROUGHT TO ACCOUNT

If Allah (ﷻ) were to punish all His creatures, He would not be unjust towards them, because they are His slaves and they belong to Him. The One Who owns something can do whatever He wants with it. But Allah will judge His slaves in a fair and just manner, such as mankind will never have seen before. Our Lord has told us in many texts the principles on which the Judgement and Reckoning on that Day will be based.

We will mention as many of these principles as we have come to know.

1) Perfect justice which is not contaminated by any element of injustice

Allah (ﷻ) will pay His slaves in full on the Day of Resurrection, with nothing lacking at all. No person will be treated with the slightest injustice, not even the equivalent of a grain of mustard seed.

﴿... ثُمَّ تُوَفَّىٰ كُلُّ نَفْسٍ مَّا كَسَبَتْ وَهُمْ لَا يُظْلَمُونَ ﴿٢٨١﴾﴾

﴿...Then every person shall be paid what he earned, and they shall not be dealt with unjustly.﴾ *(Qur'an 2: 281)*

Luqmaan said, telling his son about the justice of Allah (ﷻ):

[16] *At-Tadhkirah*, Pp. 287.

﴿ يَـٰبُنَيَّ إِنَّهَآ إِن تَكُ مِثْقَالَ حَبَّةٍ مِّنْ خَرْدَلٍ فَتَكُن فِي صَخْرَةٍ أَوْ فِي ٱلسَّمَـٰوَٰتِ أَوْ فِي ٱلْأَرْضِ يَأْتِ بِهَا ٱللَّهُ ۚ إِنَّ ٱللَّهَ لَطِيفٌ خَبِيرٌ ﴿١٦﴾ ﴾

﴾O' my son! If it be [anything] equal to the weight of a grain of mustard seed, and though it be in a rock, or in the heavens or in the earth, Allah will bring it forth. Verily, Allah is Subtle [in bringing out that grain], Well-Aware [of its place].﴿ *(Qur'an 31: 16)*

Elsewhere, Allah (ﷻ) says:

﴿ إِنَّ ٱللَّهَ لَا يَظْلِمُ مِثْقَالَ ذَرَّةٍ ... ﴿٤٠﴾ ﴾

﴾Surely, Allah wrongs not even of the weight of an atom [or a small ant]...﴿ *(Qur'an 4: 40)*

﴿ ... وَٱلْـَٔاخِرَةُ خَيْرٌ لِّمَنِ ٱتَّقَىٰ وَلَا تُظْلَمُونَ فَتِيلًا ﴿٧٧﴾ ﴾

﴾...The Hereafter is [far] better for him who fears Allah, and you shall not be dealt with unjustly even equal to the *Fateela* [a scalish thread in the long slit of a date stone].﴿ *(Qur'an 4: 77)*

﴿ وَمَن يَعْمَلْ مِنَ ٱلصَّـٰلِحَـٰتِ مِن ذَكَرٍ أَوْ أُنثَىٰ وَهُوَ مُؤْمِنٌ فَأُو۟لَـٰٓئِكَ يَدْخُلُونَ ٱلْجَنَّةَ وَلَا يُظْلَمُونَ نَقِيرًا ﴿١٢٤﴾ ﴾

﴾And whoever does righteous good deeds, male or female, and is a [true] believer [in the Oneness of Allah (Muslim)], such will enter Paradise and not the least injustice, even to the size of a *Naqeera* [speck on the back of a date stone], will be done to them.﴿ *(Qur'an 4: 124)*

And Allah (ﷻ) says:

﴿ فَمَن يَعْمَلْ مِثْقَالَ ذَرَّةٍ خَيْرًا يَرَهُۥ ۝٧ وَمَن يَعْمَلْ مِثْقَالَ ذَرَّةٍ شَرًّا يَرَهُۥ ۝٨ ﴾

﴿So whosoever does good equal to the weight of an atom [or a small ant] shall see it. And whosoever does evil equal to the weight of an atom [or a small ant] shall see it.﴾ *(Qur'an 99: 7-8)*

In these verses, Allah tells us that He will requite every person for his actions, and that nothing will be lost, and not even the smallest amount will be lacking. The word used in Arabic is *dharrah* (translated as 'an atom' or a 'small ant'), which refers to the tiny particles which can be seen in a ray of sunlight when it enters a small aperture. Not even a *fateel* or a *naqeer* of injustice will be done; the *fateel* is the thread which is found in the groove of a date-stone, and the *naqeer* is a small dent in the back of a date stone.

2) No one will be responsible for the sin of another

The principle of reckoning and requital which represents the utmost justice is that Allah will requite His slaves for their actions; if they are good, then (the consequences will be) good, and if they are bad then (the consequences will be) bad. Allah will not make anyone bear the burden of sins of another, as He (ﷻ) says:

﴿ ... وَلَا تَكْسِبُ كُلُّ نَفْسٍ إِلَّا عَلَيْهَا ۚ وَلَا تَزِرُ وَازِرَةٌ وِزْرَ أُخْرَىٰ ۚ ثُمَّ إِلَىٰ رَبِّكُم مَّرْجِعُكُمْ فَيُنَبِّئُكُم بِمَا كُنتُمْ فِيهِ تَخْتَلِفُونَ ۝١٦٤ ﴾

﴿...No person earns any [sin] except against himself [only], and no bearer of burdens shall bear the burden of another. Then unto your Lord is your return, so He will tell you that wherein you have been differing.﴾

(Qur'an 6: 164)

This is the ultimate justice and fairness. The one who is guided will reap the benefits of his guidance, and the one who is misguided will have no one to blame but himself.

﴿ مَّنِ ٱهْتَدَىٰ فَإِنَّمَا يَهْتَدِى لِنَفْسِهِۦ ۖ وَمَن ضَلَّ فَإِنَّمَا يَضِلُّ عَلَيْهَا ۚ وَلَا تَزِرُ وَازِرَةٌ وِزْرَ أُخْرَىٰ ۗ وَمَا كُنَّا مُعَذِّبِينَ حَتَّىٰ نَبْعَثَ رَسُولًا ﴿١٥﴾ ﴾

﴾Whoever goes right, then he goes right only for the benefit of his ownself. And whoever goes astray, then he goes astray to his own loss. No one laden with burdens can bear another's burden. And We never punish until We have sent a Messenger [to give warning].﴿

(Qur'an 17: 15)

This principle is one of the matters on which all the divinely revealed laws said the same thing. Allah (ﷻ) says:

﴿ أَمْ لَمْ يُنَبَّأْ بِمَا فِى صُحُفِ مُوسَىٰ ﴿٣٦﴾ وَإِبْرَٰهِيمَ ٱلَّذِى وَفَّىٰٓ ﴿٣٧﴾ أَلَّا تَزِرُ وَازِرَةٌ وِزْرَ أُخْرَىٰ ﴿٣٨﴾ وَأَن لَّيْسَ لِلْإِنسَٰنِ إِلَّا مَا سَعَىٰ ﴿٣٩﴾ وَأَنَّ سَعْيَهُۥ سَوْفَ يُرَىٰ ﴿٤٠﴾ ثُمَّ يُجْزَىٰهُ ٱلْجَزَآءَ ٱلْأَوْفَىٰ ﴿٤١﴾ ﴾

﴾Or is he not informed with what is in the Pages [Scripture] of Moosa [Moses], And of Ibraaheem [Abraham] who fulfilled [or conveyed] all that [Allah ordered him to do or convey]: That no burdened person [with sins] shall bear the burden [sins] of another. And that man can have nothing but what he does [good or bad]. And that his deeds will be seen. Then he will be recompensed with a full and the best recompense.﴿

(Qur'an 53: 36-41)

Qurṭubi said, in his *tafseer* of the *aayah* (verse):

﴿ ... وَلَا تَزِرُ وَازِرَةٌ وِزْرَ أُخْرَىٰ ... ﴿١٦٤﴾ ﴾

﴾...And no bearer of burdens shall bear the burden of another...﴿ *(Qur'an 6: 164)*

- this means that no one who is carrying (a burden) will bear the burden of another, and no soul will be taken to task for the sins of another. Each soul will be brought to account for its own sins and will have to bear the consequences of its own evildoing. The root of the word *wizr* (translated as burden, i.e. of sin) means something heavy, such as when Allah (ﷻ) says:

﴿ وَوَضَعْنَا عَنكَ وِزْرَكَ ﴿٢﴾ ﴾

﴾And removed from you your burden [*wizrak*].﴿ *(Qur'an 94: 2).*

Here, however, the meaning is sin... This *aayah* was revealed concerning Al-Waleed ibn al-Mugheerah, who used to say, 'Follow my way and I will carry your burdens (of sin).' This was mentioned by Ibn 'Abbaas. It was also said that it is revealed to refute the Arabs of the *Jaahiliyah* who believed that a man could be responsible for the burden of his father and son, or the mistakes of his allies.[17]

Those who will bear other loads besides their own

Some people may disagree with the idea that no person will carry the sins of another, by quoting the verses:

﴿ وَلَيَحْمِلُنَّ أَثْقَالَهُمْ وَأَثْقَالًا مَّعَ أَثْقَالِهِمْ ... ﴿١٣﴾ ﴾

﴾And verily, they shall bear their own loads, and other loads besides their own...﴿ *(Qur'an 29: 13)*

﴿ لِيَحْمِلُوٓا۟ أَوْزَارَهُمْ كَامِلَةً يَوْمَ ٱلْقِيَـٰمَةِ ۙ وَمِنْ أَوْزَارِ ٱلَّذِينَ يُضِلُّونَهُم بِغَيْرِ عِلْمٍ ... ﴿٢٥﴾ ﴾

[17] *Tafseer al-Qurṭubi*, 4/157.

﴿That they may bear their own burdens in full on the Day of Resurrection, and also of the burdens of those whom they misled without knowledge...﴾ *(Qur'an 16: 25)*

What they quote is in accordance with the texts that we have mentioned; it does not contradict them at all. These texts indicate that a person will bear the burden of the sins that he commits, as well as the sins of those whom he misguides by his words and deeds, just as those who call people to true guidance will receive the reward for what they do as well as the like of the reward of those who follow their guidance and benefit from their knowledge. So the fact that those misguided people misguide others is an action on their part for which they will have to face the consequences.[18]

3) Showing the people the deeds that they had sent forth

One of the ways in which Allah (ﷻ) will leave His creation with no excuses, and will manifest His justice, is that He will show them what they had sent forth, of both righteous deeds and evil deeds, so that they may pass judgement on themselves, and then they will have no excuse. Allah (ﷻ) says:

﴿ ... إِلَى اللَّهِ مَرْجِعُكُمْ جَمِيعًا فَيُنَبِّئُكُم بِمَا كُنتُمْ تَعْمَلُونَ ﴿١٠٥﴾ ﴾

﴿...The return of you all is to Allah, then He will inform you about [all] that which you used to do.﴾

(Qur'an 5: 105)

﴿ يَوْمَ تَجِدُ كُلُّ نَفْسٍ مَّا عَمِلَتْ مِنْ خَيْرٍ مُّحْضَرًا وَمَا عَمِلَتْ مِن سُوٓءٍ تَوَدُّ لَوْ أَنَّ بَيْنَهَا وَبَيْنَهُۥٓ أَمَدًا بَعِيدًا ... ﴿٣٠﴾ ﴾

﴿On the Day when every person will be confronted with

---

[18] We have discussed this matter in greater detail in our book *Maqaaṣid al-Mukallafeen.*

all the good he has done, and all the evil he has done, he will wish that there were a great distance between him and his evil...﴾ *(Qur'an 3: 30)*

﴿ عَلِمَتْ نَفْسٌ مَّا قَدَّمَتْ وَأَخَّرَتْ ﴿٥﴾ ﴾

﴾[Then] a person will know what he has sent forward and [what he has] left behind [of good or bad deeds].﴿ *(Qur'an 82: 5)*

﴿ ... وَوَجَدُوا۟ مَا عَمِلُوا۟ حَاضِرًا ۗ وَلَا يَظْلِمُ رَبُّكَ أَحَدًا ﴿٤٩﴾ ﴾

﴾...And they will find all that they did, placed before them, and your Lord treats no one with injustice.﴿ *(Qur'an 18: 49)*

The way in which the people will be shown what they sent forth of deeds will be by means of their being given the books of their deeds, which they will read. Our Lord has told us that He has appointed two angels to each one of us, to record our righteous and evil deeds. When a person dies, a seal is placed on his book, and when the Day of Resurrection comes, each person will be given his book and will be told, 'Read your book; you are sufficient as a reckoner against yourself this Day.'

Allah (ﷻ) says:

﴿ وَكُلَّ إِنسَـٰنٍ أَلْزَمْنَـٰهُ طَـٰٓئِرَهُۥ فِى عُنُقِهِۦ ۖ وَنُخْرِجُ لَهُۥ يَوْمَ ٱلْقِيَـٰمَةِ كِتَـٰبًا يَلْقَىٰهُ مَنشُورًا ﴿١٣﴾ ٱقْرَأْ كِتَـٰبَكَ كَفَىٰ بِنَفْسِكَ ٱلْيَوْمَ عَلَيْكَ حَسِيبًا ﴿١٤﴾ ﴾

﴾And We have fastened every man's deeds to his neck, and on the Day of Resurrection, We shall bring out for him a book which he will find wide open. [It will be said to him]: 'Read your book. You yourself are sufficient as a reckoner against you this Day.'﴿ *(Qur'an 15: 13-14)*

This is a book which includes all of a person's deeds, great and small alike:

﴿ وَوُضِعَ ٱلْكِتَـٰبُ فَتَرَى ٱلْمُجْرِمِينَ مُشْفِقِينَ مِمَّا فِيهِ وَيَقُولُونَ يَـٰوَيْلَتَنَا مَالِ هَـٰذَا ٱلْكِتَـٰبِ لَا يُغَادِرُ صَغِيرَةً وَلَا كَبِيرَةً إِلَّآ أَحْصَىٰهَا ۚ وَوَجَدُوا۟ مَا عَمِلُوا۟ حَاضِرًا ۗ وَلَا يَظْلِمُ رَبُّكَ أَحَدًا ﴿٤٩﴾ ﴾

﴾And the Book [one's Record] will be placed [in the right hand for a believer in the Oneness of Allah, and in the left hand for a disbeliever in the Oneness of Allah], and you will see the *Mujrimoon* [criminals, polytheists, sinners], fearful of that which is [recorded] therein. They will say: 'Woe to us! What sort of Book is this that leaves neither a small thing nor a big thing, but has recorded it with numbers!' And they will find all that they did, placed before them, and your Lord treats no one with injustice.﴿ *(Qur'an 18: 49)*

4) Multiplication of *ḥasanaat* (good deeds) but not of *sayi'aat* (bad deeds)

It is one aspect of Allah's mercy that He multiplies the reward for righteous deeds:

﴿ إِن تُقْرِضُوا۟ ٱللَّهَ قَرْضًا حَسَنًا يُضَـٰعِفْهُ لَكُمْ وَيَغْفِرْ لَكُمْ ۚ ... ﴿١٧﴾ ﴾

﴾If you lend to Allah a goodly loan [i.e. spend in Allah's Cause], He will double it for you, and will forgive you...﴿ *(Qur'an 64: 17)*

The least amount by which the *ḥasanah* will be multiplied is ten:

﴿ مَن جَآءَ بِٱلْحَسَنَةِ فَلَهُۥ عَشْرُ أَمْثَالِهَا ۖ ... ﴿١٦٠﴾ ﴾

﴾Whoever brings a good deed [Islamic Monotheism and deeds of obedience to Allah and His Messenger] shall have ten times the like thereof to his credit...﴿

(Qur'an 6: 160)

But the recompense for *sayi'ah* (a bad deed) will simply be one like it:

﴿ ... وَمَن جَآءَ بِٱلسَّيِّئَةِ فَلَا يُجْزَىٰٓ إِلَّا مِثْلَهَا ... ﴿١٦٠﴾ ﴾

﴾...And whoever brings an evil deed [polytheism, disbelief, hypocrisy, and deeds of disobedience to Allah and His Messenger] shall have only the recompense of the like thereof...﴿ *(Qur'an 6: 160)*

This is indicative of His justice, may He be exalted.

It is narrated by Al-Ḥaakim in his *Mustadrak* and by Aḥmad in his *Musnad*, with a *ṣaḥeeḥ isnaad*, that Abu Dharr (رضي الله عنه) said: "The trusted truthful [i.e., the last Prophet (ﷺ)] told us that his Lord told him:

'The *ḥasanah* is for ten like it or more, and the *sayi'ah* is one, or I will forgive it. And if you meet Me with sins nearly as great as the earth, so long as you did not associate anything in worship with Me, I will meet you with forgiveness nearly as great as the earth.'"[19]

Among the actions for which the Messenger (ﷺ) has told us that the reward will be multiplied ten times is reading Qur'an. According to the hadith narrated by Tirmidhi and Ad-Daarimi with a *ṣaḥeeḥ isnaad* from Ibn Mas'ood, the Messenger of Allah (ﷺ) said:

"Whoever reads one letter of the Book of Allah, will have one *ḥasanah* for it, and each *ḥasanah* will be rewarded tenfold. I do not say that *'Alif-laam-meem'* is

---

[19] *Silsilat al-Aḥaadeeth aṣ-Ṣaḥeeḥah*, hadith no. 128.

one letter. *Alif* is a letter, *laam* is a letter and *meem* is a letter."

- Tirmidhi said: this is a *ṣaḥeeḥ ḥasan* hadith whose *isnaad* is *ghareeb.*[20]

Our Messenger (ﷺ) has also told us that *dhikr* will be rewarded tenfold. In the *Sunans* of Tirmidhi, Nasaa'i and Abu Dawood it is narrated from 'Abdullah ibn 'Amr ibn al-'Aaṣ (may Allah be pleased with them both) that the Messenger of Allah ﷺ said:

> "There are two characteristics which no Muslim attains but he will enter Paradise. They are easy, and those who do them are few: glorifying Allah (saying *Subḥaan Allah*) after every prayer ten times, and praising Him (saying *Al-Ḥamdu Lillaah*) ten times, and magnifying Him (saying *Allahu Akbar*) ten times." I saw the Messenger of Allah (ﷺ) counting them on his hand. He said: "That is one hundred and fifty on the tongue, and one thousand and five hundred in the Balance. And when you go to bed, glorify Him and magnify Him and praise Him one hundred times. That will be one hundred on the tongue and one thousand in the Balance. Who among you does one thousand and five hundred *sayi'aat* in one day?" They said, "How should we not count it?" He said: "The *Shayṭaan* (Satan) comes to one of you whilst he is praying and says, 'Remember such and such, remember such and such,' until he finishes his prayer, then he may not recite the *dhikr*, or he (the *Shayṭaan*) comes to him whilst he is lying in bed and does not leave him until he makes him fall asleep." - This is narrated by Tirmidhi and Nasaa'i.

---

[20] *Mishkaat al-Maṣaabeeḥ*, 1/661, hadith no. 2137.

According to a report narrated by Abu Dawood, after he (ﷺ) said "in the Balance" the first time, he said:

> "And magnify Him (say *Allahu Akbar*) thirty-four times when you go to bed, and praise Him (say *Al-Ḥamdu Lillaah*) thirty-three times, and glorify Him (say *Subḥaan-Allah*) thirty-three times. That is one hundred on the tongue and one thousand in the Balance." I saw the Messenger of Allah (ﷺ) counting them on his hand. They said, "O' Messenger of Allah, how come are they easy, and how come those who do them are so few?" He said, "The *Shayṭaan* (Satan) comes to one of you when he is going to sleep, and makes him sleep before he can say them, and he comes to him when he is praying and reminds him of his affairs before he can say them."[21]

Our Messenger (ﷺ) told us in the hadith of the *Israa'* narrated by Bukhari and others about how he went back and forth between his Lord and Moosa (Moses), when each time Moosa told him to go back to his Lord and ask Him to reduce the number of prayers required, until they became five instead of fifty. At the end of that He (ﷻ) said:

> "My word does not change, as it is enjoined upon you in *Umm al-Kitaab*, every *ḥasanah* will have the reward of ten like it, so they are fifty in *Umm al-Kitaab* and five enjoined upon you." So he went back to Moosa, who said, "What did you do?" He said, "It is reduced for us, and for every *ḥasanah* we will be given the reward of ten like it."

Or they may be multiplied more than that, to a level of seven hundred, or even more. An example of that is the reward of the one

[21] *Jaami' al-Uṣool*, 4/372, hadith no. 2418.

who spends for the sake of Allah. Allah (ﷻ) says:

﴿ مَّثَلُ ٱلَّذِينَ يُنفِقُونَ أَمْوَٰلَهُمْ فِى سَبِيلِ ٱللَّهِ كَمَثَلِ حَبَّةٍ أَنۢبَتَتْ سَبْعَ سَنَابِلَ فِى كُلِّ سُنۢبُلَةٍ مِّائَةُ حَبَّةٍ ۗ وَٱللَّهُ يُضَٰعِفُ لِمَن يَشَآءُ ۗ وَٱللَّهُ وَٰسِعٌ عَلِيمٌ ﴿٢٦١﴾ ﴾

﴿The likeness of those who spend their wealth in the way of Allah, is as the likeness of a grain [of corn]; it grows seven ears, and each ear has a hundred grains. Allah gives manifold increase to whom He wills. And Allah is All-Sufficient for His creatures' needs, All-Knower.﴾ *(Qur'an 2: 261)*

Ibn Katheer said:

"This is an example of the generosity of Allah, as He multiplies the reward of those who spend for His sake, seeking His pleasure. The *ḥasanah* will be multiplied between ten and seven hundred times. And Allah (ﷻ) says: ﴿The likeness of those who spend their wealth in the way of Allah...﴾ *(Qur'an 2: 261)* Sa'eed ibn Jubayr said: This means, in obedience to Allah. Makḥool said: this means spending in jihad, buying steeds of war (cf. 8:60) and preparing weapons, etc. It was narrated from Ibn 'Abbaas that jihad and Ḥajj multiply the dirhams spent on them by seven hundred."[22]

In his *tafseer* of the *aayah*, Ibn Katheer mentioned the hadith narrated by Muslim, Nasaa'i and Aḥmad from 'Abdullah ibn Mas'ood. It states that a man gave a haltered camel in charity for the sake of Allah. The Messenger of Allah (ﷺ) said:

"It will be brought forth on the Day of Resurrection with seven hundred other haltered camels."

[22] *Tafseer Ibn Katheer*, 1/561.

This is the version narrated by Aḥmad and Nasaa'i; the version narrated by Muslim says: A man brought a haltered camel and said, "O' Messenger of Allah, this is for the sake of Allah." He (ﷺ) said:

> "For this you will have seven hundred camels on the Day of Resurrection."[23]

Among the actions which will be multiplied beyond measure, to an extent known only to the One Who gives the reward, is fasting. According to the hadith narrated by Bukhari, Muslim and Aḥmad from Abu Hurayrah (رضي الله عنه), the Prophet (ﷺ) said:

> "Every good deed of the son of Adam will be multiplied between ten and seven hundred times, but Allah says, 'Except for fasting, because it is for Me and I will give the reward for it.'"[24]

The reason why the one who fasts will be given (reward) without measure is that fasting requires *ṣabr* (patience), and those who are patient will be given reward without measure. Allah (سبحانه وتعالى) says:

﴿... إِنَّمَا يُوَفَّى ٱلصَّٰبِرُونَ أَجْرَهُم بِغَيْرِ حِسَابٍ ﴿١٠﴾﴾

> ﴿...Only those who are patient shall receive their reward in full, without reckoning.﴾ *(Qur'an 39: 10)*

Qurṭubi said: "The scholars said: 'Every reward will be measured and weighed out, except (the reward for) fasting, which will be poured out and heaped up.'"[25]

Patience includes patience in the face of disasters, grief and distress in this world, by means of which Allah tests His slaves:

---

23 Ibid, 1/562.

24 *Mishkaat al-Maṣaabeeḥ*, 1/613, hadith no. 1959.

25 *Tafseer al-Qurṭubi*, 15/240.

﴿ وَلَنَبْلُوَنَّكُم بِشَيْءٍ مِّنَ ٱلْخَوْفِ وَٱلْجُوعِ وَنَقْصٍ مِّنَ ٱلْأَمْوَٰلِ وَٱلْأَنفُسِ وَٱلثَّمَرَٰتِ ۗ وَبَشِّرِ ٱلصَّٰبِرِينَ ﴿١٥٥﴾ ٱلَّذِينَ إِذَآ أَصَٰبَتْهُم مُّصِيبَةٌ قَالُوٓا۟ إِنَّا لِلَّهِ وَإِنَّآ إِلَيْهِ رَٰجِعُونَ ﴿١٥٦﴾ أُو۟لَٰٓئِكَ عَلَيْهِمْ صَلَوَٰتٌ مِّن رَّبِّهِمْ وَرَحْمَةٌ ۖ وَأُو۟لَٰٓئِكَ هُمُ ٱلْمُهْتَدُونَ ﴿١٥٧﴾ ﴾

﴾And certainly, We shall test you with something of fear, hunger, loss of wealth, lives and fruits, but give glad tidings to *Aṣ-Ṣaabiroon* [the patient]. Who, when afflicted with calamity, say: 'Truly, to Allah we belong and truly, to Him we shall return.' They are those on whom are the *Ṣalawaat* [i.e. who are blessed and will be forgiven] from their Lord, and [they are those who] receive His Mercy, and it is they who are the guided ones.﴿ *(Qur'an 2: 155-157)*

When the people who were safe from disasters (in this world) see how great is the reward of the patient, they will wish that their skins would have been torn with iron combs so that they might have attained the reward of the patient. In *Sunan at-Tirmidhi* it is narrated from Jaabir, and in *Mu'jam aṭ-Ṭabaraani* it is narrated with a *ḥasan isnaad* from Ibn 'Abbaas, that the Messenger of Allah (ﷺ) (Blessings and Peace be upon him) said:

> "The people who were safe (in this world) will wish, on the Day of Resurrection, that their skins would have been torn with iron combs, when they see the reward of the people who suffered trials." [26]

Another aspect of Allah's bounty is that when the believer intends to do a good action, but does not do it, it is recorded for him as one complete *ḥasanah*. If he intends to do an evil action, then he does not

---

[26] *Ṣaḥeeḥ al-Jaami' aṣ-Ṣagheer*, 5/111, hadith no. 5360.

do it because he fears Allah, then it will be recorded for him as one complete *ḥasanah*. In *Ṣaḥeeḥ Bukhari* it is narrated from Ibn 'Abbaas (ﷺ) that the Prophet (ﷺ) said narrating about his Lord:

> "Allah ordered (the appointed recording angels) to write down both good deeds (*ḥasanaat*) and bad deeds (*sayi'aat*), then He explained how that was to be done. Whoever resolves to do a good deed but does not do it, Allah will record it with Him as one complete *ḥasanah*. If he resolves to do it and does do it, then Allah will record it with Him as between ten and seven hundred *ḥasanaat* or many more. Whoever resolves to do a bad deed and does not do it, Allah will record it with Him as one complete *ḥasanah*. If he resolves to do it and do it, Allah will record it for him as one *sayi'ah*."[27]

Exchanging *sayi'aat* for *ḥasanaat*

The mercy and bounty of Allah towards His slaves will reach such an extent that He will exchange their *sayi'aat* for *ḥasanaat*. In the hadith narrated by Muslim in his *Ṣaḥeeḥ* from Abu Dharr, it says: The Messenger of Allah (ﷺ) said:

> "I know the last of the people of Paradise to enter Paradise, and the last of the people of Hell to emerge from the Fire. It will be a man who will be brought forth on the Day of Resurrection, and it will be said, 'Show him the least of his sins.' It will be said to him, 'Did you not do such and such on such a day...?' He will say, 'Yes.' He will not be able to deny it, and he will be scared that his major sins will also be shown to him. Then it will be

[27] Ibid, *Kitaab ar-Riqaaq, Baab man hamma bi ḥasanah aw sayi'ah, Fatḥ al-Baari*, 11/323.

said to him, 'In the place of every *sayi'ah* you have a *ḥasanah*. He will say, 'My Lord, I did things that I do not see here' - and I saw the Messenger of Allah (ﷺ) smiling so broadly that his eyeteeth could be seen."[28]

5) The testifying of witnesses against the *kuffaar* and *munaafiqeen*

The greatest witness against mankind on the Day of Resurrection will be their Lord and Creator, from Whom nothing of their circumstances is hidden or concealed.

Allah (ﷻ) says:

﴿ ... وَلَا تَعْمَلُونَ مِنْ عَمَلٍ إِلَّا كُنَّا عَلَيْكُمْ شُهُودًا إِذْ تُفِيضُونَ فِيهِ ... ﴿٦١﴾ ﴾

﴿...Nor you [O' mankind] do any deed [good or evil], but We are Witness thereof, when you are doing it...﴾ *(Qur'an 10: 61)*

﴿ ... إِنَّ ٱللَّهَ كَانَ عَلَىٰ كُلِّ شَىْءٍ شَهِيدًا ﴿٣٣﴾ ﴾

﴿...Truly, Allah is Ever a Witness over all things.﴾ *(Qur'an 4: 33)*

But Allah likes to leave no excuse for His creation, so He will send witnesses against the liars and rejecters, so that they will have no excuse at all. Many *aayaat* (verses) refer to the witnesses who will testify against mankind, such as:

﴿ إِنَّا لَنَنصُرُ رُسُلَنَا وَٱلَّذِينَ ءَامَنُوا۟ فِى ٱلْحَيَوٰةِ ٱلدُّنْيَا وَيَوْمَ يَقُومُ ٱلْأَشْهَـٰدُ ﴿٥١﴾ ﴾

---

[28] Muslim, 1/177, hadith no. 190.

﴿Verily, We will indeed make victorious Our Messengers and those who believe [in the Oneness of Allah - Islamic Monotheism] in this world's life and on the Day when the witnesses will stand forth, [i.e. Day of Resurrection].﴾ *(Qur'an 40: 51)*

﴿ ... وَجِاْيٓءَ بِٱلنَّبِيِّـۧنَ وَٱلشُّهَدَآءِ ... ﴿٦٩﴾ ﴾

﴿...And the Prophets and the witnesses will be brought forward...﴾ *(Qur'an 39: 69)*

The first ones who will bear witness against the nations will be their Messengers. Each Messenger will testify against his nation and state that he conveyed the Message.

﴿ فَكَيْفَ إِذَا جِئْنَا مِن كُلِّ أُمَّةٍۭ بِشَهِيدٍ وَجِئْنَا بِكَ عَلَىٰ هَـٰٓؤُلَآءِ شَهِيدًا ﴿٤١﴾ ﴾

﴿How [will it be] then, when We bring from each nation a witness and We bring you [O' Muhammad] as a witness against these people?﴾ *(Qur'an 4: 41)*

﴿ وَيَوْمَ نَبْعَثُ فِي كُلِّ أُمَّةٍ شَهِيدًا عَلَيْهِم مِّنْ أَنفُسِهِمْۖ وَجِئْنَا بِكَ شَهِيدًا عَلَىٰ هَـٰٓؤُلَآءِ ... ﴿٨٩﴾ ﴾

﴿And [remember] the Day when We shall raise up from every nation a witness against them from amongst themselves. And We shall bring you [O' Muhammad] as a witness against these...﴾ *(Qur'an 16: 89)*

The phrase "a witness against them from amongst themselves" refers to the Messengers, because the Messenger for every nation is one of them, as Allah (ﷻ) says:

﴿ لَقَدْ جَآءَكُمْ رَسُولٌ ... ﴿١٢٨﴾ ﴾

﴿Verily, there has come unto you a Messenger [Muhammad] from amongst yourselves...﴾

(Qur'an 9: 128)

﴿ وَنَزَعْنَا مِن كُلِّ أُمَّةٍ شَهِيدًا فَقُلْنَا هَاتُوا۟ بُرْهَـٰنَكُمْ ... ﴿٧٥﴾ ﴾

﴿And We shall take out from every nation a witness, and We shall say: 'Bring your proof.'...﴾ *(Qur'an 28: 75)*

Just as they will testify that they conveyed the Message to their nations, so too they will testify that their nations disbelieved:

﴿ ۞ يَوْمَ يَجْمَعُ ٱللَّهُ ٱلرُّسُلَ فَيَقُولُ مَاذَآ أُجِبْتُمْ ۖ قَالُوا۟ لَا عِلْمَ لَنَآ ۖ إِنَّكَ أَنتَ عَلَّـٰمُ ٱلْغُيُوبِ ﴿١٠٩﴾ ﴾

﴿On the Day when Allah will gather the Messengers together and say to them: 'What was the response you received [from men to your teaching]?' They will say: 'We have no knowledge, verily, only You are the All-Knower of all that is hidden [or unseen].'﴾

(Qur'an 5: 109)

﴿ فَلَنَسْـَٔلَنَّ ٱلَّذِينَ أُرْسِلَ إِلَيْهِمْ وَلَنَسْـَٔلَنَّ ٱلْمُرْسَلِينَ ﴿٦﴾ فَلَنَقُصَّنَّ عَلَيْهِم بِعِلْمٍ ۖ وَمَا كُنَّا غَآئِبِينَ ﴿٧﴾ ﴾

﴿Then surely, We shall question those [people] to whom it [the Book] was sent and verily, We shall question the Messengers. Then surely, We shall narrate unto them [their whole story] with knowledge, and indeed We have not been absent.﴾ *(Qur'an 7: 6-7)*

Ibn Katheer said, commenting on the first of these *aayaat* (5:109): "Here Allah tells us what He will say to the Messengers on the Day of Resurrection about the response of the nations to whom they were sent. Concerning the phrase uttered by the Messengers - 'We have no knowledge' - Mujaahid, Al-Ḥasan al-Baṣri and Aa-Suddi said: 'They will say that because of the horrors of that Day...' Ibn 'Abbaas said, (this means), 'We have no knowledge except that knowledge that You know better than we do about it.' Ibn Jareer narrated this view and it was the view which he favoured. Undoubtedly it is a good view, and it has to do with having the proper etiquette before Allah, i.e., 'We have no knowledge in comparison with Your knowledge which encompasses all things; even if we give our answer and are sure of our answer, but there are some whose outward appearance we could see but we had no knowledge of their inner feelings, but You are the Omniscient Who knows all things and can see all things, so our knowledge is nothing compared to Your knowledge.'"[29]

Then the nations will deny their Messengers and each nation will say, no warner came to us. Then this ummah - the ummah of Muhammad (ﷺ), will come forth and testify that the Messengers did convey the Message, as Allah (ﷻ) says:

﴿ وَكَذَٰلِكَ جَعَلْنَٰكُمْ أُمَّةً وَسَطًا لِّتَكُونُوا۟ شُهَدَآءَ عَلَى ٱلنَّاسِ وَيَكُونَ ٱلرَّسُولُ عَلَيْكُمْ شَهِيدًا ... ﴿١٤٣﴾ ﴾

﴿Thus We have made you [true Muslims - real believers of Islamic Monotheism, true followers of Prophet Muhammad and his Sunnah (legal ways)], a just [and the best] nation, that you be witnesses over mankind and the Messenger [Muhammad] be a witness over you...﴾
(Qur'an 2: 143)

Bukhari narrated in his *Ṣaḥeeḥ* in *Kitaab at-Tafseer* the hadith from Abu Sa'eed al-Khudri (رضي الله عنه) who said, The Messenger of Allah (ﷺ) said:

---

[29] *Tafseer Ibn Katheer*, 2/676.

"Nooḥ (Noah) will be called on the Day of Resurrection and he will say, 'Here I am at Your service, O' Lord.' (Allah) will say, 'Did you convey (the Message)?' He will say, 'Yes.' It will be said to his nation, 'Did he convey (the Message) to you?' They will say, 'No warner came to us.' He will say, 'Who will bear witness for you?' (Nooḥ) will say, 'Muhammad and his ummah.' So they will bear witness that he did convey the Message, and the Messenger will be a witness over you. This is what Allah says:

﴾Thus We have made you [true Muslims - real believers of Islamic Monotheism, true followers of Prophet Muhammad and his Sunnah (legal ways)], a just [and the best] nation, that you be witnesses over mankind and the Messenger [Muhammad] be a witness over you...﴿

(Qur'an 2: 143)[30]

Ibn Ḥajar mentioned that the hadith was recorded by Aḥmad, Nasaa'i and Ibn Maajah with the wording,

"A Prophet will come on the Day of Resurrection, and with him will be one man; another Prophet will come and with him will be two men; and another Prophet will come and with him will be more than that. And it will be said to them, 'Did this man convey (the Message) to you?' They will say, 'No.' It will be said to the Prophet, 'Did you convey (the Message)?' He will say, 'Yes.' It will be said to him, 'Who will testify for you?'..."

Ibn Ḥajar also mentioned that in some reports of the hadith it adds:

"It will be said, 'What did he teach you?' They will say,

---

[30] Bukhari, 13, *Kitaab at-Tafseer*, 8/171.

'Our Prophet told us that the Messengers had conveyed the Message, and we believed him.'"[31]

Also among the witnesses will be the earth, and days and nights; they will testify about what was done to them and against them. Wealth will testify against its owner. Qurṭubi devoted a chapter to this subject in his *Tadhkirah*, in which he mentioned the hadith narrated by Tirmidhi from Abu Hurayrah (رضي الله عنه), who said: The Messenger of Allah (ﷺ) recited this *aayah* -

﴿ يَوْمَئِذٍ تُحَدِّثُ أَخْبَارَهَا ﴿٤﴾ ﴾

﴾That Day it [the earth] will declare its information [about all that happened over it of good or evil].﴿

(Qur'an 99: 4)

He (ﷺ) said, "Do you know what 'its information' is?" They said, "Allah and His Messenger know best." He said, "Its information means that it will testify against every man and woman about what they did on its surface. It will say, 'On such and such a day they did such and such. That is 'its information'.'"

- Tirmidhi said: this is a *ghareeb ṣaḥeeḥ ḥasan* hadith.

The angels of the Most Merciful will also testify against a person, the angels who used to record his deeds, both righteous and evil. Allah (سبحانه وتعالى) says:

﴿ وَجَاءَتْ كُلُّ نَفْسٍ مَّعَهَا سَائِقٌ وَشَهِيدٌ ﴿٢١﴾ ﴾

﴾And every person will come forth along with an [angel] to drive [him] and an [angel] to bear witness.﴿

(Qur'an 50: 21)

---

[31] *Fatḥ al-Baari*, 8/172.

The one who will drive him and the one who will bear witness are two angels who are appointed to deal with this person.

The angels will testify against the people and state what they used to do.

﴿... وَيَقُولُ ٱلْأَشْهَـٰدُ هَـٰٓؤُلَآءِ ٱلَّذِينَ كَذَبُوا۟ عَلَىٰ رَبِّهِمْ ... ﴿١٨﴾﴾

﴾...And the witnesses will say, 'These are the ones who lied against their Lord!'...﴿ *(Qur'an 11: 18)*

If a person persists in arguing and disbelieving his Lord and the witnesses who have testified against him, Allah will appoint a witness against him from his own self, so a man's own limbs and faculties will testify against him, as explained above.

4 - WHAT PEOPLE WILL BE QUESTIONED ABOUT

People will be questioned about the gods whom they used to worship and their response to the Messengers, as we have explained above.

They will also be questioned about the deeds they did, the luxuries they enjoyed in this world, their promises and covenants, their hearing, seeing and hearts. These are the matters which we will discuss here.

1) *Kufr* and *shirk*

The most serious matter about which people will be questioned is their *kufr* and *shirk*. Allah will question them about the partners and rivals which they used to worship instead of Allah, as Allah (ﷻ) says:

﴿وَقِيلَ لَهُمْ أَيْنَ مَا كُنتُمْ تَعْبُدُونَ ﴿٩٢﴾ مِن دُونِ ٱللَّهِ هَلْ يَنصُرُونَكُمْ أَوْ يَنتَصِرُونَ ﴿٩٣﴾﴾

﴾And it will be said to them: 'Where are those [the false

gods whom you used to set up as rivals with Allah] that you used to worship. Instead of Allah? Can they help you or [even] help themselves?'》 *(Qur'an 26: 92-93)*

﴿ وَيَوْمَ يُنَادِيهِمْ فَيَقُولُ أَيْنَ شُرَكَآءِيَ ٱلَّذِينَ كُنتُمْ تَزْعُمُونَ ﴿٦٢﴾ ﴾

《And [remember] the Day when He will call to them and say: 'Where are My [so-called] partners whom you used to assert?'》 *(Qur'an 28: 62)*

They will be questioned about their worship of [false gods] other than Allah, when they offered sacrifices to the gods whom they used to worship:

﴿ وَيَجْعَلُونَ لِمَا لَا يَعْلَمُونَ نَصِيبًا مِّمَّا رَزَقْنَٰهُمْ ۗ تَٱللَّهِ لَتُسْـَٔلُنَّ عَمَّا كُنتُمْ تَفْتَرُونَ ﴿٥٦﴾ ﴾

《And they assign a portion of that which We have provided them unto what they know not [false deities]. By Allah, you shall certainly be questioned about [all] that you used to fabricate.》 *(Qur'an 16: 56)*

And they will be questioned about their rejection of the Messengers:

﴿ وَيَوْمَ يُنَادِيهِمْ فَيَقُولُ مَاذَآ أَجَبْتُمُ ٱلْمُرْسَلِينَ ﴿٦٥﴾ فَعَمِيَتْ عَلَيْهِمُ ٱلْأَنۢبَآءُ يَوْمَئِذٍ فَهُمْ لَا يَتَسَآءَلُونَ ﴿٦٦﴾ ﴾

《And [remember] the Day [Allah] will call to them, and say: 'What answer gave you to the Messengers?' Then the news of a good answer will be obscured to them on that Day, and they will not be able to ask one another.》 *(Qur'an 28: 65-66)*

2) What they did in this world

On the Day of Resurrection, a man will be asked about all the deeds which he did in this world, as Allah (ﷻ) says:

﴿ فَوَرَبِّكَ لَنَسْـَٔلَنَّهُمْ أَجْمَعِينَ ﴿٩٢﴾ عَمَّا كَانُوا۟ يَعْمَلُونَ ﴿٩٣﴾ ﴾

﴿So, by your Lord, [O' Muhammad], We shall certainly call all of them to account. For all that they used to do.﴾

(Qur'an 15: 92-93)

﴿ فَلَنَسْـَٔلَنَّ ٱلَّذِينَ أُرْسِلَ إِلَيْهِمْ وَلَنَسْـَٔلَنَّ ٱلْمُرْسَلِينَ ﴿٦﴾ ﴾

﴿Then surely, We shall question those [people] to whom it [the Book] was sent and verily, We shall question the Messengers.﴾ *(Qur'an 7: 6)*

In *Sunan at-Tirmidhi*, it is narrated from Abu Barzah al-Aslami (رضي الله عنه) that the Messenger of Allah (ﷺ) said:

> "A man will not be let go on the Day of Resurrection until he has been asked about four things: his life and how he spent it, his knowledge and what he did with it, his wealth and how he earned it and spent it, and his body and how he used it."[32]

In *Sunan at-Tirmidhi* it is also narrated from 'Abdullah ibn Mas'ood (رضي الله عنه) that the Prophet (ﷺ) said:

> "The son of Adam will not be released from his Lord's presence on the Day of Resurrection until he has been questioned about five things: his life and how he spent it,

---

[32] *Jaami' al-Uṣool*, 10/436, hadith no. 7969. The editor said: Tirmidhi said: this is a *ṣaḥeeḥ ḥasan* hadith. *Shaykh* Naaṣir (al-Albaani) also stated that it was *ṣaḥeeḥ*, in *Ṣaḥeeḥ al-Jaami'*, 6/148, hadith no. 7177.

> his youth and how he used it, his wealth and how he earned it and spent it, and what he did with the knowledge he gained."[33]

The one who ponders these *aḥaadeeth* will realize the reason why the Messenger (ﷺ) encouraged Muslims to acquire little wealth, because the more wealth a person has, the longer his reckoning will be. The less wealth a person has, the shorter his reckoning will be and the sooner he will reach Paradise. The Messenger (ﷺ) told us that the poor *Muhaajireen* will enter Paradise forty years before the rich *Muhaajireen*. Muslim narrated that Abu 'Abdul-Raḥmaan al-Ḥubali said: "Three people came to 'Abdullah ibn 'Amr ibn al-'Aaṣ whilst I was with him, and said: 'O' Abu Muhammad, by Allah we are not able to do anything, we have no money, no livestock and no possessions.' He said, 'Whatever you want: if you wish, you can come back to us and we will give you whatever Allah makes easy for you, or if you wish, we can tell the *sulṭaan* about your situation, or if you wish, you can be patient. I heard the Messenger of Allah (ﷺ) say:

> "On the Day of Resurrection, the poor *Muhaajireen* will enter Paradise forty years before the rich *Muhaajireen*."'"[34]

3) The luxuries that they enjoyed

On the Day of Resurrection, Allah will question His slaves about the blessings that He granted them in this world, as He (سبحانه وتعالى) says:

﴿ ثُمَّ لَتُسْـَٔلُنَّ يَوْمَئِذٍ عَنِ ٱلنَّعِيمِ ﴿٨﴾ ﴾

---

[33] Ibid, 10/437, hadith no. 7970. This is a *ḥasan* hadith as the editor of *Jaami' al-Uṣool* stated. *Shaykh* Naaṣir also classed it as *ḥasan* in *Ṣaḥeeḥ al-Jaami'*, 6/148, hadith no. 7176.

[34] Muslim, 4/2285, hadith no. 2979.

﴿Then, on that Day, you shall be asked about the delight [you indulged in, in this world]!﴾ *(Qur'an 102: 8)*

- i.e., the delights of a full stomach, cool water, the shade of dwellings, an even-tempered nature and the joy of sleep. Sa'eed ibn Jubayr said: even taking honey. Mujaahid said: (they will be asked) about every delight or joy of this world. Al-Ḥasan al-Baṣri (may Allah be merciful to him) said: these delights include lunch and dinner. Abu Qulaabah said: these delights include eating ghee and honey with soft bread. It is narrated that Ibn 'Abbaas said: the joy of a healthy body, hearing and sight.[35]

The delights referred to in the *aayah* are not limited to those mentioned in these various interpretations, because the kinds of joy and delight are innumerable.

﴿ ... وَإِن تَعُدُّوا۟ نِعْمَتَ ٱللَّهِ لَا تُحْصُوهَآ ... ﴿٣٤﴾ ﴾

﴿...And if you count the Blessings of Allah, never will you be able to count them...﴾ *(Qur'an 14: 34)*

Some kinds of delight are essential, and others are extras or luxuries, and this varies from one person to another. At some times there may be things that are not known to the people of other eras, and in one country there may be things that are unknown to the people of other countries. People will be questioned about all of that.

Tirmidhi narrated with his *isnaad* from Abu Hurayrah that he said: The Messenger of Allah (ﷺ) said:

"The first question that a person will be asked about the delights (of this world) on the Day of Resurrection will be: 'Did We not give you good health? Did We not give

[35] *Tafseer Ibn Katheer*, 7/364.

you cool water to drink?'"[36]

Some people do not realize the great blessings that Allah (ﷻ) has bestowed upon them. They do not appreciate the blessing of having water to drink and food to eat, or the blessings that Allah has bestowed upon them in their homes, spouses and children. They think that luxury means having palaces, gardens and fancy means of transportation. A man asked 'Abdullah ibn 'Amr ibn al-'Aaṣ, "Are we not among the poor *Muhaajireen*?" 'Abdullah said to him, "Don't you have a wife to whom you return at the end of the day?" He said, "Yes." He said, "Don't you have a house to live in?" He said, "Yes." He said, "Then you are one of the rich." He said, "I have a servant." He said, "Then you are one of the kings."[37]

Bukhari narrated that Ibn 'Abbaas said: The Messenger of Allah (ﷺ) said:

> "There are two blessings which many people do not appreciate: good health and free time."[38]

What this means is that they fail to appreciate these two blessings fully, and they do not fulfil the duties associated with them, and whoever does not fulfil the duties associated with a thing does not appreciate it fully.

In *Musnad Aḥmad* it is narrated that the Messenger of Allah (ﷺ) said:

> "There is nothing wrong with being rich for those who fear Allah, but for those who fear Allah, good health is

[36] *Mishkaat al-Maṣaabeeḥ*, 2/656, hadith no. 5196. The editor of *Al-Mishkaat* said: its *isnaad* is *ṣaḥeeḥ*.

[37] Muslim, 4/2285, hadith no. 2979.

[38] *Mishkaat al-Maṣaabeeḥ*, 2/648, hadith no. 5155.

better than riches. And peace of mind is also a blessing."[39]

In some *aḥaadeeth*, the Prophet (ﷺ) explained some of the forms that the questioning about worldly luxuries will take, when Allah confronts His slaves with these questions on that Day. In Muslim it is narrated from Abu Hurayrah that the Prophet (ﷺ) said:

"The Lord will meet His slave and will say, 'O' So and so, did I not honour you and make you prominent, and give you a wife, and subjugate horses and camels to you, and cause you to become a leader?' He will say, 'Indeed.' Allah will say, 'Did you think that you would meet Me?' He will say, 'No.' Allah will say, 'I will forget you as you forgot Me.' Then He will meet a second (slave) and will say, 'O' So and so, did I not honour you and make you prominent, and give you a wife, and subjugate horses and camels to you, and cause you to become a leader?' He will say, 'Indeed.' Allah will say, 'Did you think that you would meet Me?' He will say, 'No.' Allah will say, 'I will forget you as you forgot Me.' Then He will meet a third (slave), and will say something similar. The slave will say, 'O' Lord, I believed in You and in Your Book and Your Messengers. I prayed and fasted and gave in charity,' and he will praise himself. Allah will say, 'Let us pause here.' Then it will be said to him, 'Now We shall send to you a witness against you.' He will think to himself, who is that who can bear witness against me? Then Allah will place a seal over his mouth, and it will be said to his

---

[39] Ibid, 2/676, hadith no. 5290. The editor attributed it to Ibn Maajah, and said, its *isnaad* is *ṣaḥeeḥ*.

> thigh and his flesh and bones, 'Speak!' So his thigh and his flesh and bones will speak about his deeds, and thus proof will be established against him from himself. That will be the hypocrite with whom Allah will be angry."[40]

The questioning about blessings and luxuries will be to question whether a person was grateful for the blessings that Allah bestowed upon him. If he gave thanks, then he will have fulfilled the duty required by that blessing. If he refused to give thanks and was ungrateful, Allah will be angry with him. Muslim narrated on the authority of Anas that the Messenger of Allah (ﷺ) said:

> "Allah will be pleased with His slave if, when he eats some food he praises Him for it, and when he drinks something, he praises Him for it."[41]

4) Promises and covenants

Allah (ﷻ) will question His slaves about the promises and covenants they made:

﴿ وَلَقَدْ كَانُوا۟ عَـٰهَدُوا۟ ٱللَّهَ مِن قَبْلُ لَا يُوَلُّونَ ٱلْأَدْبَـٰرَ ۚ وَكَانَ عَهْدُ ٱللَّهِ مَسْـُٔولًا ﴿١٥﴾ ﴾

> ﴾And indeed they had already made a covenant with Allah not to turn their backs, and a covenant with Allah must be answered for.﴿ *(Qur'an 33: 15)*

Every covenant among people that does not involve anything that is *ḥaraam*, Allah will ask them whether they fulfilled it:

﴿ ... وَأَوْفُوا۟ بِٱلْعَهْدِ ۖ إِنَّ ٱلْعَهْدَ كَانَ مَسْـُٔولًا ﴿٣٤﴾ ﴾

---

[40] Narrated by Muslim in his *Ṣaḥeeḥ*, 4/2280, hadith no. 2968.

[41] *Mishkaat al-Maṣaabeeḥ*, 2/446, hadith no. 4200.

> ﴾...And fulfil [every] covenant. Verily, the covenant will be questioned about.﴿ *(Qur'an 17: 34)*

5) Hearing, sight and hearts

Allah will question His slaves about everything that they say, hence He warns them against speaking without knowledge:

﴿ وَلَا تَقْفُ مَا لَيْسَ لَكَ بِهِۦ عِلْمٌ ۚ إِنَّ ٱلسَّمْعَ وَٱلْبَصَرَ وَٱلْفُؤَادَ كُلُّ أُو۟لَٰٓئِكَ كَانَ عَنْهُ مَسْـُٔولًا ﴿٣٦﴾ ﴾

> ﴾And follow not [O' man, i.e., say not, or do not, or witness not] that of which you have no knowledge. Verily, the hearing, and the sight, and the heart of each of those ones will be questioned [by Allah].﴿
> *(Qur'an 17: 36)*

Qataadah said: "Do not say, 'I saw' when you did not see, or 'I heard' when you did not hear, or 'I know' when you do not know, for Allah will ask you about all of that."[42]

Ibn Katheer said: "The implication of what is mentioned in the *aayah* is that Allah forbids us to speak without knowledge, i.e., conjecture or suspicion which is based on imagination. As Allah (سُبْحَانَهُ وَتَعَالَىٰ) says:

﴿ يَٰٓأَيُّهَا ٱلَّذِينَ ءَامَنُوا۟ ٱجْتَنِبُوا۟ كَثِيرًا مِّنَ ٱلظَّنِّ إِنَّ بَعْضَ ٱلظَّنِّ إِثْمٌ ... ﴿١٢﴾ ﴾

> ﴾O' you who believe! Avoid much suspicion; indeed some suspicions are sins...﴿ *(Qur'an 49: 12)*

And according to the hadith:

> "Beware of suspicion, for suspicion is the falsest of speech."

---

[42] *Tafseer Ibn Katheer*, 4/308.

In *Sunan Abi Dawood* it says,

> "What a bad thing it is for a man to keep saying, 'They say'."

According to another hadith:

> "The worst type of lies is for a man to claim that he saw something which his eyes did not see."

And in *Ṣaḥeeḥ al-Bukhari* it says,

> "Whoever claims to have seen a dream that he did not see, will be commanded on the Day of Resurrection to tie two grains of barley together, and he will not be able to do it."[43]

5 - THE FIRST OF HIS DEEDS FOR WHICH A PERSON WILL BE BROUGHT TO ACCOUNT

The first of his duties towards Allah for which a person will be brought to account will be his *ṣalaah* (prayer). If his prayer is good he will succeed and prosper, otherwise he will be a loser and doomed. In *Sunan at-Tirmidhi* and *Sunan an-Nasaa'i* it is narrated that Abu Hurayrah (رضي الله عنه) (may Allah be pleased with him) said: I heard the Messenger of Allah (ﷺ) say:

> "The first of his deeds for which a person will be brought to account on the Day of Resurrection will be his *ṣalaah* (prayer). If it is good then he will succeed and prosper, and if it is bad then he will be a loser and doomed. If anything is lacking from his obligatory prayers, the Lord will say, 'Look and see whether my slave has any

---

[43] Ibid.

> voluntary (prayers), and use that to make up whatever is missing from his obligatory prayers.' Then all of his deeds will be reviewed in like manner."[44]

In *Sunan Abi Dawood* it is narrated from Abu Hurayrah that the Prophet (ﷺ) said:

> "The first of their deeds for which the people will be brought to account on the Day of Resurrection will be their *ṣalaah* (prayer). Our Lord will say to His angels, 'Look at the prayer of My slave, whether it is complete?' If it is complete, it will be recorded as being complete, and if anything is lacking, He will say, 'Look and see whether My slave offered any voluntary prayers.' If he did any voluntary prayers, He will say, 'Complete My slave's obligatory prayers from his voluntary prayers.' Then all other deeds will be reviewed."[45]

6 - THE DIFFERENT KINDS OF RECKONING, AND EXAMPLES THEREOF

1) The different kinds of reckoning

The ways in which people will be brought to account will vary. For some the reckoning will be hard. They are the *kuffaar* and evildoers, who associated others in worship with Allah for which He had not sent down any authority. They rebelled against the laws of Allah, and disbelieved in the Messengers. Some of the sinners among the people

---

[44] *Jaami' al-Uṣool*, 10/434, hadith no. 7964. In *Ṣaḥeeḥ al-Jaami'* it is attributed to Tirmidhi, Nasaa'i and Ibn Maajah, and classed as *ṣaḥeeḥ*. *Ṣaheeḥ al-Jaami'*, 2/184, hadith no. 2016.

[45] *Jaami' al-Uṣool*, 10/435, hadith no. 7965. In *Ṣaheeḥ al-Jaami'*, *Shaykh* Naaṣir attributed it to Abu Dawood, Aḥmad, Nasaa'i and Ḥaakim, and said, it is *ṣaḥeeḥ*. *Ṣaheeḥ al-Jaami'*, 2/352, hadith no. 2568.

of *Tawḥeed* will face a lengthy and difficult reckoning because of the number and magnitude of their sins.

Some people will enter Paradise without being brought to account. They are a small group numbering no more than seventy thousand. They are the elite of this ummah, those who reach the pinnacle of faith, piety, righteousness and jihad. They will be described in more detail when we discuss the people of Paradise. For some people the reckoning will be easy. They are the ones whose record will not be discussed or checked. They will be shown their sins, then they will be forgiven for them. This is the meaning of the *aayah* (verse):

﴿ فَأَمَّا مَنْ أُوتِيَ كِتَٰبَهُۥ بِيَمِينِهِۦ ۝٧ فَسَوْفَ يُحَاسَبُ حِسَابًا يَسِيرًا ۝٨ ﴾

﴾Then as for him who will be given his Record in his right hand, He surely, will receive an easy reckoning.﴿ *(Qur'an 84: 7-8)*

Bukhari and Muslim narrated from 'Aa'ishah that the Messenger of Allah (ﷺ) said:

> "No one will be called to account on the Day of Resurrection but he will be doomed." I said, 'O' Messenger of Allah, does not Allah say, ﴾Then as for him who will be given his Record in his right hand, He surely, will receive an easy reckoning.﴿ *(Qur'an 84: 7-8)*?' The Messenger of Allah (ﷺ) said: 'That is only the presentation of the account, but no one will have his account questioned (in detail) on the Day of Resurrection but he will be doomed.'"[46]

---

46 Bukhari: *Kitaab ar-Riqaaq, Baab min nooqasha al-ḥisaab 'udhdhib, Fatḥ al-Baari*, 11/400; Muslim: 4/2204, haidht no. 2876. This version is narrated by Bukhari.

An-Nawawi said, commenting on this hadith: "The meaning of having his account questioned in detail is that he will be examined thoroughly. Al-Qaaḍi said: the word 'punished' has two meanings. One is that the very process of being shown one's sins and having them discussed in detail will be a punishment, because of the rebuke implicit in that. The second is that it will lead to the punishment in the Fire. This is supported by the word 'doomed' in the second report, instead of 'punished.' This is the view of Al-Qaaḍi (Iyaaḍ).

An-Nawawi said: this second meaning is the correct one. It means that shortcomings are common among people, and whoever is examined thoroughly and is not forgiven, will be doomed and will enter Hell, but Allah will forgive and overlook sins less than *shirk* for whomsoever He wills."[47]

Ibn Ḥajar narrated that Qurṭubi said concerning the meaning of the phrase "That is only the presentation of the account": "The account mentioned in the *aayah* is when the deeds of the believer are shown to him, so that he will recognize how Allah blessed him by concealing those sins in this world, and by forgiving him for them in the Hereafter."[48]

What is meant by the presentation - as is apparent from these *aḥaadeeth* - is the presentation of the believers' sins to them, so that they may appreciate the extent of Allah's blessing upon them when He forgives them for them.

2) Examples of these kinds of reckoning

In the Sunnah of the Prophet (ﷺ) there are narrated scenes of the discussion of accounts, presentation and rebuke which Allah, the Almighty, All-Glorious, will give to His slaves. We will give three

---

[47] An-Nawawi's commentary on Muslim, 17/208.
[48] *Fatḥ al-Baari*, 11/402.

examples for each of these three kinds of reckoning from the *ṣaḥeeḥ* Sunnah.

a) Discussing the sins of those who show off

Muslim, Tirmidhi and Nasaa'i narrated that Shafiy ibn Maati' al-Aṣbaḥi (may Allah have mercy on him) said: "I entered Madeenah, and saw a man around whom people had gathered. I said, 'Who is this?' They said, 'Abu Hurayrah.' So I approached him and sat down in front of him, whilst he was speaking to the people. When he became silent and was alone, I said to him: 'I abjure you by Allah, that you tell me a hadith which you heard from the Messenger of Allah (ﷺ), that you understood and learned.' Abu Hurayrah said, 'I shall do that, I shall tell you a hadith that the Messenger of Allah (ﷺ) told me, which I learned and understood.' Then Abu Hurayrah started to gasp, and we sat for a while, then he recovered and said: 'I shall tell you a hadith that the Messenger of Allah (ﷺ) told me in this house, when there was no one else with us but me and him.' Then Abu Hurayrah started to gasp again, then he recovered and wiped his face, and said: 'I shall tell you a hadith that the Messenger of Allah (ﷺ) told me when he and I were in this house, and there was no one else with us but me and him.' Then Abu Hurayrah started to gasp intensely, then he leaned forward as if he were about to fall on his face, so I supported for a long time, until he recovered, then he said: The Messenger of Allah (ﷺ) told me:

> 'On the Day of Resurrection, Allah will come down to His slaves to pass judgement between them, and every nation will be kneeling. The first one to be called forth will be a man who had learned the whole of the Qur'an, a man who was killed for the sake of Allah, and a man who had a lot of wealth. Allah will say to the one who had learned the whole of the Qur'an, 'Did I not teach you what I had revealed to My Messenger?' He will say,

> 'Yes, O' Lord.' Allah will say, 'What did you do with that which I taught you?' He will say, 'I used to stand (in prayer and recite) it during the night and during the day.' Allah will say to him, 'You are lying,' and the angels will say to him, 'You are lying.' Allah will say to him, You only wanted it to be said that So and so is a reader (of the Qur'an), and that was said.'
>
> Then the one who had a lot of wealth will be brought, and Allah will say to him, 'Did I not bestow abundantly upon you, so that you had no need of anybody else?' He will say, 'Yes, O' Lord.' Allah will say, 'What did you do with that which I gave you?' He will say, 'I used to uphold the ties of kinship, and give in charity.' Allah will say to him, 'You are lying,' and the angels will say to him, 'You are lying.' Allah will say to him, 'You only wanted it to be said that So and so is generous, and that was said.'
>
> Then the one who was killed for the sake of Allah will be brought, and Allah will say, 'What were you killed for?' He will say, 'I was commanded to engage in jihad for Your sake, so I fought until I was killed.' Allah will say to him, 'You are lying,' and the angels will say to him, 'You are lying.' Allah will say to him, 'You only wanted it to be said that So and so is brave, and that was said.'
>
> Then the Messenger of Allah (ﷺ) struck my knees and said, 'O' Abu Hurayrah, these three will be the first among the creation of Allah for whom the Fire will be heated on the Day of Resurrection.''''

Al-Waleed Abu 'Uthmaan al-Madaa'ini said: "Uqbah ibn Muslim told me, that Shafiy was the one who met Mu'aawiyah and told him about this."

Abu ‘Uthmaan said: “And al-‘Alaa’ ibn Abi Ḥakeem told me that he was the executioner of Mu‘aawiyah, and a man visited him and told him this hadith from Abu Hurayrah. Mu‘aawiyah said: “If this is what will be done to these people, then how about the rest of the people?” Then Mu‘aawiyah wept intensely, until we thought that he was about to die, and we thought that this man had brought him bad news. Then Mu‘aawiyah recovered, and wiped his face, and said: ‘Indeed Allah (ﷻ) and His Messenger spoke the truth.

﴿مَن كَانَ يُرِيدُ ٱلْحَيَوٰةَ ٱلدُّنْيَا وَزِينَتَهَا نُوَفِّ إِلَيْهِمْ أَعْمَٰلَهُمْ فِيهَا وَهُمْ فِيهَا
لَا يُبْخَسُونَ ﴿١٥﴾ أُو۟لَٰٓئِكَ ٱلَّذِينَ لَيْسَ لَهُمْ فِى ٱلْءَاخِرَةِ إِلَّا ٱلنَّارُ وَحَبِطَ مَا
صَنَعُوا۟ فِيهَا وَبَٰطِلٌ مَّا كَانُوا۟ يَعْمَلُونَ ﴿١٦﴾﴾

﴾Whosoever desires the life of the world and its glitter, to them We shall pay in full [the wages of] their deeds therein, and they will have no diminution therein. They are those for whom there is nothing in the Hereafter but Fire, and vain are the deeds they did therein. And of no effect is that which they used to do.﴿

(Qur’an 11: 15-16).’”

- This is narrated by Tirmidhi.

According to the report narrated by Muslim and Nasaa’i from Sulaymaan ibn Yasaar: “The people left Abu Hurayrah, and Naatil the Syrian said to him: ‘O’ *shaykh*, tell me a hadith that you heard from the Messenger of Allah (ﷺ).’ He said, ‘Yes, I heard the Messenger of Allah (ﷺ) say:

‘The first of the people upon whom judgement will be passed on the Day of Resurrection will be a man who was martyred. He will be brought forth and reminded of the blessing that he was given, and he will acknowledge it. (Allah) will say, ‘What did you do with it?’ He will say, 'I fought for Your sake until I was martyred.' (Allah) will say, 'You are lying. You fought so that it might be said, he is brave, and it was said.' Then the command will be given, and he will be dragged on his face and thrown into Hell. Then there will be a man who acquired knowledge and taught it, and recited the Qur'an. He will be brought forth and reminded of the blessing that he was given, and he will acknowledge it. (Allah) will say, 'What did you do with it?' He will say, 'I acquired knowledge and taught it, and recited the Qur'an for Your sake.' (Allah) will say, 'You are lying. You acquired knowledge so that it might be said, he is a knowledgeable man, and it was said.' Then the command will be given, and he will be dragged on his face and thrown into Hell. Then there will be a man to whom Allah gave in abundance, all kinds of wealth. He will be brought forth and reminded of the blessing that he was given, and he will acknowledge it. (Allah) will say, 'What did you do with it?' He will say, 'I did not leave any way in which You love charity to be given, but I spent for Your sake in that way.' (Allah) will say, 'You are lying. You did that so that it might be said, he is generous, and it was said.' Then the command will be given, and he will be dragged on his face and thrown into Hell.''''

b) The Lord will show the slave his sins

It is narrated that 'Abdullah ibn 'Umar (رضي الله عنه) said: I heard the Messenger of Allah (ﷺ) say:

"Allah will bring the believer close to Him and shelter him and cover him, then He will say, 'Do you acknowledge such and such a sin, do you acknowledge such and such a sin?' He will say, 'Yes, O' Lord,' until he will have acknowledged his sins, and he will think to himself that he is doomed. Then Allah will say, 'I concealed it for you in the world, and I forgive you for it this Day.' Then he will be given the book of his good deeds. But as for the *kaafireen* and *munaafiqeen*, the witnesses will say:

﴿... هَٰٓؤُلَآءِ ٱلَّذِينَ كَذَبُواْ عَلَىٰ رَبِّهِمْۚ أَلَا لَعۡنَةُ ٱللَّهِ عَلَى ٱلظَّٰلِمِينَ ١٨﴾

﴾...These are the ones who lied against their Lord! No doubt! the Curse of Allah is on the *Ẓaalimoon* [polytheists, wrongdoers, oppressors].﴿

(Qur'an 11: 18).'"[49]

Qurṭubi said concerning the phrase "will shelter him": this means He will cover him with kindness and generosity, and will speak to him gently and converse with him in a conciliatory manner. Allah will say to him, 'Do you acknowledge?' and he will say, 'Yes, O' Lord, I acknowledge.' Then Allah will remind him of His blessings and show His favour upon him by saying, 'I concealed it for you in the world and I did not expose it, and I forgive you for it this Day.'"[50]

c) Allah will rebuke His slave for the shortcomings he committed

The Messenger (ﷺ) has told us that the Lord will rebuke His slaves on the Day of Resurrection. In *Saheeh Muslim* it is narrated that Abu Hurayrah (رضي الله عنه) stated: The Messenger of Allah (ﷺ) said:

---

[49] Bukhari: *Kitaab al-Maẓaalim, Baab Qawlihi ta'aala,* ﴾*Alaa la'nat Allaahi 'ala aẓ-Ẓaalimeen*﴿, *Fatḥ al-Baari*, 5/96; Muslim, 4/2120, hadith no. 2768.

[50] *At-Tadhkirah*, Pp. 263.

"Allah will say on the Day of Resurrection, 'O' son of Adam, I fell sick and you did not visit Me.' He will say, 'O' Lord, how could I visit You when You are the Lord of the Worlds?' Allah will say, 'Did you not know that My slave So and so was sick, and you did not visit him? Do you not know that if you had visited him, you would have found Me with him?' 'O' son of Adam, I asked you for food and you did not feed Me.' He will say, 'O' Lord, how could I feed You when You are the Lord of the Worlds?' Allah will say, 'Did you not know that My slave So and so asked you for food, and you did not feed him? Did you not know that if you had fed him, you would have found that with Me?' 'O' son of Adam, I asked you to give Me to drink, and you did not give Me to drink.' He will say, 'O' Lord, how could I have given you to drink when You are the Lord of the Worlds?' Allah will say, 'Did you not know that My slave So and so asked you to give him to drink, and you did not give him to drink? If you had given him to drink, you would have found that with Me.'"[51]

7 - HOW THE PEOPLE WILL BE GIVEN THEIR BOOKS

At the end of the Reckoning, each person will be given his book containing a complete record of the deeds which he did in this life. The ways in which the people will be given their books will vary. The believer will be given his book in his right hand, from the front, and his reckoning will be easy, then he will return to his family in Paradise in joy:

---

[51] *Mishkaat al-Maṣaabeeḥ*, 1/486, hadeeth no. 1528.

﴿ فَأَمَّا مَنْ أُوتِيَ كِتَابَهُ بِيَمِينِهِ ﴿٧﴾ فَسَوْفَ يُحَاسَبُ حِسَابًا يَسِيرًا ﴿٨﴾
وَيَنقَلِبُ إِلَىٰ أَهْلِهِ مَسْرُورًا ﴿٩﴾ ﴾

﴾Then as for him who will be given his Record in his right hand, He surely, will receive an easy reckoning, And will return to his family in joy!﴿

(Qur'an 84: 7-8)

When the believer will look at what his record contains, of *Tawḥeed* and righteous deeds, he will be happy and will rejoice, and he will raise his voice to announce this joy.

﴿ فَأَمَّا مَنْ أُوتِيَ كِتَابَهُ بِيَمِينِهِ فَيَقُولُ هَاؤُمُ اقْرَءُوا كِتَابِيَهْ ﴿١٩﴾ إِنِّي ظَنَنتُ أَنِّي
مُلَاقٍ حِسَابِيَهْ ﴿٢٠﴾ فَهُوَ فِي عِيشَةٍ رَّاضِيَةٍ ﴿٢١﴾ فِي جَنَّةٍ عَالِيَةٍ ﴿٢٢﴾ قُطُوفُهَا
دَانِيَةٌ ﴿٢٣﴾ كُلُوا وَاشْرَبُوا هَنِيئًا بِمَا أَسْلَفْتُمْ فِي الْأَيَّامِ الْخَالِيَةِ ﴿٢٤﴾ ﴾

﴾Then as for him who will be given his Record in his right hand will say: 'Here! read my Record! Surely, I did believe that I shall meet my Account!' So he shall be in a life, well-pleasing. In a lofty Paradise, the fruits in bunches whereof will be low and near at hand. Eat and drink at ease for that which you have sent on before you in days past!﴿ *(Qur'an 69: 19-24)*

As for the *kaafir* (disbeliever), *munaafiq* (hypocrite) and people of misguidance, they will be given their books in their left hands from behind their backs. At that point the *kaafir* will raise his voice with cries of woe, praying against himself.

﴿ وَأَمَّا مَنْ أُوتِيَ كِتَابَهُ وَرَاءَ ظَهْرِهِ ﴿١٠﴾ فَسَوْفَ يَدْعُو ثُبُورًا ﴿١١﴾ وَيَصْلَىٰ سَعِيرًا
﴿١٢﴾ ﴾

﴾But whosoever is given his Record behind his back, He will invoke [for his] destruction, And he shall enter a blazing Fire, and made to taste its burning.﴿

(Qur'an 84: 10-12)

﴾ وَأَمَّا مَنْ أُوتِيَ كِتَٰبَهُۥ بِشِمَالِهِۦ فَيَقُولُ يَٰلَيْتَنِى لَمْ أُوتَ كِتَٰبِيَهْ ﴿٢٥﴾ وَلَمْ أَدْرِ مَا حِسَابِيَهْ ﴿٢٦﴾ يَٰلَيْتَهَا كَانَتِ ٱلْقَاضِيَةَ ﴿٢٧﴾ مَآ أَغْنَىٰ عَنِّى مَالِيَهْ ۜ ﴿٢٨﴾ هَلَكَ عَنِّى سُلْطَٰنِيَهْ ﴿٢٩﴾ خُذُوهُ فَغُلُّوهُ ﴿٣٠﴾ ثُمَّ ٱلْجَحِيمَ صَلُّوهُ ﴿٣١﴾ ﴿

﴾But as for him who will be given his Record in his left hand, will say: 'I wish that I had not been given my Record! And that I had never known how my Account is! Would that it had been my end [death]! My wealth has not availed me; My power [and arguments to defend myself] have gone from me!' [It will be said]: 'Seize him and fetter him; Then throw him in the blazing Fire.'﴿

(Qur'an 69: 25-31)

When the people are given their books, it will be said to them:

﴾ هَٰذَا كِتَٰبُنَا يَنطِقُ عَلَيْكُم بِٱلْحَقِّ ۚ إِنَّا كُنَّا نَسْتَنسِخُ مَا كُنتُمْ تَعْمَلُونَ ﴿٢٩﴾ ﴿

﴾This Our Record speaks about you with truth. Verily, We were recording what you used to do [i.e. Our angels used to record your deeds].﴿ *(Qur'an 45: 29)*

8 - QURṬUBI'S DEPICTION OF THE SCENE OF THE RECKONING

Qurṭubi said, describing the scene of the Reckoning:

"When the people are resurrected from their graves to the place (of Judgement), they will stand therein for as long as Allah (ﷻ) wills, barefoot and naked. Then the time of reckoning will come when Allah wills to bring them to account. He will command that the books in which the honourable scribes (angels) recorded the deeds of mankind be brought forth. Among them will be some who will be given their books in their right hands. These are the blessed (those who are to enter Paradise). Others will be given their books in their left hands or from behind their backs. They are the doomed (those who are to enter Hell). At that point each person will read his book.

Imagine yourself when the books fly forth and the Balance is set up, and you are called by name before all of creation: where is So and so the son of So and so? Come to have your record examined before Allah. Angels will be dispatched to fetch you, and they will bring you closer to Allah. There will be no problem posed by the similarity of names to your name and your father's name. You will know that you are the one who is being called. Your heart will be filled with fear and your limbs will start to tremble. You will start to panic, your colour will change and your heart will sink. You will be taken through the ranks to your Lord, to be examined by Him and to stand before Him. The eyes of all creatures will be upon you, and you will be standing before them all. Your heart will sink and you will be filled with intense terror, because you will know what is going to happen.

Imagine yourself, standing before your Lord, holding in your hands the book that speaks of your deeds. It will not overlook any terrible deed that you did and concealed, or any secret that you kept. You will read the book's contents nervously, with a broken heart, faced with terrors from in front and behind. How many forgotten terrible actions will you remember now! How many bad deeds which you had concealed will be made known now! How many deeds which you took for granted were sincere and acceptable will now be thrown back at you in that place and cancelled out, after you had pinned such great hopes on them! How much regret will fill your heart and how sorry you will feel for your negligence in obeying your Lord!

The one who is given his book in his right hand will know that he is one of the people of Paradise, and will say, "Here, read my Record!"

when Allah gives him permission to read his book. If he was a leader of goodness who called others to good and enjoined it upon them, and persisted in doing it regularly, he will be called by his name and the name of his father. He will come forth and a white book will be brought out for him, in the middle of which are his *sayi'aat* and on the outside of which are his *ḥasanaat*. He will start by reading the record of his *sayi'aat* and he will be scared; his face will turn yellow and his colour will change. When he reaches the end of his book, it will say, 'These are your *sayi'aat*, and you are forgiven for them.' He will be filled with great joy, then he will turn the book over and will read his *ḥasanaat*, and his joy will only increase further. At the end of the book, he will find the words, these are your *ḥasanaat*, which are multiplied for you. Then his face will turn white, and a crown will be brought and placed on his head. He will be dressed in two garments and every joint of his body will be adorned. He will grow to a height of sixty cubits, which was the height of Adam, and it will be said to him, 'Go to your companions and tell them the glad tidings, tell them that each one among them will have the same.' When he turns away, he will say,

﴿... هَآؤُمُ ٱقْرَءُوا۟ كِتَٰبِيَهْ ﴿١٩﴾ إِنِّى ظَنَنتُ أَنِّى مُلَٰقٍ حِسَابِيَهْ ﴿٢٠﴾﴾

﴾...Here! Read my Record! Surely, I did believe that I shall meet my Account!﴿ *(Qur'an 69: 19-20)*

Allah (ﷻ) says,

﴿فَهُوَ فِى عِيشَةٍ رَّاضِيَةٍ ﴿٢١﴾﴾

﴾So he shall be in a life, well-pleasing.﴿ *(Qur'an 69: 21)*,

- i.e., a good life, which he will be pleased with.

﴿فِى جَنَّةٍ عَالِيَةٍ ﴿٢٢﴾﴾

﴾In a lofty Paradise.﴿ *(Qur'an 69: 22)*

- means, in the heavens.

﴿ قُطُوفُهَا دَانِيَةٌ ﴿٢٣﴾ ﴾

﴾The fruits in bunches whereof will be low and near at hand.﴿ *(Qur'an 69: 23)*

- means, its fruits will be close to them. He will say to his companions, 'Do you recognize me?' They will say, 'You have been overwhelmed with the honour of Allah, who are you?' He will say, 'I am So and so the son of So and so. Let every one among you have the glad tidings of a similar reward.'

﴿ كُلُوا وَاشْرَبُوا هَنِيٓـًٔا بِمَآ أَسْلَفْتُمْ فِي ٱلْأَيَّامِ ٱلْخَالِيَةِ ﴿٢٤﴾ ﴾

﴾Eat and drink at ease for that which you have sent on before you in days past!﴿ *(Qur'an 69: 24)*

- means, what you stored up for yourself during the life of this world.

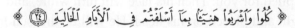

If a man was a leader of evil, who called others to evil and enjoined it upon them, and persisted in doing it regularly, he will be called by his name and the name of his father. He will come forth and a black book will be brought out for him, in the middle of which will be his *ḥasanaat* and on the outside of which are his *sayi'aat*. The reckoning will start with his *ḥasanaat*, which he will read and will think that he will be saved. When he reaches the end of his book, it will say, these are your *ḥasanaat*, and they are rejected. Then his face will turn black, and he will be overwhelmed with grief and despair. Then he will turn the book over and read his *sayi'aat*. His grief will only increase further, and his face will turn even blacker. When he reaches the end of the book, he will find the words, these are your *sayi'aat*, which are multiplied for you - i.e., the punishment will be multiplied for him, it does not mean that things that he did not do will be added to his record. Then he will be taken to the Fire; his eyes will turn blue and his face will turn black, and he will be clothed in garments of pitch.

It will be said to him, 'Go to your companions and tell them that each of them will have the same.' So he will go off, saying,

﴿ وَأَمَّا مَنْ أُوتِيَ كِتَٰبَهُۥ بِشِمَالِهِۦ فَيَقُولُ يَٰلَيْتَنِى لَمْ أُوتَ كِتَٰبِيَهْ ﴿٢٥﴾ وَلَمْ أَدْرِ مَا حِسَابِيَهْ ﴿٢٦﴾ يَٰلَيْتَهَا كَانَتِ ٱلْقَاضِيَةَ ﴿٢٧﴾ ﴾

﴾I wish that I had not been given my Record! And that I had never known how my Account is! Would that it had been my end!﴿ *(Qur'an 69: 25-27),*

- meaning, my death.

﴿ هَلَكَ عَنِّى سُلْطَٰنِيَهْ ﴿٢٩﴾ ﴾

﴾My power [and arguments to defend myself] have gone from me!﴿ *(Qur'an 69: 29).*

Ibn 'Abbaas (رضي الله عنه) interpreted this as meaning, 'I have no argument with which to defend myself.' Then Allah (تعالى) will say:

﴿ خُذُوهُ فَغُلُّوهُ ﴿٣٠﴾ ثُمَّ ٱلْجَحِيمَ صَلُّوهُ ﴿٣١﴾ ﴾

﴾Seize him and fetter him; Then throw him in the blazing Fire﴿ *(Qur'an 69: 30-31)*

- i.e., let him enter Hell.

﴿ ثُمَّ فِى سِلْسِلَةٍ ذَرْعُهَا سَبْعُونَ ذِرَاعًا فَٱسْلُكُوهُ ﴿٣٢﴾ ﴾

﴾Then fasten him with a chain whereof the length is seventy cubits!﴿ *(Qur'an 69: 32).*

Allah knows best the exact nature of these cubits. Al-Ḥasan and Ibn 'Abbaas said, it is seventy of the angels' cubits.

'Then fasten him' it is said, (this means) his neck will be fastened in it, then he will be dragged by it. If one link of this chain were to be placed on a mountain, it would melt.

He will call out to his companions, 'Do you recognize me?' They will say, 'No, but we see the grief on your face. Who are you?' He will say, 'I am So and so the son of So and so, and each of you will have the same as I have.'

As for those who will be given their books from behind their backs, their left shoulders will be dislocated and their arms will be placed behind them, with which they will take their books. Mujaahid said: their faces will be moved to the backs of their heads, and they will read their books in that state.

Imagine yourself, if you are one of the blessed, going out before all of creation with a joyful face, having attained perfection and beauty, with your book in your right hand, seized under the arms by an angel who will call out before the people, 'This is So and so the son of So and so, he has attained happiness and will never feel sorrow again.' But if you are one of the doomed, your face will turn black and you will pass the people with your book in your left hand, or behind your back. You will utter cries of woe and an angel will seize you under the arms and call out before all the people: 'So and so is doomed to a state of misery and will never feel happy again!'"[52]

[52] *At-Tadhkirah*, Pp. 255.

CHAPTER ELEVEN
SETTLING SCORES AMONG ALL CREATURES

On the Day of Resurrection, Allah (ﷻ) the Just, will settle the score between the oppressed and his oppressor, so that there will be no outstanding wrongs among people. Scores will be settled even among the animals. If two sheep butted heads, and one had no horns and the other did, then the score will be settled between them. Muslim narrated from Abu Hurayrah (رضي الله عنه) that the Prophet (ﷺ) said:

> "All creatures' rights will be restored to them on the Day of Resurrection, to such an extent that the hornless sheep will settle its scores with the horned sheep."[1]

If a person committed aggression against another by hitting him, the score will be settled on the Day of Resurrection by the victim hitting his attacker. According to the *ṣaḥeeḥ* hadith narrated by Bukhari in *Al-Adab al-Mufrad*, and by Al-Bayhaqi in *As-Sunan*, Abu Hurayrah (رضي الله عنه) said: The Messenger of Allah (ﷺ) said:

> "Whoever hits someone with a whip unjustly, the score will be settled against him on the Day of Resurrection."[2]

In *Mu'jam aṭ-Ṭabaraani al-Kabeer*, it is narrated that 'Ammaar said: The Messenger of Allah (ﷺ) said:

> "Whoever beats his slave unjustly, the score will be settled against him on the Day of Resurrection." - its *isnaad* is *ṣaḥeeḥ*.[3]

---

[1] Muslim: 1997, hadith no. 2582.

[2] *Ṣaḥeeḥ al-Jaami' aṣ-Ṣagheer*, 5/319, hadith no. 6250.

[3] Ibid, 5/319, hadith no. 6252.

If a person accuses his slave of *zinaa*, the punishment will be carried out against him on the Day of Resurrection, if he is lying. Muslim narrated that Abu Hurayrah (ﷺ) said: Abu'l-Qaasim (ﷺ) said:

> "Whoever accuses his slave of *zinaa*, the punishment will be carried out against him on the Day of Resurrection, unless the matter is as he said."[4]

1 - HOW SCORES WILL BE SETTLED ON THE DAY OF RESURRECTION

When the Day of Resurrection comes, a man's wealth and capital will be his *ḥasanaat* (good deeds). If he had done wrong to any people, they will take from his *ḥasanaat* to the extent that he mistreated them. If he does not have any *ḥasanaat*, or if his *ḥasanaat* run out, then some of their *sayi'aat* (bad deeds) will be taken and added to his burden.

Bukhari narrated on the authority of Abu Hurayrah (ﷺ) that the Messenger of Allah (ﷺ) said:

> "Whoever wronged his brother with regard to his honour or any other matter, should seek his forgiveness today, before there are no longer any dinars or dirhams; and if he has any righteous deeds, they will be taken from him, in accordance with the wrong he did; and if he has no *ḥasanaat*, some of the *sayi'aat* of his counterpart will be taken and added to his burden."[5]

This person whose *ḥasanaat* are taken from him by the people, and then has their *sayi'aat* placed on his own back, is the one who is

---

[4] Muslim: 3/1282, hadith no. 1660.

[5] Bukhari: *Kitaab al-Maẓaalim, Baab man kaanat lahu maẓlamah 'inda rajul, Fatḥ al-Baari, 5/101*

bankrupt, as the Messenger (ﷺ) called him. Muslim narrated from Abu Hurayrah (رضي الله عنه) that the Messenger of Allah (ﷺ) said:

> "Do you know who is the one who is bankrupt?" They said, "The bankrupt is the one who has no money and no possessions." He said, "Among my ummah, the one who is bankrupt is the one who will come on the Day of Resurrection with prayer and fasting and zakah (to his credit), but he will come having insulted this one, slandered that one, consumed the wealth of this one and shed the blood of that one, and beaten that one. So they will all be given some of his *ḥasanaat*, and when his *ḥasanaat* run out, before judgement is passed, some of their sins will be taken and cast onto him, then he will be cast into the Fire."[6]

If a debtor died when he still owed money to people, they will take from his *ḥasanaat* whatever is in accordance with what he owes them. In *Sunan ibn Maajah* it is narrated with a *ṣaḥeeḥ isnaad* that Ibn 'Umar (رضي الله عنه) stated: The Messenger of Allah (ﷺ) said:

> "Whoever dies owing a dinar or a dirham, it will be paid from his *ḥasanaat*, for then there will be no dinars or dirhams."[7]

If people wronged one another, the score will be settled between them. If they mistreated one another equally, then there will be no score to settle. If one of them is still owed something by the other, he will take what he is entitled to.

In *Sunan at-Tirmidhi* it is narrated that 'Aa'ishah said: "A man came and sat in front of the Messenger of Allah (ﷺ), and said, 'O'

---

[6] Muslim: 4/1998, hadith no. 2581.

[7] *Ṣaḥeeḥ al-Jaami' aṣ-Ṣagheer*, 5/537, hadith no. 6432.

Messenger of Allah, I have two slaves who tell me lies, betray and disobey me, and I insult them and beat them. What is my position with regard to them?' The Messenger of Allah (ﷺ) said:

> 'On the Day of Resurrection, their betrayal, disobedience and lying will be measured against your punishment of them. If your punishment is commensurate with their wrongs, then there will be no score to settle. If your punishment of them was less than their sins deserved, then this will count in your favour. If your punishment of them was more than their sins deserved, then the score will be settled against you.' The man turned away and started to weep. The Messenger of Allah (ﷺ) said to him, 'Have you not read the words of Allah?' -
>
> ﴿ وَنَضَعُ ٱلْمَوَٰزِينَ ٱلْقِسْطَ لِيَوْمِ ٱلْقِيَٰمَةِ فَلَا تُظْلَمُ نَفْسٌ شَيْـًٔا ۖ وَإِن كَانَ مِثْقَالَ حَبَّةٍ مِّنْ خَرْدَلٍ أَتَيْنَا بِهَا ۗ وَكَفَىٰ بِنَا حَٰسِبِينَ ﴿٤٧﴾ ﴾
>
> ﴿And We shall set up Balances of justice on the Day of Resurrection, then none will be dealt with unjustly in anything. And if there be the weight of a mustard seed, We will bring it. And Sufficient are We to take account.﴾
>
> *(Qur'an 21: 47).*'"[8]

Because *ẓulm* (oppression) is such a serious matter, it is better for those who fear that Day to give up oppression and avoid it. The Messenger (ﷺ) has told us that oppression will be darkness on the Day of Resurrection. Bukhari and Muslim narrated from 'Abdullah ibn 'Umar that the Prophet (ﷺ) said:

> "Oppression (*ẓulm*) will be darkness (*ẓulumaat*) on the

---

[8] *Mishkaat al-Maṣaabeeḥ*, 3/66, hadith no. 5561. It is also narrated in *Ṣaḥeeḥ al-Jaami'*, 6/327, hadith no. 7895, where it attributed to Aḥmad and Tirmidhi.

Day of Resurrection."[9]

Muslim narrated from Jaabir ibn 'Abdullah that the Messenger of Allah (ﷺ) said:

> "Beware of oppression (*ẓulm*), for oppression will be darkness (*ẓulumaat*) on the Day of Resurrection."[10]

2 - THE ENORMITY OF BLOODSHED

One of the most serious of matters before Allah (ﷻ) is when people shed one another's blood in ways that have not been prescribed by Allah. According to the *ṣaḥeeḥ* hadith narrated by Tirmidhi from Ibn Mas'ood, the Prophet (ﷺ) said:

> "A man will come holding another by the hand, and will say, 'O' Lord, this man killed me.' Allah will say, 'Why did you kill him?' He will say, 'I killed him so that the glory would be for You.' Allah will say, 'It is for Me.' Another man will come holding another by the hand, and will say, 'O' Lord, this man killed me.' Allah will say, 'Why did you kill him?' He will say, 'So that the glory might be for So and so,' Allah will say, 'It is not for So and so,' and he will carry his sin."[11]

In the *Sunans* of Tirmidhi, Abu Dawood and Ibn Maajah it is narrated that Ibn 'Abbaas said: The Messenger of Allah (ﷺ) said:

> "The one who would be killed will bring his killer on the Day of Resurrection, holding his forelock in his hand, and with his veins running with blood. He will say, 'O'

---

[9] Bukhari: *Kitaab al-Maẓaalim, Baab aẓ-Ẓulm Ẓulumaat Yawm al-Qiyaamah, Fatḥ al-Baari*, 5/100; Muslim, 4/1969, hadith no. 2579.

[10] Muslim: 4/1969, hadith no. 2578.

[11] *Ṣaḥeeḥ al-Jaami' aṣ-Ṣagheer*, 6/324, hadith no. 7885.

> Lord, ask this man why he killed me,' until he brings him near to the Throne."[12]

Because of the seriousness of the matter of bloodshed, it will be the first thing on which judgement will be passed among mankind.

Bukhari, Muslim, Tirmidhi and Nasaa'i narrated from 'Abdullah ibn Mas'ood (ﷺ) that the Prophet (ﷺ) said:

> "The first thing concerning which judgement will be passed among the people on the Day of Resurrection will be bloodshed."[13]

Ibn Ḥajar said in his commentary on the hadith: "This hadith indicates the seriousness of the issue of bloodshed, because the matter which is attended to first is the most important, and the seriousness of any sin is connected to its negative consequences and its impact on the common good."[14]

There is no contradiction between this hadith and the hadith which says that the first thing for which a person will be brought to account is his *ṣalaah* (prayer). Ibn Ḥajar al-'Asqallaani said: "This does not contradict the hadith of Abu Hurayrah which he attributed to the Prophet (ﷺ),

> 'The first thing for which a person will be brought to account on the Day of Resurrection will be his prayer,'"

- narrated by the compilers of *Sunan*, because the former has to do with matter pertaining to interactions with people, whilst the latter has to do with worship of the Creator. Nasaa'i reconciled the two reports in his hadith narrated from Ibn Mas'ood, where the wording is:

---

[12] Ibid, 6/324, hadith no. 7887.

[13] *Jaami' al-Uṣool*, 10/ 436, hadith no. 7968.

[14] *Fatḥ al-Baari*, 11/397.

"The first thing for which a man will be brought to account will be his *ṣalaah*, and the first matter concerning which judgement will be passed among the people will be bloodshed."[15]

3 - THE SETTLING OF SCORES AMONG THE ANIMALS

"Allah will settle the scores among all His creatures, jinn, men and animals. On that Day, the hornless beast will settle its score with the beast with horns, until there will be nothing left to be settled. Then Allah will say, 'Be dust!' At that point the *kaafir* will say,

﴿ ... يَٰلَيۡتَنِي كُنتُ تُرَٰبَۢا ﴿٤٠﴾ ﴾

﴾...Would that I were dust!﴿ *(Qur'an 78: 40).*"

This hadith is narrated by Ibn Jareer in his *Tafseer*; his *isnaad* goes back to Abu Hurayrah, who attributed it to the Prophet (ﷺ). According to another report also narrated by Ibn Jareer from Abu Hurayrah, the Messenger of Allah (ﷺ) said:

"Allah will gather together all of His creatures, every animal and bird and human, and He will say to the animals and birds, 'Be dust!' At that point the *kaafir* will say: ﴾...Would that I were dust!﴿ *(Qur'an 78: 40).*"

Ibn Jareer also narrated that 'Abdullah ibn 'Amr said: "When the Day of Resurrection comes, the arena of gathering will be spread out and the animals and beasts will be gathered. Then scores will be settled among the animals, so that the sheep without horns will settle the score with the sheep that has horns. When all scores among the animals would be settled, 'He will say to them, 'Be dust!'' At that

[15] Ibid, 11/396.

point the *kaafir* (disbeliever) will say, ﴾...Would that I were dust!﴿ *(Qur'an 78: 40).*"

Muslim narrated in his *Ṣaḥeeḥ* from Abu Hurayrah that the Messenger of Allah (ﷺ) said:

> "All rights will be restored to their owners on the Day of Resurrection, so that even the sheep without horns will settle the score with the sheep that has horns."

Aḥmad narrated in his *Musnad* with an *isnaad* whose men are the men of *ṣaḥeeḥ* from Abu Hurayrah, that the Prophet (ﷺ) said:

> "The scores among all creatures will be settled, so that the animal without horns will settle its score with the animal with horns, and ants will settle their scores with other ants."

In *Al-Musnad* it is also narrated from Abu Hurayrah, who attributed it to the Prophet (ﷺ):

> "By the One in Whose hand is my soul, scores will be settled among all things on the Day of Resurrection, even two sheep who butted heads with one another."

Aḥmad narrated with a *ṣaḥeeḥ isnaad* from Abu Dharr that the Messenger of Allah (ﷺ) saw two sheep butting heads and said,

> "O' Abu Dharr, do you know why they are butting heads?" He said, "No." He (the Prophet) said, "But Allah knows and He will settle the score between them."[16]

---

[16] *Shaykh* Naaṣir narrated these *aḥaadeeth* and discussed their *isnaad* in *Silsilat al-Aḥaadeeth aṣ-Ṣaḥeeḥah*, 4/606, hadith no. 611.

How will scores be settled among the animals when they are not responsible for their actions?

The issue that the animals will be gathered and the scores among them will be settled was deemed problematic by many scholars. An-Nawawi explained this issue in his commentary on *Ṣaheeḥ Muslim*:

"This clearly indicates that the animals will be gathered on the Day of Resurrection, and that they will be brought back to life just as the accountable humans will be brought back to life, as will the children and the insane, and those whom the call did not reach. There is much evidence in the Qur'an and Sunnah to indicate this. Allah (ﷻ) says:

﴿وَإِذَا ٱلْوُحُوشُ حُشِرَتْ ۝٥﴾

﴿And when the wild beasts shall be gathered together.﴾ *(Qur'an 81: 5).*

If there is a *shar'i* text which appears to mean something, and there is nothing to prevent us from taking it as it appears to be - such as rational objections or the existence of a conflicting text - then we should take it as it appears to be. The scholars said: it is not a condition of the gathering and resurrection that the creatures should be rewarded or punished. The settling of scores between horned and hornless animals is not based on accountability, for animals are not accountable for their deeds; rather it is simply the matter of settling scores. And Allah knows best."

Shaykh Naaṣiruddeen al-Albaani said, after quoting these comments of An-Nawawi: Something similar was mentioned, more briefly, by Ibn al-Malik in *Mabaariq al-Azhaar* (2/293). *Shaykh* 'Ali al-Qaari' quoted from him in *Al-Marqaah* (4/761):

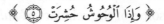

"If it is said that sheep are not accountable, so how can scores be settled among them? We say that Allah is the One Who does whatever He wills, and He is not to be questioned about His actions. The purpose behind it is to show His slaves that no rights are ever lost, that the one who has been wronged will take his rights from his oppressor."

Al-Qaari' said: "This is a sound view, a good way of looking at it. But describing (Allah's) wisdom as 'purpose' is not appropriate. The point of the matter is that this settling of scores eloquently points to perfect justice among all of those who are responsible. If this is the case with animals who are not accountable, then how about rational creatures, whether they are noble or ignoble, strong or weak?"

Shaykh Naaṣir commented on this by saying: "It is most unfortunate that some of the scholars of *kalaam* reject all of these *aḥaadeeth* on the basis of their opinions, and it is very strange that the scholar Al-Aloosi favours this view! After quoting the hadith of Abu Hurayrah narrated by Muslim and Aḥmad, in his *tafseer* of the *aayah*, ﴿And when the wild beasts shall be gathered together.﴾ *(Qur'an 81: 5)*, in his *tafseer* entitled *Rooḥ al-Ma'ani* (9/3006), he says:

'Ḥujjat al-Islam al-Ghazaali and a group (of other scholars) tended to think that no creatures would be gathered apart from mankind and the jinn, because they (those other creatures) are not accountable and they do not deserve this honour (of Resurrection) in any way, and there is no text in the Qur'an or reliable Sunnah to indicate that the animals will be resurrected. The report of Muslim and Tirmidhi, although it is *ṣaḥeeḥ*, was not narrated by way of explaining this *aayah*. It may be a metaphor for perfect justice. This is the view that I tend to favour, but I cannot be definitely sure that those who favour the first view are wrong, because in general they have evidence for their view. And Allah knows best.'"

I (*Shaykh* Naaṣir) said: This is what he said - may Allah forgive us and him. It is very strange on his part, because it is different from what we know of him in the book of his that we have mentioned, where he interprets the Qur'an in the right way, following the methodology of the *Salaf* without any element of misinterpretation or denying the attributes of Allah. What made him interpret this hadith in a different manner is the apparent meaning, which he took to be a metaphor for total justice. Is this not a rejection of the hadith that clearly states that the hornless sheep will settle its score with the horned sheep? Following the scholars of *kalaam*, he says that this is a metaphor!... i.e., that the hornless sheep will not settle its score. All of this might be said if we limit ourselves to discussing only the report narrated by Muslim. But if we look at other reports, such as *hadith al-tarjamah*, the hadith of Abu Dharr and others, then these offer definitive proof that the settling of scores mentioned in these *aḥaadeeth* is real and is not metaphorical. May Allah have mercy on Imam an-Nawawi, to whose comment I referred earlier: 'If there is a *shar'i* text which appears to mean something, and there is nothing to prevent us from taking it as it appears to be - such as rational objections or the existence of a conflicting text - then we should take it as it appears to be.'

I say: he (An-Nawawi) intended to refute the misinterpretation referred to above. Because of such misinterpretations, the philosophers and many of the scholars of *kalaam* such as the Mu'tazilah and others denied that the believers would see their Lord on the Day of Resurrection, and that He is over the Throne, and that He comes down to the first heaven every night, and that He will come (to pass judgement) on the Day of Resurrection, and other *aayaat* and *aḥaadeeth* which speak of His attributes.

In conclusion, the view that the animals will be gathered and that they will settle the scores among them is the correct view, and no other view is permissible. It comes as no surprise that the majority were of this view, as Al-Aloosi himself mentioned at the end of his *Tafseer* (9/

281). This was also the view stated by Ash-Shawkaani in his *tafseer* of the *aayah* in *Soorah at-Takweer*, in his *Tafseer Fatḥ al-Qadeer* (5/377), where he says:

"The beasts are the animals that live in the wild. The meaning of 'gathered together' is resurrected, so that they might settle their scores with one another, and the hornless animal might settle its score with the one with horns."[17]

4 - WHEN WILL THE BELIEVERS SETTLE SCORES AMONGST THEMSELVES?

In Bukhari it is narrated from Abu Sa'eed al-Khudri (رضي الله عنه) that the Messenger of Allah (ﷺ) said:

> "When the believers have been saved from the Fire, they will be detained at a bridge between Paradise and Hell, where they will settle any scores that existed among them in this world. Then when they have been purified, they will be granted permission to enter Paradise. By the One in Whose hand is the soul of Muhammad, any one of them will be more familiar with his dwelling in Paradise than he was with his house in this world."[18]

---

[17] *Silsilat al-Ahaadeeth aṣ-Ṣaheeḥah*, by *Shaykh* Naaṣiruddeen al-Albaani, 4/612.
[18] Bukhari: *Kitaab al-Maẓaalim, Baab Qiṣaaṣ al-Maẓaalim, Fatḥ al-Baari*, 5/96.

CHAPTER TWELVE
THE BALANCE

1 - DEFINITION

At the end of that Day, the Balance will be set up to weigh people's deeds. Qurṭubi said: "When the Reckoning would have been completed, the deeds will be weighed. The weighing will be for the purpose of requital, so it should come after the Reckoning. The Reckoning will be an evaluation of people's deeds, then the weighing will be to determine their values so that reward or punishment may be awarded accordingly."[1]

The texts indicate that the Balance is a real scale, whose vast size is known only to Allah (سبحانه وتعالى). Al-Ḥaakim narrated from Salmaan that the Prophet (ﷺ) said:

> "The Balance will be set up on the Day of Resurrection, and even if the heavens and the earth were to be weighed in it, they would fit. The angels will say, 'O' Lord, who will be weighed in this?' Allah will say, 'Whoever I will among My creation.' The angels will say, 'Glory be to You, we did not worship You as You deserved to be worshipped.'"[2]

It is a precise scale, which does not give any discrepancy, whether more or less, in its measurements.

﴿ وَنَضَعُ ٱلْمَوَٰزِينَ ٱلْقِسْطَ لِيَوْمِ ٱلْقِيَٰمَةِ فَلَا تُظْلَمُ نَفْسٌ شَيْـًٔا ۖ وَإِن كَانَ مِثْقَالَ حَبَّةٍ مِّنْ خَرْدَلٍ أَتَيْنَا بِهَا ۗ وَكَفَىٰ بِنَا حَٰسِبِينَ ﴿٤٧﴾ ﴾

---

[1] *At-Tadhkirah*, Pp. 309.

[2] *Silsilat al-Aḥaadeeth aṣ-Ṣaḥeeḥah*, 2/656, hadith no. 941.

﴾And We shall set up Balances of justice on the Day of Resurrection, then none will be dealt with unjustly in anything. And if there be the weight of a mustard seed, We will bring it. And Sufficient are We to take account.﴿ *(Qur'an 21: 47)*

The scholars differed to whether it is one scale or many. Some of them thought that each person would have his own scale, or that for each deed there would be a scale, because Allah (ﷻ) says: ﴾And We shall set up Balances of justice on the Day of Resurrection...﴿ *(Qur'an 21: 47).*

Others thought that the Balance is one, and that the plural form in the *aayah* is intended to refer to the number of deeds or of persons.

After describing the scholarly debate, Ibn Ḥajar stated his view that the Balance is one, and said: "The fact that so many people will have their deeds weighed should not be an issue, because the way things will be on the Day of Resurrection is different to the way they are in this world."[3]

As-Safaareeni related: "Al-Ḥasan al-Basri said: each person who is accountable will have his own scale. Some of them said: the more correct view is that there will be many scales on the Day of Resurrection, not just one, because Allah says, ﴾And We shall set up Balances...﴿ *(Qur'an 21: 47)* and:

﴿ فَمَن ثَقُلَتْ مَوَٰزِينُهُۥ ... ﴿١٠٢﴾ ﴾

﴾Then, those whose scales [of good deeds] are heavy...﴿ *(Qur'an 23: 102).*

He said: on this basis, it is not far-fetched to say that for actions of the heart there will be a scale, and for actions of the body there will be a

---

[3] *Fatḥ al-Baari*, 3/537.

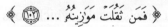

scale, and for the actions of the tongue there will be a scale. Ibn 'Atiyah narrated this and said: the view of the majority differs from that. Every person will be weighed individually, but the scale is one. Some of them said that the reason why the plural form is used in the *aayah* is because of the great number of people whose deeds will be weighed. This is a good point."[4]

2 - THE BALANCE ACCORDING TO *AHL AS-SUNNAH*

According to *Ahl as-Sunnah*, the Balance is a real scale in which the deeds of the people will be weighed. The Mu'tazilah and a small number of *Ahl as-Sunnah* held a different view.

Ibn Ḥajar said: "Abu Isḥaaq al-Zajjaaj said: the *Ahl as-Sunnah* are unanimously agreed on belief in the Balance, and that the deeds of mankind will be weighed in it on the Day of Resurrection., and that it has a 'tongue' and two pans in which deeds will be weighed. The Mu'tazilah rejected the idea of the Balance, and said that it was a metaphor for justice. They went against the Qur'an and Sunnah, because Allah has told us that He will set up the Balance in order to weigh the deeds (of His creatures), and to show them their deeds so that they might be witnesses against themselves.

Ibn Foorak said: 'The *Mu'tazilah* denied the Balance, on the grounds that abstract things cannot be weighed, because they have no physical manifestation.'

He said, 'Some of the scholars of *kalaam* narrated from Ibn 'Abbaas that abstract things will be given a physical form and will be weighed.'

Some of the *Salaf* said that the Balance means justice and judgement. Aṭ-Ṭabari attributed this opinion to Mujaahid.

---

[4] *Lawaami' al-Anwaar al-Bahiyyah*, 2/186.

The correct view is the one stated by the majority.

The Balance was mentioned in Al-Ḥasan's presence, and he said: it has a tongue and two pans."[5]

Qurṭubi attributed the interpretation of the Balance as meaning justice to Mujaahid, Aḍ-Ḍaḥḥaak and Al-A'maash.[6]

Perhaps these scholars interpreted the Balance as referring to justice in *aayaat* (verses) such as the following:

﴿ وَٱلسَّمَآءَ رَفَعَهَا وَوَضَعَ ٱلْمِيزَانَ ۝٧ أَلَّا تَطْغَوْا۟ فِى ٱلْمِيزَانِ ۝٨ وَأَقِيمُوا۟ ٱلْوَزْنَ بِٱلْقِسْطِ وَلَا تُخْسِرُوا۟ ٱلْمِيزَانَ ۝٩ ﴾

﴾And the heaven He has raised high, and He has set up the Balance. In order that you may not transgress [due] balance. And observe the weight with equity and do not make the balance deficient.﴿ *(Qur'an 55: 7-9)*

In the context of these *aayaat*, the Balance means justice, and Allah (ﷻ) is enjoining His slaves to deal with one another in a just manner. But the Balance which will be set up on the Day of Resurrection has been mentioned in the *mutawaatir aḥaadeeth*, and it is a real scale, as is the apparent meaning of the Qur'an.[7]

Imam Aḥmad refuted those who denied the Balance by pointing out that Allah mentioned the Balance in the *aayah*:

﴿ وَنَضَعُ ٱلْمَوَٰزِينَ ٱلْقِسْطَ لِيَوْمِ ٱلْقِيَٰمَةِ ... ۝٤٧ ﴾

﴾And We shall set up Balances of justice on the Day of Resurrection...﴿ *(Qur'an 21: 47)*

---

[5] *Fatḥ al-Baari*, 13/578.

[6] *At-Tadhkirah*, Pp. 313.

[7] *An-Nihaayah* by Ibn Katheer, 2/34.

And the Prophet (ﷺ) also mentioned the Balance, and whoever rejects the Prophet's words rejects the words of Allah.[8]

Shaykh al-Islam (Ibn Taymiyah) proved that the Balance is not a metaphor for justice, but is a real scale in which deeds will be weighed against the Qur'an and Sunnah. He said:

"The Balance is that in which deeds will be weighed, it does not mean justice as is indicated by the Qur'an and Sunnah, for example the *aayaat*:

﴿ فَمَن ثَقُلَتْ مَوَٰزِينُهُۥ ... ﴿١٠٢﴾ ﴾

﴾Then, those whose scales [of good deeds] are heavy...﴿ *(Qur'an 23: 102)*

﴿ وَمَنْ خَفَّتْ مَوَٰزِينُهُۥ ... ﴿١٠٣﴾ ﴾

﴾And those whose scales [of good deeds] are light...﴿ *(Qur'an 23: 103)*

﴿ وَنَضَعُ ٱلْمَوَٰزِينَ ٱلْقِسْطَ لِيَوْمِ ٱلْقِيَٰمَةِ ... ﴿٤٧﴾ ﴾

﴾And We shall set up Balances of justice on the Day of Resurrection...﴿ *(Qur'an 21: 47)*

Bukhari and Muslim narrated that the Prophet (ﷺ) said,

> 'Two words which are light on the tongue but will weigh heavily in the Balance, and they are beloved to the Most Merciful: *'Subḥaan Allah wa bi ḥamdih, Subḥaan Allah il-'Aẓeem* (Glory and praise be to Allah, Glory be to Allah the Almighty)."

- And he (ﷺ) said concerning the calves of 'Abdullah ibn Mas'ood,

---

[8] *Fatḥ al-Baari*, 13/538.

'In the Balance they will weigh more than Uḥud.'

In Tirmidhi and elsewhere there is the hadith about the piece of paper, which has been rated as *ṣaḥeeḥ* by Tirmidhi, Al-Ḥaakim and others, about a man who will be brought forth (on the Day of Resurrection), and ninety-nine sheets (of records of his deeds) will be spread out for him, each of which will be as vast as the eye can see. They will be put in one pan (of the Balance), then a piece of paper on which are the words *Laa ilaaha ill-Allah* will be brought. The Prophet (ﷺ) said,

> 'The pan in which the sheets are, will shoot up, and that piece of paper will weigh heavily.'

This and similar reports make it clear that deeds will be weighed on scales to show whether the good deeds outweigh the bad deeds or vice versa. This is what justice means, and this is how justice may be established, as is the case with scales in this world.

As for how this weighing will be carried out is like asking how any of the matters of the unseen will come to pass (i.e., it is known only to Allah)."[9]

Qurṭubi refuted those who denied the Balance and misinterpreted the texts which mention it. He said: "Our scholars said: if the Balance can be interpreted according to what they suggested, then we could interpret the *Ṣiraaṭ* as referring to the true religion, Paradise and Hell as referring to the grief or joy that may befall the soul but not the body, the *shayaaṭeen* (Devils) and jinn as referring to bad characteristics, and the angels as referring to good characteristics. All of that is incorrect, because it is a rejection of what was taught by the Truthful one [the Prophet (ﷺ)]. In *Aṣ-Ṣaḥeeḥayn* (Bukhari and Muslim) it says that he will be given the record of his good deeds, then he will be given a piece of paper. This indicates that the Balance

---

[9] *Majmoo' al-Fataawa Shaykh al-Islam*, 4/302.

is real, and that what will be weighed is the books of deeds, as we have explained. And Allah is the source of strength."[10]

3 - WHAT WILL BE WEIGHED IN THE BALANCE

Scholars differed as to what will be weighed on that Day. The different opinions are:

1) That which will be weighed on that Day are the deeds themselves. They will take on a physical shape and will be placed in the Balance. This is indicated by the hadith of Abu Hurayrah (رضي الله عنه) in *Aṣ-Ṣaḥeeḥ*, according to which he said: The Messenger of Allah (ﷺ) said:

> "Two words which are light on the tongue but will weigh heavily in the Balance, and they are beloved to the Most Merciful: *'Subḥaan Allah wa bi ḥamdih, Subḥaan Allah il-'Aẓeem* (Glory and praise be to Allah, Glory be to Allah the Almighty).'"[11]

Many texts indicate that deeds will be brought forth on the Day of Resurrection, in a form which is known best to Allah. For example, the Qur'an will come forth on the Day of Resurrection as an intercessor for its companions (those who read and acted upon it). *Soorah al-Baqarah* and *Soorah Aal 'Imraan* will come forth looking like two clouds or two patches of mist, or like two flocks of birds spreading their wings, defending those who read and acted upon them. Muslim narrated that Abu Umaamah said: I heard the Messenger of Allah (ﷺ) say:

> "Read the Qur'an, for it will come forth on the Day of Resurrection as an intercessor for its companions. Read

---

[10] *At-Tadhkirah*, 314.

[11] Bukhari: *Kitaab at-Tawḥeed, Baab Wa naḍa' al-Mawaazeen al-Qisṭa li Yawm il-Qiyaamah, Fatḥ al-Baari*, 13/537.

> the two shining ones - *Soorah al-Baqarah* and *Soorah Aal 'Imraan*, for they will come forth looking like two clouds or two patches of mist, or like two flocks of birds spreading their wings, defending their companions."[12]

Muslim also narrated that An-Nawaas ibn Sam'aan said: I heard the Messenger of Allah (ﷺ) say:

> "The Qur'an will come forth on the Day of Resurrection with its people who used to act in accordance with it. *Soorah al-Baqarah* and *Soorah Aal 'Imraan* will come forth like two clouds, or two patches of shade with light in between, or like two flocks of birds spreading their wings, defending their companions."[13]

This view is described as most correct and supported by Ibn Ḥajar al-'Asqallaani, who said: "The correct view is that deeds are the things that will be weighed. Abu Dawood and Tirmidhi narrated a hadith from Abu'd-Darda', which is classed as *saheeh* by Ibn Ḥibbaan, in which the Prophet (ﷺ) said:

> 'Nothing will be placed in the Balance on the Day of Resurrection which will weigh more heavily than good manner and attitude.'"

2) That which will be weighed is the doer of the actions himself. The texts indicate that people will be weighed on the Day of Resurrection, and they will be heavy or light according to their faith, not according to the size of their bodies or how much flesh and fat they have. In *Ṣaḥeeḥ Bukhari* it is narrated from Abu Hurayrah that the Messenger of Allah (ﷺ) said:

---

[12] *Mishkaat al-Maṣaabeeḥ*, 1/656, hadith no. 2120.

[13] Ibid, hadith no. 2121.

> "A huge fat man will be brought forth on the Day of Resurrection, and he will weigh no more before Allah than a mosquito's wing. He said, recite:
>
> ﴿... فَلَا نُقِيمُ لَهُمْ يَوْمَ ٱلْقِيَٰمَةِ وَزْنًا ﴿١٠٥﴾﴾
>
> ﴿...And on the Day of Resurrection, We shall assign no weight for them﴾ *(Qur'an 18: 105).*"[14]

A slim, weak man, with thin calves, will be brought and his weight will be like the weight of mountains. Aḥmad narrated in his *Musnad* from Zur ibn Ḥubaysh from Ibn Mas'ood, that he was a man with thin calves. He was buffeted about by the wind, and the people laughed at him. The Messenger of Allah (ﷺ) asked,

> "What are they laughing at?" They said, "O' Prophet of Allah, they are laughing at his thin calves." He said, "By the One in Whose hand is my soul, they will weigh more heavily than Uḥud in the Balance."

- Ibn Katheer said: this is narrated only by Aḥmad; its *isnaad* is *jayyid qawiy.*[15]

3) That which will be weighed is the records of deeds. Tirmidhi narrated in his *Sunan* from 'Abdullah ibn 'Amr ibn al-'Aaṣ (رضي الله عنه) that the Messenger of Allah (ﷺ) said:

> "Allah will select a man from my ummah before all of creation on the Day of Resurrection, and will spread out for him ninety-nine sheets [of the record of his deeds], each one extending as far as the eye can see. Then He will say, 'Do you deny any part of this? Have My

[14] Bukhari: *Kitaab at-Tafseer, Tafseer Soorah al-Kahf, Fatḥ al-Baari*, 8/426.
[15] *An-Nihaayah* by Ibn Katheer, 2/29.

> recording scribes been unjust towards you?' The man will say, 'No, O' Lord.' Allah will say, 'Have you any excuse?' The man will say, 'No, O' Lord.' Allah will say, 'Yes indeed, you have a *ḥasanah* (stored) with Us, and there will be no injustice this Day.' And He will bring forth a piece of paper on which is written *Ashhadu an laa ilaha ill-Allah wa ashhadu anna Muḥammadan Rasoolallah*. He will say, 'Weigh this.' The man will say, 'O' Lord, what is this piece of paper compared to all these records?' Allah will say, 'You will not be wronged.' Then the sheets will be placed in one pan and the piece of paper in the other; the pan with the sheets will fly up and the pan with the piece of paper will weigh heavily, and nothing will outweigh the name of Allah."[16]

Qurṭubi favoured this opinion, and said: "The correct view is that the books in which the deeds are recorded may be heavy or light in the Balance... Ibn 'Umar said: the books of deeds will be weighed. It is proven that these books are physical entities. Allah will make it so that when one of the pans outweighs the other, this will show whether the person is to enter Paradise or Hell."[17]

As-Safaareeni said, "The truth is that what will be weighed are the records of deeds. This was regarded as being correct by Ibn 'Abdul-Barr, Qurṭubi and others. *Shaykh* Mar'i described it as the correct view in his book *Al-Bahjah*, and the majority of the *mufassireen* favoured this view. Ibn 'Atiyah narrated this view from Abu'l-Ma'aali..."[18]

---

[16] *Jaami' al-Uṣool*, 10/459, hadith no. 7981. The editor of *Al-Jaami'* said: its *isnaad* is *ṣaḥeeḥ*. It has been narrated by Ibn Maajah, by Ibn Ḥibbaan in his *Ṣaḥeeḥ*, and by Al-Ḥaakim, Al-Bayhaqi and others.

[17] *At-Tadhkirah*, Pp. 313.

[18] *Lawaami' al-Anwaar al-Bahiyyah*, 2/187.

Perhaps the truth is that what will be weighed is the person, his deeds and the record of his deeds. The texts that we have quoted indicate that each of these three will be weighed; the fact that a particular text says that one of these things will be weighed does not rule out the idea that any of the others will also be weighed. Reconciling the texts implies that all of the three things mentioned will be weighed.

This has been regarded as preferred and correct by *Shaykh* Ḥaafiẓ al-Ḥakami. He said: "What is apparent from the texts - and Allah knows best - is that the doer of the deed, the deed and the record of his deed will all be weighed, because the *aḥaadeeth*, which serve to explain the Qur'an, mention all of these things, and there is no contradiction between them. This is also indicated in the report narrated by Aḥmad (may Allah have mercy on him) from 'Abdullah ibn 'Amr. It tells the story of the person for whom a piece of paper will be brought forth. He said: the Messenger of Allah (ﷺ) said:

> 'The scales will be set up on the Day of Resurrection, and a man will be brought forth and placed in one pan, then everything that was recorded against him will be placed in the other. The scale will tip against him, and it will be said, 'Send him to the Fire.'
> When he will turn back, a voice will cry out from the presence of the Most Merciful, saying, 'Do not hasten! There is something left for him.' A piece of paper will be brought forth on which would be written *Laa ilaaha ill-Allah*, and it will be placed in the pan with the man and the balance will tip in his favour."'

This indicates that the person will be placed in one pan along with his *ḥasanaat* and his record of good deeds, and his *sayi'aat* and record of bad deeds will be placed in the other pan. This is the way to reconcile

[19] *Ma'aarij al-Qubool*, 2/272.

all the *aḥaadeeth* about the weighing in the Balance. To Allah be praise and blessings.[19]

4 - DEEDS WHICH WILL WEIGH HEAVILY IN THE BALANCE

The thing which will weigh most heavily in the Balance for a person is manner and good attitude. It is narrated from Abu'd-Darda' that the Prophet (ﷺ) said:

> "The heaviest thing that will be placed in a person's Balance on the Day of Resurrection is good manner, and Allah hates the obscene immoral person."

- This is narrated by Tirmidhi who said, this is a *ṣaheeḥ hasan* hadith. The first part is also narrated by Abu Dawood.[20]

In *Ṣaḥeeḥ Bukhari, Ṣaḥeeḥ Muslim* and *Sunan at-Tirmidhi* it is narrated from Abu Hurayrah that the Prophet (ﷺ) said,

> "Two words which are light on the tongue but will weigh heavily in the Balance, and they are beloved to the Most Merciful: *Subḥaan Allah wa bi ḥamdih, Subḥaan Allah il-'Aẓeem* (Glory and praise be to Allah, Glory be to Allah the Almighty)."[21]

Muslim narrated on the authority of Abu Maalik al-Ash'ari that the Messenger of Allah (ﷺ) said:

> "Purity is half of faith, and (saying) '*Al-Ḥamdu Lillaah* (Praise be to Allah)' fills the scale, and saying '*Subḥaan Allah wa'l-ḥamdu Lillaah* (Glory be to Allah and praise be to Allah)' fills what is between heaven and earth."[22]

---

[20] *Mishkaat al-Maṣaabeeḥ*, 2/630, hadith no. 5081.

[21] *Jaami' al-Uṣool*, 4/397, hadith no. 2462.

[22] Muslim, 1/203, hadith no. 223.

Bukhari, Nasaa'i and Aḥmad narrated from Abu Hurayrah that the Prophet (ﷺ) said:

> "Whoever keeps a horse for the sake of Allah, out of faith in Allah and believing in His promise, its eating and drinking, its defecation and urination, will all be *ḥasanaat* in his Balance on the Day of Resurrection."[23]

---

[23] *Ṣaḥeeḥ al-Jaami' aṣ-Ṣagheer*, 5/229, hadith no. 5843.

CHAPTER THIRTEEN
AL-ḤAWḌ - THE CISTERN

Allah (ﷻ) will honour His slave and Messenger Muhammad (ﷺ) in that great gathering by giving him a huge, vast cistern whose water is whiter than milk and sweeter than honey, with a fragrance finer than musk. The vessels for drinking will be like the stars of the sky. This good water will come from the river of *Al-Kawthar*, which Allah has given to His Messenger (ﷺ) in Paradise. The ummah of the Chosen Prophet (ﷺ) will come to drink from it, and whoever would drink from it would never feel thirsty again.

The scholars differed as to the location of the cistern. Al-Ghazaali and Qurṭubi thought that it will be before the people pass over *Aṣ-Ṣiraaṭ* in the arena of the Day of Judgement, basing that view on the fact that some of those who would drink from it will be taken to Hell. If it were after *aṣ-ṣiraaṭ* they would not be able to reach it.[1]

Ibn Ḥajar assumed that Bukhari's view was that the cistern will be after *Aṣ-Ṣiraaṭ*, because Bukhari narrated the *aḥaadeeth* about the cistern after the *aḥaadeeth* about the intercession, and the *aḥaadeeth* about the setting up of the *Aṣ-Ṣiraaṭ*.[2]

What Qurṭubi said is preferable and correct. And Ibn Ḥajar has examined the evidence of the two groups in his valuable book *Fatḥ al-Baari*.[3]

---

[1] *At-Tadhkirah*, Pp. 302.

[2] *Fatḥ al-Baari*, 11/466.

[3] Ibid, 11/466.

1 - THE *AḤAADEETH* NARRATED CONCERNING THE CISTERN

The *aḥaadeeth* narrated concerning the cistern are *mutawaatir*, and there is no doubt among the scholars of hadith that they are indeed *mutawaatir*. More than fifty *Ṣaḥaabah* narrated these *aḥaadeeth* from the Messenger (ﷺ), and their names were mentioned by Ibn Ḥajar.[4]

Here, we will quote some of these *aḥaadeeth* narrated by Al-Khaṭeeb at-Tabrizi in his *Mishkaat*:[5]

1) 'Abdullah ibn 'Amr, narrated that the Messenger of Allah (ﷺ) said:

> "My cistern is (as big as) a month's journey, and its corners are like the same.[6] Its water is whiter than milk and its fragrance is better than musk. Its drinking-vessels are like the stars of the sky. Whoever drinks from it will never feel thirsty again." (Bukhari and Muslim)

2) Abu Hurayrah (رضي الله عنه) related that the Messenger of Allah (ﷺ) said:

> "My cistern is greater than the distance between Aylah[7] and 'Aden. It is whiter than snow and sweeter than honey with milk. Its drinking-vessels number more than the stars, and I will prevent other people from coming to it just as a man prevents the camels of other people from coming to his trough." They said, "O' Messenger of Allah, will you recognize us on that Day?" He said,

---

[4] *Fatḥ al-Baari*, 11/468.

[5] *Mishkaat al-Maṣaabeeḥ*, 3/68.

[6] i.e., it is square, with all its sides of equal length.

[7] i.e., the city of 'Aqabah in Jordan.

> "Yes, you will have a sign that no other nation has. You will come to me with white faces and limbs from the traces of *wuḍoo'*."

3) According to a report also narrated by him (Muslim) from Anas, he (ﷺ) said:

> "In it you will see vessels of gold and silver, as numerous as the stars in the sky."

4) According to another report narrated by Muslim from Thawbaan, he [the Prophet (ﷺ)] was asked about its drink. He said,

> "It is whiter than milk and sweeter than runny honey. It has pipes leading into it from Paradise, one of gold and the other of silver."

2 - THOSE WHO WILL COME TO THE CISTERN AND THOSE WHO WILL BE PREVENTED FROM DOING SO

Many *aḥaadeeth* have been narrated in which the Messenger (ﷺ) described those who will come to his cistern to drink, and those who will be prevented from drinking from it. We will mention here some of the reports narrated by Ibn al-Atheer in *Jaami' al-Uṣool*:[8]

1) Bukhari and Muslim narrated that 'Abdullah ibn Mas'ood (رضي الله عنه) stated: The Messenger of Allah (ﷺ) said:

> "I will be the first one among you to reach the cistern, and some men among you will come to me, but when I offer them something to drink, it will be snatched away from them in front of me. I will say, 'O' Lord, my companions!' He will say, 'You do not know what they did after you were gone.'"

[8] *Jaami' al-Uṣool*, 1/468.

2) They also narrated from Anas ibn Maalik (ﷺ) that the Messenger of Allah (ﷺ) said:

> "Some men among my companions will come to the cistern, and when I would see them and they would reach me, they would be snatched away in haste from me. I would say, 'O' Lord, my companions!' And He will say to me, 'You do not know what they did after you were gone.'"

According to another report by Bukhari and Muslim, he (the Prophet) (ﷺ) said:

> "Some people from among my ummah will come to me... and I will say, 'Doomed is the one who changed after I was gone.'"

3) They also narrated from Abu Ḥaazim (may Allah have mercy on him) that Sahl ibn Sa'd (ﷺ) said: I heard the Messenger of Allah (ﷺ) say,

> "I will be the first among you to reach the cistern. Whoever would come to it would drink, and whoever would drink would never be thirsty again. People will come to me whom I will recognize and they will recognize me, then they will be taken away from me."

Abu Ḥaazim (may Allah have mercy on him) said: Al-Nu'maan ibn Abi 'Ayyaash heard this when I was recounting this hadith to them, and he said, 'Is this what you heard Sahl saying?' I said, 'Yes.' He said, 'I bear witness that I heard Abu Sa'eed al-Khudri (ﷺ) adding something more,' he said,

> "And he (the Prophet) would say, 'They belong to me.' And it would be said, 'You do not know what they did

after you were gone.' And I will say, 'Doomed, doomed is the one who changed after I was gone.'" (Bukhari and Muslim)

4) They - Bukhari and Muslim - also narrated from Abu Hurayrah (رضي الله عنه) that Messenger of Allah (ﷺ) said:

> "A group of my Companions - or he said, a group from my ummah - will come to me on the Day of Resurrection, and they will be pushed away from the cistern. I will say, 'O' Lord, my companions!' He will say, 'You have no knowledge of what they did after you were gone. They became apostate and turned on their heels.'" According to another report: "They will be taken away."

Bukhari narrated that the Messenger of Allah (ﷺ) said:

> "Whilst I would be standing at the cistern, a group of people will come, and when I recognize them a man will come and stand between me and them. He will say, 'Let's go!' I will say, 'Where to?' He will say, 'To the Fire, by Allah.' I will say, 'What is wrong with them?' He will say, 'They became apostate and turned on their heels.' Then another group will come, and when I would recognize them a man will come and stand between me and them. He will say, 'Let's go!' I will say, 'Where to?' He will say, 'To the Fire, by Allah.' I will say, 'What is wrong with them?' He will say, 'They became apostate and turned on their heels.' And I will not see anybody saved from among them except a few."

Muslim narrated that the Messenger of Allah (ﷺ) said:

> "My ummah will come to me at the cistern, and I will be keeping the rest of the people away from it, just as a man keeps the camels of other people away from his own camels." They said, "O' Prophet of Allah, will you not recognize us?" He said, "Yes, you will have a sign that no one else will have. You will come with white faces and limbs from the traces of *wuḍoo'*. But a group of you will be prevented from coming to me, and they will not reach me. I will say, 'O' Lord, these are from among my companions.' Then an angels will come and say, 'Do you know what they did after you were gone?'"

According to another report he (ﷺ) said:

> "My cistern is vaster than the distance between Aylah and 'Aden. It is whiter than snow and sweeter than honey with milk. Its vessels are more in number than the stars. I will keep the people away from it just as a man keeps the other people's camels away from his trough." They said, "O' Messenger of Allah, will you recognize us on that Day?" He said, "Yes, you will have a mark that no other nation will have. You will come to me with white faces and limbs."

Qurṭubi narrated in his *Tadhkirah* some of the *aḥaadeeth* that we have quoted here, then he said: "Our scholars (may Allah have mercy on them all) said: 'Everyone who turns apostate from the religion of Allah or innovates in it something that Allah is not pleased with and does not permit, will be one of those who are turned away from the cistern and kept away from it. Those who will be most forcefully turned away will be those who went against the *jamaa'ah* of the Muslims and left their path, such as the *Khawaarij* with their various paths, and the *Raafiḍis* (Rawafiḍ) with their various forms of misguidance, and the *Mu'tazilah* with their various whims and desires. All of these are people who introduced changes into the religion.

The same applies to the oppressors who go to extremes in their injustice, who conceal the truth and kill and humiliate its people, and who openly commit major sins and take sin lightly, and all the followers of miguidance, whims and desires and *bid'ah* (reprehensible innovation).

Some may be kept away for a while, then brought close after being forgiven, if their changes were in the matter of deeds and not in the matter of beliefs (*'aqeedah*). Some will be known by the light of *wuḍoo'*, then it will be said to them, 'May you be doomed, if they were among the *munaafiqeen* (hypocrites) at the time of the Messenger of Allah (ﷺ), who made an outward display of faith whilst concealing *kufr* in their hearts. The Prophet (ﷺ) will take them at face value, then their true nature will be revealed and it will be said to them, 'You are doomed.' No one will spend eternity in Hell except the one who blatantly reject/rejected the truth and who does/did not have even a mustard-seed's worth of faith in his heart."[9]

[9] *At-Tadhkirah*, Pp. 306.

insignificance and the *Murjiah* with their various whims and desires. All of these are people who introduced changes into the religion.

The same applies to the oppressors who go to extremes in their injustice, who conceal the truth and kill and humiliate its people, and who openly commit major sins and take sin lightly, and all the followers of misguidance, whims and desires and bid'ah (reprehensible innovation).

Some may be kept away for a while, then brought close after being forgiven, if their changes were in the matter of deeds and not in the matter of beliefs (*'aqeedah*). Some will be known by the light of *wudoo'*, then it will be said to them: 'May you be doomed, if they were among the *munaafiqeen* (hypocrites) at the time of the Messenger of Allah (ﷺ) who made an outward display of faith whilst concealing *kufr* in their hearts. The Prophet (ﷺ) will take them at face value, then their true nature will be revealed and it will be said to them, "You are doomed." No one will spend eternity in Hell except the one who blatantly reject/rejected the truth and who does/did not have even a mustard-seed's worth of faith in his heart."[1]

[1] *At-Tadhkirah*, p. 300

CHAPTER FOURTEEN
THE FINAL GATHERING TO THE PLACE OF ETERNAL ABODE: PARADISE OR HELL

1 - EVERY NATION WILL BE TOLD TO FOLLOW THAT WHICH IT USED TO WORSHIP

At the end of this Day, the people will be gathered either to Paradise or to Hell. These are the final places which people will reach. The Messenger (ﷺ) told us that at the end of that Day, each nation will be told to follow the god they used to worship. So those who used to worship the sun will follow the sun, and those who used to worship the moon will follow the moon. For those who used to worship idols, their gods will be made to appear before them and will walk before them and they will follow them. Those who used to worship Pharaoh will follow him. Then these false gods will all fall into the Fire, one after the other, and their worshippers will tumble into Hell after them, as Allah (ﷻ) says concerning Pharaoh:

﴿ يَقْدُمُ قَوْمَهُۥ يَوْمَ ٱلْقِيَـٰمَةِ فَأَوْرَدَهُمُ ٱلنَّارَ ۖ وَبِئْسَ ٱلْوِرْدُ ٱلْمَوْرُودُ ﴿٩٨﴾ ﴾

﴿He will go ahead of his people on the Day of Resurrection, and will lead them into the Fire, and evil indeed is the place to which they are led.﴾

(Qur'an 11: 98)

After that there will be no one left except the believers and a few of the People of the Book. Among the believers will be the hypocrites who were with them in this world. Then their Lord will come to them and will say to them, "What are you waiting for?" They will say, "We are waiting for our Lord." They will know Him by the Shin when it is laid bare to them. At that point they will fall down prostrating to Him, except for the hypocrites who will be unable to do so.

﴿ يَوْمَ يُكْشَفُ عَن سَاقٍ وَيُدْعَوْنَ إِلَى ٱلسُّجُودِ فَلَا يَسْتَطِيعُونَ ﴿٤٢﴾ ﴾

﴾[Remember] the Day when the Shin shall be laid bare [i.e. the Day of Resurrection] and they shall be called to prostrate themselves [to Allah], but they [hypocrites] shall not be able to do so.﴿ *(Qur'an 68: 42)*

Then the believers will follow their Lord. The *ṣiraaṭ* will be set up, and the believers will be given their lights, and they will cross the *ṣiraaṭ*. But the light of the hypocrites will be extinguished, and it will be said to them, 'Go back to your rear and seek a light!' Then a wall will be put up between them, with a gate therein. Inside it will be mercy, and outside it will be torment. (cf. Qur'an 57: 13) The believers will cross *Aṣ-Ṣiraaṭ* at speeds commensurate with their faith and righteous deeds.

Muslim narrated in his *Ṣaḥeeḥ* from Abu Sa'eed al-Khudri, that the Prophet (ﷺ) said:

> "When the Day of Resurrection comes, a *muadh-dhin* will call out, 'Let every nation follow that which it used to worship.' There will be no one left who used to worship idols and stone altars, but they will all fall into the Fire, until there is no one left except those who used to worship Allah, righteous and immoral alike, and what is left of the People of the Book. The Jews will be called and it will be said to them, 'What did you use to worship?' They will say, 'We used to worship 'Uzayr the son of Allah.' It will be said to them, 'You have lied, for Allah has not taken a wife or son. What do you want?'

They will say, 'We are thirsty, O' Lord. Give us to drink.' It will be said to them, 'Why don't you go and drink there?' then they will be all gathered into Hell like a stampeding flock, and they will fall into the Fire. Then the Christians will be called, and it will be said to them, 'What did you use to worship?' They will say, 'We used to worship the Messiah, the son of Allah.' It will be said to them, 'You have lied, for Allah has not taken a wife or son. What do you want?' They will say, 'We are thirsty, O' Lord. Give us to drink.' It will be said to them, 'Why don't you go and drink there?' then they will all be gathered into Hell, like a stampeding flock, and they will fall into the Fire. Then when there is no one left except those who used to worship Allah, whether they were righteous or immoral, the Lord of the Worlds will come to them in a form different to that in which they had previously seen Him. He will say, 'What are you waiting for? Every nation is following that which they used to worship.' They will say, 'O' our Lord, we kept away from the people in the world at the time when we needed them the most and we did not go with them.' He will say, 'I am your Lord.' They will say, 'We seek refuge with Allah from you! We will not associate anything with Allah.' This will be repeated two or three times, until some of them are about to turn on their heels. Then He will say, 'Is there any sign between you and Him by which you will recognize Him?' They will say, 'Yes.' Then the Shin will be laid bare, and there will be no one left who used to prostrate to Allah willingly and sincerely, but Allah will grant him permission to prostrate, and there will be no one left who used to prostrate only to avoid trouble or to show off, but Allah

> will make his spine into one solid piece, so that whenever he wants to prostrate, he will fall on his back. Then they will raise their heads, and He will have changed into the form in which they had seen Him the first time. He will say, 'I am your Lord.' And they will say, 'You are our Lord.'
>
> Then the bridge will be set up over Hell, and the intercession will take place, and they will say, 'O' Allah, save us, save us.'
>
> It was said, 'O' Messenger of Allah, what is the bridge?' He said, 'It is the void in which one is likely to slip. In it there are hooks and tongs and spikes like the thorns of the plant in Najd which is called *As-Sa'daan*. The believers then will pass over it within the twinkling of an eye, like lightning or the wind or birds, and like fine horses and camels. Some will escape and be safe, some will be scratched (by the hooks etc.) and let go, and some will be piled up in the Fire of Hell."[1]

Muslim also narrated from Abu Hurayrah, concerning the description of the passing over the *ṣiraaṭ*, that the Messenger of Allah (ﷺ) said:

> "Trustworthiness and ties of kinship will be sent, and will stand at either side of the *ṣiraaṭ*, to the right and the left. The first of you will cross it like lightning." I said, "May my father and my mother be sacrificed for you! How can it be like lightning?" He said, "Have you not seen lightning, how it goes and comes back in the blinking of an eye? Then (some will pass) like the wind, or like birds and fast horses, and the speed at which

[1] Muslim: *Kitaab al-Eemaan, Baab Ma'rifat Ṭareeq ar-Ru'yah*, 1/167, hadith no. 183.

> people cross will be according to their deeds. And your Prophet will be standing on the *ṣiraaṭ* saying, 'O' Lord, save, save!' until the people's deeds will be failing in strength, and a man will come who could only move by crawling. At the edges of the *ṣiraaṭ* will be hooks, hanging ready to catch anyone whom they are commanded (to catch). Some will be scratched and saved, and some will be piled up in Hell."[2]

And Muslim narrated in his *Ṣaḥeeḥ* from Abu Zubayr, that he heard Jaabir ibn 'Abdullah being asked about the passing over Hell. He said:

> "We will come on the Day of Resurrection like this, like this,[3] - and look at that - above the people. And the nations will be called by their idols and that which they used to worship, one by one. Then our Lord will come to us and will say, 'Who are you waiting for?' They will say, 'We are waiting for our Lord.' He will say, 'I am your Lord.' They will say, 'Let us see You.' Then He will manifest Himself to them, smiling.
>
> Then He will set out with them and they will follow Him. Each one among them, believer or hypocrite, will be given a light, then they will follow Him. On the

---

[2] Muslim: *Kitaab al-Eemaan, Baab Adnaa Ahl al-Jannah*, 1/187, hadith no. 195.

[3] Ibn Ḥajar said in his comment on this hadith: "The origin of this phrase is a mis-spelling by the narrator of the word *kawm* (hill). He wrote *kadha wa kadha* (like this, like this) because he was not sure that he had understood it. Then he wrote, 'Look at that', telling the reader to examine the narration and think about whether his wording was correct. All of that was included in the narration (of the hadith) a long time ago." *At-Takhweef min an-Naar*, Pp. 199. He mentioned that the correct version is as narrated in *Al-Musnad* and the books of Sunnah: "On the Day of Resurrection we will be on a hill above the people, and the nations will be called by their idols..."

> bridge over Hell there will be hooks and spikes, which will catch whomever Allah wills. Then the light of the hypocrites will be extinguished, and the believers will be saved; the first group among them will have faces like the moon on the night when it is full, seventy thousand who will not be brought to account. Then those who will follow them will be like the light of the stars in the sky...”[4]

Bukhari and Muslim narrated from Abu Hurayrah that the Messenger (ﷺ) said, replying to the *Saḥaabah* when they asked him whether they would see Allah:

> “Do you have any doubt that you see the moon on the night when it is full and there are no clouds in front of it?” They said, “No, O’ Messenger of Allah.” He said, “Then you will see Him on the Day of Resurrection in the same way. Allah will gather the people and will say, ‘Whoever used to worship anything, let him follow it.’ So all those who used to worship the sun, or the moon, or the false gods, will follow (their gods). Then this ummah will be left, with its hypocrites among them. Then Allah will come to them in a Form other than that which they know, and He will say, ‘I am your Lord.’ They will say, ‘We seek refuge with Allah from you. This is where we will stay until our Lord comes to us. When our Lord comes to us, we will know Him.’ Then Allah will come to them in the form which they know, and He will say, ‘I am your Lord.’ They will say, ‘You are our Lord,’ and they will follow Him, and the bridge

[4] Muslim: *Kitaab al-Eemaan, Baab Adnaa Ahl al-Jannah manzilatan*, 1/175, hadith no. 191.

will be set up over Hell."

The Messenger of Allah (ﷺ) said: "I will be the first one who will cross it, and the prayer of the Messengers that Day will be, 'O' Allah, save, save!' On it will be spikes like the thorns of *as-sa'daan*. Have you not seen the thorns of *as-sa'daan*?" They said, "Yes indeed, O' Messenger of Allah." He said, "They are like the thorns of *as-sa'daan*, but no one knows how huge they are except Allah. They will hit people according to their deeds: some will be doomed because of their deeds, and some will cut into pieces and will fall into Hell, then they will be saved..."[5]

These *ṣaḥeeḥ* texts clearly point to a number of matters. They refer to the gathering of the *kuffaar* to Hell, the progress of the believers towards Paradise across the *ṣiraaṭ*, and the separation of the believers from the hypocrites. They also refer in a general sense to the meaning of the passing over Hell which Allah mentions in the *aayah*,

﴿ وَإِن مِّنكُمْ إِلَّا وَارِدُهَا ... ﴿٧١﴾ ﴾

﴾There is not one of you but will pass over it [Hell]...﴿ *(Qur'an 19: 71)*

We will discuss this matter in more detail in the following pages.

2 - THE GATHERING OF THE *KUFFAAR* TO HELL

There are many texts which depict for us how the *kuffaar* will be gathered to Hell, they and their gods which they used to worship.

---

[5] Bukhari: *Kitaab ar-Riqaaq, Baab aṣ-Ṣiraaṭ jasr jahannam, Fatḥ al-Baari*, 11/444. Muslim: *Kitaab al-Eemaan, Baab Ma'rifat Ṭareeq ar-Ru'yah*, 1/163, hadith no. 182. This version is narrated by Bukhari.

1) For example, they will be driven like flocks of cattle, group by group, and they will be harshly treated and shouted at from all sides, as the herdsman does with his cattle or sheep.

﴿ وَسِيقَ ٱلَّذِينَ كَفَرُوٓاْ إِلَىٰ جَهَنَّمَ زُمَرًا ... ﴿٧١﴾ ﴾

﴾And those who disbelieved will be driven to Hell in groups...﴿ *(Qur'an 39: 71)*

﴿ يَوْمَ يُدَعُّونَ إِلَىٰ نَارِ جَهَنَّمَ دَعًّا ﴿١٣﴾ ﴾

﴾The Day when they will be pushed down by force to the fire of Hell, with a horrible, forceful pushing.﴿ *(Qur'an 52: 13)*

﴿ وَيَوْمَ يُحْشَرُ أَعْدَآءُ ٱللَّهِ إِلَى ٱلنَّارِ فَهُمْ يُوزَعُونَ ﴿١٩﴾ ﴾

﴾And [remember] the Day that the enemies of Allah will be gathered to the Fire, then they will be driven [(to the Fire), former ones being withheld till their later ones will join them].﴿ *(Qur'an 41: 19)*

The meaning of the word *yooza'oon* (translated here as 'will be driven') is, they will be gathered; the keepers of Hell will gather the first of them with the last of them, as human beings do with their livestock.

2) The texts indicate that they will be gathered to Hell on their faces, not on their feet as they used to walk in this world. Allah (ﷻ) says:

﴿ ٱلَّذِينَ يُحْشَرُونَ عَلَىٰ وُجُوهِهِمْ إِلَىٰ جَهَنَّمَ أُوْلَٰٓئِكَ شَرٌّ مَّكَانًا وَأَضَلُّ سَبِيلًا ﴿٣٤﴾ ﴾

﴾Those who will be gathered to Hell [prone] on their faces, such will be in an evil state, and most astray from the [Straight] Path.﴿ *(Qur'an 25: 34)*

Bukhari and Muslim narrated from Anas ibn Maalik that a man said, "O' Messenger of Allah, how will the *kaafir* be gathered on his face on the Day of Resurrection?" He said,

> "Is not the One Who made him walk on his feet in this world Able to make him walk on his face on the Day of Resurrection?" Qataadah said: "Indeed He is, by the glory of our Lord."[6]

In addition to being gathered in this horrible fashion on their faces, they will also be gathered blind, not seeing anything, mute, not saying anything, and deaf, not hearing anything.

﴿... وَنَحْشُرُهُمْ يَوْمَ ٱلْقِيَٰمَةِ عَلَىٰ وُجُوهِهِمْ عُمْيًا وَبُكْمًا وَصُمًّا ۖ مَّأْوَىٰهُمْ جَهَنَّمُ ۖ كُلَّمَا خَبَتْ زِدْنَٰهُمْ سَعِيرًا ﴿٩٧﴾﴾

> ﴾...And We shall gather them together on the Day of Resurrection on their faces, blind, dumb and deaf; their abode will be Hell; whenever it abates, We shall increase for them the fierceness of the Fire.﴿ *(Qur'an 17: 97)*

3) Their torment will be increased by the fact that they will be gathered with their false gods and their helpers and followers.

﴿ ۞ ٱحْشُرُوا۟ ٱلَّذِينَ ظَلَمُوا۟ وَأَزْوَٰجَهُمْ وَمَا كَانُوا۟ يَعْبُدُونَ ﴿٢٢﴾ مِن دُونِ ٱللَّهِ فَٱهْدُوهُمْ إِلَىٰ صِرَٰطِ ٱلْجَحِيمِ ﴿٢٣﴾﴾

> ﴾[It will be said to the angels]: 'Assemble those who did wrong, together with their companions [from the devils] and what they used to worship, instead of Allah, and lead them on to the way of flaming Fire [Hell].'﴿
> *(Qur'an 37: 22-23)*

---

[6] Bukhari: *Kitaab ar-Riqaaq, Baab al-Ḥashr, Fatḥ al-Baari*, 11/377; Muslim: 4/2161, hadith no. 2806. This version is narrated by Muslim.

4) Thus they will be overwhelmed, humiliated and belittled:

﴿ قُل لِّلَّذِينَ كَفَرُوا۟ سَتُغْلَبُونَ وَتُحْشَرُونَ إِلَىٰ جَهَنَّمَ ۚ وَبِئْسَ ٱلْمِهَادُ ﴿١٢﴾ ﴾

﴾Say [O' Muhammad] to those who disbelieve: 'You will be defeated and gathered together to Hell, and worst indeed is that place of rest.'﴿ *(Qur'an 3: 12)*

5) Before they even reach the Fire, its sounds will be roaring in their ears, and this will fill their hearts with terror.

﴿ إِذَا رَأَتْهُم مِّن مَّكَانٍۭ بَعِيدٍ سَمِعُوا۟ لَهَا تَغَيُّظًا وَزَفِيرًا ﴿١٢﴾ ﴾

﴾When it [Hell] sees them from a far place, they will hear its raging and its roaring.﴿ *(Qur'an 25: 12)*

6) When they reach the Fire and see its horrors with their own eyes, they will be filled with regret and will wish that they could go back to this world so that they might be believers.

﴿ وَلَوْ تَرَىٰٓ إِذْ وُقِفُوا۟ عَلَى ٱلنَّارِ فَقَالُوا۟ يَـٰلَيْتَنَا نُرَدُّ وَلَا نُكَذِّبَ بِـَٔايَـٰتِ رَبِّنَا وَنَكُونَ مِنَ ٱلْمُؤْمِنِينَ ﴿٢٧﴾ ﴾

﴾If you could but see when they will be held over the [Hell] Fire! They will say: 'Would that we were but sent back [to the world]! Then we would not deny the *Aayaat* [proofs, evidences, verses, lessons, revelations, etc.] of our Lord, and we would be of the believers!'﴿

(Qur'an 6: 27)

But they will not find any way out from the Fire:

﴿ وَرَءَا ٱلْمُجْرِمُونَ ٱلنَّارَ فَظَنُّوٓا۟ أَنَّهُم مُّوَاقِعُوهَا وَلَمْ يَجِدُوا۟ عَنْهَا مَصْرِفًا ﴿٥٣﴾ ﴾

﴾And the *Mujrimoon* [criminals, polytheists, sinners], shall see the Fire and apprehend that they have to fall therein. And they will find no way of escape from there.﴿

(Qur'an 18: 53)

7) At that point they will be ordered to enter Hell, and the Compeller (Allah) will be angry with the humiliated losers:

﴿ فَٱدْخُلُوٓاْ أَبْوَٰبَ جَهَنَّمَ خَٰلِدِينَ فِيهَا ۖ فَلَبِئْسَ مَثْوَى ٱلْمُتَكَبِّرِينَ ﴿٢٩﴾ ﴾

﴾So enter the gates of Hell, to abide therein, and indeed, what an evil abode will be for the arrogant.﴿

(Qur'an 16: 29)

No man or jinn will be saved from the Fire except the pious who had faith in Allah and believed in the Messengers and followed the Message that was sent down to them from their Lord.

﴿ فَوَرَبِّكَ لَنَحْشُرَنَّهُمْ وَٱلشَّيَٰطِينَ ثُمَّ لَنُحْضِرَنَّهُمْ حَوْلَ جَهَنَّمَ جِثِيًّا ﴿٦٨﴾
ثُمَّ لَنَنزِعَنَّ مِن كُلِّ شِيعَةٍ أَيُّهُمْ أَشَدُّ عَلَى ٱلرَّحْمَٰنِ عِتِيًّا ﴿٦٩﴾ ثُمَّ لَنَحْنُ أَعْلَمُ
بِٱلَّذِينَ هُمْ أَوْلَىٰ بِهَا صِلِيًّا ﴿٧٠﴾ وَإِن مِّنكُمْ إِلَّا وَارِدُهَا ۚ كَانَ عَلَىٰ رَبِّكَ حَتْمًا
مَّقْضِيًّا ﴿٧١﴾ ثُمَّ نُنَجِّى ٱلَّذِينَ ٱتَّقَواْ وَّنَذَرُ ٱلظَّٰلِمِينَ فِيهَا جِثِيًّا ﴿٧٢﴾ ﴾

﴾So by your Lord, surely, We shall gather them together, and [also] the *Shayaaṭeen* [(devils) with them], then We shall bring them round Hell on their knees. Then indeed We shall drag out from every sect all those who were worst in obstinate rebellion against the Most Gracious [Allah]. Then, verily, We know best those who are most worthy of being burnt therein. There is not one of you but will pass over it [Hell]; this is with your Lord, a Decree which must be accomplished. Then We shall save those who used to fear Allah and were dutiful to Him. And We shall leave the *Ẓaalimoon* [polytheists and

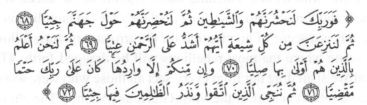

wrongdoers] therein [humbled] to their knees [in Hell].﴿
(Qur'an 19: 68-72)

Sayyid Quṭb said, commenting on these verses:

"Allah swears by Himself - which is the greatest and most majestic of oaths - that they will be gathered together after death, and this is a matter which is certain: ﴾So by your Lord, surely, We shall gather them together...﴿ And they will not be alone: ﴾...And [also] the *Shayaaṭeen* [(devils) with them]...﴿ They will not be alone; the *shayaaṭeen* will be with them. The *shayaaṭeen* are the ones who used to whisper doubts to them. The relationship between them is that of leader and follower... Here a vivid picture is drawn, of them kneeling around Hell in abject humiliation: ﴾...then We shall bring them round Hell on their knees.﴿ This is a terrifying picture, of these vast innumerable crowds gathered to Hell, kneeling around it, staring at its horrors, with its heat touching them, waiting to be seized at any moment and thrown into it, waiting on their knees in humiliation and fear... this is a scene of humiliation for the arrogant tyrants, followed by a scene where the most rebellious will be dragged forth: ﴾Then indeed We shall drag out from every sect all those who were worst in obstinate rebellion against the Most Gracious [Allah].﴿ The phrasing (of the original Arabic) is quite emphatic, depicting the shade and sound of this terror, followed by the image of their being flung into the Fire, which concludes this awful scene.

Allah knows who will be the first to be dragged into it; no one will be taken in a random fashion from these innumerable crowds that have been gathered, the numbers of which are known to Allah one by one. ﴾Then, verily, We know best those who are most worthy of being burnt therein.﴿ They will be chosen to be the first group to be thrown in."[7]

[7] *Fa Ẓilaal al-Qur'an*, 4/2317.

This *aayah* - ﴾There is not one of you but will pass over it [Hell]...﴿ *(Qur'an 19: 71)* - affected the attitude of the righteous and kept them awake at night. It changed their whole life and kept them from laughing and enjoying their (physical) pleasures to the full. Ibn Katheer mentioned that when Abu Maysarah went to bed he said, "Would that my mother had never given birth to me!" Then he wept. He was asked, "Why are you weeping O' Abu Maysarah?" He said, "Allah has told us that we will pass over it (Hell), but He has not told us that we will be saved from falling into it." 'Abdullah ibn al-Mubaarak narrated that Al-Ḥasan al-Baṣri said: "A man said to his brother, 'Have you heard that you will pass over the Fire?' He said, 'Yes.' He said, 'Have you heard that you will be saved from falling into it?' He said, 'No.' He said, 'Then why do you laugh?' He said, 'I never saw him laugh until they day he died.' Ibn 'Abbaas said to a man who was discussing with him, 'You and I, O' Abu Raashid, will pass over it, so wait and see whether we will be saved from falling into it or not.'"[8]

3 - HOW THE BELIEVERS WILL CROSS *AṢ-ṢIRAAṬ* AND HOW THE BELIEVERS WILL BE RID OF THE HYPOCRITES

When the atheist *kuffaar* - disbelievers - and the misguided *mushrikeen* will be taken to the house of destruction, Hell, in which they will burn - and what an evil place it is to settle in (cf. 14: 28-29), there will be left in the arena of the Resurrection the monotheistic followers of the Messengers, among whom will be people who committed sins, and the hypocrites. Darkness will be cast upon them ahead of the bridge, as is stated in the hadith narrated by Muslim from 'Aa'ishah (may Allah be pleased with her), who said: The Messenger (ﷺ) was asked, "Where will the people be on the Day when the earth is changed into another earth and the heavens?" He said,

[8] *Tafseer Ibn Katheer*, 4/476.

"They will be in darkness ahead of the bridge."

The commentator on *Aṭ-Ṭaḥaawiyah*[9] said: "In this place the hypocrites will be separated from the believers. They will stay behind, and the believers will go ahead. A barrier will be placed between them which will prevent them from reaching them. Al-Bayhaqi narrated with his *isnaad* from Masrooq that 'Abdullah said: 'Allah will gather the people on the Day of Resurrection... Some of them will be given light like a mountain, in front of him; some will be given more light than that. Some will be given their light like a palm-tree, to their right, and some will be given less that that, on their right. The last one to be given light will be given on his big toe, in front of him, which will shine on and off. When it will shine, he will move forward, and when it will be extinguished he will stand still. He and they will move forward across the *ṣiraaṭ*, and the *ṣiraaṭ* will be like the edge of a sword, a void in which one is likely to slip. It will be said to them, 'Carry on as much as your light enables you to.' Some of them will cross it like a falling star (i.e., very fast), others will cross it like the wind, or like the blinking of an eye, or like a man running or jogging, according to the level of his deeds. Then the one whose light is on his big toe will cross it, with one hand slipping and the other holding on, and one foot slipping and the other hanging on, with the Fire hitting his sides, until when they pass it and reach safely, they will say, 'Praise be to Allah who has saved us from you (Hell) after we had seen you. We have been given what no one else has been given.'"[10]

---

[9] *Sharḥ aṭ-Ṭaḥaawiyah*, Pp. 470.

[10] *Shaykh* Naaṣir said in his commentary on the *aḥaadeeth* of *Sharḥ aṭ-Ṭaḥaawiyah* (470): "It is *ṣaḥeeḥ* and narrated by Al-Ḥaakim. I think that Al-Bayhaqi narrated it via a different *isnaad*. Al-Ḥaakim said: It is *ṣaḥeeḥ* according to the conditions of the two *Shaykhs* (Bukhari and Muslim), and Adh-Dhahabi agreed with him. The *Shaykh* explained that there is some weakness in one of the narrators, who was *mudallis* but he was cross-examined and said *ḥaddathanaa* (i.e., clearly stated that he heard the hadith), so the hadith is *ṣaḥeeḥ*.

Allah (ﷻ) has told us about this scene, when the believers will cross *aṣ-ṣiraaṭ*. He says:

﴿يَوْمَ تَرَى ٱلْمُؤْمِنِينَ وَٱلْمُؤْمِنَـٰتِ يَسْعَىٰ نُورُهُم بَيْنَ أَيْدِيهِمْ وَبِأَيْمَـٰنِهِم بُشْرَىٰكُمُ
ٱلْيَوْمَ جَنَّـٰتٌ تَجْرِى مِن تَحْتِهَا ٱلْأَنْهَـٰرُ خَـٰلِدِينَ فِيهَا ۚ ذَٰلِكَ هُوَ ٱلْفَوْزُ ٱلْعَظِيمُ ﴿١٢﴾
يَوْمَ يَقُولُ ٱلْمُنَـٰفِقُونَ وَٱلْمُنَـٰفِقَـٰتُ لِلَّذِينَ ءَامَنُوا۟ ٱنظُرُونَا نَقْتَبِسْ مِن نُّورِكُمْ قِيلَ
ٱرْجِعُوا۟ وَرَآءَكُمْ فَٱلْتَمِسُوا۟ نُورًا فَضُرِبَ بَيْنَهُم بِسُورٍ لَّهُۥ بَابٌۢ بَاطِنُهُۥ فِيهِ ٱلرَّحْمَةُ
وَظَـٰهِرُهُۥ مِن قِبَلِهِ ٱلْعَذَابُ ﴿١٣﴾ يُنَادُونَهُمْ أَلَمْ نَكُن مَّعَكُمْ ۖ قَالُوا۟ بَلَىٰ وَلَـٰكِنَّكُمْ
فَتَنتُمْ أَنفُسَكُمْ وَتَرَبَّصْتُمْ وَٱرْتَبْتُمْ وَغَرَّتْكُمُ ٱلْأَمَانِىُّ حَتَّىٰ جَآءَ أَمْرُ ٱللَّهِ وَغَرَّكُم
بِٱللَّهِ ٱلْغَرُورُ ﴿١٤﴾ فَٱلْيَوْمَ لَا يُؤْخَذُ مِنكُمْ فِدْيَةٌ وَلَا مِنَ ٱلَّذِينَ كَفَرُوا۟ ۚ مَأْوَىٰكُمُ
ٱلنَّارُ ۖ هِىَ مَوْلَىٰكُمْ ۖ وَبِئْسَ ٱلْمَصِيرُ ﴿١٥﴾﴾

﴿On the Day you shall see the believing men and the believing women - their light running forward before them and by their right hands. Glad tidings for you this Day! Gardens under which rivers flow [Paradise], to dwell therein forever! Truly, this is the great success! On the Day when the hypocrites men and women will say to the believers: 'Wait for us! Let us get something from your light!' It will be said: 'Go back to your rear! Then seek a light!' So a wall will be put up between them, with a gate therein. Inside it will be mercy, and outside it will be torment. [The hypocrites] will call the believers: 'Were we not with you?' The believers will reply: 'Yes! But you led yourselves into temptations, you looked forward for our destruction; you doubted [in Faith] and you were deceived by false desires, till the Command of Allah came to pass. And the chief deceiver [Satan] deceived you in respect of Allah.' So this Day no ransom shall be taken from you [hypocrites], nor of those who disbelieved [in the Oneness of Allah Islamic

> Monotheism]. Your abode is the Fire. That is your *mawla* [friend - proper place], and worst indeed is that destination.'﴿ *(Qur'an 57: 12-15)*

Allah tells us that the believing men and women who were guided by the light of this great religion in this world, will be given light on the Day of Resurrection which will show them the way to the Gardens of Delight (Paradise) and will help them to avoid the obstacles and stumbling-blocks on that slippery path. There they will receive the glad tidings of Gardens of Delight, which the hypocrites will be denied, those who claimed in this world that they were with the believers and were on their side, but in reality they were against them and were not guided as they were, and did not follow their path of light, and they denied themselves the light of the Qur'an in this world. The hypocrites will ask the believers to wait for them so that they can avail themselves of their light. But at this point they will be tricked, just as they used to trick the believers in this world. It will be said to them, 'Go back and seek a light.' So the hypocrites will retreat to the rear, and the believers will advance to the front. Thus the two parties will become distinct. Then Allah will set up between them a wall in which there will be a gate; within that wall will be mercy, and outside it will be torment. Then the destination of the believing men and women will be Paradise, and the destination of the hypocrites, men and women, will be Hell.

Allah (ﷻ) tells us of the supplication of the believers when their light runs forth ahead of them and on their right; it will be, 'O' Lord, keep perfect our light for us.' Allah (ﷻ) says:

﴿... يَوْمَ لَا يُخْزِى ٱللَّهُ ٱلنَّبِىَّ وَٱلَّذِينَ ءَامَنُوا۟ مَعَهُۥ ۖ نُورُهُمْ يَسْعَىٰ بَيْنَ أَيْدِيهِمْ وَبِأَيْمَٰنِهِمْ يَقُولُونَ رَبَّنَآ أَتْمِمْ لَنَا نُورَنَا وَٱغْفِرْ لَنَآ ۖ إِنَّكَ عَلَىٰ كُلِّ شَىْءٍ قَدِيرٌ ﴿٨﴾﴾

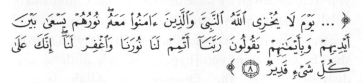

﴾...The Day that Allah will not disgrace the Prophet [Muhammad] and those who believe with him. Their Light will run forward before them and [with their Records Books of deeds] in their right hands. They will say: 'Our Lord! Keep perfect our Light for us [and do not put it off till we cross over the *Ṣiraaṭ* (a slippery bridge over the Hell) safely] and grant us forgiveness. Verily, You are Able to do all things.'﴿

(Qur'an 66: 8)

Mujaahid, Aḍ-Ḍaḥḥaak, Al-Ḥasan al-Baṣri and others said: this is what the believers will say when, on the Day of Resurrection, they see that the light of the hypocrites has been extinguished.[11]

4 - THE ONES WHO WILL CROSS THE *ṢIRAAṬ* ARE THE BELIEVERS, NOT THE *MUSHRIKEEN*

The *aḥaadeeth* that we have quoted indicate that the *kaafir* nations will follow the false gods that they used to worship, and those gods will lead their worshippers to the Fire, which they will fall into. Then there will be left the believers, and among them the hypocrites and believers who sinned. These are the ones for whom the *ṣiraaṭ* will be set up.

I have not seen in any of the books of the scholars who noted that which we have stated above, that the *ṣiraaṭ* will be only for the believers and not for anyone else such as the *kuffaar, mushrikeen* or atheists - apart from Ibn Rajab al-Ḥanbali (may Allah have mercy on him), who said in his book *At-Takhweef min an-Naar*:

"Note that that the people will be divided into the believers who worshipped Allah Alone, associating nothing in worship with Him,

---

[11] *Tafseer Ibn Katheer*, 7/61.

and the *mushrikeen* who worshipped others alongside Allah. The *mushrikeen* will not cross the *ṣiraaṭ*, rather they will fall into Hell before the *ṣiraaṭ* is set up."[12] He quoted some of the same *aḥaadeeth* as we have quoted here, including the hadith of Abu Sa'eed al-Khudri narrated in *Ṣaheeḥayn* (Bukhari and Muslim), then he said: "This hadith clearly states that everyone who openly worshipped anything other than Allah, such as those among the People of the Book who worshipped the Messiah or 'Uzayr, will join the *mushrikeen* in falling into the Fire before the *ṣiraaṭ* is set up. But each group of the *mushrikeen* who worshipped idols or the sun or moon etc. will follow that which they used to worship in this world, and they will fall into the Fire along with their objects of worship. The Qur'an indicates this in reference to Pharaoh:

﴿ يَقْدُمُ قَوْمَهُۥ يَوْمَ ٱلْقِيَـٰمَةِ فَأَوْرَدَهُمُ ٱلنَّارَ وَبِئْسَ ٱلْوِرْدُ ٱلْمَوْرُودُ ﴿٩٨﴾ ﴾

﴿He will go ahead of his people on the Day of Resurrection, and will lead them into the Fire, and evil indeed is the place to which they are led.﴾

(Qur'an 11: 82)

But those among the People of the Book who worshipped the Messiah and 'Uzayr, will be detained among the people who claimed to be followers of the Prophets, then they will be led to the Fire later on.

It is narrated in another hadith that for those who used to worship the Messiah, the *qareen* (devil-companion) of the Messiah will appear to them, and they will follow him. Something similar will happen in the case of those who used to worship 'Uzayr. In the hadith about the Trumpet it says that an angel will appear to them in the form of the

---

[12] *At-Takhweef min an-Naar*, Pp. 187.

Messiah, and another angel will assume the form of 'Uzayr. After that there will be no one left except those who worshipped Allah alone to all outward appearances, whether they were sincere or hypocrites, from this ummah and others. Then the hypocrites will be distinguished from the believers by their being prevented from prostrating, and by the light which will be given only to the believers."[13]

This is a sound view expressed by this writer, may Allah have mercy on him.

5 - THE MEANING OF THE "PASSING OVER" HELL

Some of the scholars think that what is meant by the "passing over" Hell mentioned in the *aayah* (verse) -

﴿ وَإِن مِّنكُمْ إِلَّا وَارِدُهَا ۚ كَانَ عَلَىٰ رَبِّكَ حَتْمًا مَّقْضِيًّا ﴿٧١﴾ ﴾

﴿There is not one of you but will pass over it [Hell]; this is with your Lord, a Decree which must be accomplished.﴾ *(Qur'an 19: 71)*

- is entering Hell. This is the view of Ibn 'Abbaas (رضي الله عنه)[14], and he quoted as evidence for that the *aayah* in which Allah (سبحانه وتعالى) says concerning Pharaoh:

﴿ يَقْدُمُ قَوْمَهُ يَوْمَ الْقِيَامَةِ فَأَوْرَدَهُمُ النَّارَ ... ﴿٩٨﴾ ﴾

﴿He will go ahead of his people on the Day of Resurrection, and will lead them into the Fire...﴾ *(Qur'an 11: 98)*

And the *aayaat* (verses):

---

[13] *At-Takhweef min an-Naar*, Pp. 188

[14] Ibid, Pp. 20.

﴿ وَنَسُوقُ ٱلْمُجْرِمِينَ إِلَىٰ جَهَنَّمَ وِرْدًا ﴿٨٦﴾ ﴾

﴾And We shall drive the *Mujrimoon* [polytheists, sinners, criminals, disbelievers in the Oneness of Allah] to Hell, in a thirsty state [like a thirsty herd driven down to water].﴿ *(Qur'an 19: 86)*

﴿ لَوْ كَانَ هَٰٓؤُلَآءِ ءَالِهَةً مَّا وَرَدُوهَا ... ﴿٩٩﴾ ﴾

﴾Had these [idols] been *aalihah* [gods], they would not have entered there [Hell]...﴿ *(Qur'an 21: 99)*

And Muslim al-A'war narrated that Mujaahid said concerning the *aayah* -

﴿ وَإِن مِّنكُمْ إِلَّا وَارِدُهَا ... ﴿٧١﴾ ﴾

﴾There is not one of you but will pass over it [Hell]...﴿ *(Qur'an 19: 71)*

- this means, enter it.[15]

Some of the scholars said that what is meant by passing over Hell is crossing the *ṣiraaṭ*. The commentator on *Aṭ-Ṭahaawiyah* said: "The *mufassireen* differed as to what was meant by 'passing over' in the *aayah* (verse), ﴾There is not one of you but will pass over it [Hell]...﴿ *(Qur'an 19: 71)* - The most apparent and strongest meaning is that it refers to crossing the *ṣiraaṭ*. Allah (ﷻ) says: ﴾Then We shall save those who used to fear Allah and were dutiful to Him. And We shall leave the *Ẓaalimoon* [polytheists and wrongdoers] therein [humbled] to their knees [in Hell].﴿ *(Qur'an 19: 72)*.

It is narrated in *Aṣ-Ṣaḥeeḥ* that the Prophet (ﷺ) said:

---

[15] *At-Takhweef min an-Naar*, Pp. 200.

"By the One in Whose hand is my soul, no one who made the pledge of allegiance (*bay'ah*) under the tree will enter Hell." Hafṣah stated: "I said, 'O' Messenger of Allah, doesn't Allah say, ﴾There is not one of you but will pass over it [Hell]...﴿ *(Qur'an 19:71)*?' He said, 'Have you not heard Him say, ﴾Then We shall save those who used to fear Allah and were dutiful to Him. And We shall leave the *Ẓaalimoon* [polytheists and wrongdoers] therein [humbled] to their knees [in Hell].﴿ *(Qur'an 19: 72).*"

The Messenger of Allah (ﷺ) indicated that passing over Hell does not necessarily imply entering it, and that being saved from evil does not necessarily imply that that evil has taken place; what it implies is that the means of evil are available. When a person's enemy tries to destroy him but fails to do so, it is said that Allah saved him from him. Hence Allah (ﷻ) says:

﴿ وَلَمَّا جَآءَ أَمْرُنَا نَجَّيْنَا هُودًا ... ﴿٥٨﴾ ﴾

﴾And when Our Commandment came, We saved Hood...﴿ *(Qur'an 11: 58)*

﴿ فَلَمَّا جَآءَ أَمْرُنَا نَجَّيْنَا صَٰلِحًا ... ﴿٦٦﴾ ﴾

﴾So when Our Commandment came, We saved *Ṣaaliḥ*...﴿ *(Qur'an 11: 66)*

﴿ وَلَمَّا جَآءَ أَمْرُنَا نَجَّيْنَا شُعَيْبًا ... ﴿٩٤﴾ ﴾

﴾And when Our Commandment came, We saved Shu'aib...﴿ *(Qur'an 11: 94)*

The punishment did not befall them, but it befell others, and if Allah had not decreed for them the means of salvation, what befell the others would have befallen them too. The same applies to those who will pass over Hell, crossing on *aṣ-ṣiraaṭ*. Then Allah will save those who feared Him and He will leave the evildoers humbled to their knees therein (in Hell). According to the hadith of Jaabir mentioned above, the Prophet (ﷺ) explained that this is the passing over Hell on *aṣ-ṣiraaṭ*."[16]

In fact there will be two separate occasions on which people will pass over Hell. The first will be when the *kuffaar*, the people of Hell, pass over it. This passing over undoubtedly implies entering it, as Allah says concerning Pharaoh: ﴾He will go ahead of his people on the Day of Resurrection, and will lead them into the Fire, and evil indeed is the place to which they are led.﴿ *(Qur'an 11: 98)* i.e., evil indeed is the place which they will enter.

And the second occasion will be when the people of *Tawheed* pass over it, on the *ṣiraaṭ* as mentioned in the *aḥaadeeth* quoted above.

6 - THE REAL NATURE OF *AṢ-ṢIRAAṬ* AND THE BELIEF OF *AHL AS-SUNNAH* CONCERNING IT

As-Safaareeni said: "In Arabic, the word *ṣiraaṭ* means a clear path or way.

In shari'ah, it means a bridge which will be set up over Hell, which the first and the last (of the people) will pass over. It is a bridge between Paradise and Hell."[17]

The commentator on *Aṭ-Ṭaḥaawiyah* has described his beliefs concerning the *ṣiraaṭ* which is mentioned in the *aḥaadeeth*. He said:

"We believe in the *ṣiraaṭ*, which is a bridge over Hell. When the people have left the place of standing they will reach a place in which the darkness will be cast upon them, just before the *ṣiraaṭ*, because

[16] *Sharḥ al-'Aqeedah aṭ-Ṭaḥaawiyah*, Pp. 471.

[17] *Lawaami' al-Anwaar al-Bahiyyah*, 2/189.

'Aa'ishah (may Allah be pleased with her) said: 'The Messenger of Allah (ﷺ) was asked, 'Where will the people be on the Day when the earth is changed into another earth and the heavens?' He said,

'They will be in darkness before the bridge.''''[18]

As-Safaareeni (may Allah have mercy on him) explained the views of different sects concerning the *ṣiraaṭ*, and discussed whether the *ṣiraaṭ* is metaphorical or something real. Then he stated the view of the followers of truth as indicated by the texts. He said: "Belief in the *ṣiraaṭ* is unanimously agreed upon, but the followers of truth affirm it in accordance with its apparent meaning, that it is a bridge set up above Hell, sharper than the edge of a sword and thinner than a hair. This apparent meaning was rejected by Al-Qaaḍi 'Abdul-Jabbaar al-Mu'tazili and many of his followers, on the grounds that it could not be crossed, or so they claimed, and that if it were possible, it would involve hardship, and there will be no torment for the believers and the righteous on the Day of Resurrection. What it meant was the path to Paradise, as indicated in the *aayah* (verse),

﴿ سَيَهْدِيهِمْ وَيُصْلِحُ بَالَهُمْ ۝٥ ﴾

﴾He will guide them and set right their state.﴿

(Qur'an 47: 5)

- and the way to Hell, as indicated in the *aayah*,

﴿ ... فَاهْدُوهُمْ إِلَىٰ صِرَاطِ الْجَحِيمِ ۝٢٣ ﴾

﴾...And lead them on to the way of flaming Fire [Hell].﴿

(Qur'an 37:23).

Some of them interpreted it as referring to clear evidence and permissible things, and the evil deeds which they will be questioned

---

[18] *Sharḥ aṭ-Ṭahaawiyah*, Pp. 469.

about and rebuked for. All of this is false and is a myth, because we are obliged to interpret the texts in accordance with what they really mean. Crossing over the *ṣiraaṭ* is no more strange or amazing than walking on water or flying through the air or hovering in the air. The Prophet (ﷺ) answered the question about the *kaafir* being made to walk on his face by noting that the Power of Allah is able to bring such a thing to pass. Al-'Allaamah al-Quraafi denied that the *ṣiraaṭ* is thinner than a hair and sharper than the edge of a sword; he was preceded in that by his *shaykh*, Al-'Izz ibn 'Abdus-Salaam. The truth is that *ṣaḥeeḥ* reports were narrated concerning the *ṣiraaṭ*, and they are to be interpreted as they appear to be, without any misinterpretation, as they were reported in *Ṣaḥeeḥayn* (Bukhari and Muslim) and in the books of *Musnad* and *Sunan* and *Ṣaḥeeḥ*, where innumerable reports state that it is a bridge set up over Hell, over which all creatures will pass, and the ways in which they will cross it will vary."[19]

Qurṭubi mentioned the view of those who say that the *ṣiraaṭ* is a metaphor, and who twist the meaning of the clear texts. He said:

"Some of those who discussed the *aḥaadeeth* which describe the *ṣiraaṭ* as being thinner than a hair and sharper than a sword said that this referred to how easy or difficult it will be, depending on the person's obedience or disobedience (towards Allah), and no-one knows the details of that except Allah, because deeds are hidden and are not clear. It is customary to describe something that is hidden and subtle as being narrow, and describing it as being as narrow as a hair is in this sense. Describing it as being sharper than a sword refers to the fact that the precise instruction that comes from Allah to the angels to let people cross the *ṣiraaṭ* will be carried out as swiftly and precisely as a blow from a sword, because they hasten to carry out the

[19] *Lawaami' al-Anwaar al-Bahiyyah*, 2/192.

commands of Allah. This command cannot be undone, just as when a sword strikes something, that blow cannot be undone. But if it is said that the *ṣiraaṭ* itself is sharper than a sword and thinner than a hair, that can be refuted by the description of the angels standing at either side of it, and of the hooks and spikes that are on it, and that among those who cross will be some who do so on their bellies, and some who will slip then stand up. Some of those who cross it will be given light the size of their feet. All of that indicates that those who cross it will have room to put their feet, and it is known that the width of a hair would not permit any of these things."[20]

Then he refuted their comments by saying:

"What this person mentions may be refuted by many reports, which we have to believe in. The One Who is able to make birds hover in the air is able to make the believer able to run or walk across it. We should not turn away from taking these reports as real and interpret them as metaphors, except when it is impossible to do so, which is not the case because of the reports that have been narrated concerning this matter, the interpretation of which has been transmitted by trustworthy Imams. Whoever is not given light by Allah will have no light."[21]

7 - THE LESSON LEARNED FROM CROSSING THE *ṢIRAAṬ*

Qurṭubi said: "Think now of how your heart will be filled with terror when you see the *ṣiraaṭ* and how narrow it is, then your gaze falls upon the blackness of Hell beneath it. Then your ears are filled with the angry roaring of Hell, and you are commanded to walk on the *ṣiraaṭ*, even though you are so weak, your heart is pounding, your feet are trembling and your back is so weighed down with the burden

[20] *At-Tadhkirah*, Pp. 332.

[21] Ibid, 333.

of your sins that you can hardly walk on the land, let alone the narrow edge of the *ṣiraaṭ*. How will it be when you put one of your feet upon it, and you feel how sharp it is, and you are forced to lift your other foot, and other people are ahead of you, slipping and stumbling, and the keepers of Hell are grabbing them with hooks and spikes, and you can see them tilting their heads down towards Hell and lifting their feet. What a terrifying scene it will be. How difficult it will be to cross this narrow space!"[22]

He also said [23]: "Imagine yourself, when you are on the *ṣiraaṭ*, and you look at Hell beneath you, black and filled with darkness, with its intense heat and leaping flames, and you are alternately walking and crawling across it."

---

[22] Ibid, 332.
[23] Ibid, 330.

REFERENCES

At-Takhweef min an-Naar by Al-Ḥafiẓ Abul Faraj ibn al-Jawzi, *Al-Makatabat al-'Ilmiyah*, Beirut.

At-Tadhkirah fee Aḥwal al-Mawta wa Umoor al-Aakhirah by Qurṭubi, *Al-Maktabat as-Salafiyah*, al-Madeenah al-Munawwarah.

Tafseer al-Aaloosi, Idarat aṭ-Ṭaba'ah al-Muneeriyah.

Tafseer Ibn Katheer, Dar al-Andalus, Beirut, First Ed. 1385/1996.

Tafseer al-Qurṭubi, Dar al-Kitaab al-'Arabi, Cairo.

Jamiy' al-Uṣool fee Aḥadeeth ar-Rasool by Ibn al-Atheer Ed. by Abdul Qaadir al-Arna'ooṭ, *Maktabah al-Ḥalwani*, First Ed. 1392/1972.

Ar-Rooḥ by Ibn al-Qayyim, *Al-Maktabat al-'Ilmiyah*, Beirut.

Silsilat al-Aḥadeeth aṣ-Ṣaḥeeḥah by *Shaykh* Naṣiruddin al-Albani, *Al-Maktab al-Islami*, Beirut, First Ed.

Sharḥ al-'Aqeedah aṭ-Ṭaḥaawiyah, by Muhammad ibn Muhammad ibn Abi al-'Izz al-Ḥanafi, *Al-Maktab al-Islami*, Beirut, Fourth Ed. 1391/1971.

Ṣaḥeeḥ al-Bukhari, text from *Fatḥ al-Baari*, *Al-Maktabah as-Salafiyah*, Cairo, First Ed.

Ṣaḥeeḥ al-Jamey' aṣ-Ṣagheer, by Suyooṭi, Ed. Muhammad Naṣiruddin al-Albani, *Al-Maktab al-Islami*, Beirut, First Ed. 1388/1969.

Ṣaḥeeḥ Muslim, Ed. by Muhammad Fuwad Abdul Baqi, *Daar Iḥyaa' al-Kutub al-'Arabiya*, Beirut, Second Ed. 1972.

Al-'Ahd al-Qadeem wal-'Ahd al-Jadeed (Old and New Testament).

Fatḥ al-Baari, Ibn Ḥajar al-'Asqalani, *Al-Maktabah as-Salafiyah*, Cairo, First Ed.

Fee Ẓilaal al-Qur'an, Sayyid Quṭb, *Daar ush-Shurooq*.

Lisaan al-'Arab, Ibn Manẓoor, Ed. Yusuf Khayyaṭ and Nadeem Mur 'Ashli, *Daar Lisaan al-'Arab.*

Lawaami' al-Anwaar al-Bahiyah, by Safaareeni, State of Qatar, First Ed.

Majmoo' al-Fataawa Shaykh al-Islam Ibn Taymiyah, Compiled by Ibn Qaasim, Saudi Arabia, First Ed.

Mishkaat al-Maṣaabiḥ by Al-Khaṭeeb at-Tabreezi, *Al-Maktab al-Islami*, Damascus. First Ed. 1381/1961.

Ma'arij al-Qubool by Shaykh Ḥaafiẓ Ḥukmi, *Ar-Riyasah al-'Aammah li Idaaraat al-Buḥooth al-'Ilmiyah*, Riyadh.

Maqaaṣid al Mukallifeen, 'Umar Sulayman al-Ashqar, *Maktabat al-Falaaḥ*, Kuwait.

Nihaayat al-Bidaayah wan-Nihaayah by Ibn Katheer, *Maktabat an-Nahdiyah al-Ḥadeethah*, Riyadh, First Ed. 1968.

GLOSSARY

Al-'Aalameen	العالمين	:	Sing. *'Aalam*; Worlds, Universe, Mankind, jinn and all that exists
Aalihah	آلهة	:	Sing. *Ilaah*; gods, deities
Aayah	آية	:	Pl. *Aayaat* Verse, Sign, Proof
Adhaan	أذان	:	Call for the prayer
Aḥaadeeth (Hadiths)	أحاديث	:	Sing. hadith; sayings of the last Prophet
Ahl as-Sunnah wal Jama'ah	أهل السنة والجماعة	:	The bulk of the majority of the Muslims who adhere to the ways of the last Prophet and his immediate followers - *Ṣaḥaabah*
Al-Akhirah	الآخرة	:	The Hereafter
'Alaqah	علقة	:	A clot
Al-Ba'th	البعث	:	Resurrectoin
Al-Barzakh	البرزخ	:	Lit. Barrier; The interval between death and resurrection
Al-Birr	البِرّ	:	Piety, righteousness
Ad-Daar al-Aakhirah	الدار الآخرة	:	The home of the Hereafter, the everlasting abode
Al-Ghaashiyah	الغاشية	:	Lit. The Overwhelming; Name of a chapter of the Qur'an
Al-Ḥaaqqah	الحاقة	:	Lit. The Inevitable; Name of a chapter of the Qur'an

Al-Ḥawḍ	الحوض	:	Lit. The Cistern; this refers to the river owned by the last Prophet in the next world
Al-Ḥisaab	الحساب	:	The Reckoning
Al-Muqaam al-Maḥmood	المقام المحمود	:	An elevated position in the Hereafter for the last Prophet
Al-Qaari'ah	القارعة	:	The Striking Hour, Name of a chapter of the Qur'an
Al-Qiyaamah	القيامة	:	Resurrection, Hereafter
Al-Qiyaamah al-Kubra	القيامة الكبرى	:	The Great Resurrection
Al-Waaqi'ah	الواقعة	:	The Event, Name of a chapter of the Qur'an
Anṣaab	أنصاب	:	Stone altars
'Aqeedah	عقيدة	:	Belief, Creed, Dogma
Ash-Shafaa'ah	الشفاعة	:	Intercession
'Aṣr	عصر	:	Afternoon, Afternoon prayer
Aṣ-Ṣaakhkhah	الصَّآخَّة	:	The Trumpet-blast
Aṣ-Ṣaḥeeḥayn	الصحيحين	:	The two Hadith compilations known as Bukhari and Muslim
Aṣ-Ṣiraaṭ	الصراط	:	Lit. Way, path; A bridge over Hell
Aṣ-Ṣoor	الصور	:	The Trumpet, it will be blown before resurrection
Awliya'	أولياء	:	Sing. *Wali*; Friends, Supporters, Guardians

Bid'ah	بدعة	:	Reprehensible innovation in religion, heresy
Ḍa'eef	ضعيف	:	Lit. Weak; A term used to differentiate the hadith narrations
Daa'iyah	داعية	:	Preacher, caller to Allah, missionary
Dharrah	ذرة	:	Small particle of sand, Small ant
Dirham	درهم	:	Name of a currency
Du'aa'	دعاء	:	Supplication
Ḍuḥaa	ضحى	:	The forenoon, Name of the prayer after Sunrise, Name of a chapter of the Qur'an
Eemaan	إيمان	:	Belief, faith
Faaḥisha	فاحشة	:	Pl. *Fawaaḥish*; Obscene, Vulgar, Evil and wrong deed
Fiṭrah	فطرة	:	Nature
Fujjar	فجّار	:	Sing. *Faajir*; The Wicked, disbelievers, sinners and evildoers
Ghalool	غلول	:	Stealing from the war booty
Ghayb	غيب	:	Unseen
Haawiyah	هاوية	:	Lit. Pit; Name of Hell, Hell
Ḥaraam	حرام	:	Forbidden, illegal
Ḥasan	حسن	:	Good, a term in hadith discipline for a reliable hadith but in lesser degree than a *ṣaḥeeḥ* (authentic) hadith
Ḥasanaat	حسنات	:	Good deeds
Iblees	إبليس	:	Satan, Devil

Iḥraam	إحرام	:	State of purity (and wearing two white sheets as lower and upper garments by male) for Ḥajj and/or Umrah
'Ilm al-Kalaam	علم الكلام	:	Scholasticism, Science of divinity
Isbaal	إسبال	:	Letting one's garment hang down below the ankles
Isnaad	إسناد	:	Attribution to a chain of narrators of hadith
Jaahiliyah	جاهلية	:	Ignorance, non-Islamic, period before the prophethood of Muhammad
Jamaa'ah	جماعة	:	Congregation, community
Jihaad	جهاد	:	Lit. Struggle; struggle for the establishment of Islamic order, fighting in the cause of Allah
Kaleemullah	كليم الله	:	Lit. One who speaks with Allah; the title of the Prophet Moses
Khaleel ar-Raḥmaan	خليل الرحمٰن	:	Close friend of the All-Gracious
Khaleelullah	خليل الله	:	Close friend of Allah, title of the Prophet Ibraaheem (Abraham)
Khawaarij	خوارج	:	Sing. *Khaarji*; Lit. Secedors; A group of persons deserting the camp of the Caliph 'Ali in the battle of Siffeen. It later developed into a sect declaring every sinning person a *Kaafir* — disbeliever
Khayr	خير	:	Goodness, wealth

Kuffaar	كفار	:	Sing. *Kaafir*; Disbelievers
Kufr	كفر	:	Disbelief
Marfoo'	مرفوع	:	Lit. Elevated; A term in hadith discipline for a narration of a hadith wherein the Companion says, "the Messenger of Allah said"
Mawla	مولى	:	Lord, Freed slave, friend, owner
Mawqoof	موقوف	:	A hadith when the narrating Companion narrates without mentioning the name of the Prophet, or expresses his own opinion
Miskeen	مسكين	:	Poor
Mu'tazilah	معتزلة	:	A deviating sect in Islam adhering to the belief that sin puts a believer in the middle of *kufr* and Islam i.e., he is neither a disbeliever nor a Muslim. This sect is said to be founded by Waaṣil ibn 'Aṭa'
Muḍghah	مضغة	:	A lump of chewed flesh
Muadh-dhin	مؤذن	:	One who makes prayer call
Mufassir	مفسّر	:	Pl. *Mufassireen*; Exegete, commentator of Qura'nic text
Mufsidoon	مفسدون	:	Sing. *Mufsid*. Who commit great crimes, oppressors, tyrants
Muhaajireen	مهاجرين	:	Sing. *Muhaajir*; Migrants, people leaving a place for the sake of Islam. Originally it refers to the migration of the last Prophet and his

			Companions from Makkah to Madeenah
Muhsinoon	محسنون	:	Sing. *Muhsin*; Good-doers, chaste, virtuous, followers of Islam in its totality
Mujrim	مجرم	:	Criminal, sinner, polytheist
Munaafiq	منافق	:	Pl. *Munafiqeen*; Hypocrite
Muṣḥaf	مصحف	:	Copy of the Qur'an, the revealed book
Musnad	مسند	:	A term in hadith discipline for the compilation of hadiths. Hadith compilation arranged Companion wise
Mustaḥabb	مستحب	:	Recommended, a term in Fiqh
Mutawaatir	متواتر	:	Lit. Continuous; A term in hadith discipline for a hadith reported by various chains of narrators
Muttaqoon	متقون	:	Sing. *Muttaqi*; The pious
Nifaaq	نفاق	:	Hypocrisy
Nuṭfah	نطفة	:	Semen, mixed drops of male and female sexual discharge
Qareen	قرين	:	Jinn companion
Qiblah	قبلة	:	Direction to which a Muslim turns to when praying, Ka'bah
Raafiḍi	رافضي	:	Pl. *Rawaafiḍ*; A general term used for the *Shia'h* sect
Rabb	رب	:	Lord and Master, Sustainer and

			Guardian, Sovereign and Ruler
Rooḥ	روح	:	Soul, Spirit, this is also used for archangel Gabriel (Jibreel)
Ruboobiyyah	ربوبية	:	Divinity, Divine Lordship
Ṣabr	صبر	:	Patience
Ṣadaqah	صدقة	:	Charity, also Zakah
Ṣaḥaabah	صحابة	:	Sing. *Ṣaḥaabi*; Companions of the last Prophet
Ṣaḥeeḥ	صحيح	:	A term in hadith discipline for a most authentic hadith, sound, reliable
Ṣalaah	صلاة	:	Prayer (obligatory/optional)
Salaam	سلام	:	Peace, greeting
Salaf	سلف	:	The pious predecessors, the believers of the early generation
Saraabeel	سرابيل	:	Garments
Sayi'aat	سيئات	:	Sing; *Sayi'ah*; Bad deeds
Shaheed	شهيد	:	Martyr, killed in the way of Allah
Shar'i	شرعي	:	Legal, according to Islamic law
Shayṭaan	شيطان	:	Satan, Devil
Shirk	شرك	:	Polytheism, associating deity with and besides Allah
Ṣiddeeqeen	صديقين	:	Sing. *Ṣiddeeq*; Lover of truth, the people whose sincerity of faith is beyond doubts. Their position

			comes next to the Prophets, like Abu Bakr
Sunnah	سنة	:	The Prophet's example, or way of life. Everything he said, did, approved of or condemned
Ṭaaghoot	طاغوت	:	Lit. one who exceeds legitimate limits. In the Qur'an it refers to creature who exceeds limits of his creatureliness and arrogates to himself godhead and Lordship. First stage of man's error is *fisq*, second stage is that of *kufr* and the last stage where man not only rebels against Allah but also imposes his rebellious will on others. False gods. Leaders calling to establish non Islamic orders etc. False deities, false leaders
Tafseer	تفسير	:	Exegesis; commentary and explanation of the verses of the Qur'an
Talbiyah	تلبية	:	A ritual utterings in the 'Umrah and Ḥajj saying: *Labbayk Allahumma Labbayk....*
Taqwa	تقوى	:	Piety, righteousness
Tawḥeed	توحيد	:	Islamic Monotheism, believing in one and the only god, Allah
Thareed	ثريد	:	An Arab dish of the time of the Prophet; porridge prepared with cereals, meat and/or vegetable
Thiqaat	ثقات	:	Sing. *Thiqah*; A term in hadith

			discipline meaning trustworthy
Uhud	أحد	:	A mountain near Madeenah
Uloohiyyah	الوهية	:	Divinity
Wudoo'	وضوء	:	Ablution, ritual cleansing
Yawm ad-Deen	يوم الدين	:	The Day of Recompense
Yawm al-Faṣl	يوم الفصل	:	Day of Decision
Yawm al-Ḥasrah	يوم الحسرة	:	The Day of grief and regrets
Yawm al-Ḥisaab	يوم الحساب	:	The Day of Reckoning
Yawm al-Jama'	يوم الجمع	:	The Day of Assembling
Yawm al-Jidaal	يوم الجدال	:	The Day of Pleading
Yawm al-Khulood	يوم الخلود	:	The Day of Eternal life
Yawm at-Taghaabun	يوم التغابن	:	The Day of Mutual loss and gain
Yawm at-Tanaad	يوم التناد	:	The Day when there will be mutual calling
Yawm al-Wa'eed	يوم الوعيد	:	The Day whereof warning had been given
Zakah	زكوة/ زكاة	:	An annual obligatory prescribed charity (or poor due) by a Muslim in possession of riches, merchandise, agricultural produce, livestock, trading goods etc. over a prescribed limit - a certain minimum called *niṣaab*, A pillar of Islam. Rate of payment varies according to the kind of possession. Details to be found in *Fiqh* books. Way of

			distribution to be found in the Qur'an 9: 60
Ẓaalimoon	ظالمون	:	Sing. *Ẓaalim*; Wrongdoers, tyrants
Zinaa	زنا	:	Illegal sexual act, adultery, fornication
Ẓulm	ظلم	:	Oppression, tyranny, injustice

INDEX OF THE QUR'AN

28 - Al-Qaṣaṣ	**88**/20, **83**/23, **88**/41, **62**/263, **65**/263, **64**/267, **78**/271, 273, **75**/292, **62**/296, **65-66**/296.
29 - Al-'Ankaboot	**64**/23, **55**/32, **19-20**/96, **36**/119, **12-13**/186, **13**/278.
30 - Ar-Room	**56**/25, **25**/26, **27**/96, **50**/109, **55**/134, **12**/167.
31 - Luqmaan	**25**/84, **33**/91, **28**/94, **33**/131, **13**/174, **16**/275.
32 - As-Sajdah	**25**/27, **10**/99, **12**/272.
33 - Al-Aḥzaab	**66-68**/193, **15**/302.
34 - Saba'	**3**/88, **29-30**/92, **40-41**/174, **31-33**/187.
35 - Faaṭir	**9**/63, **9**/109, **24**/115.
36 - Yaa-seen	**49-50**/42, **49-51**/48, **51-53**/61, **81**/98, **78-83**/100, **51-52**/160.
37 - Aṣ-Ṣaaffaat	**21**/27, **19-35**/177, **22-23**/363, **23**/377.
38 - Ṣaad	**26**/33, **27-28**/110, **79-81**/115, **55-64**/188.
39 - Az-Zumar	**56-58**/30, **68**/41, 44, 48, 53, 61, **71**/114, **67**/136, 138, **69**/260, **65**/269, **31**/273, **10**/286, **69**/290, **71**/362.
40 - Ghaafir/Al-Mu'min	**27**/33, **18**/34, **15**/36, **32**/37, **64**/43, **57**/98, **32-33**/121, **39-41**/121, **43**/121, **18**/129, **18**/163, **47-48**/185, **10**/193, **51**/289.
41 - Fuṣṣilat	**39**/109, **19-21**/190, **29**/194, **6-7**/268, **19**/362.
42 - Ash-Shoora	**45**/22, **7**/35, **29**/69, **18**/90.
43 - Az-Zukhruf	**83**/92, **11**/109, **67**/173, **68-69**/215.
44 - Ad-Dukhaan	**56**/54.
45 - Al-Jaathiyah	**28**/262, **29**/315.
46 - Al-Aḥqaaf	**33**/98.
47 - Muhammad	**5**/377.

78 - An-Naba' **17**/27, **40**/70, 168, 327, **20**/140, **19**/146.

79 - An-Naaziyaat **34**/29, **6-7**/48, **8-9**/129, **46**/134, **34**/161.

80 - 'Abasa **33**/28, **33-37**/130.

81 - At-Takweer **5**/69, 148, **3**/140, **6**/141, **1**/143, 145, **2**/144, **4**/147, **6**/148, **7**/148, **8**/150, **10**/150, **11**/151, **12**/151, **13**/151, **14**/152, **5**/329.

82 - Al-Infiṭaar **14-19**/27, **3**/141, **1**/142, 145, 146, **2**/144, **5**/152, **5**/280.

83 - Al-Mutaffifeen **4-6**/127, **6**/166.

84 - Al-Inshiqaaq **1-2**/142, **1**/145, **7-8**/306, **7-8**/314, **10-12**/314.

88 - Al-Ghaashiyah **1**/31.

89 - Al-Fajr **21**/139.

90 - Al-Balad **11-13**/226.

94 - Ash-Sharḥ **2**/278.

99 - Al-Zalzalah **6**/38, **7-8**/276, **4**/294.

101 - Al-Qaari'ah **1-3**/26, **5**/140, **6-11**/264.

102 - At-Takaathur **8**/298.

SYMBOLS' DIRECTORY

(سبحانه وتعالى) : *Subḥaanahu wa Ta'aala* - "The Exalted."

(ﷺ) : *Ṣalla-Allahu 'Alayhi wa Sallam* -
"Blessings and Peace be upon him."

(عليه السلام) : *'Alayhis-Salaam* - "May Peace be upon him."

(رضي الله عنه) : *Raḍi-Allahu 'Anhu* - "May Allah be pleased with him."

INDEX OF HADITH

Muslim	*Kitaab al-Jannah waṣ-Ṣifaat Na'eemiha wa Ahliha*	5102	71
		5127	73
		5108	165
Muslim	*Kitaab Ṣifaat al-Qiyamah wal-Jannah wan-Naar*	4999	80
		4995	137
Muslim	*Kitaab Ṣifaat al-Qiyamah wal-Jannah wan-Naar*	5022	270
Muslim	*Kitaab al-Ḥayḍ*	473	80, 359
Muslim	*Kitaab al-Eemaan*	315	68
		156	201
		300	236
		296	236
		286	237
Muslim	*Kitaab al-Eemaan*	284	239
		285	242
		287	243
		288	247, 358
		278	359
		277	288
		269	356
Muslim	*Kitaab az-Zuhd war-Raqaa'iq*	5270	191, 301
		5271	192
		5291	298
		5290	299
Muslim	*Kitaab az-Zakah*	1647	197
Muslim	*Kitaab al-Aadaab*	3994	198
Muslim	*Kitaab al-Jihaad was-Siyar*	3265	206

Tirmidhi	*Kitaab Tafseer al-Qur'an*	2835	282
		3281	299
		3089	324
		2955	325
Tirmidhi	*Kitaab al-Jumu'ah*	450	46
Tirmidhi	*Kitaab al-'Ilm*	2573	200
Tirmidhi	*Kitaab Faḍaail al-Jihaad*	1586	223
	Kitaab Faḍaail al-Jihaad	1581	224
		1558	231
		1559	231
Tirmidhi	*Kitaab ad-Da'waat*	3333	282
Tirmidhi	*Kitaab al-Eemaan*	2563	338, 341
Abu Dawood	*Kitaab aṣ-Ṣalaat*	883	46, 50, 64
		733	305
Abu Dawood	*Kitaab as-Sunnah*	4118	64
Abu Dawood	*Kitaab al-Janaa'iz*	2707	71
Abu Dawood	*Kitaab al-Libaas*	3571	204
Abu Dawood	*Kitaab al-Adab*	4230	211
		4404	283
Abu Dawood	*Kitaab al-Aṭ'imah*	3328	212
Abu Dawood	*Kitaab al-'Itq*	3451	230
Aḥmad	*Musnad al-Anṣaar*	20355	200
		21022	219
		21516	220
		20744	234
		22144	300
Aḥmad	*Musnad al-Mukaththireen*	9836	202
		9837	203

Note: The above given reference nos. of hadith are from the CD programme "Hadith Encyclopedia" by Harf Information Technology.

TRANSLITERATION CHART

أ	a
آ . ى	aa
ب	b
ت	t
ة	h or t (when followed by another Arabic word)
ث	th
ج	j
ح	ḥ
خ	kh
د	d
ذ	dh
ر	r
ز	z
س	s
ش	sh
ص	ṣ
ض	ḍ
ط	ṭ

ظ	ẓ
ع	‘
غ	gh
ف	f
ق	q
ك	k
ل	l
م	m
ن	n
هـ – ه – ـه	h
و	w
و (as vowel)	oo
ي	y
ي (as vowel)	ee
ء	’ (Omitted in initial position)

َ	Fatḥah	a
ِ	Kasra	i
ُ	Ḍammah	u
ّ	Shaddah	Double letter
ْ	Sukoon	Absence of vowel

Notes

Notes

Notes

Notes